Louis Austin and the Carolina Times

JERRY GERSHENHORN

Louis Austin and the Carolina Times
A Life in the Long Black Freedom Struggle

The University of North Carolina Press *Chapel Hill*

This book was published with the assistance of the Z. Smith Reynolds Fund of the University of North Carolina Press.

The University of North Carolina Press has been a member of the
Green Press Initiative since 2003.

Library of Congress Cataloging-in-Publication Data
Names: Gershenhorn, Jerry, author.
Title: Louis Austin and the Carolina times : a life in the long black freedom struggle / Jerry Gershenhorn.
Description: Chapel Hill : University of North Carolina Press, [2018] | Includes bibliographical references and index.
Identifiers: LCCN 2017033927 | ISBN 9781469638768 (cloth : alk. paper) | ISBN 9781469638775 (ebook)
Subjects: LCSH: Austin, L. E. (Louis Ernest), 1898–1971. | Carolina times (Durham, N.C.) | African American journalists—North Carolina—Durham—Biography. | African American newspapers—North Carolina—Durham. | North Carolina—Race relations.
Classification: LCC PN4874.A86 G47 2018 | DDC 070.92 [B]—dc23
LC record available at https://lccn.loc.gov/2017033927

Jacket illustration: Louis Austin reading the *Carolina Times*, 1947 (courtesy of the North Carolina Collection, Durham County Library).

Portions of chapter 2 were previously published as "A Courageous Voice for Black Freedom: Louis Austin and the *Carolina Times* in Depression-Era North Carolina," *North Carolina Historical Review* 87:1 (2010): 57–92. Portions of chapter 3 were previously published as "Double V in North Carolina: *The Carolina Times* and the Struggle for Racial Equality during World War II," *Journalism History* 32:3 (2006): 156–67. Both are used here with permission.

For Barbara

Contents

Acknowledgments

Thanks so much to the women and men who assisted in the research and writing of this book. Archivists play a critical role in the life of a historian. I am very fortunate to know and work with André Vann, university archivist, North Carolina Central University. If anyone knows more about African American history in North Carolina, I have yet to meet that individual. In addition to sharing his knowledge, he was a big help in finding photographs for this book. Lynn Richardson, who recently retired as the curator of the North Carolina Collection at Durham County Library, has been very helpful with the research for this book. Elizabeth Shulman of Durham County Library provided photographs from the library's Durham Historic Photo Archives. Archivists and librarians from Wilson Library at the University of North Carolina at Chapel Hill, the David M. Rubenstein Rare Book & Manuscript Library at Duke University, the State Archives in Raleigh, New York's Schomburg Center for Research in Black Culture, the Schlesinger Library at the Radcliffe Institute for Advanced Study at Harvard University, the Library of Congress, the R. D. Woodruff Library at Atlanta University, the J. Murrey Atkins Library at the University of North Carolina at Charlotte, the University of Maryland's Hornbake Library, the Charles Young Research Library at the University of California at Los Angeles, and Halifax County Library were also critical to the success of my research. The North Carolina Digital Heritage Center, an outstanding resource for historians, has digitized and made available to the public many North Carolina newspapers, including the *Carolina Times*, easing the strain on an aging researcher's eyes after years of looking at microfilm.

I received funding from the Schomburg Center's Scholars-in-Residence Program, which provided the opportunity for extended research in the center's outstanding collections. For two years, I held the Julius L. Chambers Endowed Professorship at North Carolina Central University, which provided research funding as well as a course release, which has been immensely helpful in completing the writing of this book.

This study could not have been written without the inspired work of many outstanding scholars who have produced important studies related to North Carolina's black freedom struggle. These fine scholars include William Chafe, Christina Greene, the late Ray Gavins, Glenda Gilmore, Marcellus Barksdale,

Charles McKinney Jr., Jacquelyn Dowd Hall, Walter Weare, Tim Tyson, David Cecelski, the late Leslie Brown, Osha Gray Davidson, Davison Douglas, Devin Fergus, Jim Leloudis, Robert Korstad, Kenneth Janken, Sarah Thuesen, Brandon Winford, Timothy Minchin, Robert Cannon, and Willie Griffin.

Grateful acknowledgment to the *North Carolina Historical Review (NCHR)* and *Journalism History* for permission to reprint portions of articles published in those journals here. Special thanks to Anne Miller, editor of the *North Carolina Historical Review,* for providing me the benefit of her editorial expertise dating back to 2001 when I published my first article on North Carolina history in the *NCHR,* one of the best state historical journals in the country. Thanks also to Patrick Washburn, former editor of *Journalism History,* for his careful reading and useful comments on an earlier version of chapter 3.

Thanks to Kenneth Edmonds and the late Vivian Edmonds for sitting for interviews and sharing their memories about their grandfather and father. Thanks to Kenneth for generously sharing some of his personal photographs.

Thanks to my colleagues, the fine historians and teachers, past and present, in the Department of History at North Carolina Central University, for their support and friendship, including Percy Murray, Freddie Parker, Carlton Wilson, the late Sylvia Jacobs, Lydia Lindsey, Lolita Brockington, J. Ranaldo Lawson, Jim Harper, Phil Rubio, Terry Mosley, Baiyina Muhammad, Joshua Nadel, Jarvis Hargrove, Tony Frazier, Charles D. Johnson, and Sean Colbert-Lewis. Thanks to Yolanda Robinson, the Department of History's outstanding administrative assistant, for all her help. Special appreciation to Percy Murray, who has been instrumental in my success as a historian.

Thanks to my students at North Carolina Central University, who participated in my classes in North Carolina history. Over the years, both undergraduate and graduate students have offered incisive comments and asked compelling questions about the life of Louis Austin, which have improved this book. Thanks in particular to Leonard Cicero, who served as my research assistant several years ago.

Thanks to my editor at the University of North Carolina Press, Brandon Proia, for his support in bringing this work to publication. He has provided expert editorial advice. It has been great to have him in my corner throughout this process. I'm also grateful to Dino Battista, Susan Garrett, and Ian Oakes of UNC Press for their work in support of this book. Thanks to Tim Tyson and an anonymous reader, who provided thoughtful and insightful commentary on the manuscript. Their suggestions have helped me to strengthen this work in several areas. Thanks to JodieAnne Sclafani and Ellen Lohman for their meticulous copyediting.

Thanks to my family for their support. Thanks to my father, Barry Gershenhorn, whose interest and involvement in politics stimulated my own interest many years ago. Thanks to my mother, Rhoda Gershenhorn, for all she did for me. I wish that she were still with us. Thanks to my brothers, Ira and Alan, and my sister, Susan, for their interest and encouragement. Thanks to my wife's family for their support.

Thanks to Barbara Barr, my partner in life for over thirty years. Without her, I would never have become a historian and this book would not exist. She has been a one-woman support system. When I needed a sounding board, she listened. When I needed emotional support, she comforted me. When I needed intellectual input or editorial advice, I could count on her insightful mind and excellent ear for language. This book is dedicated to her.

Louis Austin and the Carolina Times

Introduction

Our eternal goal must be equality. . . . We will teach it and thunder it from the pulpit until every child achieves it.

—Louis Austin

In 1933, a young North Carolinian man named Thomas Raymond Hocutt dreamed of becoming a pharmacist. As he completed his undergraduate studies at Durham's North Carolina College for Negroes, he was forced to reckon with the fact that only the all-white University of North Carolina at Chapel Hill (UNC) housed a pharmacy program. At the very same time, three young civil rights activists, two attorneys and a journalist, were searching for a brave African American who would agree to challenge Jim Crow higher education. The attorneys were Conrad Pearson and Cecil McCoy, who practiced law in Durham. The journalist was thirty-five-year-old Louis Austin, editor of the *Carolina Times*, the black news weekly in Durham.

After Hocutt agreed to apply to UNC, the four men drove from Durham to Chapel Hill to register the young man for the March quarter of classes. Austin introduced Hocutt to university registrar and dean of admissions Thomas Wilson: "This is Mr. Hocutt, a new student . . . who needs his class schedule and class assignment." After the startled registrar recovered his composure, he denied Hocutt admission because of his race, and Pearson and McCoy filed suit in state court.[1] In the short term, the case did not succeed. But these young men's actions launched the NAACP's (National Association for the Advancement of Colored People) legal struggle that would culminate with the U.S. Supreme Court's landmark *Brown v. Board of Education* decision in 1954, declaring that segregated public education was unconstitutional.

Louis Austin's part in the *Hocutt* case was characteristic of his decades-long role as a leader in the long black freedom struggle in North Carolina.[2] Although he grew up in an era of bleak possibilities and grave dangers for blacks in the state, he courageously challenged racial injustice throughout his life. In 1898, the year of his birth, white supremacists murdered African Americans and violently overthrew the biracial government of Wilmington, North Carolina. Two years later, white Democrats amended the state's constitution to disfranchise black voters. Nonetheless, by the time he drew his last breath seven decades later, in 1971, Louis Austin had helped transform the racial landscape of the state, the region, and the nation.

DURING THE TWENTIETH CENTURY, black journalists played an essential role in the struggle for equal rights in America. While the most prominent black newspapers—the *Chicago Defender* and the *Pittsburgh Courier*—were published in the North, several southern black newspapers also played a pivotal role in the fight against white supremacy. Operating in the nation's most racially oppressive section, determined black publishers, editors, and journalists illuminated racial discrimination, while advocating black voter registration and equal educational opportunity. A few black southern journalists pursued a more radical agenda and directly challenged racial segregation.[3] Austin, who edited and published the *Carolina Times* from 1927 to 1971, was one of the most fearless and effective of these journalists. He boldly challenged white supremacy and racial segregation for over four decades, from the years prior to World War II through the modern civil rights era.

Not all southern black journalists consistently opposed racial oppression or even advocated for racial integration.[4] Percy Greene, editor of Mississippi's *Jackson Advocate*, fought for black voting rights during the 1940s, but during the late 1950s and 1960s, he collaborated with the segregationist Mississippi State Sovereignty Commission, denouncing the *Brown v. Board of Education* decision and the Montgomery Bus Boycott.[5] Cornelius A. Scott, editor of the *Atlanta Daily World*, promoted voter registration campaigns during the 1940s but opposed direct action protests, including sit-ins, during the 1960s.[6] In North Carolina, the *Charlotte Post*, headed by publisher and editor J. S. Nathaniel Tross, a minister of the African Methodist Episcopal Zion Church, opposed the integration of public schools, supported North Carolina governor Luther Hodges's efforts to delay integration, and criticized Martin Luther King Jr. Tross claimed that sit-ins merely exacerbated racial conflict, without benefit to the black community.[7]

In contrast, Austin was part of a cadre of black journalists in the South who played leading roles in the fight for racial equality, refusing to moderate or reverse their stance in the face of white harassment or pressure. These crusading black journalists routinely fought for the rights of African Americans by employing "a powerful and compelling form of advocacy journalism."[8] The groundwork laid by these journalists helped accelerate the movement for equal rights in the 1950s and 1960s. In South Carolina, John McCray, publisher of the *Charleston Lighthouse*, and E. A. Parker, publisher of the *Sumter People's Informer*, merged their newspapers in 1941 to create the *Lighthouse and Informer* as an organ in the fight for equal salaries for black teachers in South Carolina. Three years later, McCray and journalist Osceola McKaine formed the Progressive Democratic Party to increase black political influence in South Carolina.[9] In Arkansas, L. C. and Daisy Bates were staunch activists, using the *State Press* (Little Rock) to aid in the black freedom struggle. They championed the *Brown v. Board of Education* decision, and Daisy Bates notably advised the nine black students who desegregated Central High School in Little Rock in 1957.[10] In Oklahoma, Roscoe Dunjee, editor of the *Oklahoma City Black Dispatch*, advocated legal action to desegregate higher education and housing, ensure voting rights for black people, and equalize teachers' salaries.[11]

Like McCray, McKaine, Dunjee, and the Bateses, Austin played a key role in stimulating and sustaining the black freedom struggle before the emergence of the modern civil rights movement. This study, which uses the life of Louis Austin as a lens through which to view the long black freedom struggle in North Carolina, reveals the important role played by the southern black press.[12] Though not a comprehensive study of the freedom struggle in North Carolina, this narrative does offer a window into black activism in many parts of the state, especially in the towns and cities in the piedmont and the east regularly covered by the *Carolina Times*. Moreover, although the newspaper was based in Durham, it was widely distributed and read in much of North Carolina.

Recently, historians have emphasized black civil rights activism during the 1930s and 1940s.[13] In her important article "The Long Civil Rights Movement," Jacquelyn Hall argued that the black freedom struggle began well before the 1950s. She maintained that "the . . . 'long civil rights movement' . . . took root in the liberal and radical milieu of the late 1930s."[14] Unlike Hall and others, I employ the term "long black freedom struggle" instead of "long civil rights movement." Though a significant number of African Americans took effective action during the 1930s and 1940s, this did not constitute a mature social movement, which would include local movements, with local and national leadership, indigenous organizations and institutions, and strong communication networks.[15] However, many of these traits were not present at a critical mass during the 1930s and 1940s. For example, the most important civil rights organization during these decades, the NAACP, had limited membership in North Carolina. Further, during these years, mass action was the exception, not the norm. There were local indigenous organizations, like the Durham Committee on Negro Affairs (DCNA) and local chapters of the NAACP, but they rarely mobilized massive participation during the

Depression and World War II eras. In North Carolina, nonetheless, Louis Austin personified the long black freedom struggle, fighting for racial justice and black empowerment from the Great Depression to the Black Power era.

While this study is centered on the life of Louis Austin, it is also the story of Durham attorney Conrad Pearson, who, beginning in 1933, fought for over three decades to integrate higher education and public schools in North Carolina. It is the story of black college students in Greensboro at Bennett College and North Carolina A&T (North Carolina Agricultural and Technical College), who boycotted segregated movie theaters in 1938. It is the story of Vella Lassiter, who successfully sued the Greensboro-Fayetteville Bus Lines in 1939 after she was roughed up by the white driver for refusing to move to the back of the bus. It is the story of Private Booker T. Spicely, who was shot and killed by a white bus driver for transgressing the color line on a Durham bus in 1944. It is the story of Mack Ingram, who was convicted of raping a white woman in Yanceyville, North Carolina, in 1951, even though he never got closer to her than seventy-five feet. It is the story of Rev. Douglas Moore and six young men and women, who staged an anti-segregation sit-in at an ice cream parlor in Durham in 1957. It is the story of Joycelyn McKissick, who helped desegregate Durham High School in 1959 and led protests to integrate restaurants. It is the story of Caswell County farmer and parent Jasper Brown, who in 1963 fought off a carload of white segregationists who sought to punish him for sending his children to a previously all-white school. Indeed, it is the story of countless African Americans across North Carolina fighting for freedom and equality.

BORN IN 1898 in rural Halifax County in eastern North Carolina, Louis Ernest Austin grew up in an era marked by appalling oppression of African Americans. In a world where whites instructed blacks to stay in their subordinate "place," Austin's father instilled in his son the values of self-respect and dignity and the importance of a solid education. Raised in the African Methodist Episcopal Church, he learned that all people were equal in the eyes of God. And growing up in a county with a history of a relatively large number of black landowners and elected officials may have contributed to the young man's fighting spirit. To pursue higher education, Austin moved to Durham in 1921 to attend the National Training School, now North Carolina Central University. There he encountered a black community with a thriving black middle class and many successful black businesses, notably North Carolina Mutual Life Insurance Company and the Mechanics and Farmers Bank, two of the largest black-owned financial institutions in the nation.

In 1927, Austin purchased the *Carolina Times*, founded in 1921, providing a voice for the black community, during a time when white newspapers regularly ignored or demonized black people in their pages. The young editor transformed the newspaper into a vital part of the black freedom struggle in North Carolina. Despite many excellent studies, most people still believe that during the decades prior to the Montgomery Boycott (1955–56), black protest was quiescent. But Austin was anything but quiescent. An extraordinarily outspoken and dynamic leader, he fearlessly attacked anyone, including prominent blacks and whites, who stood in the way of freedom and equality for all people. He exemplified the *Carolina Times'* motto, "The Truth Unbridled." Austin's advocacy did not stop with the written word. On occasion, he flouted Jim Crow law and bragged about it, leading many to wonder that he was not stopped by an assassin's bullet. For example, during the early 1930s, Austin attended a concert at the racially segregated Carolina Theater in Durham with his wife and sister-in-law. Although blacks were required to sit in the balcony, Austin disregarded the usher and sat in the main seating area, which was for whites only. After the concert, "Austin openly bragged in public that white people would never force him to sit in the buzzard roost with the 'Uncle Tom' leaders of the Negro race."[16]

During the 1930s, Austin initiated a new strategy in the black freedom struggle, as he employed legal tactics to challenge segregation and counseled African Americans to leave the Republican Party for the Democratic Party to increase black political influence in the one-party state. He led voter registration drives, campaigned for public office, pursued integration of higher education in the courts, lobbied for equal pay for black teachers and equal funding for black schools, demanded equal economic opportunity for African Americans, and denounced police brutality. In 1935, Austin cofounded the Durham Committee on Negro Affairs (DCNA), which promoted black political participation and worked to improve black life in Durham. Austin was elected justice of the peace as a Democrat in 1934, a victory that was hailed by the *Pittsburgh Courier* as the beginning of the New Deal in the South.

During World War II, Austin was the leading North Carolina advocate for the Double V strategy, fighting for victory at home against racist injustice while supporting U.S. efforts against the Axis Powers abroad. In doing so, Austin emphasized the contrast between the U.S. government's wartime rhetoric of fighting for freedom in Europe and Asia while acquiescing to or promoting the oppression of blacks on the home front and in the armed services. Unlike many black leaders in North Carolina who refused to employ confrontational tactics, Austin backed A. Philip Randolph's March on Washington Movement, which compelled President Franklin D. Roosevelt to issue an executive order banning racial discrimination in defense plants. When white employers still refused to hire African Americans, Austin called them "contemptible jackasses" who were "throttling this nation's effort to save our shores."[17] He also denounced the U.S. armed forces' racially oppressive treatment of black soldiers as "unsafe, unsound and damnable."[18] Despite being harassed by several federal government agencies, including the Federal Bureau of Investigation and the Internal Revenue Service, unlike several black newspaper editors, Austin refused to tone down his attacks on the state and federal governments for perpetuating racial injustice. In 1944, Austin revitalized the Durham branch of the NAACP after a white bus driver murdered a black soldier. The bus driver, who was exonerated by an all-white jury, shot the soldier for objecting to Jim Crow seating on the bus. Austin's wartime use of the politics of protest helped lay the groundwork for the postwar civil rights movement.

The decade leading up to the *Brown v. Board of Education* decision was pivotal for the black freedom struggle. In January 1951, Austin told a Winston-Salem audience of African Americans celebrating the eighty-eighth anniversary of the Emancipation Proclamation, "Our eternal goal must be equality. . . . We will teach it and thunder it from the pulpit until every child achieves it."[19] Working with the DCNA, Austin played a crucial role in increasing black voter registration. In 1945, Austin staged the first campaign in the twentieth century by an African American to win a seat on the Durham City Council. Although he lost, his campaign laid the groundwork for subsequent runs by African Americans, leading to the election of the first black member of the Durham City Council in 1953. Austin fought for integrated public facilities, organizing an integrated football game in Durham, which national newspapers pronounced the first racially integrated football game in the South. Austin continued to prioritize the fight for equitable public education for African Americans in the postwar years. He pursued a dual strategy, pressing for integration, particularly in higher education, while fighting for equal funding for black public schools. When North Carolina's white public officials opposed civil rights, Austin was quick to denounce them, as he did in 1949, calling a speech by Senator Clyde Hoey "a long asinine diatribe against Negroes."[20]

Unlike some older black activists, Austin sustained his position in the forefront of the movement for justice and equal opportunity during the modern civil rights movement. During the 1950s and 1960s, he joined with a new generation of activists who fought for integration of public schools, lunch counters, and restaurants; equal access to employment opportunities; and voting rights. Unlike many other black leaders in Durham, he immediately and enthusiastically embraced a sit-in that began in 1957, three years before the more celebrated Greensboro lunch counter sit-ins. Austin continued to endorse litigation, but now advocated civil disobedience and direct action, publicizing sit-ins, boycotts, and marches, and serving as an important advisor to young activists. When white movie theater owners defended racial segregation, Austin called their comments "weak, stupid and about as asinine as any we have ever heard by so-called intelligent persons."[21] He also backed a boycott of white retail businesses that refused to hire black workers by publishing the names of those businesses in the *Carolina Times*. This strategy helped compel white businesses to hire African Americans.

During these years, Austin worked relentlessly for public school integration, as North Carolina government officials implemented policies to delay enforcement of the *Brown* decision. When southern white conservatives cried out for states' rights in rejecting the *Brown* decision, Austin denounced their claim as a sham, whose sole purpose was to perpetuate white supremacy. He spoke truth to power when he asserted that states' rights meant "the right . . . to compel Negroes to go to inferior schools. . . . It means the right to attack and rape Negro women. . . . It even means the right to lynch, to force Negroes to enlist in the armed service, fight for democracy and then deny them the fruits of their sacrifices."[22] During the mid-1960s, Austin's efforts along with those of thousands of freedom fighters compelled the U.S. Congress to pass the Civil Rights Act of 1964 and the Voting Rights Act of 1965.

During the second half of the 1960s, Austin developed a complex relationship with the Black Power movement. During these years, he continued to fight for school integration and black political power. He worked closely with the Durham Committee on Negro Affairs, leading to the election of increasing numbers of black officials in Durham and throughout the state. When, in the midst of public school integration, white officials shut down many black schools and fired black principals and teachers, Austin publicized these injustices and backed lawsuits to protect black educators' jobs. While he criticized the Black Panthers and other organizations that employed violent rhetoric and advocated black nationalism, Austin championed the efforts of local activist Howard Fuller, who led an antipoverty agency in Durham called Operation Breakthrough and was considered a militant by many during that era. Austin encouraged Fuller to confront a recalcitrant black upper class while battling powerful white leaders. The *Carolina Times* spoke out in favor of striking workers at Duke University and supported black citizens' rent strikes and actions against the Durham Housing Authority, which failed to address racial discrimination in public housing. In 1971, the year of his death, Austin was still speaking out for equity in education when he challenged white-dominated school boards' practice of firing black principals as public schools were integrated.

IN 1958, MARTIN LUTHER KING JR. called the black press "the conscience of our nation." He explained, "It has become angry for people who dare not express anger themselves. It has cried for Negroes when the hurt was so great that tears could not be shed. . . . It has been a crusading press and that crusade has, from its beginning in 1827, been the cry of 'Freedom.'"[23] In defining the role of the black press, Dr. King perfectly described the role played by Louis Austin and the *Carolina Times*, which voiced the anger of black Carolinians, and turned that anger into action, in a forty-year crusade for freedom.

CHAPTER ONE

No Man Is Your Captain

The Making of an Agitator

One day, when he was about seven years old, a few years after the turn of the twentieth century, Louis Austin grabbed his shoeshine brush and approached a white man who had just entered his father's barber shop. Mimicking some of the older boys, young Louis said to the customer, "Shine, capt'n, Shine, capt'n." Louis's father, William, abruptly stopped sharpening his straight razor before giving a customer a shave, turned to his oldest child, and reprimanded him, "Son, never let me hear you say those words again. No man is your captain. You are the captain of your own soul."[1] No one in the shop said a word, as William told his son that he should never accept "second class status."[2] It was a lesson that the younger Austin never forgot.

LOUIS ERNEST AUSTIN was born in a one-room house in Enfield, in Halifax County, in eastern North Carolina, on January 24, 1898.[3] Enfield is about seventy miles northeast of Raleigh, the state capital. The grandson of slaves, Austin was the oldest child of William Louis Austin and Carrie Johnson Austin, who had three other children: Maude, born in about 1906; Jesse, born in about 1910; and Lodius, born in 1915.[4]

In the oppressive racial climate of early twentieth-century North Carolina, Austin and his siblings learned the values of self-respect and equality from their father, who was born twenty-five miles south of Enfield, in Tarboro, Edgecombe County, North Carolina, in about 1868.[5] Although Austin's father only completed two years of school, he learned to read and write. A gifted violinist, the elder Austin ran a farm, and a barbershop for white customers in Enfield.[6] Although whites commonly showed no respect for black men, Louis's strong-minded father commanded and received respect from whites, as well as blacks. Louis recalled that his father was the first one in his family to hold his head up high, refusing to grovel in front of anyone. William enjoyed the respect and love of his family and community. At a time when white southerners generally disrespected black men by refusing to call them by their last name or use the salutation "Mr.," William Austin's white customers in the barber shop called him Mr. Austin or Austin.[7] William's self-respect was based on his belief that all people were equal before God. A devout Christian, he had "great faith in God," which he imparted to his children.[8]

To ensure that his children would hold their heads high as he did, William Austin refused to "let his children work for white people." Louis Austin recalled growing up on a farm: "When our crops were finished, sometimes the children would say, 'Now Dad we can go over and make some money working for these white farmers.' But Dad would always reply, 'I'll never let you do that. No child of mine will ever work for a white man and bow down his head to the yoke. I had rather for him to starve than to do that.'"[9]

Little is known of William Austin's father, Granville Austin, except that he had been a slave in Edgecombe County, North Carolina, which is adjacent to Halifax County. In a 1958 interview, Louis Austin said that his grandfather died in Virginia, although he did not know when. According to Louis, William Austin never knew his father, so he "had to make [his] own way."[10]

Louis Austin's mother was born Carrie Johnson in Edgecombe County, during the late 1870s.[11] Louis was told that Carrie's father was a white man who had two families, a white family in South Carolina and a black family in North Carolina. In a 1958 interview, Louis Austin said that Carrie's father "married" a black woman in Edgecombe County. Of course, this "marriage" was not legal in North Carolina, where interracial marriage was banned. Austin told a researcher that this "wh[ite] man [was not] much of anything."[12] He told his grandson, Kenneth Edmonds, that Carrie's father was Irish, with a face full of freckles, which skipped a generation and appeared on Louis's daughter Vivian's face.[13] According to North Carolina death records, Carrie's father was Alvin Johnson and her mother's name was Emma. The 1880 U.S. Census indicates that twenty-five-year-old Emma Johnson (Carrie's mother) worked as a farm laborer while residing in Lower Conetoe, in Edgecombe County. Emma lived with her four daughters, including four-year-old Carrie, and one son.[14] According to Kenneth Edmonds, Carrie was "fair-skinned" with "thin wispy hair."[15]

The confidence, determination, and self-respect exhibited by Austin and his father may have been rooted in Halifax County's tradition of African Americans' self-reliance and relative prosperity. In 1860, with the largest free black population in the state, Halifax County had many successful free black farmers. In fact, "the 62 free Negro farmers who owned real property before the Civil War outnumbered the free black farmers in the other [nearby] ten counties combined."[16] After the war, African Americans predominated in the population of Halifax County, and enjoyed a degree of economic success beyond that in nearby counties. In 1900, two years after Louis's birth, 64.1 percent (19,733) of the county's population was black, and 20 percent of black farm operators were nontenants.[17] The two most important crops were cotton and corn, with peanuts and tobacco becoming increasingly important. Although it was considered a plantation county, Halifax's black population owned an average of 1.8 acres per capita in 1910, which was more land than blacks owned in surrounding counties.[18] Thus, during Louis Austin's childhood years, his family lived in a region where blacks were generally more prosperous than in surrounding counties.

Halifax County, which was part of the Second Congressional District, known as the "Black Second," also had a history of significant black political influence during the late nineteenth century. With strong black support, the Second District regularly elected Republicans, including African Americans, like James O'Hara, who served from 1883 to 1887, and George H. White, who served from 1897 to 1901.[19] So in the years surrounding Austin's birth, his family lived in a district represented by a black member of Congress.[20] Living in an area that had a record of relative black economic strength and political influence may have contributed to William Austin's inner strength and dignity.

Black political and economic influence in North Carolina suffered a precipitous decline during the early twentieth century. Intent on destroying a progressive political alliance of white Populists and black Republicans, which controlled the North Carolina General Assembly from 1894 to 1898, white supremacist Democrats employed violence, intimidation, fraud, and racist propaganda in the political campaigns of 1898 and 1900 to retake control of the state. The most violent episode, the infamous Wilmington Racial Massacre of 1898, occurred just a few months after Austin's birth. In Wilmington, on the North Carolina coast, about 160 miles south of Enfield, white vigilante Democrats killed and wounded hundreds of blacks while overthrowing the Republican government of that city.[21] In 1898 in Durham, where Austin would live most of his life, according to a local newspaper account, "Passions became so heated that a black man rumored to have been living with a white woman (allegedly the wife of a Republican) was lynched and his body left hanging along the roadside between Durham and Chapel Hill to serve as a ghastly lesson in white supremacy, a lesson which [white] Durhamites proved they could teach as well as anyone."[22]

Although blacks in Halifax County were relatively prosperous, the town of Enfield was quite poor and stagnated economically during the late 1890s. Two years before Austin's birth, the local newspaper, the *Enfield Progress*, described the town in exceedingly pessimistic terms: "It had no banking establishment. It had no schools. It had no adequate protection against fire. It had only three brick buildings. It had no supply of pure water. It had no opera-house, no town hall, no telephone system, no wholesale store. . . . The town existed; it did not really live. Inaction and stagnation had done their deadly work. Enfield looked upon the past without interest, upon the future without hope."[23]

By the early 1900s, however, Enfield was enjoying an economic and social transformation with the opening of tobacco warehouses, a textile mill, and two banks. In 1905, the town could boast two artesian wells, two fire engines, and schools that served 400 black and white students. The town now had blacksmiths, saloons, butcher shops, dry goods stores, grocery stores, and many other retail establishments. There was substantial construction of residential and commercial buildings. This economic revitalization generated a threefold increase in the town's population, from 361 in 1900 to 1,167 in 1910.[24]

In 1900, when Austin was two years old, North Carolina effectively disfranchised African Americans by passing amendments to the state constitution requiring payment of a poll tax and passing a literacy test to vote. A grandfather clause was also passed, which excluded men from having to take the literacy test if their grandfather had voted before 1868, the year black men began voting in North Carolina after the adoption of the Fourteenth Amendment to the U.S. Constitution. Thus, the grandfather clause exempted whites from having to take the literacy test, while requiring blacks to do so. The white supremacist Democrats would dominate the state and the South for the next six decades. In 1901, after North Carolina disfranchised African Americans, the Second Congressional District, like the rest of the state's districts, elected Democrats, the party of white supremacy in those years. George White, who represented the Second District until 1901, was the last black U.S. congressman from the South until the 1960s.[25] North Carolina would not elect another black member of Congress until 1992. Consequently, Austin grew up in a time when African Americans in North Carolina and throughout the South were regularly denied voting rights and economic opportunity and were victimized by educational inequality and by white violence.

Although William Austin had only two years of formal education, or perhaps because his own education had been so meager, he recognized the value of education and instilled that value in his children. Like black children throughout the South, the Austin children attended segregated schools that were woefully underfunded compared with white schools. From 1906 to 1910, North Carolina's white students received about 2½ times the funding per capita as did the state's black students.[26] Like its black students, the state's black teachers were also mistreated. In 1910, white teachers' average salary per student taught was over 2½ times that for black teachers in North Carolina.[27]

During the early twentieth century, black and white children in Halifax County received their early education in one-room schoolhouses, and Austin likely did as well. Like in the rest of the state, the black schools in Halifax County received substantially less funding than did the white schools. In 1899, the assessed value of all the black schools in the county, which had a majority-black population, was less than 10 percent of the assessed value of the county's white schools. During the first decade of the twentieth century, when Austin began school, there was little improvement in any of the schools in the county.[28]

As a teenager, Louis sought to continue his education beyond primary school, but the state did not provide any financing for public secondary education for African Americans. It was not until 1918 that the state government would begin to fund black high schools.[29] In contrast, by 1908, white high schools had become a "recognized part of the general school organization" in North Carolina. At that time, there were 213 white high schools, including 132 county schools and 81 city or town schools.[30]

Unlike most African Americans in North Carolina, Austin was able to attend a private secondary school, but given the limited financial resources of the black community, the school was in poor repair. Austin, who even as a young man exuded confidence and spoke out against injustice no matter the consequences, viewed this school as unacceptable. Finally, he could no longer remain silent about the deplorable conditions in his school. He "walked into" the school superintendent's office and "told him that the school was a disgrace and the building should be burned down." After word got around that Austin had "sassed" the superintendent, his parents decided that young Austin would be better off leaving Enfield, so they sent him to the Joseph Keasby Brick Agricultural and Normal School in Edgecombe County to finish his high school education.[31] Each day, Austin walked three miles to the Brick School.[32]

The Brick School, which offered primary and secondary education, was founded in 1895 by the American Missionary Association, with a donation of a 1,400-acre farm and $5,000 from Julia Brewster Brick, the widow of a wealthy civil engineer. Upon her death in 1903, she gave a substantial bequest to the school, which was named in memory of her husband, Joseph Keasby Brick. The first president of the school, Thomas Sewell Inborden, an 1891 graduate of Fisk University, infused the school with his philosophy emphasizing industrial and agricultural education, as well as academic instruction. Students at the school farmed a variety of crops, including cotton, peanuts, cabbage, potatoes, apples, strawberries, and peaches. Brick provided a six-year academic program in secondary education starting with the seventh grade for students preparing to go to college or to teach in the public schools. When Austin arrived for the 1915–16 academic year, the school had 336 students; forty-seven attended the secondary school. Secondary school students like Austin studied English, the sciences, agriculture, mathematics, Latin, civics, economics, and biblical history. Although Austin was seventeen years old when he arrived at the Brick School, he enrolled in the seventh grade, which was likely a result of the limited schooling available to black students in Enfield. He attended eighth grade classes during the 1916–17 school year.[33]

In 1950, Austin returned to the school to give an address during the "grand national reunion." At that time, Brick officials boasted of its alumni, who had gone on to successful careers as "ministers, physicians, dentists, lawyers, editors and publishers, morticians, building contractors, college professors, [and] public school teachers."[34]

After graduating from the Brick School, Austin enrolled at Kittrell College, located in the small town of Kittrell, about fifty miles east of Enfield.[35] Founded in 1885, Kittrell College was affiliated with and funded by the African Methodist Episcopal Church. When Austin arrived at Kittrell, Cadd G. O'Kelly was the president of the college.[36] Born in 1865, O'Kelly graduated from Lincoln University, with A.M. and D.D. degrees. By the time Austin arrived at Kittrell, O'Kelly had extensive teaching and administrative experience in secondary and higher education. He had previously taught at Kittrell and at Slater State Normal School (now Winston-Salem State University) and served as principal of Kittrell and Slater. After a brief tenure as vice president of Durham's National Religious Training School and Chautauqua from 1911 to 1912, O'Kelly returned to Kittrell, serving as president from 1912 to 1917.[37]

Kittrell emphasized industrial education and teacher training.[38] During O'Kelly's first stint as principal of Kittrell from 1896 to 1898, he introduced "domestic arts and industrial features in the teacher training program."[39] In 1916, Kittrell enrolled 284 students, with only two students in the college department. Most of the students were in the elementary school grades. Most likely, Austin took high school classes at Kittrell. The school employed twelve teachers, all black, seven women and five men.[40] Austin likely attended Kittrell at least in part because of O'Kelly's influence. When O'Kelly left Kittrell, so did Austin. Austin was a strong supporter of Kittrell throughout his life. In 1965, he headed a fundraising campaign and helped establish the Kittrell Foundation.[41]

Austin transferred to the National Training School (NTS) in Durham in 1917 after the Durham school hired O'Kelly as its vice president.[42] The NTS had been founded seven years earlier by James E. Shepard as the National

Religious Training School and Chautauqua for the Colored Race (NRTS). Born in 1875, Shepard initially sought to educate black ministers, but by the time Austin arrived, the school's mission had been broadened. In its early years, the NRTS suffered severe financial difficulties, and two years before Austin's arrival, the school's property had been sold to the Golden Belt Realty Company. Then, in May 1916, Shepard repurchased the school from Golden Belt, and the school's name was changed to the NTS. While the NRTS had had an all-black board of trustees with a white advisory board, the NTS board of trustees included several members from the white-owned Golden Belt Realty Company. After the repurchase, Shepard remained president of the school. In the fall of 1916, the school enrolled 123 students, just three in the college department. It employed eighteen teachers, all black, eight men and ten women.[43]

Austin arrived in Durham soon after the United States had entered World War I. He registered for the draft on September 12, 1918. On his registration form, he listed his occupation as barber.[44] During World War I, the United States held four draft registration days, beginning in June 1917, when ten million men over the age of twenty-one were registered. In June 1918, a second registration day was held for those men who had reached age twenty-one during that year. The last two registration days were held in August and September of 1918, with Austin registering in September, but he was too young to be drafted, as he had not yet reached his twenty-first birthday.[45] Two months later, the war was over.

Austin's arrival in Durham marked his first experience of urban living. His reaction to urban life was likely similar to that of one of his classmates at NTS, Asa Spaulding, who had grown up in rural Columbus County, North Carolina. Spaulding was related to two of Durham's leading black businessmen. Aaron Moore, his great-uncle, was Durham's first black doctor and one of the founders of North Carolina Mutual Life Insurance Company (NC Mutual). Charles Clinton Spaulding, Asa's second cousin, also worked for NC Mutual and would later serve as the company's president. Nonetheless, when Asa arrived in Durham in 1918, he could not help but be impressed by the city, with its "automobiles, street lights, rows of houses along the city blocks of paved . . . streets."[46]

While Austin attended NTS, his parents and siblings joined him in Durham. Louis lived with his father, who ran a barbershop; his mother; and his younger siblings, Maude, Jesse, and Lodius.[47] During those years, Louis followed his father's profession, at times working as a barber. He later recalled that he "should have been a barber . . . but felt cooped in." He felt that he "could not express" himself "freely to whites," and Louis Austin was not one to hold his tongue.[48]

Austin graduated in 1921 from the Academy Department of the NTS (equivalent to a high school graduation), but he did not graduate alongside his class.[49] According to Austin's daughter, Austin had irritated the school's president, James Shepard, by playing a number of practical jokes. On one occasion, Austin and his friends put a pig in a piano, and another time, they put a wagon on the roof of a house on campus. Consequently, Shepard waited several years before conferring Austin and his practical-joker friends their diplomas.[50] In the 1920 NTS catalogue, Austin is listed among the eighteen third-year students in the Academy Department, which had a four-year program. Several of Austin's classmates went on to successful careers in business and education, including real estate and insurance entrepreneur Henry McKinley Michaux Sr., of Adako, North Carolina. In 1920, the school's College Department included three freshmen, three sophomores, one junior, and two seniors. There were thirty students in the Commercial Department, twenty-eight students in the Music Department, and eight students in the Domestic Art Department. Notable students in these departments included James T. Taylor, who would have a long career as a professor and an administrator at North Carolina College for Negroes (NCCN), the successor to NTS; Ruth Rush, who would serve as dean of women at NCCN; and Annie Day Shepard, daughter of James Shepard. The board of trustees, a majority of whom were white, included two blacks, James Shepard and W. G. Pearson, a businessman and the principal of Durham's black high school, Hillside Park.[51]

In 1921, the NTS was the only accredited high school for African Americans in Durham. At that time, the North Carolina Department of Public Instruction (DPI) recognized ten black schools in the state as providing instruction above the high school level, including NTS and Kittrell College.[52] The DPI recognized ten black high schools as "standard high schools" with classifications of IA, IB, IIA, and IIB, with IA the highest rating. Six black high schools had an IA rating, including NTS. The Brick School and Kittrell College were both rated IIA.[53]

While at school in Durham, Austin also worked as an insurance agent for NC Mutual selling insurance in eastern North Carolina.[54] Founded in 1898 by black Durhamites John Merrick, the owner of several barbershops, and physician Aaron Moore, by 1921, NC Mutual was the largest black-owned insurance company in the world. It was also the center of a thriving black business district in downtown Durham, which included the Mechanics and Farmers Bank, the Mutual Savings and Loan Association, and the Bankers Fire Insurance Company. These financial institutions were formed to serve the black community when, as they regularly did, white companies refused to grant fire insurance, home mortgages, and other loans to African Americans.[55] A strong black middle class emerged in Durham as a result of such successful African American businesses.

While Durham in the late 1910s and 1920s enjoyed a reputation for a thriving black middle class because of the presence of vibrant black financial concerns, it was also in many ways a typical southern town. African Americans were victimized by Jim Crow law, and suffered from economic, political, and legal oppression and white violence. Three years after Austin arrived in Durham, "a black Durham laborer was lynched for alleged assault of a white girl in Person County. An angry crowd took the presumed attacker from the sheriff's custody and hanged him on a tree in a black cemetery."[56] A white Durhamite road construction company owner named Nello Teer "courageously wrote to the paper about what he labeled a 'ghastly mistake.' He explained that Edward Roach, the lynched man, had worked for him on a project near Roxboro, and on the day of the assault had fallen ill and been excused from work by the foreman. On his way to Mount Tirzah station to catch a train back to town, he had been apprehended, not told what the charges were against him, prevented from communicating with Teer, who could have cleared him, and promptly taken in hand by a masked mob and executed." North Carolina officials "offered a $400 reward for the apprehension and conviction of each member of the mob," but "no one came forward to inform on the culprits."[57]

In addition to the danger of violent attacks by whites, Durham was a very unhealthy place for African Americans. In 1920, the city's death rate for blacks was 29.9 per thousand compared with 10 per thousand for whites. From 1927 to 1928, close to one-third of "black babies died" before age one. Fewer than one in eight African Americans "lived past the age of sixty . . . [and] statistics for 1927–28 showed that 64 percent of blacks died before the age of forty." A 1926 investigation by the Durham Business League revealed that in Durham "80 percent of blacks lived in rental housing, substandard, cheaply constructed, overcrowded, badly lighted and ventilated, and lacking in sanitary arrangements." Most black homes did not have indoor plumbing, and outhouses were "standard fixtures in black neighborhoods."[58] The 1926 study explained, "The difference in black and white health was attributable to blacks' poor housing, lack of sewerage, years of poor nutrition, and general medical neglect."[59]

Nonetheless, during the early 1920s, Austin advanced his career in insurance and also pursued an interest in journalism. By 1925 he had become manager of the insurance department of the Mechanics and Farmers Bank.[60] After he graduated from the NTS, he also served as sports editor for the local black newspaper, the *Standard Advertiser*, founded by Charles Arrant and first published in August 1921.[61]

African Americans had published newspapers and periodicals in North Carolina since the late nineteenth century. Examples include the *African Methodist Episcopal Zion Quarterly Review*, which was first published in 1882; the *Banner Enterprise*, started in 1883, published by the North Carolina Industrial Association; the *African Methodist Episcopal Church Review* (1885–1913); and the *AME Zion Star of Zion*, first published in 1883 and perhaps earlier.[62]

In Durham, there were several black newspapers prior to the founding of the *Standard Advertiser*. The first three were all closely associated with or controlled by NC Mutual. First was the *North Carolina Mutual*, which became known as the *Durham Negro Observer* by 1906. The third black newspaper was called the *Durham Reformer*. All three were published by NC Mutual, and served as the company's newspaper, while also serving Durham's black community.[63]

The *Reformer* had first been published by the Richmond-based Grand United Order of the True Reformers, a mutual benefit society founded by ex-slave and former Union Army soldier William Washington Browne. Under Browne's leadership, the Reformers created a successful insurance business that "claimed 100,000 members and had spread their operations to eighteen states." Browne's death in 1900 contributed to the demise of the Reformers by 1910.[64] Around 1910, NC Mutual "purchased the defunct *Reformer* from the failing True Reformers." The insurance company moved the Reformer Publishing Company to Durham, and also hired its Richmond editor, W. S. Young.[65] A member of the family that published the *Norfolk Journal and Guide* (Virginia), "Young managed the paper for a year and then bought it from the Mutual and continued to operate it until about 1918."[66]

According to most accounts, the founder of the *Standard Advertiser* was Charles J. Arrant, who was born in Pine Bluff, Arkansas, about 1888.[67] Prior to starting the newspaper, Arrant had earned his living as an actor and a comedian. Arrant arrived in Durham, in mid-1921, with a traveling theater company. He came to Durham with his wife and their ward, Rosa Lee Walters.[68] According to an article in the *Chicago Defender*, Arrant was influenced by friends "to leave the stage for a business career," and embarked on a journalism career.[69] However, a November 1921 article in the *Baltimore Afro-American* claims different origins for the paper. This article reported that "Billy Parent (Mr. Rareback) in association with Mr. Horace Van Hook" published "a nice little local paper [in Durham] called the *Colored Advertiser*."[70] Perhaps Arrant changed the paper's name when he assumed control.

In any event, under Arrant's leadership, the *Standard Advertiser* took a strong interest in black voter registration. In April 1922, when very few blacks were registered to vote, blacks in Durham formed the Colored Voters League to increase black voter registration. The officers of the organization were funeral director J. C. Scarborough, president; Dr. Stanford L. Warren, vice president; attorney R. McCants Andrews, secretary; Dr. Joseph N. Mills, assistant secretary; and William O'Kelly, treasurer.[71] In October 1922 the league met at the *Standard Advertiser*'s office to make plans to register 500 black voters in Durham County. The league hoped to use increased black political influence to pressure the city council and county commissioners to pave streets in the main black section of Durham, known as Hayti; hire black probation officers; and provide free books to the black public schools, among other things.[72] Meanwhile, one of the town's white daily newspapers, the *Durham Morning Herald*, warned black voters not to "become too vigorous in their use of the ballot" lest they arouse a violent response from the town's whites to keep blacks in their subordinate position.[73]

Two months later, Arrant's tenure at the newspaper was tragically terminated when, on Sunday, December 3, 1922, he was killed in a shootout with a local mobster.[74] According to the *Chicago Defender*, Arrant was murdered by Durham's "notorious vice lord" Dave McNeil, who confronted Arrant because of the journalist's anti-crime campaign. Arrant led a community effort to clean up crime in a rough section of Durham, known as Mexico. Prior to the shootout, Arrant and McNeil had fought after the editor took exception to "remarks made about him by McNeil. . . . Arrant overpowered McNeil, relieving him of his .45 caliber special Colt revolver, with which he later killed the vice lord," reported the *Chicago Defender*.[75] The following day the two men met near Arrant's home,"[76] "at the corner of Pettigrew street and Branch Alley."[77] The *Chicago Defender* described the altercation between McNeil and Arrant: "McNeil slapped the editor, at the same time drawing a .38 caliber revolver from his pocket and opened fire. Arrant drew at the same time and sent a charge through McNeil's abdomen. Both men fell to the pavement mortally wounded, but continued firing until their guns were emptied." They were taken to the hospital, Arrant dying in less than an hour, and McNeil surviving for two days before succumbing to his wounds.[78] The *Durham Morning Herald*, however, suggested a different reason for the dispute between Arrant and McNeil, stating that Arrant took exception to McNeil's harassment of Rosa Lee Walters, who was "reared and employed by Arrant."[79] In any event, Arrant's funeral was held at Mount Vernon Baptist Church in Durham.[80]

Following Arrant's death, the *Standard Advertiser* was edited by Richard Spiller, a Baptist minister.[81] Born in 1851, Spiller had served as pastor of the Bank Street Baptist Church in Norfolk, Virginia, from 1876 to 1884. In 1884, Spiller tried to change the church's tradition wherein the black congregation sat in segregated seating based on skin complexion, with dark-complexioned blacks on one side and light-complexioned blacks on the other side of the church. Former slaves had to "sit in the gallery." When Spiller was unable to convince the congregation to integrate seating, he led "a group of sixteen former slaves and dark-skinned members" out of that church and they formed the Queen Street Baptist Church, which he pastored until 1890.[82] Spiller later pastored the First Baptist Church in Hampton, Virginia, from 1888 to 1905, and started the People's Building and Loan Association there.[83] Prior to publishing the *Standard Advertiser*, Spiller lobbied the *Durham Morning Herald* to publish information about the successes of the black community in Durham. Like other mainstream (white) newspapers, the *Durham Morning Herald* generally ignored the black community, with the exception of reporting on black crime. In December 1922, Spiller persuaded the white paper to publish his report on successful black businesses in Durham, including NC Mutual, the Mechanics and Farmers Bank, the Bankers Fire Insurance Company, and others.[84] Under Spiller's direction, the *Standard Advertiser* was closely connected to NC Mutual, with its office in 1923 located at 106½ West Parrish Street, which also housed offices of NC Mutual.[85] Spiller died in 1929 in Durham at age eighty-five.[86]

During the mid-1920s, E. G. Harris, a Standard Life Insurance agent who had managed the paper under Spiller, ran the paper.[87] By 1926, with Harris serving as editor, the paper had changed its name to the *Carolina Times*, with offices in downtown Durham, at 203½ East Chapel Hill Street.[88] Prior to working for Durham's black newspaper, Harris had served in 1921 as field secretary of the newly formed North Carolina Negro Historical Association, which planned to "gather and publish records and doings of Negroes all over the State." The association was formed to build on the work of R. McCants Andrews, an African American lawyer in Durham, who had recently authored a biography of John Merrick (1859–1919), one of the founders of NC Mutual. James Shepard organized the meeting that created the association, with Andrews serving as secretary. Other officers included educators Charlotte Hawkins Brown, who founded Palmer Memorial Institute in Sedalia, North Carolina; Thomas S. Inborden of the Brick School, who served as president; and former two-term U.S. congressman Henry P. Cheatham, who served as vice president.[89]

Meanwhile, just one year after Louis Austin completed his studies at the NTS and while he was working in insurance and journalism, his father died. In May 1922, William Austin succumbed to heart disease and kidney disease at age fifty-three. After his father's death, Austin lived with his mother and siblings, at 509 Dunbar Street, near Fayetteville Street, which was the main black business street in the Hayti section of Durham.[90] Austin's father's death made oldest child Louis the chief financial provider for his mother, who never held a job outside the home, and his three younger siblings. Louis's youngest brother, Lodius, who was only seven years old when his father died, later recalled that Louis was like a father to him. At the time of William Austin's death, Louis's brother Jesse was twelve years old and his sister, Maude, was sixteen.[91]

Four years after his father's death, on June 26, 1926, Austin married Stella Vivian Walker, who was from Muskogee County, Oklahoma, where she had been born in 1900 to Coleman Walker Sr., who operated a large wheat farm, and Eliza J. Walker. Stella attended elementary school in Muskogee County. At age fourteen she began high school at Tuskegee Institute, in Tuskegee, Alabama, where she would later take college courses and work in scientist George Washington Carver's laboratory. When Walker arrived at Tuskegee, Booker T. Washington, who died the following year, was still presiding over the institution he had founded. In 1921, after completing her studies, Walker moved to Durham to work as a first grade teacher in the public schools.[92] According to an FBI report, based on information gleaned from the local draft board in 1944, Louis and Stella married in Muskogee, Oklahoma. After her marriage, Stella taught in the Durham public schools for many years. Like her husband, Stella was an active member of St. Joseph's African Methodist Episcopal (AME) Church, and she regularly taught Sunday school. She and Louis had one child, a daughter, Vivian Louise, who was born in August 1927.[93]

The year 1927 proved to be a particularly momentous year in Louis Austin's life, as it brought another auspicious beginning for the young man from Enfield. Richard L. McDougald, vice president of the Mechanics and Farmers Bank, concluded that the men running the *Carolina Times*, including Harris, were not competent to operate the paper because of a tendency toward an immoderate consumption of alcohol, and sought out Austin to buy the paper. Austin knew McDougald from school and through their common association with NC Mutual. McDougald had graduated from the NTS in 1918, three years before Austin. He arranged for Austin to obtain a $250 loan from the Mechanics and Farmers Bank to purchase the paper from Harris.[94] So it was that Louis Austin embarked on a forty-four-year run as the publisher and editor of the *Carolina Times*.[95]

CHAPTER TWO

We Have Got to Fight for Our Rights
Advocacy Journalism in the Great Depression

Once he took the reins, Austin quickly transformed the *Carolina Times* into a bullhorn for racial justice and equality. He declared, "The *Carolina Times* is the mouthpiece of Negro Durham."[1] A devout Christian, Austin believed that it was his moral duty to expose the suffering and injustice doled out to African Americans and to wage war against those who denied African Americans the rights and opportunities enjoyed by white Americans.[2] For Austin, like for many African Americans, the message of the Bible was a message of freedom and equality. All God's children had the right to be treated with dignity and respect. Austin's Christianity—he was a longtime member and trustee of St. Joseph's African Methodist Episcopal (AME) Church in Durham—could not abide racist oppression and mistreatment.[3]

In a time when white newspapers provided little coverage of the black community, with a disproportionate emphasis on black crime, black newspapers like the *Carolina Times* provided an indispensable voice for the black community. As editor, Austin carried on the legacy of the country's first black newspaper, New York's *Freedom's Journal*, which in its first issue in 1827 announced its purpose: "We wish to plead our own cause. Too long have others spoken for us. Too long has the public been deceived by misrepresentation in the things which concern us dearly."[4] Austin's daughter, Vivian Edmonds, who published the *Times* after her father's death in 1971, put the role of the black press simply but astutely: "The black press records 'what the white press won't.' "[5]

The *Carolina Times* engaged in advocacy journalism by speaking out for racial justice, while reporting on events that were ignored in white newspapers but were important to black North Carolinians. With his decisions about what stories to include in the paper as well as in his editorials, Austin advocated for black political influence, economic and educational opportunity, legal equality, and justice in all areas of life. Advocacy journalism has a long history in America.[6] In the era of the American Revolution, patriot journalists denounced British legislation and backed independence. During much of the nineteenth century, newspapers promoted the party line of one or the other major political party. The yellow or sensationalist journalism that began in the 1890s emphasized crime and sex stories to attract more readers and initiated crusades against social injustice for the same purpose.[7] During the first decade of the twentieth century, investigative journalists known as muckrakers publicized corrupt practices by politicians and big businesses and the dangerous working conditions faced by miners and railroad workers, leading to prosecutions of corrupt public officials and the passage of legislation that regulated big business practices.[8] During the 1930s, the American Society of Newspaper Editors endorsed interpretive journalism, paving the way for syndicated columnists, who analyzed local, national, and international politics.[9] Like its counterparts in the white and black press, the *Carolina Times* employed columnists, but its main source of interpretation was provided by the editorials penned by Louis Austin.

While Austin took an advocacy position in his editorials, a common journalistic practice, his paper did not explicitly reject objectivity as a goal. Articles in the *Times* did not overtly take a position. By devoting significant space in the paper to articles that reported cases of discrimination against blacks, the *Times* sought to shine a light on racial oppression to demonstrate the false picture painted by white-owned newspapers and white politicians, who routinely ignored or endorsed racial discrimination or claimed that it did not exist. By deciding what to cover, white and black newspapers ostensibly took a political position.

While white newspaper editors may have claimed that they were objective, in order to appear unbiased, it is important to note as sociologist Michael Schudson has observed, "The principle of objectivity on the news pages 'was not an ideal but a mystification' among newspaper editors."[10] Typically, white newspapers in North Carolina advocated the status quo in race relations, while the *Times* sought the opposite. By ignoring or praising the poor funding of black schools, the suppression of the black vote, and the denial of equal employment opportunity, to name just a few examples, white papers reinforced racial oppression. They also perpetuated negative stereotypes in their portrayals of African Americans. In 1947, the Hutchins Commission on Freedom of the Press, headed by University of Chicago chancellor Robert Hutchins, indicted the mainstream white press for its inadequate and unfair coverage of African Americans and other minorities.[11]

Austin's outspokenness, which often alienated advertisers, meant that the newspaper faced an ongoing struggle to survive financially. As that of other black newspapers with outspoken editors, advertising income of the *Carolina Times* was often diminished when black or white businesses withdrew advertisements in response to Austin's editorials attacking racial segregation, racist oppression, and black and white leaders who blocked the path to racial justice. At times, the paper's financial condition was so dire that Austin could not afford to pay his brother Lodius, who worked for many years as his linotype operator.[12] In 1948, Austin reported, "Our income is dependent absolutely on advertising and circulation, and the advertising is never too great when you try to maintain a progressive editorial policy."[13] But Austin refused to cater to advertisers, observing that "the average reader has a way of sensing insincerity and will quit supporting a newspaper that sells out to business interests."[14] And Austin was no sellout. Consequently, at times, powerful blacks in Durham canceled advertisements or made it difficult for Austin to get loans when they opposed his tactics or editorials.[15] At other times, realizing the important service that the *Times* gave to the black community, black financial institutions, notably the Mechanics and Farmers Bank and North Carolina Mutual (NC Mutual), and black businessmen, including C. C. Spaulding, loaned money or aided Austin in other ways to help him meet expenses.[16]

Spaulding, who served as NC Mutual president from 1923 to 1952, was a key supporter of Austin and the *Carolina Times*. Although they often clashed on the proper tactics to improve the lives of African Americans, they "had great respect for one another." According to historian Walter Weare, "on at least three occasions," NC Mutual "advanced the *Times* advertising money or loans to bail it out of insolvency." When the NC Mutual board of directors questioned Spaulding's support for the *Times*, he claimed that his backing was necessary to "have a paper we can controll, [sic] so to speak."[17] However, no one, not even Spaulding, could control what Austin published in the paper. Indeed, Austin was quick to criticize Spaulding or any of Durham's black businessmen when he disagreed with them, which was not infrequently.

During the 1920s and 1930s, like many black businesses in Durham, the *Carolina Times* struggled to survive in that era's oppressive racial climate and dire economic conditions. Jim Crow law and practice also facilitated the growth of some black businesses, as many white businesses refused to serve black customers. Consequently, many black businesses flourished during the 1920s, and although the Depression took its toll, many black businesses survived that decade. A 1938 survey reported that Durham had 146 black-owned businesses, including 117 sole proprietorships, thirteen partnerships, and sixteen corporations, with a total of 117 part-time employees and 248 full-time employees.[18] That same year, with the Durham Chamber of Commerce excluding black businesses, black businessmen began their own organization called the Durham Business and Professional Chain to promote the interests of black businesses. James J. Henderson, an executive with NC Mutual, presided over the organization during its first eight years, from 1938 to 1946. Austin, like Henderson, a member of St. Joseph's AME Church, was an active participant in the Business and Professional Chain from its inception, and would serve as president in 1953.[19]

During the Depression, Austin struggled to keep the newspaper afloat but carefully guarded his independence. In 1932, when Claude Barnett, who in 1919 had founded the Associated Negro Press (ANP), told Austin that T. E. McKinney, dean of Johnson C. Smith College in Charlotte, North Carolina, had offered to pay the *Carolina Times'* subscription to the press service, Austin rejected McKinney's help. Austin told Barnett that he did not want anyone else paying his bills. If his finances improved, he would renew his subscription with the ANP.[20]

Austin's relationship with Barnett was not a smooth one. In 1928, when the *Times* was late in its payments to the ANP, Barnett proposed to forgive Austin's debt as a favor to NC Mutual, with which they had an ongoing business relationship. Barnett thought that NC Mutual would appreciate this proposal because it would make the *Carolina Times* "morally obligated" to the insurance company.[21] Barnett's statement indicates he did not know Austin well, because the young editor would not permit himself or his newspaper to be beholden to anyone or anything. In fact, NC Mutual vacillated between being supportive of Austin and withholding support from him. By May 1929, NC Mutual had stopped paying Austin's bills with the ANP, but in October 1929, the insurance company decided to once again cover the *Times'* subscription costs with the news service.[22]

In 1932, after Barnett sent Austin "political propaganda for the Republican Party," Austin refused to publish it unless it was paid for as advertising. Barnett told Austin that he would not pay to publish. He may have assumed that Austin was fishing for a Republican subsidy, as he told Austin "even if any subsidy should exist for papers this year, that it might not reach the southern papers." Barnett noted that in a previous campaign, Republican Party officials told him that their "policy was not to interfere in the South."[23] The Republican Party had a long tradition of providing subsidies to black newspapers that supported Republican candidates. In 1904, for instance, Booker T. Washington advised the Republican Party "which black newspapers to subsidize in return for supporting the Republican candidates."[24] When, in 1919, Claude Barnett created the ANP, he arranged to receive subsidies from the Republican Party.[25]

Although Austin often asserted his independence from economic pressure, he did apparently accept the common practice whereby the Republican Party subsidized black newspapers. As he was a Republican anyway, he may have felt no conflict of interest in accepting Republican money, or he may have considered the subsidies just another form of payment for advertising. In a letter to Chicago-based National Features Services in late September 1932, Austin vowed that no political propaganda would be published without payment. He declared, "If the *Carolina Times* is to be omitted in the pay-offs as it was in the 1928 campaign, we prefer not to receive your releases. We were promised remuneration for carrying publicity for the Republican Party, but were side-stepped."[26] Given the newspaper's ongoing financial difficulties, Austin could not afford to give the Republican Party free publicity.

WHILE AUSTIN USED the *Carolina Times* to advocate for racial justice, he did not limit his activism to the pages of his newspaper. On occasion, he took direct action against racial segregation and racial injustice. During the 1930s, he attended a concert by the black tenor Roland Hayes at the racially segregated Carolina Theater in Durham with his wife and sister-in-law, "forced his way past the usher and took seats on the ground floor which" were "reserved for whites." After the concert, "Austin openly bragged in public that white people would never force him to sit in the buzzard roost with the 'Uncle Tom' leaders of the Negro race."[27] He also flouted other Jim Crow practices. Sometimes he drank from the "white" water fountain, and occasionally he sat in the "white" section of the Durham bus station.[28]

On several occasions, he organized picketing of white-owned stores that refused to hire black clerks. In 1932, Austin led a campaign to pressure white-owned grocery stores in Hayti, the main black section of Durham, to hire black clerks.[29] In February 1936, he helped initiate a boycott of white-owned grocery stores in Hayti, which did not employ black workers. Austin chaired the Durham Civic Committee, which sponsored the successful boycotts. Picketers brandished signs reading, "Don't Buy Where We Can't Work." According to one report, the Atlantic & Pacific Tea Company's (A&P) refusal to hire black workers led to the almost total loss of any black business. The protest succeeded in forcing the store to hire and continue employing black clerks for years. In 1942, Austin told a Duke University student that A&P feared another picketing campaign if it did not employ black clerks. Similarly, Kroger's grocery store hired black workers after just a couple of days of picketing, when its business dried up because of the boycott.[30]

Because Austin was so dismissive of whites' notions of proper racial etiquette, many whites viewed him as an anomaly and a radical who had little support, but, in fact, his words and deeds made him a hero to many African Americans. In a speech to an African Methodist Episcopal Zion Church conference in Durham, Austin exclaimed, "We have got to fight for our rights." The audience greeted Austin's words with thunderous applause, punctuated by comments like "Austin is right," "He doesn't bite his tongue," and "He is not afraid to tell them." The audience's response to Austin's speech was in marked contrast to the tepid response to speeches by other orators, including NC Mutual president C. C. Spaulding, the leading black businessman in the state.[31] In 1939, a visiting researcher reported that many African Americans "admired" Austin because of "his vitriolic editorials against the policies of the powers that be."[32] Austin's sister-in-law DeNina Austin admired Louis's courage, calling him a "fighter" who "looked for challenges." She said, "He'd walk where angels feared to tread."[33]

In 1932, in an interview for the *Pittsburgh Courier*, Austin contrasted his editorial approach with that of other southern black newspapers. He explained that many "Negro newspapers in the South are not only suppressed by fear of the opposite group, but are also suppressed by leaders of their own race, who refuse to support a newspaper that does not know the art of 'soft peddling.' This publication speaks with authority." Regardless of the opposition, Austin refused to soft peddle his views on racial inequality or his reporting on racial oppression.[34] When old-style white supremacists like newspaper publisher Josephus Daniels, new-style white moderates like University of North Carolina sociologist Guy Johnson, or older and more moderate black leaders like C. C. Spaulding criticized his words or actions, Austin refused to temper his confrontational tactics. As William Chafe showed in his study of the modern civil rights movement in Greensboro, North Carolina, confrontation and defiance, not civility and accommodation, were needed to break white supremacy's stranglehold on the South.[35] Austin took to heart Frederick Douglass's admonition: "Power concedes nothing without a demand. It never did, and it never will."[36]

From the early days of his tenure at the *Carolina Times*, Austin's outspoken and fearless attacks on racial injustice often placed him in harm's way. When in 1929 he published editorials in support of a black family under attack for purchasing a home in a white neighborhood, Austin received menacing phone calls, some threatening to burn his house down. The Ku Klux Klan threw rocks and bottles at his house and burned a cross on his lawn. But Austin refused to back down. He once told an interviewer of a time when he was "ordered out of town [he did not say by whom]." Undaunted, Austin visited the man who had threatened him, "just to let him know that I would still be here any time he wanted me." That night, a group of Austin's friends "gathered to stand guard and defend" him. No attack ensued.[37] In 1932, a columnist for the *Pittsburgh Courier* proclaimed that Austin's "brand of courage . . . is rare in the South."[38] Similarly, in 1933, a columnist for the *Baltimore Afro-American* called Austin "fearless and determined."[39]

Austin's impatience with cautious blacks and purportedly liberal whites made him a strong critic of the interracial movement. The southern Commission on Interracial Cooperation (CIC), formed in 1919, sought to alleviate interracial tensions and preserve peaceful race relations, but never opposed segregation.[40] The North Carolina Commission on Interracial Cooperation (NCCIC), the state chapter of the CIC, included moderate black and white businessmen and educators, like C. C. Spaulding and white sociologist Guy Johnson, but it was dominated by its white members. It met regularly during the 1930s but rarely took action. An important exception occurred when the NCCIC sued to force bus companies in North Carolina to carry black passengers and received a favorable ruling from the state supreme court.[41]

However, the organization was typically marked by passivity. For instance, at the 1934 annual meeting, L. R. Reynolds, director of both the Virginia and North Carolina CICs, urged a discussion emphasizing "the necessity of the exercise of patience [by African Americans] . . . and a less critical attitude toward the deficiencies of the educational system and other aspects of governmental and social life."[42] Reynolds demonstrated his paternalism toward blacks in a letter he wrote to North Carolina Governor Clyde Hoey in 1938, when he compared blacks to children. He told the governor, "As long as our children were at our feet we knew where they were, but when they grew to the point where they could drive an automobile our anxieties were multiplied many fold."[43]

Although he was not privy to this correspondence, Austin plainly saw the limitations of the NCCIC and particularly the white men who dominated it. In January 1934, Austin indicted the NCCIC for failing to fight for racial justice. He declared, "The Inter-racial Commission of North Carolina ought to disband. . . . The Commission has done, and is doing nothing, to prove itself of value to the Negroes of North Carolina."[44] In his inimitable way, Austin observed that a more appropriate name for the NCCIC would be the "North Carolina *Circus* on Interracial Cooperation."[45] In contrast, the *Norfolk Journal and Guide* took issue with Austin's view, noting that the CIC "made it possible for North Carolina Negroes to break down resistance on the part of bus lines to hauling Negro passengers in that State."[46]

For Austin, interracial organizations like the NCCIC rendered black leadership impotent. He contended that Durham's black leaders were "too friendly with the white people to be real leaders. You cannot maintain friendship with the oppressors and attempt to still solve the problems of the op-pressed." At a 1929 meeting of the NCCIC, Austin demonstrated his willingness to stand up to white leaders who were "feared" by some because of their power, by denouncing "N.C. Newbold, white director of Negro education in North Carolina." For this act, Austin was "expelled" from the organization.[47]

Nonetheless, at a meeting of the NCCIC in the 1930s, Austin pressured the organization to take meaningful action on racial segregation. According to Guy Johnson, following the "usual talk, nice discussions" without "any heat, any real controversy," Austin spoke up in disgust: "I've been listening to this and I'm fed up. Nobody has put his finger on the real problem, and that is social equality. And until an organization like this has the guts to say that that is the problem and we are all willing to get up and say that this person of the other race is my equal socially and every other way, and we are willing to have equal contacts, then there is no solution to this. Why don't we get down to brass tacks?" Immediately, the usually staid group became quite agitated and sought to regain control. Johnson recalled, "Well you could just see them, fearful around the room and several people trying to get the floor, and one or two of the blacks got up and wanted it known that this man didn't represent their thinking." For the moderates in the room, Austin "was a sort of threat, he was rocking the boat. And some white man said, 'Well, this is not anything that we can do anything about, it's not our function. Let's forget it.' But there really was a stir for awhile." According to Johnson, this was the "only time" that the question of segregation was raised.[48] It is important to note that for whites, the phrase "social equality" frightened them because it raised the specter of black men and white women engaging in sexual relations or getting married, which was anathema for most whites.[49]

In 1934, Guy Johnson attacked Austin for an editorial that condemned the CIC. Johnson claimed that most members of the state's Interracial Commis-sion agreed with Austin on "principles and policies," but disagreed on "tac-tics." Johnson claimed that the CIC was the "only movement in the South which has been able to enlist in a large way the support of both whites and Negroes, an organization which is a symbol of what little progress has been made in Southern thinking on the race problem."[50] For Austin, however, the CIC was a major obstacle to meaningful progress toward civil rights in North Carolina. While Johnson argued that interracial meetings were a step toward racial progress, for Austin, these meetings were all show and no substance; confrontation, not civility, was needed to effect change. The CIC rarely took significant action against racial oppression and merely allowed a few North Carolinians to claim that they were enlightened on the race issue.

While white and black racial moderates regularly emphasized good or improving race relations in North Carolina, Austin routinely debunked the related claim that blacks in North Carolina and the South were content with their status. In 1929, when President Herbert Hoover's wife met with the wives of members of Congress, including Jessie De Priest, wife of Oscar De Priest, the newly elected congressman from Illinois and the first African American to serve in that body since 1901, there was a huge outcry from southern whites. The *Raleigh Times* and the *Raleigh News and Observer* called Mrs. Hoover's action an insult to the South. The *Carolina Times* responded by asserting that "Mrs. Hoover's actions met with the approval of the majority of blacks North and South." Moreover, Austin asserted that contrary to white southerners' claim, regardless of region, African Americans had the same "soul burnings, desires, hopes" for their race and sought "equal justice, opportunity, and citizenship." Austin explained that while they were less outspoken than their northern counterparts because of the dangers they faced, southern blacks "were more virulent in their opposition than their Northern brothers" to racial injustice. Southern blacks were not content with their oppressed status. Rather, according to Austin, they were "creatures of the hypocritical smile, of feigned goodwill, of hatred hidden by fawning."[51]

During the 1930s, like other contemporary militant black activists, Austin rejected white paternalism, and instead, championed the National Association for the Advancement of Colored People (NAACP) and legal action against racial segregation and oppression. He employed a confrontational style and attacked all racial inequities, and sought to abolish all segregated institutions. Unlike the more established older generation of black leaders in North Carolina, he publicly embraced the integrationist NAACP.[52]

Austin was an active member of the Durham branch of the NAACP, which was founded in 1919. From 1919 to 1930, John Avery, an NC Mutual executive, served as branch president. Austin regularly promoted NAACP membership in the *Carolina Times*. When interest and support for the branch flagged in 1929, Austin demanded that the black community contribute funds so that the NAACP could continue to battle racial injustice. He singled out black businessmen for failing to publicly support a viable and active local branch of the NAACP.[53] This became a recurrent theme as NC Mutual officials, led by C. C. Spaulding, regularly rejected bold action that directly confronted white oppression or challenged racial segregation.

In 1930, Austin helped promote the NAACP's campaign to defeat President Hoover's nomination of North Carolina judge John J. Parker to the U.S. Supreme Court because Parker had spoken out against black voting rights

911131517192123252729313335373941434547495153555759616365676971

7375777981838587899193959799

were "barred from [a] soup kitchen."[61] In 1932, Austin met with the Durham superintendent of schools and tried to persuade him to reverse his firing of a black supervisor.[62] In September 1939, Austin counseled black farmers to vote for a crop control measure on the ballot that would increase tobacco prices, thereby helping tobacco farmers.[63] And, as noted above, Austin led protests that compelled white grocery stores to hire black clerks.

Austin actively supported union organizing efforts among tobacco workers in North Carolina. In Durham's Liggett & Myers (L&M) tobacco mill, work was racially segregated, with one white department for machine operators, including men and women, who produced and packaged cigarettes, and two black departments, one that sorted, blended, and flavored the tobacco, and one that sorted and stemmed the tobacco.[61] In the spring of 1934, according to Marion Dries, "Austin . . . helped organize a pro-union mass meeting at Durham's YMCA" at which he encouraged black tobacco workers to join the Tobacco Workers International Union (TWIU).[65] This meeting inspired female tobacco stemmers to form the first black tobacco workers' union chapter in Durham, Local 194. However, the union local quickly declined after workers witnessed the failure of the General Textile Strike of September 1934.[66] The white workers at L&M in Durham had already organized Local 176 of the TWIU in 1933. It won a collective bargaining agreement in 1937, the first union in Durham to do so.[67] The same year, African Americans, who worked with smoking tobacco, formed Local 208 and received a charter from the TWIU, and in one year "won a signed contract, becoming the first black local in Durham to achieve this distinction." Nonetheless, wage inequities continued. At that time black workers' maximum pay in the mill was fifty cents per hour, while white workers' top pay was double that.[68]

In March 1935, several black women workers at R. J. Reynolds Tobacco Company in Winston-Salem asked Austin "to speak on how to 'organize and raise wages and standard of living,' " at a meeting at the YWCA's black branch. When white leaders heard of the meeting, "the chairman of the Community Chest threatened to withhold funds from the YWCA," leading to the cancellation of the meeting. Reynolds had a well-deserved reputation for ruthlessly opposing unionization. Workers who even uttered the word "union" were typically fired in the 1930s.[69]

In April 1939, 4,000 TWIU workers from Local 176 and Local 194 in Durham, along with TWIU workers in Richmond, Virginia, struck L&M for a closed shop and a five-cents-per-hour wage increase. After a nine-day strike, workers won a pay increase and the company's promise that it would support a closed union shop. Black workers received a two- to four-cents-per-hour wage increase. Although white and black workers had joined together in this strike, racial tensions between the locals and the workers continued.[70] Austin supported the workers, criticized the exploitation of the workers by the mill owners, and emphasized that the workers built the tobacco industry and should receive just pay for their toil. He condemned the mill owners who "would take from American citizens the right to safeguard their own health and future."[71] One black worker, William Edwards, recalled, "Whatever the company gave the white union, we tried to get [too]. It never did work. The company just wouldn't pay. They'd give the white man six cents and the black man three cents. I was angry all the time."[72]

A week after the settlement of the 1939 tobacco strike, Austin visited Duke University, and enumerated the injustices perpetuated by the Duke family. Austin noted that black workers' sweat and toil had built the Dukes' tobacco fortune, which had in turn built Duke University. But while the children of white tobacco workers might attend that university, blacks were barred from the university that their work had built. Austin asked, "Where is justice? Where is right? Where is God?"[73]

While Austin fought for economic justice for black workers, he did not always see eye-to-eye with the labor movement, which had a long history of discriminating against black workers. On one occasion, in 1939, Austin praised non-union R. J. Reynolds Tobacco Company for its treatment of black workers, which "angered white unionists who took it as a direct slap against their domination of African-American union members." White TWIU leaders threatened a boycott of the *Carolina Times*, while "black unionists remained silent. Austin reluctantly backed down." Although historian John Rice claimed that Austin "rarely . . . [mentioned] labor issues in his paper again," by the early 1940s, Austin was backing union organizing efforts at Reynolds.[74]

Although Austin was an avowed integrationist, he occasionally embraced nationalist tactics, especially during the Depression years, when, at times, he lost faith that racial justice could be achieved in America. In 1934, he praised the movement for the creation of a separate black state. The National Movement for a 49th State, a Chicago-based organization, proposed the establishment of a separate state for African Americans, where self-governing blacks would enjoy justice and economic opportunity. Austin argued that the severe repression of the black American during the Depression "is bound to result in his ultimate defeat as a citizen." He predicted that blacks would suffer a similar fate as the Jews in Germany under the Nazi regime.[75]

Perhaps the issue that Austin was most passionate about was education; he publicized inequities in the segregated public education system and fought for equal educational opportunity for blacks in North Carolina. He spoke out for equal funding for black schools and equal salaries for black teachers. But unlike more cautious black leaders in North Carolina, Austin did not hesitate to advocate legal action to enforce equity in primary, secondary, and higher education. Nor did he shy away from lawsuits to integrate public education in North Carolina.

In 1933, Austin played a key role in filing the first legal challenge to segregated higher education in the South. He joined with local black attorneys Conrad Pearson and Cecil McCoy in planning Thomas Hocutt's lawsuit, which challenged the racial exclusiveness of the University of North Carolina at Chapel Hill (UNC). A graduate of Hillside Park High School in Durham and a graduating senior at North Carolina College for Negroes (NCCN), Hocutt sought admission to UNC's pharmacy school. In agreeing to challenge Jim Crow, the young man displayed great courage. Few students were willing to risk transgressing white authority, placing themselves in the crosshairs of white violent retaliation. In 1939, attorney Thurgood Marshall reported that the NAACP was "unable to get a qualified applicant with courage to apply" to the University of Virginia to challenge segregated higher education in that state.[76]

As Pearson and McCoy prepared to file the integration lawsuit, their plan to keep it secret for the moment was subverted by NCCN president James Shepard. Pearson had told Shepard of the plans to sue UNC, but the older man, who had been "pledged to confidentiality and silence," immediately broke that confidence and leaked the story to the *Greensboro Daily News*. The report in the Greensboro paper generated substantial opposition from powerful whites. To present their side of the story, Pearson and McCoy gave an interview to the *Durham Morning Herald*.[77]

Why did Shepard conspire to sabotage the case? Although he was not satisfied with the inequitable distribution of resources and the limited economic opportunities for blacks under Jim Crow, Shepard believed that absent political power, blacks had to rely on behind-the-scenes lobbying of powerful whites in order to gain funding for black institutions or facilities for the black community. Therefore, Shepard cultivated relationships with white leaders and regularly opposed confrontational tactics, like lawsuits, that might jeopardize his working relations with whites.

So, on February 16, 1933, Shepard sent Governor J. C. B. Ehringhaus a copy of that day's editorial from the *Greensboro News* and told the governor that he was doing all he could to stop the case. He wrote, "There is quite a stir . . . in regard to the proposal of the colored lawyers to make a test case as to the admission of students . . . at the University." Shepard, who sought to establish graduate and professional programs at NCCN, suggested that the purpose of the suit was to compel the state to provide funding for black students to go out of state for programs they could not get at black schools in the state. Shepard continued, "We are seeking to bring pressure upon them not to agitate the matter for two years at least. I do not know what the outcome will be."[78] Ehringhaus replied the next day that he agreed with Shepard's position that the suit was "most unfortunate."[79]

In response to the threat against segregation law in North Carolina, white education officials, including Nathan C. Newbold, director of the North Carolina Division of Negro Education, pressured Shepard and NC Mutual president C. C. Spaulding to convince Hocutt and his allies to abandon the case. Like Shepard, Spaulding generally opposed confrontational tactics as counterproductive to peaceful race relations. Newbold asked Spaulding whether the "responsible Negro leadership [would be] a party to the embarrassment of the University." He told Spaulding, "You and your friends will know how to deal with the . . . local persons." He also suggested that North Carolina should deal with its own problems, without unnecessary outside interference. This last remark, eschewing meddling outsiders, was typical of the southern moderate view, as well as that of the more conservative southerners.[80] Southern whites regularly attributed radical tactics to outsiders, in part, to underscore their argument that southern blacks were well treated and content with their status in the South. Nothing could be further from the truth, as evidenced by the fact that Hocutt's lawsuit had nothing to do with outside interference, as local activists Austin, Pearson, and McCoy had initiated it.

Newbold intensified the pressure on Shepard to obstruct the desegregation scheme. And Shepard could not easily ignore this pressure, since Newbold was ostensibly Shepard's supervisor and he needed Newbold's support when he requested funding from the state legislature for the operations of NCCN. Shepard assured Newbold that he opposed the lawsuit. He advocated a policy whereby the government of North Carolina would pay tuition for black students to attend out-of-state professional schools and/or establish graduate and professional schools at black colleges. He also reassured Newbold that he believed that there could be no "real progress without the fullest support, confidence and good will of the white people." Of course, Shepard's position as president of a state institution made him particularly beholden to the white legislature's "good will."[81] In March 1933, Shepard suggested to the governor that the best way to stop the integration lawsuit was to either provide funds for black students to take professional programs out of state or establish such programs at NCCN.[82]

Meanwhile, UNC officials hired an attorney who urged older black leaders to stop the case from moving forward. A meeting was held at NC Mutual, where Spaulding and other black businessmen pressured Austin, Pearson, and McCoy to drop the case.[83] The discussion became quite heated. At one point, Pearson called one of Spaulding's allies, black businessman Ed Merrick, a "handkerchief head." Merrick responded by threatening to throw Pearson out the window.[84] When Spaulding argued that pursuing the case would lead to violent outbursts by whites against the black community, Hocutt's advocates refused to back down. Austin later recalled his words: "If my actions will cause a race riot, you had better grease up your muskets for I am going back Monday to pursue this cause."[85] Austin remembered that the "N[egro] big shots raised more sand at t[he] time than t[he] wh[ite] folks; [they] accused Austin of disturbing r[ace] rel[ation]s."[86]

In referring to the possibility of white violence, Spaulding likely remembered the vicious attack he had experienced less than two years earlier. In August 1931, in Raleigh, the fifty-seven-year-old Spaulding was "set upon and beaten by a dastardly white soda clerk for presuming to drink a cup of soda water in the store instead of on the street." At the time, Austin commented, "A city has a long way to go when an elderly, eminent man can be assaulted with impunity by a young white soda jerker."[87] Spaulding lost two teeth and suffered a black eye from the beating. After a brief trial, the clerk was fined $15 and court costs.[88]

Meanwhile, pressure from Shepard and Spaulding convinced the Durham branch of the NAACP to oppose Hocutt's lawsuit, even though lawyers McCoy and Pearson had taken "a large hand in the reorganization of the local branch," in early 1933. McCoy told NAACP executive secretary Walter White that the Durham branch was now "in control of a group of spineless persons who have disappointed us by scuttling to cover at the first stage of action."[89] McCoy blamed the decision on "the pressure of a few white politicians upon our so-called Negro leaders." He maintained that the *Hocutt* case had "the sympathy of the Negro in the street, as well as many other Negroes and well-thinking white people."[90]

NAACP officials at the national office were outraged by Shepard and Spaulding's opposition to the case. Of Spaulding, NAACP official George

Streator later said, "He is not worth in the final analysis a tinkers dam for fighting purposes. I have had enough dealings with him to know that he frequently capitalizes on his ability to swing things out of reach of radical Negroes. 'Call Spaulding when the radicals are on the war path' is a Durham racket.... Durham Negroes [like Spaulding and Shepard] take a big hand from the white folks for sitting on the lid and keeping the young Negroes quiet."[91] Similarly, Walter White observed of Spaulding and Shepard, "Some of the timid and conservative Negroes have promptly run to cover."[92]

Nonetheless, Hocutt, Austin, McCoy, and Pearson remained undeterred in their commitment to seek justice. They drove to the UNC registrar's office in Chapel Hill and attempted to register Hocutt for the March quarter of classes at the School of Pharmacy. There, Austin introduced Hocutt to Thomas J. Wilson Jr., registrar and dean of admissions: "This is Mr. Hocutt, a new student ... who needs his class schedule and dormitory assignment." With these words, Austin signaled that the battle had begun. After recovering his composure, Wilson quickly denied Hocutt's application for admission.[93] This scene, a black student attempting to enter an all-white university, would necessarily be repeated many times over the next three decades before the South's Jim Crow laws were toppled.

Following the registrar's denial of Hocutt's application, Pearson and McCoy filed a writ of mandamus asking that the Superior Court of Durham County order UNC to admit Thomas Hocutt. The young man's lawyers based their petition on the equal protection and due process clauses of the Fourteenth Amendment to the U.S. Constitution and the argument that North Carolina law did not explicitly mandate segregated universities. State law only specified segregated public schools, defined as elementary and secondary schools, or schools that were part of a city school system.[94]

In mid-March, Newbold renewed his pressure on Shepard, now imploring him to publicly oppose Hocutt's petition: "You and other leaders can afford ... to be more aggressively independent [of the black radical position] in this matter."[95] But Shepard rebuffed Newbold's entreaty, explaining that the "younger element of Negroes in North Carolina do not believe in the leadership of the older Negroes. They think the older Negroes represent the servile type and that a more aggressive leadership is need[ed]." Referring to his support for Judge John J. Parker's nomination for the U.S. Supreme Court in 1930, Shepard reminded Newbold, "I was denounced all over the United States and held up as one who was willing to sell his race for the favor of the white man. I have not recovered from the bitter attack upon me in that instance." Shepard insisted that "the duty of the Negro leader is to work quietly with the radical element and try to reason with them, because if he denounces them publicly he has no further influence with them."[96]

Meanwhile, white politicians, educators, and lawyers, determined to uphold segregated higher education, mobilized to defeat the lawsuit. UNC law professor Robert Wettach prepared an eight-page memorandum that listed relevant cases and laws, suggesting several strategies to deal with the matter. These included setting up separate graduate schools for blacks and paying out-of-state tuition.[97] UNC sociology professor Howard W. Odum forwarded copies of Newbold's correspondence with Shepard to UNC president Frank Porter Graham. UNC assembled the state's top white lawyers, including Wettach, UNC School of Law dean Maurice T. Van Hecke, North Carolina attorney general Dennis G. Brummitt, Brummitt's assistant, A. A. F. Seawell, and Victor Bryant, a prominent local lawyer as well as an attorney for NC Mutual.[98] The importance that the white community attached to the *Hocutt* case is clear from the prominence of the attorneys who were employed to defend segregation.

During the trial, Hocutt and his lawyers, including William H. Hastie of the NAACP, who had joined the local legal team, enjoyed enthusiastic support from most of the black community. During a pretrial conference, when UNC attorneys sought to convince Pearson and McCoy to drop the case, Hocutt's supporters chanted, "Don't give in! Don't give in!"[99] During the trial, hundreds of blacks and whites crowded the courtroom. Many African Americans were filled with pride and felt themselves part of the momentous fight that Hocutt was waging. By all accounts, Hastie's arguments were brilliant. He "swept the entire court-room off its feet with his ability and demeanor."[100] One spectator remembered that after seeing Hastie's performance, "we probably couldn't conceive of him losing. . . . We probably lost all sight of all of the discrimination that . . . he was really up against. We were so thrilled." It was a transcendent moment for many young African Americans in Durham. Although the older generation may have considered the *Hocutt* case too radical and sure to fail, the younger generation saw the case as cause for optimism, and change seemed possible.[101]

Nonetheless, Durham County Superior Court judge Maurice V. Barnhill ruled against Hocutt on two counts. First, the mandamus petition was not the proper remedy; the court could not compel UNC to admit a student as the plaintiffs had sought. It could only order the university to review Hocutt's application in an impartial manner. Second, the court ruled that Hocutt's application was incomplete because no official college transcript had been submitted with the application. NCCN president James Shepard, acquiescing to pressure from white officials, had denied Hocutt an official transcript, throwing up a roadblock to the young man's application. The court's reasoning on the second count is somewhat specious given the fact that UNC's pharmacy program was an undergraduate program. As such, only a high school transcript was required. Moreover, Hocutt's brief asserted that he had graduated from Hillside Park High School, a fact that was not contested by the defendant's attorneys. However, Hocutt's high school records could have been challenged because when he graduated from Hillside Park, it had not yet been granted a Grade A classification.[102] Of course, black schools' lower classifications were not unrelated to the limited funding they were given by the state.

Despite the court's adverse ruling, Austin emphasized the positive impact of the case: "Instead of the legal encounter disrupting interracial accord, as some feared, it has proved to the public that we are equipped with men able to represent their people in court."[103] Although the case failed to integrate UNC, it served as the opening salvo in the NAACP's legal battle to overturn segregated public education, culminating in 1954 with the *Brown v. Board of Education* decision.[104]

The case also convinced the NAACP to mount a major membership drive in North Carolina.[105] Walter White decided to create a North Carolina state branch of the NAACP in order to better focus attention on the fight for equal opportunity in higher education and equal salaries for black and white public school teachers.[106] Buoyed by black enthusiasm for the *Hocutt* case, White traveled to twelve North Carolina cities in May 1933 because he believed that "North Carolina offers opportunity for the most significant and aggressive struggle for the Negro's rights of any state in the country."[107] During his sojourn, White found that blacks in the state, especially the younger generation, were "more militant, more alert, more determined and more intelligent about their rights than ever before," and were excited about the NAACP's program to fight racial injustice.[108] In addition, White convinced NC Mutual officials, including C. C. Spaulding, to provide financial and logistical support for the organizing effort. As a result of these efforts, NAACP membership rose throughout the state with new branches established in several cities.[109] Durham's membership grew dramatically. According to branch president Joseph N. Mills, a physician, the local membership drive had signed up 500 members by February 1934.[110]

In the aftermath of the *Hocutt* case, Shepard ingratiated himself with Governor Ehringhaus by attacking Austin, thereby demonstrating Shepard's loyalty to the governor, in order to boost NCCN's chances for increased state funding. In 1934, Shepard praised Ehringhaus's speech at NCCN, telling the governor that he had "allayed racial friction for some time." He then referenced an editorial in the *Carolina Times* and tried to assure the governor that "whatever the Negro paper here may say, there is no need to take note of it by anybody. The Editor and the paper have very little influence over any group. They cannot stir up any great trouble." Despite Shepard's assertion, Austin, in fact, enjoyed the respect and trust of many blacks in Durham and throughout North Carolina. Shepard told the governor, "You can always depend upon me to do and say the thing that in my judgment will promote peace instead of discord. You made us all feel proud of you as Governor."[111] The governor replied, "Certainly there is every day less and less reason for such strife, and certainly those in high positions in the state and other outstanding responsible citizens of both races . . . will continue to do, all possible to promote good will."[112] Two weeks later, Shepard went even further in his pandering to the governor: "You again made a frank and convincing appeal for justice and harmony between the races. You are really an Apostle of Peace and Good Will. We all believe absolutely in your desire for justice and you certainly have the support of all good thinking people, white and colored."[113] While personal politics probably helped Shepard advocate for funding for NCCN, his methods helped perpetuate the status quo in race relations and racial injustice in North Carolina.

No doubt, Shepard's pandering to the governor was related to the troubles encountered by NCCN during the Depression, including declining enrollment and financial difficulties. In spring 1934, NCCN enrollment totaled 235 students, which was 17 percent below the previous year's total.[114] Budget constraints meant that Shepard could not fulfill his financial obligations to the college's teachers. He reported, "During the fiscal year 1933, we failed to pay teachers for approximately two months and one-half." While 1934 was a little better, teachers were not paid for "two-thirds of one month." Shepard complained to the governor about the paltry state appropriation of only $24,000, noting that the "salaries are entirely too low, [and] as a result, I am losing three teachers the coming session who ought not to go."[115]

As he lobbied for increased state appropriations, Shepard continued to curry favor with the governor at the expense of Austin and the *Carolina Times*. In May 1934, he wrote the governor, "Confidentially, I understand that the *Carolina Times*, the Negro paper here, is in great financial difficulties and it is going to be difficult to operate in the future. So there will be no need for anyone to think that this paper will long disturb the good feeling between the races."[116] The following month, Shepard wrote the governor, "The *Carolina*

Times . . . has failed to come out for the last two weeks. The bank refused any further credits. It is very doubtful that a paper of such type will again be published in Durham."[117] Ehringhaus thanked Shepard, noting that he was "glad to have the information."[118] Nonetheless, Austin was able to recover from the financial difficulties of the mid-1930s and the paper renewed publication, despite Shepard's prediction of the paper's demise. The paper's recovery was likely facilitated by the black financial community. As noted previously, NC Mutual bailed out the *Carolina Times* at least three times. This was likely one of them.[119] Even though Austin and Spaulding had been at odds the previous year during the deliberations of the *Hocutt* case, the older man did not hold a grudge, and continued to see the value the *Times* provided the black community.

Despite financial difficulties, Austin refused to temper his militant tactics. During the late 1930s, he continued to press for legal action to integrate higher education in the state. In 1936, Mechanics and Farmers Bank executive Richard L. McDougald, who had loaned the money to Austin to buy the paper in 1927, wrote NAACP leader Walter White urging him to dissuade local black attorneys from bringing a suit in Durham County to integrate UNC. McDougald claimed that such a lawsuit would lead to the loss of C. C. Spaulding's support for a statewide NAACP branch because whites would accuse him of "sponsoring the suit." McDougald added that he and Spaulding sought to avoid antagonizing white North Carolinians.[120] By contrast, in 1937, Austin urged the North Carolina Committee on Negro Affairs, formed the previous year, to sue in federal court for the admission of an African American to UNC.[121]

The following year, Austin supported Pauli Murray's application to integrate UNC.[122] Born in Baltimore, Maryland, in 1910, Murray grew up in Durham, and she delivered the *Carolina Times* as a youth. In the summer of 1927, she worked in the *Times*' editorial department. An outspoken young activist who rejected racial segregation, Murray graduated from Hunter College in New York City and worked for the National Urban League and the Works Progress Administration's Workers' Education Project. In November 1938, she decided to undertake graduate study, and, based on her appreciation of the race relations research of sociologists Howard Odum and Guy Johnson, she applied to UNC's graduate program in sociology.[123] The following month, President Franklin Roosevelt received an honorary degree from UNC and expressed his pride in becoming "an alumnus" of an institution that represented "American liberal thought." Murray was appalled to learn that the president of the United States had praised a racially segregated institution for being a model of liberalism. Immediately, she "poured out" her "indignation" in a two-page letter to the president, taking him to task for praising an institution that carried on the very illiberal tradition of marginalizing millions of African Americans and subjecting them to "insults, injustices, and such degradation of the spirit that you would believe impossible."[124] Murray's attempt to enroll at UNC was widely reported in black and white newspapers. By making her application so public, she risked retaliation from white supremacists. Her aunt, a schoolteacher in Durham, was "terrified of the possibility that aroused whites might burn our house down" or that she would be fired from her job.[125] Murray later told an interviewer that the "racist element of the [UNC] student body threatened to lynch any nigger who came on campus." But Pauli Murray was nothing if not brave, and she visited the campus. Fortunately, she was not attacked.[126]

Although NCCN's James Shepard told Murray that a "court case . . . would be useless," Austin observed that legal pressure impelled the state legislature to fund new construction at NCCN.[127] Murray recalled that Austin was her "greatest supporter . . . in Durham."[128] Despite Murray's efforts, UNC rejected her application.[129] Nonetheless, her application increased pressure on the state government to provide its black citizens with graduate and professional educational opportunities.

Meanwhile, in an important victory for the NAACP and black educational opportunity, the U.S. Supreme Court ruled in *Gaines v. Canada* (1938) in favor of equal, but separate, graduate and professional schools for blacks or failing that, admission of blacks to white graduate and professional schools. Austin praised this "momentous" decision, which showed "that in America the torch of liberty still feebly burns."[130] This case fulfilled, in part, the promise of the *Hocutt* case. The combination of the *Gaines* decision and Pauli Murray's very public application to UNC put pressure on white officials to take action. Murray's application to UNC was rejected on December 12, 1938, two days after the U.S. Supreme Court issued its ruling in *Gaines*. North Carolina governor Clyde Hoey, who wanted to stop integration at all costs, declared, "North Carolina does not believe in social equality between the races and will not tolerate mixed schools for the races."[131]

But, in order to avoid desegregating its white colleges, Hoey and the North Carolina General Assembly opted for the creation of graduate and professional courses at the state's largest black public colleges, NCCN and the Agriculture and Technical College in Greensboro. Austin, who correctly suspected that state funding for black graduate and professional schools would be grossly inadequate, opposed this ruse, and demanded integration.[132] The following month, Austin referenced Murray's quest to gain admission to UNC, noting that if state funding for black graduate and professional programs were inadequate, UNC would face more black applicants and lawsuits.[133] In 1939, he wrote, "The economical way, the righteous and just way, the sensible way is to admit the handful of Negroes desiring graduate work to the University of North Carolina. The damnable way, the disgraceful way, the unrighteous and unjust way is for the white people of this state to crucify their own souls upon an ignominious cross of deceit by establishing makeshift graduate courses for Negroes in Negro colleges."[134] Unlike the *Carolina Times*, some southern black newspapers expressed opposition to the integration of higher education. The *Atlanta Daily World*, while praising the *Gaines* decision, suggested that the best solution was not integration, or even a separate black law school, but a scholarship program to send blacks out of state for a legal education.[135]

Knowing that white officials in North Carolina would not choose the righteousness of integration, Austin insisted that the state legislature provide proper funding for graduate and professional programs at the state's black colleges. In 1938, Austin backed Shepard's request for $600,000 for new construction at NCCN, with about half to come from the state government and the balance from the federal government. Although Austin preferred a larger request from the state, he counseled others to defer legal action because "Dr. Shepard may be able to do more with an olive branch than others can do with branches of law."[136] This was one occasion when Austin backed Shepard's behind-the-scenes maneuvering, instead of legal tactics. The U.S. Public Works Administration, a New Deal program created during Franklin D. Roosevelt's presidency, approved $150,000 and North Carolina authorized about $130,000 for new construction at NCCN.[137] Reacting to the state legislature's insufficient appropriation, Austin now threatened that if proper funding was not forthcoming, blacks would resort to legal action.[138]

Meanwhile, Austin fought for equal education for black students and equitable salaries for black teachers in North Carolina's public schools. In 1931, the *Times* proclaimed, "Negro children are victims of one of the most injurious systems of educational discrimination in modern society."[139] Two years later, Austin told the Durham school board that the city's black public schools suffered from crowded conditions, low teacher salaries, and other inequities. He urged the board to improve black schools and equalize black teachers' salaries with those of whites.[140] One month later, in August 1933, black citizens formed a six-member committee, including businessmen C. C. Spaulding and R. L. McDougald, NCCN professor James Taylor, Julia Warren, Lyda Moore Merrick, and Austin, to lobby the all-white school board on behalf of black school needs.[141] In a 1937 editorial titled "The Educational Rape of Negroes in North Carolina," Austin published statistics revealing that in 1935–36, white public schools received about nine times the funding awarded to black public schools in North Carolina.[142] He indicted the "Old Guard" of black leaders, a reference to Spaulding and Shepard, for hurting the battle for equal education by continuing to placate "their white friends by being passive on the race question."[143] In contrast, Austin demanded legal action to ensure equitable funding for Durham's county and city schools.[144]

He also insisted that white administrators treat black teachers with respect. In July 1936, Austin admonished Durham city school superintendent W. Franklin Warren for failing to address black female teachers with the salutations Mrs. or Miss. Austin concluded, "The whole thing boils down to one and only one thing, and that is that the superintendent . . . is a little man in a big place. . . . The Negro teachers should ignore the ignorance of the superintendent and pity him for not being able to lift himself from the lowest element of his group."[145]

In 1936, Austin pressured the Durham City Council to add a twelfth grade to the black high school so that it would be on par with the city's white high school.[146] When the city council refused to act, Austin contacted Walter White of the NAACP to help Durham blacks sue the Durham Board of Education to gain a twelfth grade for Durham's black Hillside High School. Although, according to Austin, local black lawyers refused to take the case because "they all seem afraid," the threat of a lawsuit compelled the all-white Durham Board of Education to support the addition of a twelfth grade to Hillside in 1937.[147] Thus did pressure tactics gain the African American high school in Durham a twelfth grade, when most high schools in North Carolina stopped at the eleventh grade. In February 1938, Governor Hoey recommended the addition of a twelfth grade to all public high schools in the state.[148]

Austin also invigorated the battle for equal pay for black teachers in North Carolina, and unlike many of the state's black leaders, he urged legal action. In 1929, black teachers earned only 56 percent of what white teachers were paid in North Carolina.[149] When a black educator, Charles M. Eppes, attacked the NAACP in the *Greensboro Daily News* in 1933, Austin published a rejoinder supporting the NAACP and its plans for legal action on salary equity.[150] In September 1933, Walter White thanked Austin for the "superwork" he was "doing in the *Carolina Times* on the teachers' salary fight. Keep hammering away."[151]

The following month, the NAACP organized a conference in Raleigh attended by about 2,500 African Americans and perhaps a few hundred whites, who demanded equal funding for black education and black teachers.[152] One of the NAACP organizers of the conference, George Streator, called the event "by far the most significant gathering of colored people ever held in the South." According to Walter White, the conference was an important show of force that would transform the black struggle for equal education in North Carolina. Prior to this conference, the North Carolina [black] Teachers Association (NCTA) had taken no action to reduce the salary discrepancy between black and white teachers.[153] Just one month before the conference, NAACP attorney William Hastie had met with the NCTA, but he was unable to get their support. He told Walter White that the NCTA was now controlled by "a group which is pointed out as reactionary, even by [James] Shepard."[154] The huge turnout at the October 1933 conference—such meetings rarely topped 500 teachers in attendance—was indicative of a significant turn for the state's black teachers. White observed that black conservatives "have already been driven to cover and most of them are scrambling to get on the band wagon." Indeed, NAACP pressure had already persuaded the state to increase black principals' salaries by "an average of $18.00 each." However, the state meant "to try to drive the wedge between the principals and the teachers."[155] Nonetheless, NAACP support was growing, as several black principals had "told their teachers that if they did not join the N.A.A.C.P., they would have no jobs next year." In addition, several black teachers were planning to elect a more activist leader of the NCTA.[156]

White officials became increasingly alarmed at African Americans' demands for racial justice in public education, which threatened to upset the status quo in relations between the races. A 1934 report of the Committee on Race Relations of the North Carolina Conference for Social Service reported that race relations in the state had deteriorated during the previous five years. Evidence of this deterioration was the increased assertiveness of black activists and the black community in general. The report cited the *Hocutt* case and the October 1933 meeting attended by over 2,000 blacks at Raleigh City Auditorium calling for the equalization of black teachers' salaries. The report indicated that white "state and local officials . . . have been surprised, shocked" by rising black activism.[157]

Moreover, the show of force at the October NAACP conference by North Carolina's black teachers convinced Governor Ehringhaus to appoint a commission, including five members of the NCTA, to address problems facing black public schools. The commission recommended increased teachers' salaries, more state funding for black colleges, the creation of black graduate schools, and tuition grants to black students to enroll in out-of-state universities to pursue graduate study unavailable to them in North Carolina. Nonetheless, the state legislature refused to act.[158] Consequently, Austin wrote to Walter White and urged the NAACP to take legal action on the salary equalization issue.[159] White told Austin that in order to give the case a chance to succeed, it had to be carefully prepared, but the NAACP still planned to bring suit.[160]

Meanwhile, James Shepard used his influence with the NCTA to stop the filing of a salary equalization lawsuit in North Carolina. In October 1933, Shepard assured Governor Ehringhaus that legal action would not be taken. He wrote, "I want to ask you not to lose faith and confidence in the masses of Negro people. . . . After all this storm has blown over there will come a calm and I do not believe any court action is going to be taken at the present time to test the validity of salaries." He continued, "I am one of those, who believes that a strong christian appeal to the consciousness of the white people of North Carolina will bring a great deal of the relief we need. . . . The radical element among us must not be given encouragement, nor do I desire anything done that will give them further cause for agitation. I stand squarely with you in your stand to secure fair play to everybody."[161]

In 1937 and 1938, as black Virginia and Maryland teachers sued for equal salaries, Austin pressured the NCTA and the North Carolina Committee on Negro Affairs (NCCNA) to follow their lead.[162] Rencher N. Harris of the Bankers Fire Insurance Company criticized Austin's editorial attacking the North Carolina Committee for failing to effectively push for teacher salary equalization. Harris claimed that they were doing just that, citing the approval of a motion to work with the NCTA toward its goal of ending unequal salaries.[163]

But while the NCTA supported equalization rhetorically, it continued to reject the use of lawsuits. In fact, North Carolina was the only southern state where black teachers did not sue for salary equality.[164] In a 1939 radio address, James Shepard, who continued to exercise great influence over the NCTA, asserted, "However effective appeal to the federal jurisdiction may be, no Negro who covets cordial relations with his white neighbors wishes to rest his civil rights on the courts alone."[165] In April 1939, Walter White observed that North Carolina, "which boasts of being progressive is further behind in the fight for equalization of . . . teachers' salaries, than even . . . Florida, Alabama, and Louisiana." White attributed this to the NCTA's strategy of "meekly petitioning the powers-that-be," unlike Virginia, which had already "raised over $5,000 to pay the cost of court action."[166] In response to the NCTA's cautiousness, Austin denounced most of the state's black teachers, calling them "a shiftless and spineless group who are kept so by white teacher bosses who dare them to show any signs of concerted action."[167] Unlike Shepard, Austin refused to embrace civility when equity was at stake.

From 1938 to 1944, Austin urged the state assembly to increase appropriations for black teachers' salaries, publicized legal action in other southern states, and threatened legal action in North Carolina to ensure equal teacher salaries. In 1942, North Carolina's Advisory Budget Committee "recommended wiping out the salary differential between black and white teachers." In 1944 the State Board of Education "adopted a plan to equalize salaries."[168] While no lawsuit for equal teacher salaries was ever filed in North Carolina, Austin's confrontational tactics helped move the state's black teachers toward equity.

A LIFELONG ADVOCATE of black political power, Austin recognized that voting was a prerequisite for black gains in education and other fields, so he worked to increase black voter registration throughout the late 1920s and 1930s and fought efforts to limit black voting rights.[169] Although the North Carolina General Assembly repealed the poll tax in 1920, most black citizens remained disfranchised by white officials, who used discriminatory application of the literacy test and their control of voter registration to limit black voting.[170]

In 1928, Austin, like most African Americans in that era, supported the Republican Party, and consequently he backed Herbert Hoover's candidacy for president. Whites in North Carolina and throughout the South typically voted for the Democrats, because in the South the Democratic Party was the party of white supremacy. The 1928 presidential election was atypical because southern Democrats, like U.S. senator from North Carolina Furnifold Simmons, had commanded white Democrats to support Hoover, as they refused to back the Democratic nominee for president, Al Smith, because he was a Catholic. Austin noted this point, ascribing it to the "religious intolerance" of white North Carolinians.[171]

Despite the obstacles to black voting in North Carolina, Austin refused to leave politics in the hands of the white supremacists. During the late 1920s and 1930s, Austin joined forces with other leading black citizens to increase black voter registration. Early efforts by Austin and attorney R. McCants Andrews yielded little, as only fifty black voters were registered in Durham in 1928.[172]

In 1930, in an attempt to jumpstart black voter registration, Austin called the "first state-wide meeting" in North Carolina to promote black voting.[173]

Like many African Americans, in 1932, in the midst of the Great Depression and based on the failure of the Republican administration of President Herbert Hoover to reverse the economic decline, Austin "turned Abraham Lincoln's portrait to the wall" and began supporting the Democratic Party.[174] Although most African Americans had been Republicans since the Reconstruction era, blacks now sought to register to vote as Democrats because participation in the Democratic Party was the only opportunity to influence local and statewide elections in North Carolina and the South in the 1930s.[175] Furthermore, the Republican Party had done little for African Americans in recent decades. This move to the Democratic Party was also influenced by the U.S. Supreme Court ruling in May 1932 declaring the Texas white primary, which barred blacks from voting in the Democratic primary, unconstitutional.[176]

In 1932, Austin played a prominent role in an important effort by blacks in North Carolina to register thousands of new voters as Democrats.[177] In March, Austin helped organize a "state-wide non-partisan political conference" in Durham with 500 leading blacks invited. The editor declared that the conference sought to increase black political power in the state by revitalizing black interest in voting, and formulating tactics to counter roadblocks to black political participation.[178] At this conference, blacks from around the state created the North Carolina Independent Voters League, with the *Norfolk Journal and Guide* crediting Austin for its formation, and calling the *Carolina Times* the "strongest race newspaper in the South between Norfolk, Va. and Atlanta, Ga."[179] A few months later, Austin noted that "the *Carolina Times* has gone to considerable expense perfecting a political organization of Negroes in North Carolina and our publication is considered its official organ."[180] Prominent officials of the newly created voters league included Livingstone College professor W. H. Hannum, president; Palmer Memorial Institute founder Charlotte Hawkins Brown, vice president; and Durham attorney M. Hugh Thompson, chairman of the legal redress committee. C. C. Spaulding and James Shepard spoke in support of the new league at its founding meeting. Disillusioned with the Republican Party and realizing its impotence in North Carolina, black leaders asserted that they would no longer be bound to the Republican Party.[181]

The following month, there was a huge effort in Raleigh to register thousands of new black voters as Democrats. Helping to lead this effort was Raleigh's black newspaper, the *Carolina Tribune*, led by publisher-editor Hugo I.

Fontellio-Nanton, who had been mentored by Austin when he worked for the *Carolina Times*.[182] When Josephus Daniels, editor of Raleigh's most important white newspaper, the *News and Observer*, excoriated 3,000 African Americans for trying to register to vote as Democrats so they could vote in the Democratic primary, Nanton denounced Daniels and promoted the voter registration movement.[183] Furthermore, four black attorneys, three from Durham and one from Raleigh, represented black voters whose registration as Democrats was challenged.[184]

The significance of this voter registration drive and the *Tribune* and *Times'* support for it is indicated by the vociferous opposition by white Democrats and the *News and Observer*, which saw these actions as a threat to white supremacy. The *News and Observer* published articles on the voter drive almost every day from May 22 to June 6, including several blistering editorials penned by editor Daniels, who had been a leader in the 1898 white supremacy campaign by the Democrats, which overturned control of the North Carolina General Assembly by the biracial alliance of Populists and Republicans. In one editorial, Daniels asserted, "The Democratic Party in North Carolina is a white man's party." Referring to the white Democrats' campaign of violence and intimidation in 1898, which included the murder of many African Americans in Wilmington, he added that the Democratic Party's white exclusivity "came through blood and fire in allegiance to that principle. It cannot be abandoned now without peril, and small minds bent on immediate satisfactions should not be allowed to repudiate it." Daniels demanded a challenge of all unqualified black voters, based on his opinion that no blacks were qualified to vote.[185] Four days later, in a disturbing analogy, Daniels opined that blacks had "no more right to vote in a Democratic primary than a Baptist has to vote in an Episcopal convention." He asserted that white Democrats who helped blacks register as Democrats were "trying to destroy the great victory won under the leadership of [Charles] Aycock and [Furnifold] Simmons in 1898 and 1900," another reference to the vicious campaign to end black political participation in 1898 and pass constitutional amendments in 1900, which disfranchised the state's black voters.[186]

Nonetheless, the *Carolina Times* refused to back down in the face of Daniels's violent rhetoric. The Durham newspaper trumpeted blacks' successes in overturning challenges to their voter registrations when the Wake County Superior Court ruled in June 1932 that 210 black voters should be restored to the registration rolls. Indeed, this successful lawsuit, backed by the North Carolina Independent Voters League and the Raleigh Voters League, was apparently the first such success by black voters in North Carolina. The attorneys on the case were M. Hugh Thompson, Jerry Gates, and R. McCants Andrews of Durham, and Fred J. Carnage and Roger D. O'Kelley of Raleigh.[187] Tragically, Andrews, an important leader in the early black freedom struggle in North Carolina, died in July 1932 of peritonitis.[188]

Although white Democrats succeeded in invalidating many black registrants in 1932, blacks in the region continued to pursue their right to vote. In 1933, black protests, including a petition drive yielding over 300 signatures against white east Durham registrar J. C. Pope, who required blacks to "read, write, and interpret long sections of the Constitution," led to his removal.[189] By April 1933, over 1,000 African Americans in Durham were registered to vote.[190]

The impact of the rising black vote was seen in 1933, when the *Times* reported that black voters in Durham helped win passage of a tax increase that would be used to improve the city's schools. Black voters provided the winning margin and agreed to vote for the tax increase only after they won a promise that black schools would share equitably in increased revenues.[191]

In 1934, with a little trickery, Austin and movie theater owner Frederick K. Watkins won election as Democrats to be justices of the peace in Durham. Watkins was the leading operator of black theaters in North Carolina, with as many as seven at one time.[192] Watkins, who lived on Fayetteville Street in Durham, apparently styled himself the "Movie King," as these words were carved into one of the "granite topped piers" in the front of his house.[193] When Austin filed for the justice position, the head of the local Democratic Party tried to dissuade him from pursuing the office, but characteristically, Austin refused to back down.[194] Austin and Watkins assured their victories by filing for election at the last minute when Austin found out that Durham's quota for this position—North Carolina required one justice of the peace for every 1,000 citizens—was unmet, permitting them to run unopposed. The victories of Austin and Watkins were widely hailed by the black press as a turning point for African Americans in politics. The *Pittsburgh Courier* proclaimed, "For the first time in the history of the South, two colored men were elected to office on the Democratic ticket." The *Courier* asserted that their "election marks the beginning of the 'New Deal' in the South."[195] Austin's victory "established a precedent" for blacks serving as justices of the peace in Durham.[196] While serving one term, Austin presided over hundreds of cases.[197] In 1958, Austin recalled that when he served as justice of the peace, "Whites [were] upset [and] Some Negroes [were] critical—said it set r[ace] rel[ation]s back here many years."[198]

Although whites "carefully avoided bringing cases before" Austin, they were not always successful.[199] In one case, a black plaintiff sued a white driver for damages related to an automobile accident. As the white man was at fault, Austin called him to see if he would settle. When the white man dodged the call, Austin swore out a warrant. When the man came to see Austin and saw that he was black, he lost his temper and insisted on moving the case to another court, so Austin switched him to the other black justice, Watkins. After the defendant returned, Austin "told him . . . if he didn't respect the dignity and honor of this court, I would cite him for contempt, and also bind him over for Criminal Court and have him locked up," which calmed him down. Ultimately he accepted guilt for the accident and paid damages.[200]

A watershed moment in the emergence of black political influence in Durham occurred in 1935, when Austin joined with James Shepard, C. C. Spaulding, and other black leaders to form the Durham Committee on Negro Affairs (DCNA). This organization sought to register black voters, increase black political influence, and challenge inequities in education, employment, and access to public facilities.[201] The organizing meeting, held on August 15, 1935, was called by James T. Taylor of NCCN, attorney Conrad O. Pearson, Spaulding, Shepard, and Richard L. McDougald of the Mechanics and Farmers Bank. At a mass meeting that November, Spaulding was elected president, Shepard vice-president, and Taylor secretary.[202] The leadership sought "to build a coalition," so Austin, who worked for the Durham Committee for decades in various capacities, "was named to the executive committee."[203] Rencher N. Harris, W. D. Hill, and R. L. McDougald served with Austin on the initial executive committee.[204] In November 1935, at a meeting of 300 blacks at Hillside High School, Austin and McDougald urged African Americans to register to vote.[205]

By the end of its first year of operation, the DCNA had upped Durham's black voter registration totals to 1,000. One year later, an estimated 4,000 African Americans cast their votes in the November 1936 election.[206] Despite these gains, black voter registration was generally too low to elect black officials to citywide or statewide office, so the DCNA typically supported white candidates who were relatively more sympathetic to the needs of African Americans, and the *Times* published advertisements in support of those candidates.[207]

Austin also played an important role in the NCCNA, formed in 1936, which sought to advance black interests statewide.[208] NCCNA efforts helped increase black voter registration in North Carolina to about 50,000 in 1936.[209] In 1937, Austin urged the NCCNA to take legal action in the federal courts to ensure that black citizens were not denied their right to vote.[210] In April 1938, Austin called for an aggressive voter registration campaign to double the

60,000 black registrants in the state to force legislators to improve black opportunities in education, industry, and other areas.[211] Austin also lobbied the NCCNA to use its rising influence to defeat legislators opposed to the federal anti-lynching bill and the Fair Labor Standards Act, which would set a minimum wage and regulate working hours.[212] In May 1938 Austin joined with other prominent black leaders in convening a rally of black Democrats in Durham, probably the first one ever held in the city.[213]

During the 1930s, the political efforts of blacks in Durham yielded some notable victories. In May 1938, the *Carolina Times* reported that "Durham political leaders made history" by electing two African Americans, James T. Taylor, NCCN dean of men, and Nora Hughes, as Democratic Party chairman and vice-chairman of a Durham voting precinct, for the first time. Another African American, Davis B. (Dan) Martin, NC Mutual agency supervisor, was elected secretary of another Durham precinct. Because all chairmen were automatically included in the Democratic Party executive committee in Durham, an African American would serve on that body, too.[214]

In addition to his efforts to increase black voter registration, Austin ran for public office. He was one of two black candidates for local office in Durham in 1938. Attorney M. Hugh Thompson ran for a seat on the Durham County Board of Commissioners and Austin ran for the Durham County Board of Education. These candidacies were the first by African Americans for important county offices in decades.[215] Austin's candidacy failed because the state legislature refused to confirm his candidacy, a requirement during those years.[216] Although Thompson failed to win the Democratic Party nomination for a seat on the county board of commissioners, he garnered over 1,500 votes.[217] While both candidates lost, mass meetings in support of their candidacies stimulated black voter turnout, interest, and optimism that black candidates might succeed in the future.[218]

The year 1938 did yield an important political victory for Austin and the black community. When a $300,000 bond issue was floated to support construction of an airport for Durham, Austin counseled blacks to register to vote to reject it unless they were assured of equal access to the airport and its flights, which was not the case at the Raleigh and Greensboro airports. Furthermore, Austin reasoned that Durham's black schools needed a bond issue to fix their dilapidated facilities before the city needed an airport, especially one that would only serve whites.[219] To stir up opposition to the airport, Austin printed an advertisement in the *Times* that read, "Warning! Negro Voters: You are about to be taxed for an airport you will not be allowed to use. Register now and . . . vote against 'Taxation without Representation.'"[220] The bond was defeated by a three-to-one margin with, by Austin's estimates, over 90 percent of the 2,000 registered black voters rejecting the bond.[221] Austin observed that blacks and poor whites provided the crucial votes to defeat the bond, noting that this type of class-based coalition could benefit poor Carolinians of both races in the future by checking the power of the white elite.[222]

In 1939, as chairman of the political division of the NCCNA, Austin worked to stimulate black voter registration and black political influence. He urged African Americans to vote for black candidates in the upcoming primary election in Durham to ensure that their voices were heard on issues important to the black community, notably funding for black schools.[223] In August, Austin called for increased black voter registration to elect officials who would work to end job discrimination, unequal teachers' salaries, and other types of racial discrimination.[224] He also reported that in North Carolina "there are many sections in which Negroes are not allowed to register and vote. . . . There can be no freedom without the ballot and no ballot without freedom."[225] Austin's efforts for the NCCNA helped register 3,000 black voters in Durham by the end of 1939 and 75,000 black voters in North Carolina by February 1940.[226]

Besides pressing for voting rights and educational opportunity, Austin consistently backed African Americans who challenged inequitable treatment and segregation in transportation and other public facilities. In August 1939, the *Times* reported that a black teacher named Vella Lassiter sued the Greensboro-Fayetteville Bus Line for $1,250 for brutal treatment during a bus ride in March 1937. After visiting her family in Randolph County during Easter weekend, Lassiter was en route to her home in Reidsville. When she sat down near the back of the bus next to a white passenger, the bus driver tried to remove her from the bus, but she resisted. Even though there were empty seats in the front of the bus where the white passenger could have sat, Lassiter was forcibly removed from the bus by two policemen, who threw "her onto the sidewalk." Lassiter later recalled that she resisted removal because "she had bought a ticket and she was just as good as any white person."[227] She testified that she was "embarrassed, suffered mental anguish and mental anxiety and permanent injury to her left arm because of the conduct of the agent of the Greensboro-Fayetteville Bus Lines."[228] T. F. Sanders, a black attorney from High Point, and Franklin W. Williams, a black Winston-Salem attorney, represented Lassiter in the suit. The jury ruled in her favor, awarding her $300. The bus company's appeal to the North Carolina Supreme Court led to the lower court's ruling being upheld in 1939.[229]

When Ellen Harris, a black passenger on a Durham bus, was charged with violating Jim Crow law in 1938, Austin came to her defense.[230] He praised black attorneys C. J. Gates and Edward R. Avant, who defended Harris after she was arrested for refusing "to move from a seat next to the last one in the rear of the bus . . . after being asked to do so by a white passenger."[231] When Harris was found guilty, Austin criticized the judge for acquiescing to racist views.[232] On appeal, the North Carolina Supreme Court overturned the lower court's decision. The court reasoned that North Carolina law did not prohibit black and white riders from sitting on the "same bench . . . when all other seats" were occupied, even though whites generally sought to bar such an event.[233] Austin observed that this case showed "how much Negroes have suffered when they have not had the means nor the money to carry their cases to higher courts."[234] It also showed that many African Americans were willing to publicly challenge racial discrimination and abuse, using "their voices as weapons in the wars against white supremacy."[235]

During the Depression, Austin recommended boycotts of white businesses that mistreated African Americans. In 1937, after a white store owner in Hayti, the main black section of Durham, assaulted a blind African American, Austin organized blacks in picketing the store. The protest was so effective that the retailer went out of business.[236] He also publicized the efforts of the Durham Housewives League, which issued pledge cards to local blacks to patronize only black businesses and white businesses that treated blacks fairly and with respect.[237]

In 1929, Austin wrote an editorial suggesting that blacks "boycott segregated theaters." He also criticized black teachers for "entering the back door and climbing to the buzzard roost in the Carolina Theater." Years later, he recalled that after writing the editorial in 1929, "members of our editorial staff were not only criticized but nearly run out of Durham for even suggesting that Negroes boycott segregated theaters."[238]

In 1938, Austin promoted a boycott by black students at Greensboro's Bennett College and the Agricultural and Technical College of North Carolina (A&T) of white-owned movie theaters in response to the decision by the organization of white North and South Carolina movie theater owners to censor movies in which black and white actors appeared in scenes on an "equal basis." Austin told an audience at a church in Greensboro, North Carolina, that "the white man understands two languages—that of the cash register and that of the ballot box." He declared that black theatergoers could maintain their self-respect by patronizing black-owned movie theaters, while rejecting those theaters that insult African Americans by screening movies that did not accurately depict African Americans.[239] The boycott lasted at least five weeks, with regular meetings at local churches to sustain the boycott and to encourage more people to join. The boycott caused significant losses for Greensboro theaters, leading white theater owners to publicize the showing of movies with black actors playing characters "on an equal social basis."[240] Austin praised the students for their courage, noting that they would be opposed by the "old 'Uncle Toms' of the race," as well as whites.[241] He called on students around the state to join the boycott.[242]

Austin also spoke out against inequities in medical care. In May 1938, he criticized the Durham city and county governments for appropriating $25,000 for Watts Hospital, a white hospital, while rejecting a request for just $1,000 for Lincoln Hospital, Durham's black hospital, to install a new boiler.[243] When Lincoln Hospital requested $2,500 from the city and the mayor and the city stalled, demanding a budget from the hospital, Austin pointed out that no such request was made when Watts Hospital received $25,000 from the city.[244]

Austin fought to reform the justice system, speaking out for fair treatment for black defendants and for punishment of whites, who committed violence against African Americans. A study of ten North Carolina counties, including Wake and Durham Counties, revealed that for the ten years from 1930 to 1940, in trials of whites accused of killing blacks, not one white defendant had been sentenced to life imprisonment or death. By contrast, in trials of blacks accused of killing whites, 37.2 percent received life imprisonment or the death penalty.[245]

Austin advocated passage of the federal anti-lynching bill and attacked police brutality. He regularly denounced North Carolina senators Josiah Bailey and Robert Reynolds for their opposition to the federal anti-lynching bill.[246] In September 1938, after Senator Bailey gave a speech extolling white supremacy and the "Southern way," Austin declared, "Bailey continues to make a jackass of himself."[247] To try to increase congressional support for the anti-lynching bill, Austin published a report of a November 1937 poll that showed that 72 percent of Americans and 57 percent of southerners supported the bill.[248]

After a filibuster by southern senators, including Bailey and Reynolds, had succeeded in killing the anti-lynching bill, Austin sarcastically observed that North Carolina's "liberty loving senators" had helped win for the white man "the right to lynch." To drive the point home, Austin published a photograph of a naked African American hung from a tree by a lynch mob right next to his editorial. Austin asserted, tongue firmly in cheek, "Thank God the right to lynch is a white man's right. He alone enjoys the lust of human blood. He alone enjoys carrying in his pockets human toes, fingers, etc., of a dead Negro, as a reminder that he is the supreme ruler of this nation."[249]

When white policemen—there were no black policemen in Durham until 1942—brutally attacked black Carolinians, as they regularly did, Austin demanded legal action or at least disciplinary action against the police.[250] Once, according to sociologist Harry J. Walker, Austin went to Durham's city manager's office and "insisted that he suspend a policeman who slapped a colored woman in the police station."[251] In 1937, Durham police officer J. S. Whifield assaulted Vernon Farrington, an African American, for sitting next to him in a front seat on a city bus, when all rear seats were filled. The *Carolina Times* reported the attack and Austin urged the police department to issue a warrant for Whitfield's arrest.[252] The *Times* reported that a police officer at the station praised Whitfield's attack, asserting that "some of the damn niggers are getting mighty smart around here."[253]

Austin and DCNA president Spaulding met with the Durham city manager, the mayor, and other city officials, and demanded that Whitfield be disciplined. After Mayor William F. Carr reprimanded Austin for his outspoken criticism of whites, Austin told the mayor, "When you white people give Negroes justice I'll stay off you, but until you do I'm going to keep right on writing about you." Although Spaulding often tried to temper Austin's remarks, he acknowledged that the outspoken editor's tactics were effective. Spaulding commented, "Austin has a lot of people back of him, and the white people are scared to death of him."[254] The public pressure generated by the *Carolina Times* and the efforts of the Durham Committee helped lead to Whitfield's arrest, conviction ($5 fine and court costs), and suspension from police duty for four days without pay.[255]

In November 1937, the *Times* publicized Charlotte's black citizens' protest of recent assaults and killings of African Americans by policemen. In one case, the Charlotte police disingenuously claimed that a police officer fell and accidentally shot William Connor. Eyewitnesses refuted the claim that the officer fell, and reported that the victim "was shot while his arms were in the air."[256] A coroner's jury found Connor's killer guilty of "unjustifiable homicide."[257] In February 1938, Austin demanded the firing of a white policeman who shot an African American in the foot, took him to the hospital, and claimed "he was shot by an unidentified policeman."[258] In May 1939, the *Times* reported that a white policeman assaulted a black teenager and knocked him down in front of several white witnesses, who corroborated the story.[259] The policeman was given a small fine, but Austin demanded his termination, especially since he had committed a similar offense at least once before.[260]

Although the publicity generated by the *Times* surrounding cases of police brutality did not usually lead to justice, it demonstrated that the black community refused to remain silent in the face of repeated attacks. *Times* articles also provided evidence of the pervasiveness of the problem and, often, of the absurdity of some of the defenses. In May 1938, the *Times* reported that a white police officer had shot and killed a thirteen-year-old black boy. The patrolman claimed he had slipped while chasing the victim, who was allegedly "trying to break into a bakery," and shot him accidentally. Despite the improbability of the policeman's explanation, an all-white coroner's jury ruled that the shooting was an accident.[261]

The publicity brought by the *Times* to a 1938 Durham case in which T. D. Wilkie, a white ABC (Liquor) squad officer, killed James McNeil, a black tobacco worker, sparked a public outcry for justice. Wilkie and two police officers, one of whom had "a reputation for clubbing Negroes," broke into Mc-Neil's home "and clubbed and shot him to death."[262] Austin called Wilkie's attack "the most beastly killing that has occurred in the city in many years." The editor criticized the attempt by authorities to demonize the victim, and encouraged Durham citizens to protest the outrage committed by Wilkie.[263]

In the wake of the publicity produced by the *Times*, the Chapel Hill *People's Rights Bulletin*, published by the liberal Southern Committee for People's Rights, an organization of white Virginians and North Carolinians, charged North Carolina policemen with abusing their power by conducting illegal searches and executing the accused "on the spot." The *Bulletin* concluded, "There have been too many shootings of unarmed men in North Carolina by police and enforcement officers."[264] At the same time, a group of professors and administrators from UNC, including university president Frank Porter Graham, demanded an investigation.[265]

In hopes of ensuring justice in the case, black attorneys M. Hugh Thompson, C. J. Gates, Edward Avant, and C. O. Pearson represented "the state at the trial before Judge W. H. Murdock."[266] The DCNA, which called the shooting "unjustifiable homicide," raised $300 to help prosecute Wilkie.[267] Murdock ordered Wilkie brought before a grand jury.[268]

The grand jury indicted Wilkie, who claimed self-defense, on a charge of manslaughter for killing McNeil. Witnesses to the attack reported that "the raiding officers attacked McNeill [*sic*] with blackjacks both before and after the shooting, and that McNeill [*sic*] was beaten on the back of the head after he fell face downward with a bullet in his abdomen."[269] The charges against the other two ABC officers present during the shooting were "dismissed" by the judge, "who held that identification of the officers accused of slugging had not been positive." Black witnesses testified "that Wilkie shot McNeill [*sic*] upon finding that his mouth was bleeding from a glass thrown at him by Mc-Neill [*sic*]." Testimony revealed that although the ABC officers had a warrant, they "did not read it or show it upon demanding entry to the house." When the occupants delayed admitting the officers, "they forced it open and broke into the house, using violent and indecent language."[270] The grand jury bound Wilkie over for trial on the charge of manslaughter.[271]

An all-white jury found Wilkie not guilty. Austin wrote, "Twelve white men, 'tried and true,' have declared that the ABC officer had a right to shoot down James McNeal [*sic*] in the manner he did. The preponderance of evidence, presented by the prosecution, to the contrary, apparently had no influence on the jury. . . . The courts have closed the issue . . . in the same manner they usually do when a Negro is shot down by a white man in North Carolina."[272]

The failure to convict McNeil made it open season on blacks in North Carolina, which Austin publicized, hoping to shame white officials into doing something about it. In June 1939, the *Times* reported that a Charlotte police officer choked and beat a black woman he had arrested on suspicion of operating an illegal liquor house, but the cop was found not guilty.[273] In August 1939, an ABC officer, who had once been a bootlegger, brutally beat a black Durhamite with a blackjack at the home of a friend, in the police car, and at the police station, while the man was in handcuffs.[274]

In part to remedy the problem of police brutality and the failure of the courts to punish such criminal action, Austin demanded that the city of Durham hire black policemen and add African Americans to juries. In 1938, Austin noted that several southern cities, including Houston, San Antonio, Miami, and Knoxville, had hired black policemen.[275] In 1941, Austin supported the movement in Charlotte to hire black policemen. He listed the cities in other southern states, like Tampa, St. Louis, Tulsa, and Oklahoma City, that had employed black policemen.[276]

Similarly in 1936, Austin noted that blacks had "been drawn for jury service in other North Carolina cities," and urged the Durham County commissioners to authorize blacks "to serve on Durham county petit grand juries." In his request, Austin referenced the U.S. Supreme Court's decision in the Scottsboro, Alabama, case, in which the court ruled that southern states must permit blacks to serve on juries. To further buttress his case for black jurors, Austin noted the failure of white jurors to convict blacks who killed other blacks, leading to the freeing of murderers. Austin claimed that he knew of "10 killers who are now walking the streets of Durham." But the Durham County commissioners were not persuaded, and claimed that "Negro names are now in the jury boxes here."[277] Although their names may have been on the lists, black men were not called to serve on juries. In August 1938, Austin reported that not one African American had served on a Durham County jury in over thirty-five years.[278] In June 1939, Austin reiterated his call for black jurors in Durham.[279]

Police officers were not the only whites who physically abused blacks in North Carolina with impunity. In June 1938, the *Times* reported that an Edgecombe County white man, a former laundry worker, was freed by a grand jury after he had been accused of tossing burning matches at an African American whose "clothes caught fire from burning cleaning solvent," leading to his death from burns.[280]

Black women and girls, many of whom were employed as domestics in white households, were particularly vulnerable to attacks by white men. In 1936, a thirteen-year-old black girl accused Oscar King, the son of a member of the Durham County Board of Commissioners, of attempted rape. The girl had been taking care of the children of the accused, who allegedly "carried the girl off and practically tore her clothing from her body." She escaped to the home of a neighbor, who turned her over to the sheriff. The *Carolina Times* publicized the case, as did the local white daily newspapers, but no action was taken against the attacker.[281] In 1939, Austin pilloried the legal system in North Carolina when once again a white attacker of a black woman was freed. The assailant, a pastor, who threatened the woman, was found not guilty. Austin noted, cynically but accurately, "As a rule North Carolina courts do not convict white men for attacking Negro women."[282]

In July 1939, the *Times* reported that a white café employee beat a black hotel employee so badly that he lost his left eye. The judge in the case in which the victim sought $5,000 in damages had continued the case twenty-five times since the February attack, leading to widespread criticism.[283] Austin declared that the continued delays would not have occurred if the attacker had been black and the victim had been white.[284]

Throughout the interwar era, Austin fought for the rights of African Americans. By consistently publicizing and denouncing racial discrimination against black workers, students, teachers, and voters, and by advocating protest tactics and litigation, Louis Austin gave voice to the black struggle for freedom. He also helped shape a new civil rights strategy that employed confrontation, rejected accommodation, and used legal tactics and mass politics to make important gains for African Americans. As World War II brought new challenges for African Americans, Austin refused to shy away from directly confronting injustice whenever and wherever it reared its ugly head.

CHAPTER THREE

Double V in North Carolina
The Struggle for Racial Equality during World War II

During World War II, African American activists formulated a strategy that the *Pittsburgh Courier* called the Double V.[1] Even before the *Courier* first publicized the Double V slogan in February 1942, black activists and newspapers were already articulating a dual strategy in which blacks would fight for victory abroad against the Axis Powers while fighting for victory at home against the forces of white supremacy and racial oppression. The black press, according to one authority, the most powerful institution in the black community, played a key role in promoting this strategy.[2] By publicizing racial oppression, black newspapers revealed the hypocrisy in America's supposed "war for democracy."[3]

Like the larger northern black newspapers, notably the *Pittsburgh Courier* and the *Chicago Defender*, southern black newspapers played a critical role in the fight against white supremacy in America during the war. Working in the nation's most racially oppressive section, black journalists boldly attacked racial inequity. While some southern black editors, notably P. B. Young of the *Norfolk Journal and Guide*, refused to mount a direct attack on segregation, or shied away from criticizing local officials, Louis Austin fought racial oppression wherever it arose.[4] Indeed, he was the leading proponent of the Double V strategy in North Carolina. Perhaps the most outspoken of the southern black editors, Austin courageously demanded the end of racial segregation. Building on his civil rights advocacy from the 1930s, Austin continued to stimulate the politics of protest in the South by demanding an end to racial discrimination in education, politics, economics, and the armed forces. His wartime activism helped lay the groundwork for the postwar civil rights movement.

In advocating the Double V strategy, Austin joined other black journalists who rejected W. E. B. Du Bois's World War I–era admonition to African Americans to postpone the fight against racial discrimination until after the war. In his July 1918 editorial in the *Crisis*, organ of the NAACP, Du Bois had written that "while this war lasts [African Americans should] forget our special grievances and close our ranks shoulder to shoulder with our white fellow citizens" in support of the American war effort.[5] Du Bois's strategy yielded little benefit for African Americans. By most accounts, black oppression increased during and after the war, with over seventy African Americans lynched in 1919 alone.[6] During the 1940s, the post–World War I oppression was no distant memory, and many blacks took action to ensure that there would be no repeat. Indeed, black protest actions during World War II like the March on Washington Movement, NAACP membership drives and legal battles against the white primary, and the black press's attack on racial segregation and other inequities laid the groundwork for the modern civil rights movement of the 1950s and 1960s. As Patricia Sullivan has observed, "the war fueled a national movement for civil rights."[7]

In 1942, Austin articulated his goals and methods in an interview with a Duke University graduate student. The editor explained, "Our efforts are toward uplifting the Negro race by bringing about a complete race consciousness. . . . We can build up a strong belief in our rights by merely presenting the facts to the Negro public. If we want to present our wishes to the white people, however, it must be done through their paper as very few whites read a paper published by the Negroes."[8]

Austin capitalized on the nature of World War II to press for equal rights and fight against racism, articulating the Double V strategy in North Carolina. In February 1944, he contrasted the U.S. government's wartime rhetoric of fighting for freedom in Europe and Asia, while every day blacks suffered from oppression. The erstwhile editor explained that black soldiers and sailors traveling on a train from Washington, D.C. to Raleigh were "ordered out of the coach in which they were riding into a Jim Crow car merely because they were Negroes." Austin sharply drew the contrast between America's idealistic rhetoric and its racist practices: "Here in America we can claim that we have a democracy until we are blue in the face, we can sing our national anthem until we become hoarse. . . . But unless we realize the sanctity of human personality and the brotherhood of all mankind, we are going to have to pay a high price in human lives to win this war and in the end lose the peace."[9] In March 1944, Austin called for the firing of Secretary of War Henry Stimson after Stimson claimed that black troops were not used in combat because they were "unable to master efficiently the techniques of modern war weapons."[10]

In February 1945, Austin denounced the persistent humiliation of black soldiers by the U.S. military, which treated German prisoners of war better than African American soldiers. In Tampa, Florida, at MacDill Field, in January 1945, a white commanding officer ordered black soldiers out of the hospital mess hall when German POWs "refused to work if Negro military patients were fed in the same hospital mess hall with white[s]." Austin declared that only black soldiers would "continue to fight and die for a country that permits this kind of undemocratic and unchristian conduct to continue."[11]

During World War II, black newspapers exerted a large and increasing influence in the black community. With white newspapers rarely reporting on blacks unless they were celebrities (actors, musical artists, athletes) or criminals, the black community relied on the black press for news about African Americans. Black press circulation rose dramatically in the 1940s from about 1.2 million in 1940 to over 1.8 million by 1945. Moreover, those numbers understate the number of total readers, as each issue was regularly read by two to three readers, so that total readership, according to one authority, surpassed 3.5 million during the war.[12] Black readers generally agreed with black newspapers' "militant attitudes." In 1945, according to a survey by the *Chicago Defender*, "81 percent of the blacks it polled . . . did not make decisions on local and national matters until they saw what the black press wrote about the issues, and 97 percent felt that the main reason that blacks were obtaining equal rights and becoming first-class citizens was that the black newspapers had sounded a continual drumbeat against inequalities."[13]

With the largest circulation of any black newspaper in the state, the *Carolina Times*, which ran eight pages during the 1940s, played a key role in providing a voice for black Carolinians during the war. To expand its coverage and circulation, in 1939, in partnership with black journalist Trezzvant Anderson, the *Carolina Times* had opened an office in Charlotte and began printing a Charlotte edition of the paper.[14] The *Times*' circulation topped 11,000 in 1945 and reached individuals throughout North Carolina.[15] Moreover, this number understates the paper's influence because the *Times*, like other black papers, was often "passed from family to family and read aloud in barber shops, pool halls and informal civic and religious gatherings." Indeed, the content of editorials was widely discussed.[16] In a time when African Americans, particularly in the South, were assaulted and even killed for speaking out or acting against racial injustice, black readers were heartened to read Louis Austin's forthright denunciation of all types of racist oppression.

After the outbreak of war in Europe in 1939, Austin joined the chorus of black editors and columnists who saw little difference between German Nazism and British imperialism, and thus urged the United States to stay out of the war.[17] After German troops invaded Poland in September 1939, Austin asserted that "the freedom possessed by American citizens is too valuable, too precious for it to be endangered by a bunch of double crossing, double dealing European crooks whose greatest obsession is greed and power. . . .

We think all America should guard against being overcome by British propaganda and stay out of European affairs."[18] In April 1940, Austin observed that Germany was rapidly "displacing the British empire as the world's greatest robber of smaller nations." In Austin's view, Germany's invasion of weaker European nations was similar to French and British colonization of weaker African and Asian nations.[19]

After the United States entered the war, Austin continued to criticize British imperialism. He argued in August 1944 that the "greatest menace to world peace after this war . . . will be . . . the arrogance of the British Empire toward other nations of the world, both small and large."[20] In November 1944, Austin wrote an editorial titled "The British Empire Must Be Destroyed," calling Britain an "international bully." He proclaimed, "For centuries the English people have lived off the sweat and blood of others," and "the sooner [the empire of] Great Britain is destroyed, the sooner we will be able to establish peace in the world."[21]

Other black leaders in North Carolina were less willing to criticize America's allies. In September 1939, North Carolina College for Negroes president James Shepard told his students that England and France were great democracies fighting a war "to save democracy from Communism, Naziism [*sic*], [and] Fascism" and predicted that the United States would soon join this fight.[22]

After the Japanese attack on Pearl Harbor and America's entrance into the war in December 1941, black commentators quickly articulated the contradiction implicit in the federal government urging Americans to fight racism abroad while remaining silent about racism at home. In 1942, black journalist Earl Brown summarized the cynical view of many black Americans: "Because he must fight discrimination to fight for his country and to earn a living, the Negro today is angry, resentful, and utterly apathetic about the war. 'Fight for what?' he is asking. 'The war doesn't mean a thing to me. If we win I lose, so what?'" A black youth, after being drafted into the army, commented, "Just carve on my tombstone, 'Here lies a black man killed fighting a yellow man for the protection of a white man.'"[23]

Even moderate black leaders like Shepard recognized that many African Americans were not gung-ho for the war effort. Following a trip to northeastern cities in April 1942, Shepard noted that blacks had "very little enthusiasm" for the war. He found "real bitterness, disappointment and loss of hope on the part of many" African Americans, who continued to suffer from employment discrimination and violent attacks by whites. Shepard observed that the "recent horrible lynching in Missouri has stirred up a feeling of bitterness and hatred which could hardly be imagined."[24] Shepard referred to the lynching of Cleo Wright, a black oil mill worker who had been jailed after being accused of attacking a white woman. Wright was abducted by a mob and dragged behind a car, and then his body was set on fire.[25]

While some African Americans viewed blatant discrimination against blacks in employment and in the armed forces as an indication that the war was making life worse for the race, others believed that the war would yield benefits for African Americans. Indeed, many African Americans used the nature of the war and American condemnation of the Nazis' racist ideology to their rhetorical benefit in fighting racial oppression on the home front. As historian Richard Dalfiume has observed, "Hope was evident in the growing realization that the war provided the Negro with an excellent opportunity to prick the conscience of white America."[26]

Many readers of the *Carolina Times* supported the paper's advocacy of the Double V strategy. When *Times* columnist Clifford Jenkins asked ten readers if blacks should postpone the fight for equal rights until after the war, eight readers responded in the negative. (The other two were ambivalent.) Durham beautician Anna Morrow said, "If we don't strive for our rights now, we have no future." Margaret Jeffers proclaimed, "We should fight for our rights.... Every man should have equal rights and should not be pushed around." A housewife declared, "When we read of the many insults which come to our boys in the uniform, we should be moved to fight with increased energy for the things that rightfully should be ours."[27]

Many black Carolinians went beyond words in resisting racial oppression, and put their bodies on the line in fighting against racial segregation. In fact, there were extensive reports throughout the state of African American challenges to segregated bus seating. In June 1943, Stanley Winborne, chairman of the North Carolina Utilities Commission, advised North Carolina governor J. Melville Broughton that he had received many complaints from whites in eastern North Carolina "that the Negroes crowd them off the buses." Winborne reported numerous challenges to segregation in Durham, calling it "one of the worst places we have, due to the large negro population, and . . . the fact that there are a great many Northern negro soldiers at Camp Butner [a temporary military installation, eighteen miles northeast of Durham]." He noted that on "the local bus line between Durham and Camp Butner . . . it was utterly impossible . . . to enforce the segregation laws and that the police of Durham stated that they could not assist him in doing so." Winborne concluded, "It is a bad situation."[28] Black civilians in Durham also resisted Jim

Crow law. In the spring of 1943, a sixteen-year-old female high school student refused to sit in the back of a Durham bus and was arrested.[29]

In July 1943, Annie Williamson, an African American woman, flouted the Jim Crow system and sat down in an empty front seat on a crowded bus in Wilmington. When she refused to give up her seat to a white man, she was arrested and beaten mercilessly by two white policemen. Instead of the police being charged with assault, Williamson was tried and convicted of violating segregation law, assaulting the bus driver, and resisting arrest. Austin demanded that the governor take action to rectify this blatant injustice. He wrote, "Governor, what would you have done if Mrs. Williamson had been your sister, mother, daughter or wife?" Austin maintained that it was the governor's responsibility to prevent racial violence. He must administer justice, or African Americans would have no alternative but to meet violence with violence.[30] But the governor refused to take positive action, instead blaming the black press, and particularly Austin, for inciting racial tensions. Broughton claimed that the "greatest menace to race relations in the nation today is this type of inflammatory Negro press."[31] Broughton's virulent reaction to Austin's unrelenting criticism demonstrates the power of the editor's words and the threat that he posed to white officials and the status quo.

In 1940, Pauli Murray, who had sought to desegregate the University of North Carolina in 1938, and her friend Adelene McBean were arrested in Petersburg, Virginia, for refusing to sit in the back of a bus en route to Durham. When Austin heard of their imprisonment, he admonished the police and praised the two women for bravely challenging Jim Crow law. He called the police actions "a brutal mistreatment and disrespect for Negro womanhood." He noted that black leaders were typically loath to risk going to jail, and suggested that Murray and McBean represented "a new type of [black] leadership" that would bravely risk jail in the cause of civil rights.[32] After the two women were released from jail and arrived in Durham, Austin tried to convince them to help him lead a Gandhi-type resistance movement in the city. Murray characterized Austin as a descendant of "Nat Turner, and a firebrand if ever there was any." Murray and McBean decided to return to New York, as they did not believe that they were up to the huge challenge of leading a movement in the South, where they would have "to give up" the freedom they enjoyed in the North.[33]

A different type of challenge to racial segregation occurred in Durham in March 1944 when the North Carolina College for Negroes (NCCN) basketball team played a "secret game" against a team composed of Duke University medical students, many of whom had played college basketball. Led by

Coach John McLendon, NCCN had won the Colored Intercollegiate Athletic Association (CIAA) title the previous month, defeating A&T College of Greensboro, North Carolina in the final game. In the first integrated college basketball game in the South, NCCN crushed Duke's medical students by a score of 88 to 44. In order to avoid any repercussions for either team, the administrations at both schools were not told about the game. Although only the two teams and a referee were present for the game, the word did get out to several NCCN students, who watched the game through the windows (the doors to the gym were locked). Although Louis Austin was kept in the dark about the game because McLendon knew that publicity would likely lead NCCN president James Shepard to fire him, Austin's young sports editor, Lin Holloway, found out about the game and watched it though the gymnasium windows along with several students. Holloway knew "that he had one hell of a story," but he also knew that if he published the story in the *Carolina Times*, it would get back to white political and education officials who would pressure Shepard to fire McLendon. Weighing his choices, Holloway decided that the story was not worth it, so he "tore up his notes" and did not tell Austin about the game.[34]

Prior to the "secret game," several games between top black and white college basketball players had taken place in the late 1930s and early 1940s, but none farther south than Washington, D.C. For example, in 1939, CIAA champion Virginia Union, a black college from Richmond, split two games, played in Philadelphia and New York, with National Invitation Tournament champion Long Island University (LIU). The same year, Kentucky State also split two games, played in Troy, New York, and Harlem, with LIU. Two years before the "secret game," in 1942, NCCN defeated Brooklyn College 37–34, in Washington, D.C.[35]

THROUGHOUT THE WAR, the *Carolina Times* and other black newspapers attacked rampant racial discrimination in the nation's armed forces and, along with many black activists, fought for fair and equitable treatment for blacks in all branches of the armed services. In 1940 in Charlotte, North Carolina, when four black high school students and their teacher asked for enlistment information at an army recruiting station, they were told to leave because "the station was for 'whites only.'" When the teacher persisted, he was badly beaten by white soldiers. In 1944, a white doctor estimated that four out of five black draftees in Rocky Mount, North Carolina, were classified 4-F to exclude them from the army.[36] The *Pittsburgh Courier* publicized the "army's refusal to accept black volunteers." It also urged "readers to flood Congress with letters protesting 'military taxation without representation,' and initiate a congressional lobbying committee to get an anti-discrimination clause inserted in the pending . . . conscription bill."[37]

Austin denounced the army's practice of restricting black soldiers to subservient positions. In August 1940, he accused the army of deception for announcing a call for "more than 200 Negro volunteers for the engineers division at Fort Bragg," which was "in reality a call for Negroes to serve in the labor battalion." Austin said the call was intended to "mislead Negroes into joining the army only to become servants for white soldiers."[38] The same year, Austin urged the federal government to investigate "charges that Negro soldiers of the Ninth Cavalry, stationed near Junction City, Kansas," were "forced to shine boots, scrub floors, polish brass and do other menial jobs on government time." Austin demanded the end to "this dastardly discrimination" and insisted that "punishment should be meted out to those responsible for it."[39]

In September 1940, the *Carolina Times* urged Congress to ensure that blacks were included in all branches of the armed forces in the Selective Service bill then under debate.[40] Austin argued that the "practice of barring Negroes from certain branches of the national defense is sacrificing too much to the gods of prejudice in these turbulent times." He called the armed forces' discriminatory policies "unsafe, unsound and damnable."[41] Congress passed the Selective Service and Training Act, which outlawed racial discrimination in the draft and training of soldiers, but it also gave the War Department discretionary power to choose whom it wanted for the armed services. This clause was attacked by black leaders, who correctly predicted that it would be used to exclude blacks. For example, the First Army Headquarters, which encompassed New England, secretly directed the region's draft boards to induct only whites in the initial draft.[42]

During the war, Austin was classified III-A. This was the classification set up by the selective service system in April 1942 for fathers with dependents who were not working in essential war production.[43] The upper age limit for the draft was thirty-eight, so Austin was not drafted because he was in his early to mid-forties during the war.[44]

Meanwhile, increased defense spending by the federal government spurred economic growth and employment, and helped the American economy recover from the Depression, but black leaders saw that this recovery was yielding little benefit for black workers, who were regularly denied employment in defense plants.[45] In January 1941, civil rights leader A. Philip

Randolph, who headed the Brotherhood of Sleeping Car Porters, launched the March on Washington Movement. He planned a huge demonstration in the nation's capital with thousands of black protesters to pressure President Franklin Roosevelt to issue an executive order mandating equal employment opportunity in defense plants and integration of the armed forces. In March 1941, Austin joined Randolph in his support for equal employment opportunity and equal treatment in the military. Austin denounced the "discriminatory practices, sanctioned by our president, evidenced by our army and navy; the barring of Negro workers from employment in some of the country's major defense plants."[46]

Unlike Austin, many southern black leaders, including editor of the *Norfolk Journal and Guide* Plummer B. Young, educator James Shepard, and businessman C. C. Spaulding, opposed Randolph's March on Washington Movement.[47] Even the *Pittsburgh Courier*, which originated the Double V campaign, opposed the March on Washington Movement.[48] Young's biographer has observed that the Norfolk editor "saw nothing un-American in the march; nevertheless, he wondered how the demonstrations would be viewed 'in the heat of our perilous crisis.'"[49] In a press interview, Spaulding maintained that he wanted the "same thing that radicals want," but he rejected the use of "ill considered pressures which create enmity and stifle cooperation" between whites and blacks.[50]

Like Spaulding, Shepard, a self-described conservative, rejected the use of pressure tactics to achieve gains for African Americans.[51] In 1940, Shepard denounced black activists in a letter to Secretary of the Navy Frank Knox. He told Knox, "Those who seek to stir them [African Americans] up about rights and not duties are their enemies."[52] He claimed that blacks' best hope for making strides toward racial equality was to lobby sympathetic white officials for support. In a 1944 radio broadcast, while calling for equal economic opportunity, and equal treatment in the courts and on public transportation, Shepard nonetheless precluded the use of legal action to gain equality. He emphasized the goodness of white North Carolinians, asserting that because he "believe[d] in the innate righteousness of North Carolina, I am standing against recourse to litigation to end racial discrimination."[53] In a national radio broadcast in February 1944, Shepard defended racial segregation and claimed that African Americans did not want social equality. Howard University sociologist E. Franklin Frazier admonished Shepard, "What right did you have to state that the Negroes of this country did not want social equality? . . . I believe in *Social Equality*."[54]

Following Shepard's 1944 radio broadcast, Austin rejected the NCCN president's characterization of African Americans' status in North Carolina. He wrote, "We . . . repudiate any so-called Negro leaders in this state who are so unmindful of the injustices suffered by the rank and file of their race, as to broadcast to the nation that Negroes in North Carolina are not suffering almost unbearable conditions in courts, travel, schools, employment and other important factors necessary to the full realization of the democratic way of life." Austin declared that black Carolinians were "not satisfied with conditions in the state and they detest the philosophy of appeasement that has gotten them nothing but promise after promise" that blacks will receive equity and justice. He insisted that blacks would "never accept . . . second class citizenship . . . as permanent," and claimed that Shepard's pandering speech had lost him the respect of black people.[55]

After President Roosevelt's June 1941 speech excoriating defense contractors that failed to hire blacks, Austin insisted that mere rhetoric was worthless. He urged the president to back his words with action by withdrawing defense contracts from manufacturers that discriminated against blacks in hiring.[56] A few days later, under pressure from Randolph's March on Washington Movement, Roosevelt issued an executive order barring employment discrimination against blacks by defense contractors and created the Fair Employment Practices Committee to enforce the order. As a result, the march was called off. Austin praised Randolph's pressure tactics for producing this important victory for the black freedom struggle.[57]

During the war, Austin regularly published the "Platform of the *Carolina Times*," a list of ten demands that would advance the status of African Americans in North Carolina and throughout the nation. These demands included equal pay for black teachers and industrial workers, equal educational opportunities, the inclusion of blacks on juries, the hiring of black policemen, increased wages for domestic servants, "full participation" of blacks in all U.S. military branches, black participation in politics, black representatives in all branches of local, state, and national government, and upgraded housing for African Americans.[58]

One tactic used by Austin and other activists to push for substantive change on the home front was to regularly illuminate the contradictions between American official statements against German and Japanese atrocities overseas and the racist violence experienced by African Americans at the hands of white Americans. Austin pointed out that while white officials condemned Japanese soldiers for committing atrocities against Americans, they found nothing wrong with the brutal lynching of African Americans.[59] In January 1942, Austin condemned the lynching of Cleo Wright, the black Missourian, who was tortured and burned to death by a white mob.[60]

Austin publicized racial discrimination and oppression of black soldiers and workers, noting that these disgraceful actions hurt America's war effort against the Axis Powers because these types of racial discrimination were fuel for German and Japanese propaganda. In this vein, he publicized the armed forces' discrimination against blacks, the South's poor treatment of black soldiers, and employment discrimination by defense plants. By ending the discrepancy between salaries for black and white teachers, Austin argued, North Carolina could "bolster the morale of its Negro citizens and weaken that of our enemies."[61]

In April 1942, Austin renewed his attack on racial discrimination in the armed services. While urging the president and Congress to ban "all forms of discrimination" against blacks in America, Austin called it "damnable" that African Americans had to fight for opportunities to defend their country from its enemies. He denounced Secretary of the Navy Frank Knox's decision to bar African Americans from serving as commissioned officers in the navy, as a "half-hearted, gutless and spineless declaration." While white officials resisted change, pressure exerted by black activists did yield some victories, including the establishment of a training facility for black pilots in Tuskegee, Alabama, in 1941, and by mid-1942, a significant increase in the number of black soldiers enrolled in officer candidate schools and in the opportunities available to black sailors in the navy.[62]

While Austin continued his attacks on racist practices, some black newspapers began to moderate their editorials because of criticism from government officials and white editors. In spring 1942, white southern editors and publishers condemned the black press, claiming that they were instigating southern racial violence near army installations, by "demanding an overnight revolution in race relations."[63] Jonathan Daniels of the *Raleigh News and Observer*, an advisor to President Roosevelt on race issues, disparaged the Double V campaign as "extortion."[64] Several black newspapers were intimidated by these attacks. For example, the *Savannah Tribune* stopped "reprinting militant editorials from the Northern [black] papers such as the [Chicago] *Defender, Amsterdam News,* and *New York Age.*"[65]

Meanwhile, concerned about losing black support for the war, the federal government pressured black newspapers to stop their advocacy for the Double V campaign. Seven federal government agencies placed the black press under surveillance. Historian Patrick Washburn has shown that in 1942, "the black press was in extreme danger of being suppressed."[66] Historian Charles Simmons has called this "the most dangerous period in history for the survival of the Negro press." The U.S. Post Office revoked several small black newspapers' second-class mail permits. FBI agents investigated black newspapers, including the *Pittsburgh Courier*, the *Chicago Defender*, and the *Amsterdam Star-News*, as well as the *Carolina Times*, on suspicion of sedition.[67]

It is not surprising that the FBI surveilled the *Carolina Times*, with its reputation as perhaps the most radical black newspaper in the South. The newspaper was also harassed by the Internal Revenue Service (IRS) during the war. The IRS consistently audited the paper's tax returns during and after the war.[68] According to Austin's FBI file, in March 1943, the bureau decided to "conduct a discreet investigation in an effort to ascertain any subversive activities on the part" of Austin, "and consider the advisability of placing a mail-cover."[69] A mail-cover was when the FBI would record the names of correspondents with the person under surveillance without getting a warrant. The FBI suspected that Austin was a Communist. According to the FBI and the Durham Police Department, Austin told an informant that he had once been a member of the Communist Party, but he was "dropped from the Party, because he refused to sign a pledge to remain away from the church."[70] Although there is evidence that Austin sometimes worked with Communists in the cause of racial justice, there is no other evidence to corroborate the FBI's statement about Austin's alleged membership in the Communist Party. Despite the covert nature of the FBI's investigation, Austin soon realized he was under surveillance. In fact, after several visits by an FBI agent, Austin invited the agent to the Bible class he regularly taught at St. Joseph's AME Church. The FBI agent did go to the class at least once, and later told Austin that anyone with so much faith in God could not be a Communist.[71] Nonetheless, the FBI built up an extensive file on Austin as it continued to investigate him and his editorials for the remainder of the war.[72]

The FBI gathered evidence of Austin's extensive involvement in the black freedom struggle. Several white informants told the FBI that Austin was the key black agitator for racial equality in the city. The executive vice president of Durham Bank and Trust told the FBI that Austin was a "race agitator" and instigated resistance to racial segregation, notably on the buses.[73] Similarly, J. H. Borland, recorders court judge, told the FBI that Austin was "largely responsible for stirring up of Negroes" in Durham.[74] In late 1943, an informant told the FBI that Austin was "one of the most dangerous individuals in the state."[75] Another informant called Austin and his business manager, James G. Rhodes, "dangerous negroes, forever endeavoring to foment hard feelings on the part of the negroes at Chapel Hill, North Carolina, and is the type that makes test cases, such as having a negro sit in the front of a North Carolina bus, and then giving the incident a big write-up in his paper."[76] The FBI surveilled Rhodes from early 1944 till the end of the war.[77] After the war ended, the FBI closed its files on Austin, after deciding that the editor was no longer "considered sufficiently dangerous to warrant" continued surveillance.[78]

Meanwhile, in December 1942, President Roosevelt urged Walter White, executive secretary of the NAACP, to convince black editors to rein in their attacks on injustice toward blacks. White relayed Roosevelt's concerns at a meeting with twenty-four black editors (the *Carolina Times* apparently was not represented) and stressed the threat of government repression of the black press.[79] In fact, even before the meeting, several black newspapers, particularly in the South, had moderated their criticisms of racial inequities.[80] After the meeting, the *Pittsburgh Courier* reasserted its support for the Double V, but prior to the meeting it had sharply reduced the space in the paper devoted to the Double V campaign.[81] Several other papers "agreed to approach new opinions with some caution."[82] Moreover, the campaign to suppress black protest convinced several black editors at a 1943 news conference in New York to announce that they were opposed to black anti-war activity.[83] There is no evidence that Austin tempered his attacks on racial injustice.

Although there appeared to be a possibility of more stringent federal restrictions on the black press, U.S. Attorney General Francis Biddle refused to indict any black publishers for sedition based largely on his allegiance to a free press and his belief that the black press was not a significant threat. Although government investigations and harassment of the black press declined after Biddle's decision, "the FBI and the Post Office continued to investigate the black press."[84]

Unlike several other black southern newspapers, Austin refused to yield to government pressure. While he backed the war effort, he also continued his attacks on racial discrimination by the federal government, by America's European allies, and by whites in North Carolina. In 1942, he noted that the British and the Dutch were "paying in blood, sweat and tears" for their long oppression of subject peoples.[85] Meanwhile, Austin urged the United States to demand that Britain free its colonies, declaring that this was "one of the greatest opportunities that will ever come to the United States to strike a bloodless blow for unfortunate people living under British domain." He asserted, "We cannot fight a war on one hand to preserve the rights of free people while denying those rights to others."[86]

At the same time, Austin questioned the patriotism of whites whose racist practices hurt the war effort. In March 1942 he called whites, who refused to permit training programs for blacks in welding and other skills that were needed to help provide military supplies, a fifth column who were "as vicious an enemy as the most ruthless Japanese or German." Austin declared that blacks were "tired of grinning at little peanut-head men who are so busy fighting the Civil War and preserving white supremacy that they don't know that American lives are being lost."[87] In May 1942, Austin hammered away at race discrimination in hiring in defense plants and training programs, calling white supremacists "contemptible jackasses," who were "throttling this nation's effort to save our shores."[88]

Austin also supported the efforts of black factory workers to gain wage increases and improved working conditions. In 1943, he stood up for black tobacco workers in Winston-Salem in their battle for just treatment and fair wages against R. J. Reynolds Tobacco Company. Austin denounced black business leaders in Winston-Salem for attacking union leaders and insisting that Reynolds treated its black workers well. He called it "a stab in the back, inflicted upon its victims for the sole and selfish purpose of aiding these belly crawlers into the good graces of the Reynolds Tobacco Company."[89] Austin gave several speeches in 1943 to R. J. Reynolds tobacco workers in Winston-Salem, in support of their organizing efforts.[90] Moreover, the Congress of Industrial Organizations (CIO), which sought to represent the Reynolds workers, advertised in the *Carolina Times* in advance of August 1943 union elections.[91] In April 1944, Austin praised the Winston-Salem tobacco workers for choosing the CIO to represent them. He contrasted the CIO with the American Federation of Labor (AFL), which he said had "bungled" a tobacco workers' strike in Durham, noting that the AFL had a long history of mistreating black workers.[92]

In March 1945, Austin continued to criticize the AFL. He wrote, "Negro tobacco workers of Durham and elsewhere should demand immediate explanation from the American Federation of Labor Tobacco Workers International as to its jim-crow practices." Austin urged black workers to demand justice in hiring for all levels of jobs and equal access to promotions.[93]

During the war, Austin had no patience for white leaders who glossed over racial oppression. Nor did he shy away from attacking the most powerful white leaders in the state. North Carolina's wartime governor J. Melville Broughton was one of Austin's favorite targets. If one were to believe Broughton's utterances on race relations and race discrimination in North Carolina, one would have had no idea that racial discrimination was the rule in the state, not the exception. In a July 1943 speech on the occasion of the launching of the cargo ship the USS *John Merrick*, named after one of the founders of the North Carolina Mutual Life Insurance Company, Broughton asserted that the state had a long "record of racial harmony."[94] Austin reproved the governor for using Merrick's success in an "attempt to prove that conditions are ideal for Negroes in North Carolina or anywhere else." Austin further asserted, "So the Sunday School–teaching governor would perpetuate a system that accepts as right for Negroes inferior schools, discrimination on jobs, a lower wage scale, police brutality, inferior traveling conditions on public carriers, poor housing and a thousand other injustices."[95] Broughton responded by blaming "the violent and radical Negro press," which inflamed passions, for any racial problems that did exist.[96] As in the past, James Shepard did not miss an opportunity to ingratiate himself with white leaders by attacking Austin. In June 1944, Shepard wrote to Governor Broughton, "The editorial in last week's *Carolina Times* was one which causes us to hang our heads in shame. If Louis Alson [*sic*] does not attack me, he is attacking you."[97]

Despite his unrelenting criticism of racist discrimination, Austin, like other black editors, consistently advocated an unequivocal black commitment to defeat the foreign enemies of the United States.[98] In April 1942, Austin advised blacks to continue to "walk the highway of patriotism, with human dignity, in the face of racial insults." Nonetheless, Austin criticized the omission of Johnnie Roberson, the first black Durhamite to die in the armed services during World War II—he was killed earlier that year during a German torpedo attack on his destroyer off the coast of New Jersey—from the list of names on a memorial tablet of Durhamites who gave their lives in service to their country.[99]

During the war, Austin continued to denounce race relations meetings as ineffectual. After such a meeting in March 1943 at a local white church, he called for the permanent abolition of race relations meetings. Instead, he argued that more fruitful would be meetings with white workers who refused to work with black workers, and meetings with white landlords, sharecroppers, and tenant farmers who embraced white supremacy.[100] At a July 1944 conference on race relations held at North Carolina College for Negroes, Austin mounted a similar attack. He asserted, "You can't bring about a better racial understanding in this State or any other state by reading theoretical papers." Austin encouraged conference leaders to meet with factory owners, police chiefs, labor leaders, political leaders, bus drivers, and railroad workers, who regularly discriminated against African Americans.[101]

Earlier, Austin had criticized the October 1942 meeting of southern black leaders in Durham, North Carolina, and their Durham Manifesto in December 1942, which did not directly reject racial segregation.[102] Historian Raymond Gavins characterized the conferees as "middle-class moderates who assumed the right to speak for all Southern Negroes."[103] While some leaders like Benjamin Mays of Morehouse College and Gordon B. Hancock of Virginia Union University favored a more direct attack on segregation, others like P. B. Young, C. C. Spaulding, and James Shepard "argued for an expanded role for blacks within the existing defense structure and warned that having integration as a goal would undermine their positions of leadership in the South. Moreover, Young warned of a white backlash if whites perceived the conference as a platform 'to press for racial equality.' "[104] While declaring their opposition "to the principle and practice of compulsory segregation in our American society," the conferees agreed to postpone a final reckoning with segregation, instead advocating the end of the poll tax and the white primary, and supporting equal pay for teachers and equal public facilities, the passing of a federal antilynching law, and continuation of the Fair Employment Practices Committee.[105] Austin chided those in attendance for excluding black activists Walter White and A. Philip Randolph, who he said had "borne the brunt in the heat of the day and are still bearing it."[106] Furthermore, he dismissed the meeting as a chance for black intellectuals "to show off by appearing profound" and for black leaders to ingratiate themselves with white leaders.[107]

In 1944, Austin praised the U.S. Supreme Court ruling that outlawed the whites-only Democratic primary in Texas. However, he warned that this ruling would not be enough to stop "such human monstrosities as [Mississippi senator Theodore] Bilbo, [former Georgia governor Eugene] Talmadge, [South Carolina senator] Cotton Ed Smith and [former Alabama senator J. Thomas] Heflin" from denying African Americans voting rights and equal legal rights.[108]

By 1943, many African Americans decided that they could no longer stomach the incessant racial oppression leading to the eruption of race riots in over forty American cities, including Durham.[109] The Durham riot erupted when black soldiers, frustrated by relentless abuse by racist white soldiers and local whites, fought back. On April 3, 1943, a dispute "about ration books" between a black soldier from nearby Camp Butner and the white owner of a liquor store triggered violence in Hayti, a black neighborhood in Durham. During the argument, a white alcohol officer punched one of the black soldiers. The officer fled the store after about twenty black soldiers advanced toward him. Two black soldiers intervened between the officer, who had drawn his gun, and a crowd of about 100 black Durhamites. After black rioters threw bricks and rocks and destroyed storefronts, local police employed tear gas, but order was not restored until armed military trucks and military police were brought in and dispersed the crowd, late in the day.[110]

Following the riot, Austin perceptively analyzed the causes of the violence in Durham. While expressing his "condemnation of all forms of mob violence," Austin placed the responsibility for the conflict squarely on the shoulders of the alcohol law enforcement officer who acted maliciously toward the black soldier. Austin wrote, "Any officer of the law who on the least provocation wields his fist, [or] blackjack or pulls his gun appears to us to be encouraging disturbances rather than preventing them." Furthermore, Austin condemned the record of this branch of law enforcement, asserting that it had a record of doing "more killing, black-jacking and fist-mauling than all the others put together." Finally, he argued that the riot showed the need for the city to hire black police (Durham had none) to patrol the black sections of Durham.[111] A week later, the *Carolina Times* published an account written by a local African American who witnessed the previous week's riot. He recounted being arrested and brutally beaten—punched in the face, smashed in the head with a flashlight—by police officers for refusing to name those who were involved in the riot.[112] In June 1943, Austin declared that "the law of segregation" was the root cause behind race conflict in the state.[113] In July 1943, Austin participated in a panel discussion about the race riots at the University of North Carolina at Chapel Hill (UNC). The other speakers were UNC professors Guy Johnson and Eston E. Ericson, and Reverend Charles Jones of the Chapel Hill Presbyterian Church.[114]

The abuse faced by black soldiers in Durham was par for the course in North Carolina. E. Frederic Morrow, who was stationed at Camp Sutton, in Monroe (near Charlotte), North Carolina, where there were almost daily fights because of racist treatment, recalled that Monroe was a "racist hellhole." Monroe police regularly beat up black soldiers who received no protection from the U.S. Army. In September 1943, black soldiers attacked white military police who attempted to arrest one of their cohort. Some black soldiers shouted, "We may as well die here as over there."[115] The following summer, an altercation occurred when black soldiers from Camp Sutton were refused service at a café in nearby Concord. According to a War Department report, a white customer pushed one of the black soldiers as he was leaving. The black soldier then stabbed the white man. When the white counterman intervened, the black soldier stabbed him to death. The black soldiers got away despite being chased by a lynch mob.[116]

In contrast to his reaction to the Durham riot, after the June 1943 Detroit race riot left thirty-four people dead, Austin altered his analysis, now emphasizing the bankruptcy of violence, and understating the role of white provocation in causing the riot. While he consistently protested against all forms of injustice, Austin vilified both blacks and whites when they responded by resorting to violence. Relying on his Christian faith, which underpinned his philosophy of protest, he refused to condone black violence as a solution to injustice. Austin counseled blacks to lay down their weapons. Although he asserted that racial violence in numerous cities, including Durham, meant "America is now reaping the whirlwind for national neglect" of the racial oppression of African Americans, he focused on what blacks should do to defuse the conflict. He maintained that blacks could "afford to be calm and to do your part to avoid more bloodshed," because their "case before the world's bar of justice is so strong." He urged African Americans to send letters to their mayor, to their governor, and to the president. He opined that these letters written "out of the agony and endurance of the Negro soul, will do more than all the guns, the tear gas, the counterattacks, or mob rule can possibly do."[117]

Then, after the outburst of violence in Harlem in August 1943, triggered by a white policeman shooting and wounding a black soldier, Austin condemned black rioters. He asserted that the *Times* was "against mob violence" whether perpetrated by "white hoodlums" or "black hoodlums." He excoriated those who offered "flimsy excuses" for the rioters. He claimed that the riot began "when decent and law-abiding citizens did not have the moral courage to say to the lawless element, you can't live in this community and not have respect for the rights and prosperity of your fellowmen." He concluded by claiming that "Harlem got what was coming to it, and Durham is headed in the same direction."[118] Claude Barnett, head of the Associated Negro Press, reacted similarly. Barnett told black businessman C. C. Spaulding that he was most concerned about how "we can control that element," meaning the rioters, who he felt tarnished the reputations of all African Americans by their lawlessness.[119]

In contrast, New York City councilman and pastor of Harlem's Abyssinian Baptist Church Adam Clayton Powell Jr. asserted that the Harlem violence was not a race riot, but "the last open revolt of the black common man against a bastard democracy." Like Austin, Powell argued that violence was an ineffective strategy, and advocated the use of the ballot, but he stressed that the cause of the violence was "the whole sorrowful, disgraceful bloody record of America's treatment of one million blacks in uniform."[120] Percival L. Prattis of the *Pittsburgh Courier* highlighted the perverse role played by the police in the Detroit riot. When whites assaulted blacks in black neighborhoods, the white police arrested the black victims, not the white attackers. Prattis pronounced, "It is crystal clear that in no American community is the police power going to be used against the majority from which the mob comes to protect the minority from which the victims come."[121]

In devoting his response to the Detroit and Harlem riots to an attack on black violence, Austin missed an opportunity to emphasize the causes of black violence—as he had in the case of Durham—which often represented a response to pent-up frustration about economic oppression, housing discrimination, police brutality, and widespread mistreatment of black soldiers.[122]

While Austin publicly condemned black violence in response to white racist brutality, privately, the editor refused to turn the other cheek when confronted with violent attacks on himself or his family. During the early 1940s, Austin was walking with his wife and teenage daughter in downtown Durham, when a white man raised his elbow to force black people off the sidewalk. In doing so, he struck Austin's wife in the face, knocking her eyeglasses to the ground. Austin reacted quickly, moving his daughter out of the way, grabbing hold of the white man, and punching him in the face. Immediately, black friends and acquaintances gathered around Austin, and to protect him, quickly ushered him into a car to get him out of there. Nothing came of the incident.[123]

Meanwhile, the race riots led Austin to rethink his opposition to race relations meetings, which he had harshly attacked. Concerned about racial violence, in September 1943, Austin praised several meetings that supported the methods and goals of the 1942 Durham conference that yielded the Durham Manifesto. After an Atlanta conference of white racial moderates, and then biracial meetings in Richmond and Atlanta in June and August 1943, respectively, Austin complimented this "most impressive effort" in dealing with continued racial oppression and an expected upsurge of racial oppression in the postwar era. He predicted that thousands of black workers would be displaced by returning white soldiers.[124] In September 1943, Austin praised white moderates like Frank Porter Graham, Guy Johnson, and Howard Odum of UNC, for having "faced unflinchingly the bitter scorn of members of their own group in their efforts to . . . open up new frontiers of interracial goodwill in the South." He called them "the real heroes in the battle which Negroes are waging to obtain a full measure of American democracy."[125] The Richmond and Atlanta meetings set the stage for the creation of the Southern Regional Council, which historian Harvard Sitkoff called "a vehicle for anti-militant southern journalists and educators" to liberalize "race relations without fundamental change. It wanted trade unions to act fairly toward African Americans, supported the FEPC and the anti–poll tax bill, favored improving the living conditions of minorities, and approved of experimentally racially-mixed units of volunteers in the army and navy—but not desegregation in the South. It would not publicly condemn segregation until 1949."[126]

Austin counseled African Americans not to react with violence to oppression; he implored them to organize and vote to ensure change. Apparently backing away from his usual impatience with all racial injustices, he now maintained that progress was a "slow process," and he insisted that the "surest way to impede it is for individuals to force its arrival."[127] What Austin failed to say was that in North Carolina, racist white registrars and the literacy test continued to limit the number of black voters.[128] Nonetheless, Austin's agitation during the 1930s and 1940s did help spur black voter registration.[129] In 1940, he served as "chairman of the political division of the North Carolina Committee on Negro Affairs to increase the registration and voting of Race citizens in this state." By early 1940, voter registration campaigns had increased black registration totals to about 75,000, according to the *Chicago Defender*, and Austin sought to increase that number by the 1940 elections.[130] According to a more recent study, 10 percent of eligible African Americans in North Carolina were registered to vote in 1940. By 1947, that percentage had increased to 14 percent. The 1940 percentage placed North Carolina second to Tennessee among eleven southern states (excluding Kentucky). The 1947 percentage, however, placed North Carolina fifth in the South, behind Georgia, Arkansas, Texas, and Tennessee.[131]

In 1945 Austin, backed by the DCNA, mounted the first campaign in the twentieth century by an African American to win a seat on the Durham City Council. In fact, had he won, he would have been the first African American to be elected to a city council in North Carolina in the twentieth century. Austin ran an active campaign, including a speech to the city that was broadcast on local radio station WDNC. Despite his efforts, he lost to a white opponent in the May 8, 1945 Democratic primary.[132] Austin, who won the endorsement of labor leaders, garnered 969 votes.[133] After his defeat, Austin told NC Mutual executive Asa Spaulding that even though he lost the race, his "effort has served to begin a political awakening among the mass of Negroes of our city and will bear fruit in the future." He declared that he would run again in 1947 if another black candidate could not be found because he was determined to "abolish here in Durham the pernicious system of Negro taxation without Negro representation."[134] Just as in his work on the seminal legal challenge to racial segregation in higher education in the South in 1933, Austin took an important first step in overturning racial oppression in Durham, this time in the political arena.

During the war, the Durham Committee also sponsored two black candidates for the Durham county commission. While these black candidates also lost, their campaigns represented important steps toward electing black candidates to local office, laying the groundwork for electing black businessman Rencher N. Harris to the city council in 1953.[135]

PERHAPS THE MOST egregious example of racial brutality in Durham during the war was the murder of a black soldier by a white bus driver in 1944. This event not only demonstrated the murderous nature of Jim Crowism in Durham but also triggered a resurgence in African American activism, foreshadowing the civil rights struggle of the postwar era. On Saturday evening, July 8, 1944, Pvt. Booker T. Spicely, stationed at Camp Butner, boarded a Durham bus. As he got on the bus in a black neighborhood, he sat down in a forward row. When the bus stopped in a white neighborhood and several white passengers boarded, the white bus driver, Herman Lee Council—there were no black bus drivers in Durham—demanded that Spicely move to the back of the bus. At first, Spicely refused to move, and then muttered that the bus driver was only in a civilian job because he was unfit for military service. But Spicely did move back.[136] A few minutes later, as more white passengers including several white soldiers boarded the bus, "the bus driver shouted to" Spicely and a black female passenger, who "were sitting in the second seat from the back" to move to the rear seat. As they moved to the back seat, Spicely replied, "I thought I was fighting this war for Democracy." When Spicely exited the bus, he and Council exchanged words. Council then pulled out his .38-caliber pistol, got out of his seat, stepped off the bus, and shot Spicely, who was unarmed, twice, killing him.[137]

In the first edition of the *Carolina Times* following the murder of Spicely, the paper ran a banner headline, "Soldier Killer Given Bond, Bus Driver only Required to Post $2500 Bond in Brutal Slaying of Soldier." The *Times* made an "exhaustive investigation" of the case and issued its report based on interviews with a number of eyewitnesses to the killing. In his editorial, Austin noted that although blacks knew that the justice system in Durham was patently unjust toward blacks, nonetheless, blacks would not seek "revenge or violence." Austin reported that no white murderer who had killed a black person in North Carolina had ever been sentenced to the death penalty and only once had a white man been convicted of killing a black man. He noted that given this latest example of white racist brutality, blacks were "becoming less and less enthusiastic over having to fight a ruthless enemy on the battle front [overseas] and more ruthless enemy . . . on the home front."[138]

Immediately after the shooting, the U.S. War Department and the FBI conducted an extensive investigation, fearing that the shooting of a black soldier by a white bus driver would lead to violence by black soldiers and civilians. The FBI also increased its surveillance of Austin, suspecting that his militant response to the shooting might provoke more violence.[139] The Durham police chief told the War Department that after the shooting, a small crowd of African Americans "gathered at the scene" of the crime, but "no threats were heard." The crowd dispersed "when a fire broke out" at about 9:00 P.M. in downtown Durham.[140]

This was a massive fire that destroyed a large section of downtown. According to the *Raleigh News and Observer*, the fire "began in the basement of the Big Four tobacco warehouse."[141] The *Durham Morning Herald* reported that the "first alarm on the fire—which at that time was of minor proportions—was sounded at 9:12 P.M." But "by the time the local firemen arrived, the blaze had raced quickly throughout almost all of the Big Four building."[142] By midnight, the fire "had consumed all but one building in the block." The fire destroyed the "Central Leaf Tobacco Redrying Company plant and the Dillard Livery Stables, where 12 cows and four horses burned to death."[143] The fire chief credited "3,000 soldiers, sailors and marines . . . for bringing the inferno under control after three hours." According to the *Durham Morning Herald*, the Durham police and the military police "maintained complete order," while thousands watched the inferno.[144] Although there has been some speculation that African Americans started the fire in reaction to the Spicely murder, neither the newspapers nor the investigation by the War Department and FBI reported any such connection.[145] Nor did they report any rioting.

After the murder of Spicely, a dispute developed between local black moderates and the NAACP over how best to ensure that the defendant, bus driver Herman Lee Council, who had been indicted for second-degree murder, would be properly prosecuted. Spicely's brother Robert hired local black attorneys Jerry Gates and M. Hugh Thompson, both of whom had strong ties to NC Mutual and its president C. C. Spaulding. While Robert Spicely wanted NAACP involvement, the local black attorneys, under pressure from Spaulding and James Shepard, insisted that NAACP involvement would be counterproductive and instead argued that a white attorney should be employed to assist the prosecution. Shepard and Spaulding, with the help of the NCCIC, then raised $500 to hire a white attorney as co-counsel for Gates and Thompson. Spaulding wrote Robert Spicely to convince him that a "local white attorney" would be more effective in the "all white courts" in Durham.[146] NAACP attorney Edward Dudley reported that "there is considerable pressure being brought by certain individuals to keep the N.A.A.C.P. out of this case."[147] Although Robert Spicely expressly instructed Hugh Thompson to cooperate with the NAACP and its attorney Thurgood Marshall, that did not occur because of the opposition of the local black attorneys under pressure from Spaulding and Shepard.[148] From his experience serving as lead counsel in the 1933 *Hocutt* case, William Hastie knew of Spaulding and Shepard's propensity for acquiescing to the white leadership of the city. Accordingly, he warned Dudley, who went to Durham in place of Marshall because Marshall had another pressing case, that attorneys Gates and Thompson were "cautious and very responsive to suggestions from the good white folks."[149]

After arriving in Durham, the thirty-three-year-old Dudley, who had joined the NAACP legal team the year before, advised Marshall that he was not optimistic about the prosecution of the white bus driver. He noted that the "newly appointed solicitor [the district attorney] appears very weak. He is a man around 70 years old." He further reported, "Some of the local people have retained a white attorney to assist the prosecutions. (I suppose the Spaulding faction did this.)" Dudley disclosed that the Durham branch of the NAACP had done nothing on the case because the branch president worked for NC Mutual "and therefore his hands are tied." Dudley concluded that the only prominent blacks in Durham who were supportive of the NAACP were R. L. McDougald, R. N. Harris, and Louis Austin. Dudley "decided . . . not to attempt active participation in the trial itself. None of the others are going to withdraw and it is my personal opinion that a huge battery of attorneys may appear to be persecuting the defendant rather than prosecuting him. . . . The record of victories here where the prosecution had assistants is very poor." Dudley argued that if the bus driver was found not guilty, the case would be solid evidence of the need for the congressional bill that would make the killing of a soldier a federal crime.[150] The Senate had passed that bill, but in August 1944, southern members of the House Judiciary Committee had stopped the bill from advancing to the full House of Representatives.[151]

Before the trial of Council, Thurgood Marshall revealed that once again black Durham leaders Spaulding and Shepard were resisting NAACP involvement. Their opposition to NAACP action reminded Marshall of the *Hocutt* case, when Shepard and Spaulding had conspired to undermine the case. Marshall recalled that while "Virginia and Maryland took an active stand on the question of equalization of teachers' salaries, and although we had been requested by teachers in North Carolina to file suit, all of these efforts were stopped by certain Negro groups in North Carolina who believe that the only way to handle the problem is to handle it in North Carolina 'without outside influence.' " Marshall concluded, "One thing is certain and that is that the N.A.A.C.P. will not itself be intimidated by anyone, whether he be white or Negro. One of these days, North Carolina will realize that none of us can handle our problems alone."[152]

At the trial, which was held in September 1944, nine witnesses testified.[153] Council testified that he told Spicely to move to the back of the bus after he initially resisted. While Council claimed that Spicely responded with an expletive, other witnesses, including white soldiers, refuted the defendant's testimony.[154] Meanwhile, Council claimed that he shot Spicely in self-defense. However, witnesses testified that the bus driver followed Spicely when the soldier got off the bus, and shot Spicely, who was unarmed, twice.[155]

After a three-day trial, the all-white jury deliberated for only twenty-eight minutes, so short a time that the judge who had left the courthouse briefly was not there when the jury completed its deliberations, and declared Council not guilty. The verdict was met by a deathly silence from the spectators, divided equally between blacks and whites. After the trial, the bus company announced that following Council's killing of Spicely, the bus driver had not even been suspended, but had been assigned to a different route.[156] The *Baltimore Afro-American* reported that there was "general disgust over the verdict [that] was shared by many reputable white citizens," and that according to "most observers," the judge, defense, and prosecuting attorneys had fairly tried the case, but the jury committed a "miscarriage of justice."[157] The NAACP advised Spicely's family to pursue a civil suit against the bus company, but apparently no such suit was filed.[158]

Austin and other local activists sought to make sure that Booker T. Spicely had not died in vain by renewing efforts to revitalize the black freedom struggle in Durham. Toward that end, they reorganized the local NAACP branch, replacing the old leadership. They would not acquiesce to leadership by the likes of James Shepard, who after Spicely was murdered, declared, "Cooperation between the races in North Carolina is one of the things of which we are proud in this state." It was clear to Austin that "racial cooperation" perpetuated racial oppression.[159] He urged black Durhamites to unite in their outrage at the murder of Spicely and the acquittal of his murderer. The intrepid editor took the opportunity presented by an enraged black citizenry to replace the conservative NAACP leadership—dominated by C. C. Spaulding—which had contributed to the dormancy and docility of the Durham branch.[160] Prior to the Spicely murder, the Durham chapter of the NAACP had been moribund with not one member.[161] About 700 people, including

Spicely's family, attended the memorial service for Booker T. Spicely, held at St. Joseph's AME Church in Durham on September 25, 1944. At the service, the Durham branch of the NAACP was named after Spicely, to honor his memory. Austin was elected president of the branch with Rev. T. A. Grady, pastor of Ebenezer Baptist Church, elected vice president; Shaw University biology professor R. Arliner Young, secretary; and businessman R. N. Harris, treasurer. Within five months, energized by the new leadership, and with the help of national director of NAACP branches Ella Baker, the branch added 197 new members. Moreover, the branch broadened its base by adding many more working-class people.[162]

After the memorial service, Austin wrote that "Pvt. Spicely has lighted a torch in Durham that will never go out. Already the torch is burning in the rebirth of the local branch of the" NAACP, which would fight for equal rights in Spicely's name. Austin insisted that the humiliation of black soldiers, "the bitter sting of segregation, the flagrant insults of . . . white people . . . will never crush the spirit which exists in the breast of the Negro."[163] On November 6, 1944, the NAACP began a membership drive in Durham that aspired to sign up 5,000 members, with NAACP attorney George H. Johnson, a member of the Fair Employment Practices Committee, addressing 600 people at Mount Vernon Baptist Church. The *Times* reported that NAACP members were "canvassing persons throughout the city," with hopes of reaching 2,500 members within a month. Pastors of a number of black churches and the NAACP headquarters, which was housed in the office of the *Carolina Times*, at 814½ Fayetteville Street, were the key contacts for new members.[164] In addition to the revitalization of the Durham branch of the NAACP, Robert Spicely reported that the case led to the creation of an NAACP branch in Tuskegee, where Robert Spicely was employed as cafeteria manager at Tuskegee Institute.[165]

Alarmed by Austin's outspoken denunciation of anti-black violence and his leadership of the local NAACP, the FBI increased its surveillance of the journalist.[166] In September, the FBI, having uncovered no evidence that Austin or James G. Rhodes was a Communist, decided to treat Austin and Rhodes as "potentially dangerous to the internal security of the Country" solely because of their "Racial Agitation."[167] The FBI continued to surveil the two journalists for the duration of the war.

African Americans were outraged by the treatment accorded black soldiers in the South. In a letter to the editor published in the *Times* two weeks after the Spicely murder, Albert Hines wrote, "The kind of Democracy that is being issued out to Negro soldiers smells to God's high Heaven." Comparing the Spicely murder to a lynching, Hines said that in North Carolina the "white bus driver carries his gun . . . and shoots down one of the soldiers who is willing to give his life on a battle field for his country." He noted that while black soldiers were helping the United States win the war overseas, at home black soldiers were losing the battle in the South, "where . . . he lives in fear of being shot down or mobbed by the southern white man."[168]

Austin later recalled that African Americans posted stickers all over Durham with the word "Remember." This was a poignant reminder that the black community would not be silent in the face of white racist brutality. Austin noted that although the murderous bus driver was not convicted of his crime, subsequent perpetrators of similar crimes were punished.[169]

After the Spicely murder, Austin continued to promote the expansion and activism of Durham's NAACP branch. In March 1945, Austin announced a program to add 500 new members to the NAACP local that month. If successful, the branch would have had more than 1,000 members.[170] By May 1945, the Durham NAACP had succeeded in pressuring the federal government to open a post office branch in Hayti in Durham, with plans for an African American to head that post office.[171]

Austin continued to attack racial segregation, using Spicely's murder to buttress his attacks. Two weeks after Spicely was killed, Austin related the impoverishment of the South to its ill treatment of blacks: "Pay the Negro equally for his labor, take down the Jim crow signs in employment, give him equal advantages in education and let him have equal treatment in the courts and at the ballot box and he will help free the South from economic bondage."[172] In October 1944, Austin evoked God in an attack on segregation on public transit: "The segregation law which forces one man to sit in the rear of a public carrier merely because God made his skin darker than another's is diabolically wrong and that no [one] man, who possesses an ounce of righteousness, can truthfully deny."[173] In December 1944, Austin advocated legal action to address the inequities in segregated public education. He declared, "When one observes the wanton killing of Negro soldiers, the continuous strife and conflict, riots and near riots caused by the segregation law and its influence, there is sound reasoning behind the desire to rid the south of it by peaceful means, rather than to permit it to go on until dire consequences are the result."[174] Meanwhile, the FBI continued to express concern about Austin's "inflammatory" editorials dealing with racial injustice.[175]

While some black leaders reacted to the violent uprisings of 1943 and 1944 by backing away from their demands for the end of oppression of African Americans, Austin did not.[176] He continued to publicize economic discrimination against African Americans, reporting in July 1943 that there was not one black welder or skilled worker among 9,000 workers in North Carolina's shipyards. Austin urged agitation for employment for skilled black workers, while criticizing black leaders for failing to lead such a protest.[177] In September 1943, Austin told black teachers to file a lawsuit to force the state to eliminate the continuing salary differentials between black and white teachers.[178] In October 1943, Austin denounced the continued and widespread employment discrimination against blacks by the nation's railroads. He also publicized the finding of the chief counsel of the Fair Employment Practices Committee (FEPC) that African Americans "suffered continuous, wholesale and increasing discrimination in employment by most . . . American railroad systems."[179]

In 1944, when 6,000 white Pennsylvania Transportation Company workers struck in protest against eight black workers being promoted to platform jobs due to FEPC pressure, Austin was outraged. He demanded that the black workers be kept at their jobs "at all cost. To permit the striking hoodlums to oust them . . . is to bow to anarchy, bigotry, race hatred, and sure and certain forces of destruction." The federal government seized the company to break the strike and restored the black workers to their upgraded jobs.[180]

In June 1945, Austin called for congressional passage of a peacetime FEPC and a ban on the poll tax. He condemned southern congressmen, including North Carolina senators Josiah Bailey and Clyde Hoey, for opposing these bills and supporting continued "economic bondage" for blacks. Noting that meetings were being held in San Francisco to create an international organization to guarantee liberty to all peoples, Austin called it a "mockery" comparing the United States and Great Britain unfavorably to the Soviet Union, because of their suppression of the liberties of people of color.[181]

In July 1945, at a conference on race relations at North Carolina College in Durham, Austin encouraged the participants to endorse legislation that would make the FEPC permanent. Nathan C. Newbold, the white director of Negro education in North Carolina, and chairman of the conference, refused to allow a vote, instead noting that Austin's recommendation "deserve[d] study." After insisting that "North Carolina is the outstanding State in the South for inter-racial good will and cooperation," C. C. Spaulding announced that he personally favored the FEPC, but he refused to support a vote of the conferees. Austin pressed the issue, but no vote was taken.[182]

While most black newspapers had supported Randolph's March on Washington Movement (MOWM) in 1941, in subsequent years many papers criticized Randolph's movement to desegregate the armed forces for advocating continued protest actions, including a civil disobedience campaign in the North.[183] After the 1943 Detroit riots, Randolph's program was widely denounced by major civil rights leaders and the black press, based on the belief that civil disobedience would lead to more violence.[184] Nonetheless, some black Carolinians did mount direct challenges to segregation. In 1943, UNC sociologist Howard Odum observed that large numbers of young black men in North Carolina were being arrested for sitting at segregated lunch counters.[185] An official of a bus company that operated between Durham and Camp Butner reported that African Americans regularly flouted segregation law on the buses.[186] In addition, there were rumors that African Americans were arming themselves with ammunition purchased from Sears, Roebuck catalogues.[187]

After President Roosevelt issued Executive Order 8802, Randolph sought to capitalize on the MOWM's momentum and press the administration to end discrimination in the armed services. In 1942, the MOWM organized several mass protest meetings in New York, Washington, D.C., and Chicago.[188] Austin voiced approval for these pressure tactics, while criticizing black leaders who refused to fight racial oppression. Austin castigated obstructionist black leaders for "holding the race back through this long established system of sabotage." These leaders, who sought the approval of whites, opposed lawsuits designed to equalize the salaries of black and white public school teachers and remained quiet in the face of police brutality.[189] In May 1942, Austin encouraged black Durhamites to pressure the president and the armed services to create a racially integrated volunteer division of the army. The previous week, 2,000 students attended a mass meeting at New York University and called for the creation of such a division. Austin now encouraged students at North Carolina College for Negroes to join this effort. (There is no evidence that they did so.) Austin argued that the persistence of racial injustice was due in significant part to the failure of blacks to employ pressure tactics against oppression.[190]

In September 1942, Austin attacked conservative black leaders who opposed the Double V strategy, and he urged blacks to unite behind the protest tactics of Randolph.[191] Austin denounced James Shepard for writing a letter to President Roosevelt in which the educator beseeched blacks to postpone the fight for racial justice until after the war. Austin called Shepard's letter "disgusting, embarrassing, and humiliating."[192]

In the aftermath of the Harlem riot, however, Austin rejected civil disobedience. Fearing continued violence, he counseled against taking to the streets to push for change. He advised his readers that the bus was not the place to challenge Jim Crow law and that the street was not the place to challenge police brutality.[193] Nonetheless, Austin continued to challenge bus segregation

in the *Times*. In June 1943, he attacked the unjust treatment of a black teenager who was fined for violating bus segregation rules. He called the justice
system's treatment of the "young girl" "revolting," citing "the assault, arrest,
fingerprinting, and photographing of the young girl."[194] Austin concluded
that blacks could not get justice in the Durham courts even if he had "Jesus
Christ for an attorney and the twelve disciples for a jury."[195]

In a case in March 1945 in which two white soldiers were accused of raping
a black woman in a Pullman railroad car, the *Times* covered the story with a
banner headline. The soldiers were found not guilty in an army court martial
at Fort Bragg, North Carolina. The *Times* article contrasted the "smiles of victory on the faces of" the white soldiers with the victim of the alleged rape,
who sat in the courtroom "engulfed in grief and tears with only her venerable
father and the two Negro lawyers to comfort her during her hour of humiliation and woe."[196]

Nonetheless, the drive for equal rights during World War II yielded benefits that helped North Carolina's black community further its struggle after
the war. The NAACP increased its membership in North Carolina to almost
10,000 by the end of the war. At the same time, the NAACP doubled the
number of local branches in the state. Moreover, as president of the Durham
NAACP branch, Austin helped establish the North Carolina State Conference of NAACP Branches, which provided a stronger and more united base
to press forward in the fight for equal rights.[197]

Throughout the war, Austin was a staunch advocate of the Double V strategy. While urging African Americans to play their part in fighting America's
enemies overseas, he consistently pressed white governmental officials, both
locally and nationally, to enlist in the fight for democracy at home while pursuing victory abroad. He refused to support civil disobedience as a tactic after
1943 and, following the Detroit and Harlem race riots, failed to emphasize the
reasons for blacks resorting to violence in the midst of police brutality, housing and economic discrimination, and violent attacks by white citizens. But
by consistently publicizing racial discrimination against African American
soldiers, workers, students, and teachers and by advocating protest tactics
and litigation, Austin spurred a growing militant movement that would bear
more fruit after the war. During the decade after the war, Louis Austin would
play a pivotal role in the movement to desegregate public education and
other public facilities and to elect black public officials.

TOP The Rusty Seven (ca. 1921): Louis Austin (*back row, far right*) and six friends who attended the National Training School in Durham. Courtesy of North Carolina Central University Archives, Records and History Center.

BOTTOM Liggett & Myers Tobacco Company, Durham, North Carolina, Shift Change, ca. 1930. Courtesy of the Durham County Library Historic Photographic Archives.

The First Executive Commitee

J.E. Shepard
Vice-Chairman

J.T. Taylor
Secretary

R.N. Harris
Assistant Secretary

C.C. Spaulding
Chairman

L.E. Austin

R.L. McDougald
Treasurer

W.D. Hill

W.J. Kennedy
Made the motion to establish
the Durham Committee

John H. Wheeler
Past Chairman
Counted ballots
at the first meeting

Nine men who played key roles in establishing the Durham Committee on Negro Affairs, including Louis Austin, who served on the organization's founding executive committee. Courtesy of North Carolina Central University Archives, Records and History Center.

James E. Shepard, founder and president of North Carolina College for Negroes from 1910 to 1947. He often clashed with Austin on tactics to improve the lives of African Americans. Courtesy of the Durham County Library Historic Photographic Archives.

TOP Durham Bus Station, ca. May 1940. Library of Congress.

BOTTOM Hayti section of Durham, home to many of the city's black businesses, including the Biltmore Hotel, the Regal Theatre, and the Donut Shop. Courtesy of the Durham County Library Historic Photographic Archives.

Wonderland Theatre, owned by Frederick K. Watkins, who was elected justice of the peace in Durham in 1934. He and Austin were the first African Americans elected to public office as Democrats in North Carolina in that era. Courtesy of the Durham County Library Historic Photographic Archives.

TOP Louis Austin (*front left corner*), with C. C. Spaulding (*pictured to Austin's left*) and professional boxers Sugar Ray Robinson (*in uniform, pictured to Spaulding's left*) and Joe Louis (*in uniform, pictured to Robinson's left*). Also pictured, R. Kelly Bryant Jr. (*back corner, far left*), John H. Wheeler (*between Austin and Spaulding*), R. L. McDougald (*behind Robinson*), W. D. Hill (*front row, second from right*), and T. D. Parham (*front row, far right*), ca. 1944. Courtesy of the Durham County Library Historic Photographic Archives.

BOTTOM Pauli Murray, longtime friend of Austin, who sought to break the color line at the University of North Carolina in 1938. Courtesy of the Schlesinger Library, Radcliffe Institute, Harvard University.

TOP Louis Austin, reading the *Carolina Times*, 1947. Courtesy of the Durham County Library Historic Photographic Archives.

BOTTOM Paul Robeson (*standing, far left*) and Louis Austin (*sitting, second from left*), ca. 1948, during Henry Wallace's campaign for president. Courtesy of the *Carolina Times*.

TOP St. Joseph's African Methodist Episcopal Church, Durham, North Carolina. Courtesy of the André D. Vann Private Collection.

BOTTOM Charles Clinton (C. C.) Spaulding, president of the North Carolina Mutual Life Insurance Company from 1923 to 1952. Courtesy of the André D. Vann Private Collection.

TOP Vivian Austin, Louis Austin's daughter, 1946. Courtesy of Patricia A. Murray and the Durham County Library Historic Photographic Archives.

BOTTOM Vivian Austin's graduation from North Carolina College at Durham, 1948. *From left*, Louis Austin; Kathryn Walker, Stella W. Austin's sister; Vivian Austin; and Stella Walker Austin. Courtesy of the *Carolina Times*.

TOP Rencher N. Harris (*third from right*) being sworn in as the first African American on the Durham City Council, 1953. Courtesy of the Durham County Library Historic Photographic Archives.

BOTTOM John H. Wheeler addressing Governor Luther Hodges, with Austin seated next to Wheeler, 1955. Wheeler, Austin, and other African Americans opposed the governor's plans to obstruct the desegregation of public schools following the U.S. Supreme Court's *Brown v. Board of Education* decision. Courtesy of the Durham County Library Historic Photographic Archives.

Vivian Austin Edmonds, Woodrow W. Edmonds, Stella Walker Austin, and Louis Austin (*left to right*), 1957. Courtesy of the *Carolina Times*.

Floyd McKissick, native of Asheville, North Carolina, helped desegregate the University of North Carolina law school in 1951 and emerged as a key leader in the black freedom struggle in North Carolina and nationally. Courtesy of North Carolina Central University Archives, Records and History Center.

Louis Austin, ca. 1960. Courtesy of North Carolina Central University Archives, Records and History Center.

Attorneys Conrad Pearson, M. Hugh Thompson, Floyd McKissick, William Marsh Jr., and John H. Wheeler (*left to right*), who sued the Durham School Board to integrate the public schools after the *Brown* decision. Courtesy of the Durham County Library Historic Photographic Archives.

Austin with President Lyndon B. Johnson, spring 1965. Austin visited the White House with a group of black publishers, members of the National Newspaper Publishers Association. Courtesy of the *Carolina Times*.

Louis Austin, ca. 1970.
Courtesy of the *Carolina Times*.

Louis Austin, with child,
promoting the Oxford Orphanage.
Courtesy of the *Carolina Times*.

Vivian Austin Edmonds, ca. 1990s. She succeeded her father as the editor and publisher of the *Carolina Times*. Courtesy of North Carolina Central University Archives, Records and History Center.

CHAPTER FOUR

Segregation Must and Will Be Destroyed
The Black Freedom Struggle, 1945–1954

By the time World War II ended in 1945, Louis Austin had been a leading activist and voice for racial justice for almost two decades. During the first postwar decade, Austin's editorials continued to be forthright and resolute. This gutsy journalist, now in his late forties, led voter registration campaigns, ran for public office, advocated integration of higher education in the courts, lobbied for equal funding for black schools, demanded economic opportunity for African Americans, and denounced police brutality and racial injustice in the court system. From the late 1940s to the early 1950s, Austin played a key role in sustaining the black freedom struggle. In 1946, Pauli Murray praised Austin, calling him "a great citizen of America," whose contributions should be more widely known. She honored him for the sacrifices he had made and the "agonies he . . . suffered . . . to keep plugging away for truth and justice."[1]

At the close of World War II, black newspapers enjoyed tremendous and growing influence in the black community. Black press circulation in the United States reached over two million by 1947.[2] This trend was not universal among black newspapers, as the *Pittsburgh Courier* saw its circulation decline from a peak of 350,000 to 186,000 in 1954.[3] The *Carolina Times*, however, continued its wartime growth. During the first decade after the war, *Times* circulation doubled from 11,000 in 1945 to 22,144 in 1957. Throughout the 1940s and 1950s, the *Times* had the largest circulation of any black paper in North Carolina.[4] However, the paper still struggled financially, at times unable to pay its bills on time. In 1948, Austin told Claude Barnett of the Associated Negro Press, "Our income is dependent absolutely on advertising and circulation, and the advertising is never too great when you try to maintain a progressive editorial policy."[5]

In June 1950, Stella and Louis Austin celebrated the marriage of their only child, Vivian, to Woodrow Edmonds. At the time, Vivian, a graduate of North Carolina College at Durham (NCC), formerly North Carolina College for Negroes, worked for her father as city editor of the *Times*. Woodrow Edmonds, a World War II veteran and an NCC graduate, was employed as a teacher in Beaufort, South Carolina. The wedding, officiated by Rev. D. A. Johnston, pastor of St. Joseph's African Methodist Episcopal (AME) Church, was held at the Austin home in Durham. Louis Austin escorted the bride, "who wore an exquisite original white gown of nylon sheer, fashioned with a high ruffled neckline ... through the ribboned walkway." It was a well-attended wedding, with many family members traveling to Durham from across the country. Louis Austin's mother-in-law, Mrs. E. J. Walker, came from Los Angeles, California. Louis's brother Lodius and his wife came from Wilmington, North Carolina, and his other brother, Jesse, and his wife came from New York City.[6]

During the postwar years, Austin regularly used Cold War rhetoric to agitate for social, political, and economic change. He argued that racial discrimination was undemocratic and immoral, and, consequently, it damaged U.S. national security interests because it provided fodder for Soviet propaganda. While reactionary white supremacist politicians demonized racial egalitarians by labeling them Communists, Austin contended that the true threats to American national security were white supremacists, who aided the Communists by providing evidence to the Soviet Union that the United States was not the democracy it claimed to be.[7] In 1950, Austin proclaimed, "The real culprits behind the plots against our governments are those who stomp and strut about race superiority. They are the ones who need to be jailed and tried for treason."[8] In August 1950, six weeks after the outbreak of war in Korea, Austin noted the similarity between North Korean Communists and a mob of 300 white supremacists in Virginia, who attacked fifteen African Americans for transgressing the color line by swimming at Virginia Beach. Austin noted the irony and injustice of black soldiers "fighting Communists in a foreign land to preserve a form of government the full benefits of which are denied them at home."[9]

In the postwar years, Austin continued to pursue a dual strategy to improve black educational opportunities, at times pressing for integration, particularly in higher education, while fighting for equal funding for black schools and equal salaries for black teachers. The tenacious editor worked closely with the NAACP. In the first postwar decade, Austin, who had helped bring the first case to desegregate higher education in the South in 1933, urged Walter White of the NAACP to pursue another case to integrate the University of North Carolina at Chapel Hill (UNC).[10]

Austin agitated for equal facilities in public schools by publicizing the despicable conditions forced on black students in North Carolina, pressing for more state funding, and supporting public pressure, protests, and lawsuits that sought equal facilities, or failing that, integration. He also attacked double taxation on African Americans who were often required to raise half the funds for school buses and school construction despite the fact that these items were fully funded by tax revenues in white North Carolina public schools.[11]

During the late 1940s, African Americans, increasingly frustrated by the inequities in the education system, demanded a seat at the table when decisions were being made about black education in Durham. They urged the all-white school board to appoint at least one black member, when the next vacancy occurred. As black students constituted nearly half the students in the district, it was only fair that the black community have representation on the school board. In 1947, Austin joined a group of the city's leading black men and women to implore the school board to rescind its firing of six black Whitted Elementary School teachers. The board had fired the teachers for petitioning the school board to fire the school's principal, whom they charged with administering the school in a "cruel and undemocratic" manner. Invoking Cold War politics, the school board had justified its action by accusing the teachers and their allies of "Communistic activity." Tensions increased between the black community and the school board after the city council dismissed a request to rehire the teachers. The board further alienated the black community when it refused to appoint a black member to the board, which had two vacancies, even after an impassioned plea by septuagenarian NCC president James Shepard, whom white officials claimed to hold in high regard.[12]

When lobbying efforts failed, in 1949 African Americans in Durham brought suit in federal court demanding equal facilities for the city's black public schools. Austin publicized the case, providing concrete evidence that the public school system had long operated a grossly unequal system, with black schools and students suffering with inadequate resources.[13] In June 1950, the *Times* reported that a survey of Durham schools showed that the discrepancy between per capita state funding for black and white students in North Carolina during the twentieth century had actually worsened in dramatic fashion, increasing from $39.01 in 1904–5 to $441.47 in 1948–49.[14] Austin asserted that this information underscored the necessity for legal action to ensure the closing of the gap.[15] Black attorneys in Durham, including Austin's old friend Conrad Pearson, agreed and sued the city board of education. Based on overwhelming evidence of the outrageous inequities in funding and facilities, federal district court judge Johnson J. Hayes ruled in *Blue v. Durham Board of Education* (1951) that the Durham public schools had violated the Fourteenth Amendment of the U.S. Constitution and the North Carolina Constitution because African Americans were "not accorded equality of opportunity" in the city's public schools. In his ruling, the judge cited indisputable evidence of unequal school buildings, overcrowding in black schools, and black schools' weaker music, art, and library facilities. Following the court's decision, in February 1951, Austin indicted the all-white Durham City Board of Education for its failure to meet with black leaders to devise a plan to upgrade the black schools.[16]

Indeed, despite the victory in *Blue*, little was done to remedy the inequitable conditions in Durham's black schools, which remained overcrowded, with substandard facilities. Austin reported that one of Durham's black elementary schools had only four toilets for over 500 students. In late 1951, Austin declared that it was crystal clear that the state had failed to live up to the constitutional requirement that facilities be equal, as well as separate. Therefore, he recommended legal action to integrate public schools.[17]

The *Carolina Times*' reporting on the *Blue* case helped inspire many North Carolina communities to file similar suits. Black citizens in Chapel Hill, Wilmington, Burlington, Sanford, Perquimans County, and Hertford County prepared to file lawsuits. Black leaders also urged the governor to remedy the inequities in the public schools.[18] Even before the *Blue* decision was handed down, in early 1950, blacks in Plymouth (Washington County) and Wilson filed lawsuits demanding equal schools for blacks. The Plymouth lawsuit also sought equitable distribution of a $241,000 bond issue, which had been targeted for white schools only in Washington County.[19] In the summer of 1953, twenty-six parents of black students in McDowell County sued the school board for failing to provide equal school facilities for black students. On the front page, the *Times* furnished stunning evidence of that county's discriminatory practices.[20] Austin asserted that these lawsuits in the federal courts showed that North Carolina's reputation for racial liberalism was a myth and that white officials employed "one of the most vicious systems of deception ever operated against an underprivileged people."[21]

Meanwhile, the *Carolina Times* regularly revealed the gross inequities between black and white schools throughout the state. In Wilson, black schools' property was valued at only $145 per student, while white schools' property was valued at $349 per student.[22] In Northampton County, the black schools' calendar was severely limited, with schools closed from mid-September to November 1, to ensure that black children would be available to work as laborers picking cotton. Black schools received books and furniture only after the white schools had discarded them. Many black schools had broken windows, and wood-burning stoves, often with no wood. Unlike at white schools, the driveway leading to W. S. Creecy High School for Negroes in Rich Square was unpaved and often an impassable "sea of mud" during the winters. Austin was unsparing in his criticism of Northampton County's superintendent, N. L. Turner, whom he called a "narrow little man, drunk with power, stupefied with race hatred and despicable in his soul, [who] continues his reign of intimidation and meaness [*sic*], backed by his white constituency."[23]

In February 1951, Austin attacked Sanford city officials for failing to provide any school buildings for black students while whites had four city schools. Blacks in Sanford, who were forced to go to county schools, directed their major animus toward the black principal of the county school because he joined with white officials and opposed black efforts to get the city to build a school for African Americans.[24]

In August 1951, Austin revealed the gross inequities in Granville County schools. Although daily black school attendance was about 15 percent higher than that for whites, the value of white school property was about four times that for black school property. White schools had almost twice as many books in their libraries, and white schools received 70 percent more in operating expenses than did black schools. Furthermore, black schools received no funding for veterans training, but the white schools received $69,000 for this purpose.[25] Invoking the Cold War, Austin noted that the shameful treatment of black American students was fodder for Soviet propaganda, and would be used to demonstrate to the world that the United States failed to practice the democracy that it preached.[26]

When, in September 1951, Durham County school officials proposed a bond issue, Austin demanded that black officials be consulted during the planning stages to help ensure an equitable distribution of funds.[27] In 1952, Austin urged black voters to reject the bond issue unless the city council and board of education guaranteed that black schools would receive an equitable share of the proceeds and that black leaders would be consulted about the uses of the funds.[28]

When Durham's Board of Education decided to build a new black school in response to the *Blue* decision, black attorneys rejected the prospective location because there were no streets nearby and the hilly terrain limited access. Instead, they demanded the construction of two new black schools in more accessible locations.[29] In February 1952, the black attorney and banker John H. Wheeler observed that based on "past experience . . . it would probably be more than 25 years before the streets around the new site would be paved." He noted that the roads approaching three black schools built in the late 1920s and 1930s were still unpaved. In fact, it was almost impossible for cars to reach one of the schools because the dirt roads regularly became muddy and virtually impassable.[30]

Reacting to the failure of white leaders to consider black input in decisions on education and other public policies, Austin identified the Durham City Council's attitude as "Negro Citizens Be Damned." Further, he characterized the Durham Board of Education's mindset as follows: "We are running the Negro schools as we please and it's none of your business how or what we do with them."[31] In December 1951, three years after President Truman had issued an executive order that integrated the armed forces, Austin declared, "If Negro and white soldiers can eat, sleep and fight a common enemy together on a foreign battlefield, we see no reason why their children cannot go to school together in their own native land."[32]

In September 1951, the *Times* publicized the first North Carolina lawsuit to demand public school integration in a federal court. In this case, Durham attorney M. Hugh Thompson filed a lawsuit in Pamlico County in federal district court challenging public school segregation. The suit demanded admission of black students to the white schools unless the black schools were made equal to the white schools. While white student attendance was about 50 percent higher than black attendance in Pamlico's schools, the white schools were valued close to twenty times more than the black schools. One black school in the town of Oriental had but one room and only one teacher for 133 students.[33] While North Carolina attorney general Harry McMullan admitted "that schools in Oriental are unequal," Thompson described Pamlico County's black schools as "among the worst imaginable."[34] While the lawsuit did not lead to integration, it did yield results, as the state and the county quickly appropriated funds to construct a new Pamlico County Training School for black students.[35]

In November 1951, Austin praised the 700 black high school students in the eastern North Carolina town of Kinston, who staged a two-day walkout to protest poor school facilities. Austin warned school officials to equalize school facilities or face more strikes and federal lawsuits from the NAACP.[36] Then, in March 1952, black parents sued the Kinston Board of Education for failing to provide their children with equal schools.[37] The boycott and the lawsuit succeeded in persuading white officials to upgrade the black high school, with the addition of "a new library, classrooms, a gymnasium, and vocational facilities."[38]

In 1952, the *Times* continued to publicize gross inequities in public education. In April, the *Times* reported that Person County school facilities for

African Americans were horrendous. Only one of the twenty-two black schools was accredited, several had no running water, and quite a few classes were held in a gas station building. Many black schools had outhouses, muddy floors, and coal stoves for heat. By contrast, nine of eleven white county schools were accredited and had modern brick buildings and steam heat.[39] Austin termed the black school facilities "deplorable" and encouraged blacks to demand "absolute equality" between white and black schools, and if the demand was not met, they should file suit.[40] In November 1952, black parents in Person County did sue the school board for equal school facilities, represented by the attorney Thompson. The suit demanded integration of the public schools unless the black schools were made equal to the white schools.[41]

As the *Brown v. Board of Education* case was being argued before the U.S. Supreme Court in 1953, many southern states, including North Carolina, increased funding for black schools in hopes of perpetuating school segregation. In June 1953, the *Times* reported that the state government was planning a $50 million bond issue to equalize black and white school facilities. The *Times* argued that this amount was grossly inadequate, and that close to $200 million was needed to equalize the schools.[42] In July 1953, Austin was pleased to report that the NAACP's goal was now "total integration."[43]

While agitating for equitable facilities in primary and secondary schools, Austin also fought for the integration of higher education, rejecting the creation of poorly funded and inferior separate graduate and professional programs for blacks as a ruse to stop or delay integration. In October 1947, Austin denounced Tennessee governor Jim McCord's plan to create "regional professional schools for Negroes" as a tactic to delay integrated higher education. Austin argued that the proposed regional schools would not satisfy the federal courts' rulings. He noted that the "march of communism across Europe and Asia had been given impetus by the hypocrisy of many so-called promoters of democracy, who hold a copy of the United States Constitution in one hand and a copy of the jim crow law in the other."[44]

In March 1949, working with the NAACP Legal Defense Fund along with his longtime colleague in the civil rights struggle, the attorney Conrad Pearson, Austin supported North Carolina College (NCC) law students' fight for quality education. He and Pearson helped organize a demonstration at the state capitol in Raleigh by NCC students. The protesters demanded increased state funding for the law school to ensure that black law students received a legal education equal to that of white students at the UNC law school. Above all, the students protested the fact that their school was not accredited by the American Bar Association.[45] North Carolina secretary of state Thad Eure observed that this "was the first time the Capitol has been picketed."[46] According to one account, fifteen law students picketed in front of the state capitol brandishing signs reading, "This is Our Progressive State," "We Want Equal Educational Facilities Now," and "We're citizens of North Carolina, We want to Attend an Accredited Law School." The students provided evidence of the substandard conditions at the NCC law school. They noted that NCC School of Law's "library is housed in a narrow alcove where students have to climb over one another and the study tables to gain access to the books. Part of the library is located in a classroom, with the result that classes are disturbed by law students seeking books."[47] Although NCC president Alfonso Elder, who had replaced James Shepard after the latter man's death in 1947, expressed disapproval of the students' actions, he confirmed the veracity of their descriptions of the law school's facilities.[48]

NAACP successes in the U.S. Supreme Court during the late 1940s and early 1950s increased the pressure on white officials to prove that educational opportunities at black colleges were equal to those at white colleges or, failing that, face the prospects of integration. In 1948, in *Sipuel v. Oklahoma State Board of Regents*, the Supreme Court affirmed the *Gaines* decision and asserted that if a state did not provide equal educational opportunities for African Americans, then they must admit black students to the white institutions. Consequently, in 1948, Delaware, Arkansas, and Maryland announced the admittance or plans to admit black students to at least some of their public graduate and professional schools.[49] The U.S. Supreme Court decision in *Sweatt v. Painter* (1950) proved even more disastrous to segregationists. The court ruled that separate law schools must be equal in regard to faculty reputation, administration experience, alumni influence, and community standing and prestige, meaning that NCC's law school and other poorly financed black law schools could not meet the test of comparison to their well-established and well-funded white counterparts. North Carolina attorney general Harry McMullan acknowledged that the *Sweatt* decision meant that the state could not "successfully defend" segregated higher education.[50] Nonetheless, North Carolina's educators and bureaucrats rejected McMullan's view and doubled down on their strategy of improving facilities at the black colleges in hopes of forestalling the integration of white colleges.[51]

Meanwhile, in 1950, several black students filed a lawsuit seeking admission to UNC School of Law, an act that Austin publicized and praised in the pages of the *Carolina Times*.[52] Two years earlier, James R. Walker Jr., a student at NCC School of Law, had applied to transfer to the UNC law school because the former was not accredited by the American Bar Association (ABA). Walker was refused admission, and in retaliation for his application, his father, a high school teacher in Cleveland, North Carolina, was fired.[53] As the suit wound its way through the courts, the state upgraded the NCC law school so it could gain accreditation from the ABA. John Gaines Hervey, an ABA advisor on legal education, told Attorney General McMullan that adding temporary buildings to the campus until permanent facilities could be built would provide the basis to accredit the school. Consequently, McMullan suggested to NCC president Elder that he "make plans to provide the necessary temporary structures by the time of Hervey's visit in September."[54]

These changes convinced the ABA to accredit the NCC law school, leading NCC president Elder to claim that the school was the equivalent of the UNC law school. Taken aback by this specious claim, Austin called Elder a "mis-leader of his people."[55] The pugnacious editor would not let black leaders' attempts to weaken the students' case go unchallenged. When Elder told the state legislature that "his people are proud of the college and want to maintain it on a segregated but more nearly equal basis with" UNC, Austin had had enough. He pronounced, "When a Negro educator in this day and time is so dishonest as to misinform white people as to the desire of Negroes for FULL EQUALITY in education and in every other walk of life, we doubt his ability to administer the affairs of" NCC.[56]

Austin was equally unsparing in his attacks on white officials who stood in the way of black educational opportunities. As UNC fought the integration of its graduate and professional schools during the early 1950s, Austin denounced its president Gordon Gray. The son of the president of R. J. Reynolds Tobacco Company, Gray published the *Winston-Salem Journal* and served as secretary of the army from 1949 to 1950. After becoming UNC president in 1950, he played a key role in the effort to delay the integration of higher education in North Carolina. Gray succeeded Frank Porter Graham, who had left the presidency after Governor W. Kerr Scott appointed him U.S. senator from North Carolina, following the death of J. Melville Broughton.[57] When Gray was chosen to replace Graham, Austin wrote that Gray was an "excellent choice," in part because "he had been in the forefront of the battle to abolish segregation in the army."[58] In fact, Austin was misinformed, because as secretary of the army, Gray had implemented policies that delayed the integration of the army.[59] Thus, Gray's support for the continuation of segregated higher education was consistent with his actions with the U.S. Army. As UNC president, Gray claimed that the state, not the federal government, had the "right to impose certain regulations relating to sex, race, age, and geography."[60] He told the UNC Board of Trustees, "I am opposed to the admission of Negroes to our undergraduate schools or graduate and professional schools in cases where the State has attempted to provide such facilities for Negroes."[61] Austin called Gray a "slick lawyer," who sought to "keep the Negroes down, but do it as quietly as possible."[62]

Nonetheless, in March 1951, in *McKissick v. Carmichael*, a U.S. court of appeals judge ordered UNC to admit black students to its law school, leading to the desegregation of the state's oldest public institution of higher education. Relying on the U.S. Supreme Court ruling in *Sweatt v. Painter* (1950) as a precedent, the court determined that the NCC law school was not equal in library facilities, faculty reputation, and curriculum to the UNC law school.[63] Pauli Murray celebrated the appeals court decision and wrote Austin, "Hats off to you," and called it a "great day" for Austin and Murray and others who had thrown "their weight into the [integration] fight."[64] Following the decision, UNC's board of trustees voted to admit "qualified" African Americans to UNC's graduate and professional schools if those programs were not available at black state colleges. At the same time, the board appealed the court's decision to the U.S. Supreme Court, but the high court sustained the lower court's decision.[65] Consequently, in June 1951, three NCC students, Harvey Beech, J. Kenneth Lee, and Floyd McKissick, were admitted to the UNC law school. Earlier, Edward Diggs had been admitted to the UNC medical school.[66] The almost two-decades-long struggle to desegregate UNC, begun in 1933 by Austin, Hocutt, Pearson, and McCoy, had finally achieved success.

However, the trailblazing black students who desegregated UNC faced racist treatment, prompting Austin and other black activists to come to their defense. After black students were forced to sit in segregated seating at a UNC football game, the attorney Conrad Pearson announced that he would file suit to end discrimination against the black students.[67] Austin berated UNC–Chapel Hill chancellor Robert House for his "asininity" in defending the discriminatory treatment of the black students because of, in House's words, the "distinction between educational service and social recognition."[68] In response to Austin shining negative publicity on UNC, protests by white student organizations against the university's mistreatment of the black students, NAACP action, and the Durham Committee on Negro Affairs' (DCNA) fundraising drive to sue UNC in federal court, House reversed his decision, integrating seating at Kenan Stadium.[69]

Following the admission of black students to UNC School of Law, UNC officials concocted a plan to limit black enrollment at UNC by expanding graduate offerings at NCC, including the creation of a PhD program in education. Austin immediately attacked the plan and urged NCC president Alfonso Elder to speak out against the program because its purpose was to perpetuate segregation.[70] The following week, Austin published a front-page editorial opposing the PhD program. He reported that he had been told that 100 percent of NCC's faculty opposed the program because its purpose was to keep blacks out of UNC. Moreover, Austin pointed out that NCC's budget was too small to finance a PhD program, noting that NCC's existing under-graduate and graduate programs were woefully underfunded.[71]

In June 1951, Elder and the NCC Board of Trustees echoed Austin's views and opposed plans for the PhD program.[72] Elder argued that the "deficiencies in the present undergraduate and graduate programs are too great to warrant the upward extension of the program of the graduate program."[73] Instead of expanding graduate programs, NCC's president recommended that black educators concentrate on developing the school's undergraduate programs. Elder wrote, "We should strive to do only those things which our limited ap-propriations will permit us to do well."[74] Indeed, Elder insisted that NCC would not be able to offer a proper PhD program for "at least 10 years."[75] Elder and the NCC Board of Trustees sought to protect the integrity of NCC's graduate programs, and stop UNC from using the black college as a pawn in white officials' plan to delay integration.

But white officials at UNC rejected the argument that existing programs should be strengthened before new programs were added because their sole motive was to delay the integration of higher education in the state. When UNC administrators discovered that NCC officials were not enamored with the idea of expanding the graduate program, UNC chancellor Robert House and graduate dean W. W. Pierson pressured NCC officials to back the pro-gram.[76] Then, at the July 1951 emergency meeting of the UNC Board of Trustees, NCC officials were told to ask its board of trustees to support a two-year request for $100,000 per year to enhance graduate study and to establish a PhD program in education, if the 1953 General Assembly provided support for necessary facilities, library resources, and equipment. The NCC board agreed to support the PhD program and the $100,000-per-year funding re-quest, but only if it was supplemented with an additional $2,114,000 for capi-tal projects, including $1.8 million to construct new buildings for the departments of biology, education, and commerce.[77] The majority-white NCC board approved the PhD program by a vote of seven to two, with only the two black board members present at the meeting opposing the pro-gram.[78] The capital projects authorized by the board were crucial if NCC was going to provide its students a quality graduate education. NCC's inadequate facilities had long impaired student learning. For example, the Biology Department, housed in the basement of the Science Building, had very limited space, with only sixty-four seats for biology students, while enrollment in classes averaged 500. The department had only one large and two small laboratories, which had forced the department to cut lab time in half. Moreover, limited storage space meant that students had to keep dissection specimens of frogs and cats in their dormitory rooms.[79]

After the board's approval of the new program, Austin, who was not privy to the adversarial stance taken by Elder in his private discussions with UNC officials, denounced the NCC president for acquiescing to UNC demands for the creation of the PhD program. Intemperately, he called Elder "a flunky for the UNC mobsters."[80] Austin demanded that NCC, not UNC, control its own programs.[81] Furthermore, the *Carolina Times* called the program a "fire-sale priced, segregated, PhD program." The paper commented, "Serious educators over the country either gaped their mouths in astonishment or 'snickered' in ridicule at the idea of a PhD program at the local institution, and UNC and state education officials chuckled in their beards at their latest success in halting the movement of integrated education."[82]

In August 1952, Austin expanded his attack on those who had conspired to create the program and those who accepted its creation. He denounced UNC officials, who would "stop at nothing and undertake anything to carry out their pernicious schemes against freely opening the doors of UNC to Negroes." But Austin reserved even more venom for NCC president Elder because he did "not have the courage to oppose the program . . . and is deliberately allowing himself to become a party to a staggering wrong against the people of his race."[83] In October 1952, Austin was joined by the North Carolina NAACP, which proclaimed its opposition to the NCC PhD program because its purpose was to delay the integration of UNC and because the NCC facilities for the PhD program were inferior to those at UNC.[84]

In February 1953, Austin reproved Elder for his testimony before the state legislature requesting additional funds for the PhD program in which NCC's president said, "No other state has made as much progress as ours in terms of desirable race relations." Austin asserted that Elder's speech "reeked and dripped with so much hypocrisy that even the conservative morning newspaper in Durham referred to it as 'sugar-coated.'" Austin called Elder a "spineless sycophant whose one aim is to feather his own nest."[85] Similarly, the attorney Conrad Pearson opposed the funding request because its purpose was to perpetuate segregation, calling the legislature's hearings "an effrontery to all freedom loving peoples."[86]

Austin's unflagging opposition to the establishment of the PhD program must be understood in the context of the mid-twentieth-century battle for integrated education. For decades, black colleges and black public schools had been poorly funded, and black activists perceived the establishment of inferior black graduate schools as perpetuating inferior black education. In the context of the NAACP battle for integration of schools, black liberals opposed actions that would prolong racial segregation. At the 1951 annual convention of the NAACP, United Nations diplomat Ralph Bunche "voiced the general sentiment of his race on social aims of the mid-twentieth century. The Negro demands, Bunche asserted, 'complete integration as an American citizen.'" He concluded, "Segregation . . . in any form, is discrimination. To speak of 'segregated equality' among American citizens is to engage in wanton sophistry."[87]

In 1953, when the state announced plans to establish a nursing program at a black college in North Carolina, the *Times* opposed the program as another part of UNC's anti-integration scheme. Austin called the state's plan "its old program of jim crow education . . . in spite of recent Supreme Court decisions scrapping segregated education" in graduate and professional schools.[88] Moreover, Kelly Alexander, president of the North Carolina NAACP, asserted that the NAACP would file a lawsuit "if the Negro nurse schools are used to keep Negro nurse trainees out of the University of North Carolina."[89] In March 1954, Austin argued that graduate and professional programs set up at public black colleges like Florida A&M, NCC, and Tennessee State University were "backed by southern demagogues and . . . have one and only one purpose and that is to perpetuate segregation and to keep Negroes out of white educational institutions in the South."[90] Although Austin was proud of the work of black educational institutions, he would not allow white supremacists to use black institutions to limit African Americans' access to all institutions.

As in previous decades, Austin rejected the gradualism of interracialists, but during the late 1940s took another shot at working with the North Carolina Commission on Interracial Cooperation (NCCIC), serving on its executive committee in 1947.[91] Apparently, he had decided to try to help revitalize an organization that he had found wanting during the 1930s. However, his earlier disaffection with the timidity of the organization was likely rekindled when, in October 1948, the Special Committee on Principles and Aims of the NCCIC, which included C. C. Spaulding, Duke University sociology professor Edgar Thompson, and UNC sociology professor Guy Johnson, stated that because of the "strength of the attitudes and customs which underlie it, . . .

we do not contemplate, nor do we advocate, wholesale or sudden abolition" of segregation.[92]

Nonetheless, Austin found common ground with the NCCIC when it recommended that North Carolina governor W. Kerr Scott pardon Bayard Rustin and Joseph Felmet, who had been arrested in Chapel Hill in the Congress of Racial Equality (CORE) Fellowship of Reconciliation bus ride in 1947 that challenged segregation of interstate bus transportation. This challenge was designed to test the U.S. Supreme Court decision in *Morgan v. Virginia* (1946), which outlawed racial segregation on interstate travel.[93] Cyrus Johnson of the NCCIC told the governor, "Although I did not agree with their method of action," "both of them are very fine persons, well educated and dedicated to fulfilling the demands that their Christian conscience brings to them."[94] However, the governor refused to issue the pardons.[95]

In 1945, Austin served on the board of directors of the newly organized Committee for North Carolina (CNC) of the interracial Southern Conference for Human Welfare (SCHW), which was organized by Mary Price, a white liberal North Carolinian, who had worked as editorial secretary to famed *New York Herald Tribune* journalist Walter Lippmann. Other board members included UNC president Frank Porter Graham, the attorney Conrad Pearson, and the educator Charlotte Hawkins Brown. The historian John Hope Franklin also served on the CNC during the 1940s. According to Patricia Sullivan, the North Carolina committee "was probably the largest and most active state committee." This committee, like its counterparts, focused on "increasing voter registration and lobbying the state legislature," to raise the minimum wage, increase public funding for black schools, and repeal anti-union right-to-work laws.[96]

Austin also served on the Civil Rights Committee of the CNC, focusing on voter registration and get-out-the-vote campaigns.[97] In September 1947, the SCHW planned a meeting with North Carolina's top twelve black leaders, including Austin, to plan for the 1948 elections. Other participants included W. L. Greene of the North Carolina Teachers Association, T. V. Mangum of the North Carolina NAACP, Durham businessmen and DCNA leaders John Wheeler and John Stewart, Charlotte Hawkins Brown, John Hope Franklin, and James T. Taylor of NCC.[98]

During the postwar years, Austin played an important role in the movement to increase voter registration of African Americans in North Carolina. From 1947 to 1952, black voter registration grew from 75,000 to 100,000, and the percentage of blacks registered to vote rose from 15.2 percent to 18 percent. Although black voter registration rates in North Carolina increased steadily during the postwar years, other southern states surpassed it. In 1940, North Carolina had ranked first among eleven southern states, but by 1947, it had dropped to sixth, and by 1952, eighth, and its registration percentage was below the southern average for blacks of 20 percent. After 1952, black voter registration campaigns in North Carolina were increasingly effective, so that by 1960, black voter registration was 38.1 percent, ranking third in the South, which was well above the average for the South, which had stagnated at about 20 percent.[99]

In Durham, black voter registration campaigns were particularly effective in increasing black political influence. In 1946, the Durham branch of the NAACP worked with the CNC to increase black voter registration in the city by about 3,000.[100] According to a 1952 estimate, about "63 percent of the eligible Negro electorate in Durham, North Carolina, voted regularly."[101] In 1952, Austin reported that 10,000 African Americans were registered to vote in Durham, which had a population of about 25,000 blacks.[102] As the black vote increased, so did black political influence in Durham's Democratic Party organization. As early as 1936, an African American, NCC professor James Taylor, had been elected chairman of a voting precinct in Durham.[103] Because he chaired an election precinct, Taylor became a member of the Durham County Democratic Party Executive Committee. By 1952, Durham had three black precinct chairmen, who served on the Durham County Democratic Party Executive Committee. Durham County also had twenty-four black delegates and twenty-four black alternates, who went to the 1952 North Carolina Democratic Party Convention. These totals were more than that for the combined totals of all the other counties in the state. Black voter registration in Durham was also helped by the presence of black registrars in the city, beginning in 1949, which was possible because of black influence in the local Democratic Party.

Austin actively urged blacks to use the ballot to make North Carolina a more progressive state. In June 1945, at a meeting of the Tobacco Workers International Union in Durham, Austin "warned all present that they would always be 'hewers of wood and drawers of water' if they did not vote." At this meeting, the keynote speaker, Roy Trice, vice president of the Tobacco Workers International Union and past president of local 208 in Durham, called for organization of all tobacco mills. Like Austin, Trice worked with other organizations that worked to improve the lives of African Americans. For example, Trice chaired the membership committee of the Durham NAACP. Both men were also active church members, Austin at St. Joseph's AME Church and Trice as a deacon at White Rock Baptist Church.[104] During the postwar years,

Austin actively worked with the NAACP. At the state NAACP conference program in June 1945, Austin gave the "Principal Address."[105] In October 1949, Austin urged all Durham blacks to join the local branch of the NAACP.[106]

In the 1946 election cycle, Austin appealed to black North Carolinians to register to vote. Repeating his admonition that "a voteless people is a hopeless people," Austin urged blacks to "organize voting clubs, that are going to canvass your neighborhood block by block and house by house." He counseled his readers that voting was crucial to ensure just treatment of blacks in the courts, properly funded black schools, an end to police brutality, and an increase in paved streets, and "most important of all," to make sure that blacks were paid a living wage.[107]

In May 1946, Austin joined with unionists and liberals, black and white, in Winston-Salem at a political rally in support of John Folger's primary campaign for reelection to Congress against an anti-union candidate. Austin denounced Folger's opponent, Thurmond Chatham, as the "candidate of big business."[108] Austin told blacks to keep trying to register to vote "even if it brought 'again and again the embarrassment' of being denied the right to vote. 'Only at the ballot box,' he told listeners, 'does the worker, teacher, [and] lawyer have equal power—one vote.' "[109] Another speaker at the rally was Local 22 (of the Food, Tobacco, Agricultural, and Allied Workers–Congress of Industrial Organizations) business agent Gene Pratt, candidate for a seat in the state legislature. Pratt supported "repeal of the state sales tax, improvement of school facilities, better highways for farmers, and a state medical care and housing program."[110] Folger won the primary and the general election, demonstrating the power of an alliance between black and white working-class voters.[111]

In local elections in Durham in 1946, the *Durham Sun*, one of the two white-owned daily newspapers in Durham, criticized blacks for engaging in bloc voting. The *Sun* claimed that black bloc voting would "heighten race tensions" and "encourage such eruptions as the [Ku Klux] Klan." The *Carolina Times* criticized the *Sun* for its inflammatory editorial, noting that the *Sun* had "descended to the very depths of editorial lewdness in a most malicious attack on the Negro citizenry of Durham," noting that whites regularly voted as a bloc against black candidates. The *Times*, along with the DCNA, supported two African American candidates for local office. The attorney Edward R. Avant ran for prosecuting attorney, and John Holloway, an NC Mutual employee, ran for county commissioner. Avant was the first African American to run for that office, while Holloway was the third black to run for Durham County commissioner.[112] The Southern Conference for Human

Welfare focused its political efforts in the Durham area, sending "two special field workers" to support the campaigns of Avant and Holloway.[113] In the Sixth Congressional District contest, black voters helped stop Carl T. Durham from winning a majority in the Democratic primary and supported Earle Rivers in the runoff election.[114]

While blacks in the piedmont registered to vote in significant numbers in 1946, in the rural eastern part of the state, few blacks were able to do so, as they faced intimidation or loss of jobs if they tried to register. Black teachers in the east were threatened with firing if they registered to vote. In Nash County, only fifty out of a possible 8,000 black voters were allowed to vote. An exception was Vance County, which had a very active NAACP branch, and helped blacks register to vote.[115]

In September 1946, Austin castigated N. C. Newbold, head of the Division of Negro Education, for failing to reinstate black principals and teachers who were fired for advocating black rights in housing, education, and politics. In Fremont, a small town in Person County, George Harper, a high school principal, and his wife, a teacher, were fired for resisting the status quo. Principal Harper had started a credit union for blacks that helped increase home ownership from five or six to sixty-five. He also promoted voter registration and advocated increased funding to renovate the black high school. In Warrenton, G. E. Cheek, principal of the black high school, was fired for similar reasons as those for Harper.[116]

In 1947, when *Carolina Times* reporter Alexander Barnes served as a poll watcher in Fayetteville, he braved verbal abuse from many white voters. According to the *Chicago Defender*, "Through carelessness or maliciousness he was assigned to the polling place patronized by red-gallused voters from the outlying precincts." Barnes, "cigar and all, stuck it out although he admits his watching was something from a little distance." Fayetteville's first black candidate for city council, Frank L. Burns, was defeated; he received 684 votes out of a total of 2,000 votes.[117]

As black voter registration numbers rose in Durham, the DCNA delivered larger vote totals for black candidates for local office. Austin garnered 969 votes in his campaign for Durham City Council in 1945.[118] Two years later, funeral director J. C. Scarborough ran for city council in 1947 and got 2,084 votes. In 1949, insurance executive R. N. Harris received 3,437 votes.[119] In 1951, NCC professor James T. Taylor earned 4,507 votes.[120] Still, these totals were not enough to win election.

An important factor in increased black political influence in Durham in the late 1940s and early 1950s was the formation in 1947 of Voters for Better

Government (VBG), a coalition of black, labor, and liberal white voters in the county. The DCNA, led by chairman John Stewart, education committee chair John Wheeler, and political chair Davis B. (Dan) Martin, played a key role in this alliance. Local white labor leader Wilbur Hobby, another key leader in the coalition, called Martin "the greatest political organizer that I ever met, just a terrific guy." In 1948, VBG members, including Stewart and Martin, headed over half of the Democratic Party election precincts, and white VBG leader Leslie Atkins won election as chairman of the Durham County Democratic Party.[121] The increasing vote totals for black city council candidates Harris in 1949 and Taylor in 1951 were due in part to white votes won because of VBG support.[122]

During the early 1950s, black Durhamites enjoyed increased political influence within the Democratic Party in Durham County and in North Carolina, in part due to the alliance with liberal whites and labor in the VBG. In 1950, twenty-three blacks from Durham served as delegates to the state Democratic Party convention in Raleigh, including Rose Butler Browne, an education professor at NCC, who may have been the first black woman to serve as a delegate in a southern state convention of the Democratic Party.[123] The VBG dominated the Durham County Democratic Party until 1954, when the *Brown v. Board of Education* decision outlawing racial segregation in public schools divided the interracial alliance.[124]

Despite the city's large black vote, the system of voting for city council in Durham made it very difficult to elect a black candidate. In 1921, the city had established a government with six council members who represented particular wards and two at-large members. All eight members of the council were elected by voters throughout the city. Even if blacks had been registered to vote in significant numbers at that time, the fact that the majority of the city's population was white would have made it virtually impossible for blacks to be elected. A ward system, wherein citizens in a particular ward voted for a candidate from that ward, would have made it easier for a minority group to elect a representative to the council.[125] In 1947, the city council was expanded to include twelve members, six representing particular wards and the other six representing the entire city. Under this system, which continued to make it difficult to elect a black council member, all city voters could vote for any of the council candidates. The fact that whites predominated in the city and typically voted for white candidates made it difficult for black candidates to win elections.[126]

Similar practices that limited black representation were commonplace in North Carolina and throughout the South. In Winston-Salem, after Kenneth

Williams, an African American minister, was elected to the Board of Aldermen in 1947, the city redistricted so that black voters were concentrated in one district and would not be able to elect more than one member of the board. In Wilson, North Carolina, after an African American, George K. Butterfield, was elected to the city council in 1953 and 1955, the legislature changed the city to an at-large election system, and the council became all white again.[127]

In national politics, Austin backed Henry Wallace for president in 1948 and helped establish the Progressive Party in North Carolina. Wallace, the former vice president and secretary of commerce during Franklin Roosevelt's administration, ran as a Progressive. He ran to Truman's left, opposing the president's Cold War foreign policy and promising a more robust attack on racial segregation. In early 1948, the Progressive Party of North Carolina elected an "interracial slate of officers" and began to campaign for Wallace. Mary Price, whom Austin knew through their association in the CNC, chaired the state's Progressive Party. One of sixteen vice-chairmen, Austin was also one of several African Americans chosen for the executive committee of the state's Progressive Party, which adopted a peace platform. Like the national Progressive Party, it rejected the Truman Doctrine and "preparations of the Wall Street trusts for a Third World War." It also advocated repeal of the anti-labor Taft-Hartley Act and North Carolina's anti-labor laws. It demanded " 'action, not just words, in enforcement of civil rights for all people,' improved schools, higher teacher pay, increased aid to needy people and elimination of the three percent sales tax."[128]

Although Austin backed Wallace for president, he also supported Truman's civil rights program, which the president had articulated in a speech in February 1948. Truman's program included proposals for a permanent Fair Employment Practices Commission, federal protection for black voting rights, and federal anti-lynching legislation.[129] This program aroused almost universal opposition among white southerners. When North Carolina governor R. Gregg Cherry joined the Southern Governors' Conference committee to oppose civil rights legislation, Austin attacked the governor. He asserted that Cherry's action had "embarrassed, not only Negroes of this state, but all progressive white people."[130] Although Cherry opposed Truman's program, unlike most southern governors, he refused to join South Carolina governor Strom Thurmond's campaign for president, which was orchestrated in response to Truman's civil rights plan.[131]

Austin's association with the Wallace campaign and the Progressive Party of North Carolina gave him a platform to speak out on major issues to white as well as black audiences. In March 1948, Austin joined UNC students and Chapel Hill ministers, speaking out against the institution of a draft at a program at UNC. At the time, Congress was considering a universal military draft. Opposition to the draft sparked protests, including the burning of a cross.[132] The following year, Austin addressed a meeting of the Young Progressives at UNC–Chapel Hill. He discussed the Shreve-Regan bill, then pending in the North Carolina General Assembly, that would criminalize membership in the Communist Party. Attempts to pass the bill in 1949 and 1951 failed.[133]

On Sunday, April 24, 1948, the Progressive Party of North Carolina held a racially integrated meeting in Winston-Salem with 500 attendees, who lunched together. Vice presidential nominee of the Progressive Party Senator Glen H. Taylor of Idaho "condemned racial segregation." He "promised if elected to work for a civil rights bill in Congress." Moreover, the party adopted a very progressive civil rights platform that "called for admission of qualified persons to any state institution of learning; for full civil, political, and religious liberties; passage of anti-lynching legislation; state and national fair employment legislation; elimination of segregation in schools, travel, and cultural pursuits; and first class citizenship for Indians of the state."[134] The following day, Austin presided at the official founding convention of the state's Progressive Party in Winston-Salem.[135]

At its July 1948 national convention in Philadelphia, the Progressive Party condemned "segregation and discrimination in all its forms and in all places. We demand full equality for the Negro people, the Jewish people. . . . We call for a Presidential proclamation ending segregation and all forms of discrimination in the armed forces and federal employment." The party also backed an anti–poll tax law, and "special programs to raise the low standards of health, housing, and educational facilities for Negroes."[136]

In August 1948, when Wallace campaigned in Durham, the North Carolina Progressive Party held its nominating convention. During Wallace's campaign trip in North Carolina, as in his trips to other parts of the South, he backed up his rhetorical attacks on segregation with action. According to Wallace's biographers, he "refused to speak before segregated audiences, refused to sleep in segregated hotels, to eat in segregated restaurants."[137] Wallace and his advisors were booked at the Washington Duke Hotel in Durham, but they were not permitted to stay there because of the presence of black members in their group. Instead, Wallace stayed at the home of black businessman George W. Logan. Wallace's black secretary, Viola Scott, stayed at Austin's home during the visit. Other Wallace advisors stayed at the Biltmore Hotel, a black hotel in Durham.[138]

Segregationists in North Carolina reacted violently to the Wallace campaign. In Durham, "a Wallace supporter was stabbed repeatedly during a melee before Wallace was escorted by an armed guard to the podium. At one point a mob surrounded the car carrying his secretary, Mabel Cooney, breaking the windshield and screaming racial epithets because she was seated next to a black woman."[139] When Wallace stayed at Logan's house in Durham, Logan stood watch "all night in his attic window with a shotgun," while other armed men hid in the bushes to protect the candidate if there was an attack.[140]

At its convention in Durham, the North Carolina Progressive Party nominated Durham attorney Conrad Pearson as the Progressive Party's candidate for state attorney general. Mary Price was the party's nominee for governor. Austin was nominated for the state House of Representatives from Durham.[141] The final session of the convention on August 29, 1948, was held at the Regal Theater and the City Armory with 200 delegates in attendance. According to the *Durham Sun*, "this was 'probably the first time since "reconstruction days" that a Negro had appeared on a general election ballot [in Durham].'"[142] Wallace's tour of North Carolina as well as the general Progressive Party mobilization helped to stimulate voter registration and political activism among black Carolinians.[143]

Nonetheless, in North Carolina, the Progressives lost badly to the Democrats in the 1948 election. While Austin received 910 votes in his campaign for the state House of Representatives, his opponent received over 13,000 votes. Conrad Pearson garnered only 738 votes in Durham in his campaign for state attorney general. It is worth noting that Austin received more votes than Wallace, who got 563 votes in Durham in the presidential race. In contrast, Truman received 11,579 votes, Republican candidate Thomas Dewey received 4,512 votes, and Dixiecrat segregationist Strom Thurmond of South Carolina received 989 votes.[144] Truman's executive order desegregating the armed forces and his advocacy for civil rights legislation won him broad African American support.[145] After the election, Conrad Pearson expressed disappointment at his poor showing, noting, "I have been completely repudiated at the polls of Durham County in the precincts that are overwhelmingly Negro."[146]

Despite the Progressive Party's poor showing in the 1948 election, Austin continued to advocate for it and Wallace. In 1950, Austin lauded Wallace for repudiating "Communists within and without the [Progressive] party." Calling

Wallace "a great American," Austin overconfidently argued that "American citizens . . . [would] flock to it [the Progressive Party] by leaps and bounds."[147]

Meanwhile, Austin continued to denounce conservative politicians who defended segregation and white supremacy. In late 1949, he compared North Carolina politicians William B. Umstead, a former senator, and Senator Clyde Hoey unfavorably with Alabama governor James E. Folsom, who delivered a Christmas message in support of equity for blacks in his state, asking his constituents to follow "the teachings of Christianity and the ways of democracy." The differences, for Austin, demonstrated the fallacy of those who considered North Carolina a liberal state.[148] While Austin championed Truman's push for civil rights legislation, he denounced Hoey, who joined the Senate filibuster by conservative Republicans and southern Democrats to kill the bill.[149] Austin attacked Hoey's speech before the United Daughters of the Confederacy in Durham where the Senator said, "N— are not entitled to civil rights and will never get them. There were no n— on the Mayflower." Austin reported that Hoey went on "a long asinine diatribe against Negroes. . . . It was the old South with all its hatred, maliciousness, and bigotry." The forthright editor denounced "our so-called liberal white folks," who emphatically applauded Hoey's diatribe and "pathetically rol[l]icked and reveled in the slime of race baiting that befouled the air." Austin urged black voters to remember Hoey's words at election time.[150]

Austin consistently worked for and publicized voter registration campaigns for blacks, realizing that only political influence would yield significant gains for blacks in the schools, in job opportunity, and in the justice system. In 1948, he publicized a legal challenge to the Henderson County Board of Elections for denying African Americans the right to register to vote. Austin's old friend Conrad Pearson "filed charges" with the U.S. district attorney in Charlotte. The *Times* reported that Henderson County officials required African Americans to pass arbitrary tests. For example, a black woman "was required to write parts of the state Constitution from dictation for ten minutes in a noisy room and was rejected because of one misspelled word and faulty pronunciation."[151]

With the Congress considering civil rights legislation in 1950, Austin called for a doubling of black voter registration in North Carolina.[152] He asserted that only black voting would overturn racist discrimination in hiring, housing discrimination, and exploitation of black sharecroppers. He encouraged blacks to register to vote even if it meant risking one's job.[153] He backed the North Carolina NAACP plan to increase the state's black voter registration to 250,000 for the 1950 election. With blacks intimidated when they tried to register, especially in rural areas, Austin observed that fundraising and legal action would likely be key components of a successful registration campaign.[154]

In March 1950, Austin was elected chairman of the Non-Partisan Registration and Vote Committee for the North Carolina branch of the NAACP.[155] At the committee's organizing meeting, Austin emphasized plans to increase black voter registration in the state to 250,000.[156] By April 1950, the NAACP had organized three-fourths of the state's 100 counties to increase black voter registration.[157] In April 1950, Austin pressed for black voter registration so that blacks could influence the May primary. He exclaimed, "A voteless people is a hopeless people."[158]

In May 1950, Austin urged blacks to raise money to prosecute at least one case where a white registrar denied blacks the right to register to vote and threatened them with reprisals when they tried to do so, a widespread practice, particularly in eastern North Carolina. Austin reported that one registrar shut down his office when blacks tried to register to vote, but he registered whites "privately." While well-educated black pastors and teachers were denied the right to register to vote, illiterate whites were registered without taking a literacy test. Furthermore, two years earlier, white authorities had refused to act when African Americans swore out affidavits testifying to white registrars' illegal actions and gave these affidavits to a U.S. attorney.[159] The following week, black attorneys (including Conrad Pearson) representing the Registration and Vote Committee of North Carolina announced plans to sue Nash, Warren, and Wake county registrars for refusing to register black voters for the May 27 primary. As committee president Austin pronounced, "Negroes are determined to use every lawful means to force registrars to grant them their rights as American citizens." The lawyers collected affidavits from fifty residents of Warren and Nash Counties who had been denied registration.[160]

At the annual state conference of the NAACP, held in Fayetteville in June 1950, Austin reported that progress was being made in increasing black voter registration.[161] North Carolina NAACP president Kelly M. Alexander commended Austin for the fine job he was doing directing the voter registration efforts. Alexander estimated that black voter registration in the state had jumped from fewer than 50,000 to about 100,000, an increase that scared white politicians. Alexander explained, "They certainly don't want Negroes in the heart of the black belt to wake up and show political self-interest."[162]

During the 1950 campaign and in subsequent years, the *Carolina Times* office on 518 East Pettigrew Street served as headquarters for the DCNA campaigns to get black voters to the polls and to get black voters to cast ballots for DCNA choices. The DCNA made cars available to take voters to the polls.[163]

In 1950, Austin and the DCNA backed former UNC president Frank Porter Graham in the election campaign for U.S. senator from North Carolina.
Governor Kerr Scott had appointed Graham to the Senate in 1949, after the
death of Senator J. Melville Broughton. Graham's opponent in the Democratic Party primary, Willis Smith, defeated Graham by running a racist campaign, in which he demonized Graham as a racial integrationist. Austin
denounced Willis Smith for injecting "the race issue into the senatorial campaign."[164] Austin waited until right before the May 1950 primary before advising blacks to vote for Graham so that Smith could not use black support for
Graham to further insert the race issue into what Austin called "the dirtiest
Senatorial campaign that has ever been staged in North Carolina."[165] Austin
and the DCNA often followed this procedure when endorsing white candidates to avoid giving the opposition a chance to vilify a white candidate for
having black support. When white Democrats charged blacks with bloc voting for Graham, Austin countered that whites throughout the South had
voted as a bloc for the Democratic Party for decades, which made the South a
one-party region. And when blacks ran for public office, whites were sure to
vote en masse against the black candidate.[166]

Meanwhile, Austin continued to shine a light on suppression of the black
vote in North Carolina, particularly in the east. In August 1950, Austin censured white officials in Warrenton, in Warren County, for suppressing the
black vote: "Warrenton is still stumbling around with its benighted, ante-
bellum ideas that are for the most part generated in the half depraved mind of
an alcoholic."[167] In February 1951, Austin urged the state legislature to pass a
law "making it punishable by fine or imprisonment" for registrars or election
officials who prevent a qualified citizen from registering to vote or voting.[168]
In October 1952, the *Times* reported that a white Winston-Salem registrar "remarked that he never had registered a Negro and 'didn't intend to.'" The
NAACP planned to represent the woman at a hearing regarding the case.[169]

In 1951 and 1952, Austin kept his focus on increasing black voter registration in North Carolina. In late 1951, he encouraged black organizations to
mount voter registration drives with the slogan "Every Negro Man and
Woman Must Register and Vote" to influence the outcome of 1952 elections
and keep anti-black officials from office.[170] In April 1952, Austin set a goal of
registering 200,000 black voters. He advised black advocacy organizations to
withhold public endorsements for a gubernatorial candidate so that white
voters could not be mobilized to oppose the candidate preferred by African
American voters.[171] The withholding of public endorsements until just before an election was a common practice of the DCNA.[172] Although African

American voter registration in North Carolina fell well short of 200,000 in 1952, it did continue to rise, thanks in part to Austin's efforts. According to historian Steven Lawson, 100,000 blacks were registered to vote in North Carolina in 1952.[173] Furthermore, obstacles like literacy tests, poll taxes, and white Democratic Party control of the registration process made it impossible for southern black leaders to reach their goal to increase southern black voter rolls to two million.[174]

In the 1952 Democratic Party primary campaign for governor of North Carolina, Austin endorsed Hubert Olive. Olive, a superior court judge, was the candidate of the progressive wing of the North Carolina Democratic Party, and had the backing of outgoing governor Kerr Scott, who advocated increased education spending and repeal of the state's anti-labor right-to-work law.[175] Austin explained his endorsement, noting that Olive's opponent, William Umstead, "had the brass to tell the world that if elected to the office of governor, he would uphold a system of discrimination that is making our country hated by teeming millions of colored people all over the globe."[176] Nonetheless, Umstead won the election.[177]

In the 1952 presidential election, Austin criticized the leading Republican candidates. In December 1951, after presidential candidate Ohio senator Robert A. Taft spoke at North Carolina College, Austin assailed him for failing to take a position on legislation to ban racial discrimination in employment, the poll tax, or an anti-lynching bill.[178] In June 1952, Austin urged blacks to reject Dwight D. Eisenhower's candidacy because of his support for states' rights. Eisenhower had said that he believed that civil rights legislation should be decided by the states, not the federal government. With most southern state legislatures dominated by white supremacist segregationists, civil rights legislation had no chance if left to southern states.[179] However, when Eisenhower offered lip service to racial equality, asserting that he would not appoint a southerner to his cabinet who rejected the "basic tenet of our Constitution that we are created equal, regardless of race or religion," the *Durham Morning Herald* attacked Eisenhower's pledge. Austin denounced the Durham daily paper, proclaiming that its editorial was suffused with the "Southern philosophy of white supremacy."[180]

Given his criticism of the Republican candidates, it is not surprising that Austin endorsed the Democratic Party's candidate for president in 1952. He explained that he backed Illinois governor Adlai Stevenson because he supported the Democratic Party platform, which advocated federal civil rights legislation and opposition to the filibuster, used by southern Democrats to block civil rights legislation in the Senate. Austin rejected Eisenhower in part because the Republicans in the Senate, led by Robert Taft, had joined southern Democrats in blocking civil rights legislation.[181] Nationally, Stevenson won 73 percent of the black vote, which was more than Truman received in 1948. Unlike in 1948, when Truman was opposed on the left by Henry Wallace, Stevenson did not face a candidate with a progressive civil rights platform.[182]

In the early 1950s, Austin continued to work with the DCNA to win black representation in political offices in Durham. In August 1952, Austin criticized the Durham City Council for once again refusing to appoint a black member to the school board. Following the death of school board member Franklin Barfield, the attorney Conrad Pearson appeared before the city council and recommended the appointment of NCC professor James T. Taylor to the school board to represent the city's black population. Austin compared Durham unfavorably with other North Carolina cities that had black city council members—Greensboro, Fayetteville, Winston-Salem; a black deputy sheriff—Greensboro; a black on the board of education—Raleigh; and black firemen—Winston-Salem. Austin observed, "Durham, steeped in prejudice, still lives in the benighted past." He renewed his call for blacks to mobilize and elect black representatives.[183]

In 1953, Austin and the DCNA finally achieved their goal of adding an African American to Durham's city council with the election of businessman Rencher N. Harris. Voter registration efforts were crucial. In early 1953, Austin had charged the DCNA with registering 3,000 new black voters in Durham, increasing the total from 9,000 to 12,000, to help blacks elect a member of the city council for the first time.[184] The black, labor, and liberal political coalition, Voters for Better Government, endorsed Harris, who was elected in the Third Ward by a 500 vote margin over Marshall T. Mangum, a white grocery store owner. Harris estimated that about 1,200 of his 4,200-vote total came from whites. The DCNA also endorsed the reelection of Mayor Emanuel J. Evans, a white businessman, who had no opposition. Four of the five city council candidates that the DCNA supported won their races.[185]

In 1954, Austin called on the DCNA to mount a voter registration campaign to help black candidates win election to the Durham County Board of Commissioners and the board of education. That year, businessman Asa T. Spaulding ran unsuccessfully for Durham County commissioner. Austin attributed the loss to African Americans' failure to vote in large enough numbers.[186]

Nonetheless, black voters helped W. Kerr Scott defeat Alton Lennon for U.S. senator from North Carolina. Black voters rejected Lennon, whose campaign sent out leaflets from a fictitious black organization announcing black support for Scott. This tactic backfired when the Scott campaign publicized this shady practice. Scott defeated Lennon by close to 25,000 votes. With about 100,000 black voters in the state, the black vote likely turned the tide for Scott.[187]

DURING THE POSTWAR ERA, as African Americans continued to suffer from racist violence at the hands of white supremacists, including the police, Austin consistently reported these injustices in an effort to shame southern whites, while he demanded that the perpetrators be brought to justice. He also denounced the white media when it slanted its reporting of racial injustice and blamed African Americans for their own victimization.

In 1946, Austin illuminated the causes of a race riot in Columbia, Tennessee, and reproved the white press for presenting a biased and erroneous picture of this event.[188] The violence began when a white radio repairman slapped a black woman named Gladys Stephenson, after she and her nineteen-year-old-son, James Stephenson, complained about a faulty repair job for which they were overcharged. When James defended his mother from the repairman's attack, a white mob gathered, and "police arrested the Stephensons." Fearing a black insurrection, "the state patrol and national guard surrounded" a black section of Columbia, and then entered the area. The patrol and guard "shot out windows, rampaged through offices, and destroyed houses." More than 100 black residents "were arrested, and two were shot to death in jail."[189] Austin denounced the violent actions of the local, state, and national authorities, as well as indicting the white press for not holding responsible the white radio repairman who assaulted the black woman, noting that the woman's son was absolutely justified in retaliating after the attack on his mother. Austin criticized the Associated Press, noting that nothing it reports "is going to make us believe that the Negroes who were in the custody of the law and unarmed made it necessary for the police officers to shoot to kill for their (the officers) own protection."[190]

Austin regularly publicized police brutality against African Americans. In October 1949, the *Times'* front page headline read, "ABC Officers Arrested for Tieing Negro Up by Hands." A black man was handcuffed to a tree and beaten "with a flashlight, a pistol, and a stick" by two Alcohol Beverage Control (ABC) officers in Halifax County.[191] In 1952, Greenville police beat and kicked an NCC alumna. The *Times* observed that "cop brutality . . . seems to be running amuck throughout the state."[192] Austin reported that in Greenville and in Pitt County, blacks "live in all most perpetual fear of the white people whose fondest and greatest obsession is to maintain white supremacy whatever the cost. . . . In the county Negro sharecroppers and tenant farmers practically live as slaves with their white landlords quite often stealing or taking their crops and leaving the Negro no alternative but to go back and work harder to enrich his white master. So it was in Greenville that a young Negro woman of one of the most respected families was beaten, tried and convicted for having the courage to question an officer of the law about the right of way in traffic." She was waiting in her car for a pedestrian to cross the street before turning right.[193] In January 1953, a Durham policeman beat up "Clarence Jones, an innocent Negro." Despondent over his arrest and beating, Jones attempted suicide. He was later released when it was discovered he was wrongly arrested, as he was not "the person sought."[194] In June 1953, a Chapel Hill policeman brutally beat a black plasterer.[195]

With almost all court cases decided by white judges and all-white juries, it was rare for the North Carolina legal system to provide justice in cases where defendants and victims were of different races. The *Times* sought to publicize these injustices in hopes of reforming this racist system. In November 1951, the *Times* reported that a jury of twelve white men in Rockingham County, North Carolina, brought in a verdict of not guilty for a white farmer who had been charged with murdering a black farmer. The white farmer had previously been jailed for allegedly killing another tenant farmer. The autopsy report showed that the victim suffered blows to the back of his head. According to the victim's wife, who witnessed the attack, the defendant struck her husband with "two large oak tobacco sticks."[196] After the verdict, Austin asserted that no one was surprised when "an all-white jury in Rockingham County deliberated only 30 minutes before freeing a white man for the brutal murder of his Negro tenant farmer. . . . Justice in this State is a one way street when the rights of Negroes are concerned."[197]

The *Times* reported on efforts by black attorneys in North Carolina to overturn verdicts against black defendants rendered by all-white juries. In 1948, the U.S. Supreme Court had ruled that North Carolina's jury selection process yielding all-white juries was unconstitutional.[198] After this decision, North Carolina began including a small number of African Americans in its jury pools, but still rarely did blacks actually serve on juries. In 1952, black North Carolina attorneys argued before the U.S. Supreme Court on behalf of several clients on death row who had been convicted by all-white juries or by juries in which the number of black jurors had been unconstitutionally limited. Thus the defendants had been denied their constitutional rights to due process and a fair trial.[199]

Perhaps the most extraordinary example of racist prosecution of an African American was the case of a black farmer, Mack Ingram, who was convicted in 1951 of raping a white woman in Yanceyville, North Carolina, in Caswell County, even though he never got within seventy-five feet of her.[200] When Austin found out about the case, he sent Junius Scales, a white activist member of the SCHW, to investigate.[201] In the *Times*, Austin railed against the injustice perpetrated against Ingram, while praising the NAACP's North Carolina branch for coming to Ingram's defense.[202] Austin sought to get national attention for this case, which he hoped would produce pressure to release the defendant, as he was charged with a preposterous offense. Austin related the story to Ted Poston of the *New York Post*, that paper's only black reporter, who published an article that garnered national publicity for the case. Meanwhile, Scales sent a press release to North Carolina's largest newspapers. According to Scales, the *Post* article did the trick, as "the State Department in Washington was reportedly besieged from around the world for information about the 'seventy-five-foot rape,' and Yanceyville had become big news."[203] At the same time, the NAACP denounced Scales, who was a member of the Communist Party USA, and said "it was going to represent Ingram on appeal, in part to prevent the Communists from making political capital from the case."[204] Nonetheless, in November 1951, Ingram was convicted by an all-white jury and was given the maximum sentence of two years at hard labor.[205] The conviction was based on a North Carolina law that said "assault may be committed without actual physical contact if it can be proved that the defendant intended an attack against the person of another." North Carolina was apparently the only state with such a law.[206]

After Ingram's appeal resulted in a mistrial because two black jurors favored a not guilty verdict, a third trial was held in November 1952. This time, an "all-white all-male jury" convicted Ingram after deliberating for less than an hour of "simple assault ... under a law which provides that actual physical contact has no bearing on assault." He received a "six-month suspended sentence and [was] placed on five-years' probation ... for 'assault by leering.' "[207]

The *Times* reports of this story helped give it international renown, which ultimately helped Ingram win release from prison.[208] In February 1953, the North Carolina Supreme Court vacated the conviction of Ingram, ruling the law under which he was convicted unconstitutional because one can "not be convicted of a criminal offense 'solely for what may have been in his mind.' "[209]

During the postwar era, the *Times* regularly shed light on North Carolina's flawed justice system, which discriminated against African Americans. This was particularly true for the crime of rape. In November 1950, the *Times* reported that North Carolina had executed sixty-two African Americans from 1910 to 1950 for the crime of rape, but had executed only five whites. Austin declared, "The death penalty for rape is a race penalty—an oppressive bludgeon used almost exclusively against the Negro in the South."[210]

While black men were often falsely convicted of raping white women, white men were rarely convicted of raping black women. As historian Danielle McGuire has shown, white men "used rape as a 'weapon of terror' to dominate the bodies and minds of African-American men and women. Interracial rape was . . . used to uphold white patriarchal power."[211] As this was clearly the case in midcentury North Carolina, Austin provided abundant evidence in his attempt to shame white North Carolinians. In December 1950, the *Times* reported that a Halifax County grand jury refused to indict a white man accused of raping a black woman. The *Times* observed sarcastically, "Notorious Halifax County kept the record clean." According to the *Times*, North Carolina had never convicted a white man of raping a black woman.[212]

In September 1951, when six white soldiers were accused of raping a black mother near Carthage, in Moore County, North Carolina, Austin demanded that the army prosecute the guilty parties.[213] He noted that in a recent case, a white judge had "blasted" a grand jury in Hertford County "for refusing to indict a white man for rape on a 15-year-old Negro girl."[214] Publicity about the Carthage rape helped to produce an indictment and conviction of three white soldiers "who admitted ravishing a young Negro wife." But they were convicted of the crime of simple assault, not rape, and they were sentenced to only sixteen to twenty-four months in prison. Austin reported that the jury, including eleven whites and one black, "completely ignored the signed confessions and testimony of the three defendants and returned the nearest verdict possible to complete acquittal—simple assault on a female." Earlier, the Moore County sheriff had called the crime the "most 'heinous' crime committed in the State."[215]

In November 1951, the *Norfolk Journal and Guide* reprinted Austin's editorial with the title "No Punishment for White Rapists of Negro Women." Austin recounted several cases of whites accused, but not convicted, of raping black women in North Carolina. He indicted the state and the white church for their immorality, noting that "the white church has made no public outcry against a single one of these crimes. . . . The rape of a Negro woman is unimportant to the white church in the South." Austin reported that no white man had been convicted of raping a black woman even when the accused had confessed to the crime.[216]

This negative publicity related to the failure of the state to convict white rapists of black women had a salutary effect on the justice system in North Carolina. During the next two years, North Carolina courts convicted white rapists and sentenced them to significant prison time. In 1952, the *Times* reported that a white man was convicted for raping a black woman for the first time. The rapist was sentenced to eight to ten years in prison.[217] In 1953, a fifteen-year-old white teenager was sentenced to life in prison "for his confessed rape of a young Negro school girl." In a piece titled "A Surprising, but Hopeful Sign," Austin reported that this was the first time that a white rapist had received such a severe sentence for raping an African American.[218]

Nonetheless, black folk continued to suffer from white violence. In 1952, Austin spoke at a memorial service in High Point, North Carolina, for Harry T. Moore and his wife, victims of a bomb attack in Florida. Moore was a civil rights activist and NAACP leader, who had bravely protested the killing of an African American, while in custody, handcuffed to a sheriff. Austin declared, "Where one Moore is killed . . . a thousand others will rise in his place. We shall not give up this relentless fight until freedom and justice prevail."[219]

AUSTIN KNEW THAT without equal economic opportunity, black chances to improve their material conditions were futile, and so he urged African Americans to organize and fight for economic justice. In 1946, as he had during World War II, Austin allied with A. Philip Randolph in the struggle for jobs. He advocated the creation of a permanent Fair Employment Practices Committee (FEPC) to ensure that the federal government would stop racial discrimination against black workers. In March 1946, in a banner headline on the front page of the *Times*, Austin reported Randolph's plans for a march on Washington to press Congress to pass a permanent FEPC.[220] In February 1950, Austin asserted that the "Southern economy will forever be the slave of Wall Street so long as the Negro portion of the South is underpaid, poorly educated and exploited. That is why Yankeecrat senators who represent Wall Street interests are so quick to rush to the aid of southern numbscull [sic] senators like Hoey, Rankin and George when they filibuster against FEPC."[221] In May 1950, Austin reiterated his call for passage of the fair employment practices legislation to ban job discrimination against blacks. He argued that one's commitment to democracy should be measured by one's commitment to equal employment opportunity.[222] In January 1953, Austin attacked southern congressmen who opposed the FEPC. The need for such legislation was demonstrated by the fact that in Durham, blacks were "not even allowed to drive garbage trucks, but must be satisfied with handling the garbage only."[223]

Austin frequently pushed for the employment of African Americans in federal, state, and local government. In August 1950, he questioned the fact that twenty blacks took the civil service test for postal employees but Durham failed to hire one. Austin urged blacks to pressure local Democratic Party officials to support hiring blacks for city jobs, and if they failed to do so, vote those officials out of office.[224] In June 1953, Austin urged the state to appoint a black member to the newly authorized North Carolina parole board.[225]

Austin demanded that Durham hire African Americans as firefighters. In 1942, he had told a researcher that resistance to hiring black firemen was partially due to the nature of the job: "The whites could not stand to see us sit around all day and wait for a fire and get paid a salary for it."[226] In late 1949 the DCNA lobbied the city to hire a black fireman. Headed by businessman John S. Stewart, the DCNA noted that other southern cities, even in the Deep South, had black firemen.[227] Austin underscored the point that other southern cities had hired black firemen, and in one, there were plans to place an African American in charge of a fire station, while in Durham, there was not one black firefighter.[228] In 1951, Austin advised voters to defeat city officials who opposed hiring black firefighters.[229] In January 1952, the *Times* published photos of black firemen in Richmond and Winston-Salem to pressure Durham officials to break the color line in its fire department.[230] In March 1953, the *Times* reported extensive damage caused by fires in Hayti, arguing that these infernos demonstrated the need for a fire station in the black district. Austin asked, "We wonder how long the people in this section of town will have to unduly suffer the lack of municipal services which they deserve."[231] In 1954, Durham finally agreed to build a fire station in Hayti. Austin immediately demanded the hiring of black personnel at the fire station.[232] However, the first black firemen were not hired in Durham until 1958.[233]

Austin also urged city officials to promote black policemen and hire black deputy sheriffs. While Durham had ten black policemen in 1950, the same number as Charlotte, the latter city had employed a black police sergeant since 1948, while Durham had none.[234] In December 1951, Austin congratulated Durham on promoting a black officer to lieutenant and two black officers to be detectives. Austin called these promotions "the greatest recognition that has come to Negro police officers anywhere in the South."[235]

Austin regularly criticized private-sector employers, who exploited black workers. He zeroed in on the Dukes for their longtime profiteering off the backs of black tobacco workers: "Thousands of Negroes worked at starvation wages in the early days of the tobacco factories of Durham, Reidsville, Richmond, and other cities. . . . Some of those Negroes are still living and can relate incidents that will bring tears to the eyes of the most hardened heart, about how they were exploited by the Dukes. . . . Indeed the Duke family fairly marched to fame and fortunate [*sic*] upon the bleeding backs of help-less Negroes." Austin also attacked the tobacco mills for relegating blacks to the "most menial tasks" with no opportunity for promotion.[236] In 1951, Austin excoriated the tobacco industry for limiting blacks to the lowest-paid jobs, failing to promote them, and replacing them with white workers. He observed that black workers working long hours at low wages helped "build the Duke and Reynolds millions."[237]

While black workers were relegated to the lowest-paid jobs in tobacco mills, cotton mills in North Carolina and throughout the South refused to hire any African Americans, except as janitors or warehousemen. This was particularly devastating to black job opportunities because cotton mills were the largest industrial employers in the region. In 1952, Austin publicized re-search that showed that black workers were leaving the South because of lim-ited economic opportunity, notably the denial of work in factory jobs. He also pointed out that low pay and high rates of unemployment lowered blacks' purchasing power, thus hurting the southern economy.[238] In 1953, Austin denounced Asheville officials for boasting of good race relations when the city and Buncombe County effectively excluded blacks from jobs in its industries. He called for hiring of black workers.[239] In September 1953, Austin attacked black labor leaders in Durham for failing to fight harder for equal job opportunity for black workers.[240]

In 1953, Austin urged the formation of a statewide organization to fight for blacks' employment rights and opportunity. He reported that blacks, who had previously held more than one-half of all tobacco mill jobs, had been cut to about one-third of those jobs. Further, blacks were largely excluded from national, state, and local government jobs. Indeed, Durham employed only two black letter carriers.[241]

IN THE DECADE before the U.S. Supreme Court declared segregated public schools unconstitutional, Austin made some important inroads in the fight against the racial segregation of public facilities in Durham. In 1947, perhaps inspired by the breaking of the color line in major league baseball by Jackie Robinson, Austin helped arrange an integrated football game in Durham between a white team from Philadelphia and a black team from Washington, D.C. In advance of the game, Austin asked the Durham City Council to approve it. Austin later told an interviewer that the council "opposed it at first" because the councilmen feared it would "bring on a race riot." But Austin was not discouraged, and invoked the role of black and white soldiers in the recently ended world war, as he appealed to the councilmen's sense of patriotism. He asked them, "Do you mean to say that these boys, black and white, who've been fighting for one cause together and dying together can't come back home and play a game of football together in their own home land?" Austin then tried another tactic: "But the thing that really has me worried now is that I've already signed a contract, and they'll be suing me and the city for breach of contract. Now I'm a poor man; if you'll let them sue the city, then that'll be all right." Apparently, the councilmen's fear of financial loss persuaded them, and after making Austin wait, they approved the game but emphasized that it would not "be a precedent." Nonetheless, several councilmen and the head of Durham's recreation department attended the game, and despite their fears, no riot ensued.[242]

While the local white daily newspapers in Durham downplayed the game, the *Chicago Defender* hailed the game, played on Sunday, November 23, 1947, as "the first football game between Negroes and whites in the South." Three thousand fans, black and white, without segregated seating, saw the game, between the Vulpine Athletic Club of Philadelphia and the Willow Tree Athletic Club of Washington, D.C., which ended in a 6-6 tie "on a field drenched with a steady rain."[243] Austin, who served as president of the Piedmont Tobacco Bowl Corporation, which organized the game, asserted that the purpose of the game was "to show subversive elements in foreign countries that members of different races in America can play together as well as fight a common enemy together." Although he did not say so, he also likely wanted to show the South that an integrated sporting event could be played without incident. He called the game "as fine a demonstration of good sportsmanship . . . as I have ever seen."[244] When interviewed about the football game, Austin recalled that there was an interracial baseball game in Durham the previous summer between "a team of southern white men from Danville, Va." and the "Durham Eagles of the Carolina Negro Baseball league here."[245] The story of the first integrated football game in the South, reported by the Associated Press, made national news, as it was picked up by the *New York Times*.[246] It is important to point out that this integrated football game took place a full seven years before the first integrated football game in Washington, D.C., was played. That was in 1954 when the "bi-racial integrated D.C. Public Schools' all-stars" defeated the all-white St. Johns.[247]

In April 1950, Austin applauded minor league baseball teams for their efforts to advance the integration of sport. That month "the Brooklyn Dodgers

'B' Club played in the Raleigh-League Park (Devereaux Meadow) with Don Bankhead, one of Brooklyn's Negro pitchers doing most of the tossing for the Dodgers against the Raleigh Capitols of the Carolina League." Before this game, Devereaux Meadow had excluded black players from any sporting event. Austin recalled the 1947 game that he had organized, explaining that "when a white football team was matched against a Negro team here, it almost caused heart failure in recreation and city officials[,] many of whom predicted that the game would end in a race riot." It did not.[248]

Austin lobbied for the integration of baseball's professional minor leagues in the South. In April 1951, he urged the Carolina League to integrate its teams.[249] In April 1954, Austin observed that the continued segregation of minor league baseball in North Carolina was forcing teams out of business. While there had been forty-seven clubs in the state in 1948, six years later only thirteen survived. Black fans could make the difference between success and failure, according to Austin.[250] Later that month, he praised minor league teams in Burlington and Reidsville, North Carolina, for adding black players to their rosters, while advocating a DCNA-led boycott by black fans of Durham Bulls games because the team's roster still remained all-white.[251]

In 1954, Austin proposed a basketball game between NCC and Duke as one way to advance race relations, noting that games had been played at NCC and North Carolina State College in Raleigh between the Harlem Globetrotters and a white team and an integrated team.[252] In making this pitch for an NCC-Duke game, Austin did not mention the 1944 "secret game" when the NCC basketball team had played a game against a Duke University team composed of medical students on NCC's campus.[253]

In 1952, Austin reported that a high school tennis tournament was held at the University of Virginia with black and white tennis players, with all housed and fed at the campus on an equal basis. Austin noted that such an integrated tournament could not happen at the "liberal" University of North Carolina, which was fighting to stall integration of its programs and facilities.[254]

In November 1952, the *Times* reported that sixteen black golfers had challenged the exclusion of African Americans from the Charlotte city-owned Bonnie Brae golf course. The black golfers filed suit in the Superior Court of Mecklenburg County in January 1952. The Charlotte NAACP backed the case.[255] It would be another four years, however, before the first black golfer won access to the golf course.[256]

As he had during earlier years, Austin publicized black resistance to Jim Crow transportation, while urging bus companies to hire black bus drivers. In 1952, Austin exhorted Duke Power Company, which ran the city's bus system, to hire black bus drivers on its routes.[257] Two years earlier, in July 1950, Austin had published an article on Emma Bond Cheek, a Raleigh principal, who refused to move to the back of a bus en route from Raleigh to Knoxville, Tennessee. She was arrested and jailed on July 4, 1950. The charges were dropped when she showed her interstate bus ticket in court because the U.S. Supreme Court had banned racially segregated bus seating on interstate transportation in 1946.[258] In September 1950, the *Times* publicized another case of a black interstate bus passenger, who was arrested for refusing to move to the back of the bus and won his case in court.[259]

In December 1951, the *Times* reported that an elderly black woman named Hattie Howard traveling from New York to Savannah, Georgia, was forced to stand rather than sit on the back seat in Raleigh because white passengers needed seats. Howard got off the bus because she feared the bus driver would assault her. Backed by Raleigh attorneys Herman L. Taylor and William C. Raines, she planned to file a lawsuit against Atlantic Greyhound Bus Corporation.[260]

In 1953, the *Times* reported that a "dark-skinned man" who said he was not black, but a "Moorish-American of the Moslem faith," was arrested for refusing to vacate the white waiting room at the Raleigh bus station. The judge dismissed the charge because "apparently there is no law covering segregation in the waiting room."[261] In 1953, Austin urged the U.S. Court of Appeals to ban segregated seating for intrastate bus passengers.[262]

Similarly, Austin vociferously attacked racial inequities and segregation in medical facilities. In 1950, he illuminated the human costs of racial segregation, which sometimes led to a patient's death. In December of that year, the *Times* reported that a black World War II veteran was denied admission to Duke Hospital and died an hour later.[263] Earlier that year, Austin opposed the opening of a hospital for white cerebral palsy patients funded by black and white taxpayers.[264] When he learned that the Cerebral Palsy Hospital had decided to accept black patients, Austin commended state officials.[265]

In August 1950, Austin suggested that blacks who valued their dignity should refuse to go to facilities that required blacks to enter by a back or side door, as movie theaters often did.[266] In February 1951, the *Times* reported that North Carolina College students were considering launching a boycott of segregated theaters and picketing the theaters. One student referenced the Korean War and commented, "While segregated theaters in Durham probably can run indefinitely without our financial support I do not see why we should continue to pay them to insult us while our boys are fighting and dying on foreign battlefields to uphold democracy. Even the people who are engaged in war against our country would be admitted on an equal basis and cannot see why loyal Negro American citizens have got to be asked to go around to a side or back door."[267] Austin praised the planned boycott as "almost too good to believe." He called the plans signs of "an awakening of Negro college students in North Carolina that is long past due." Austin called Jim Crow theaters "an insult to Negroes everywhere" that could be shut down "if Negroes would muster enough self-respect to stay out of them."[268]

In a tactical reversal, in February 1952, Austin agreed with the decision of the DCNA to reject a "proposed boycott of segregated theaters in Durham." Austin claimed that not enough blacks would support the boycott, and a failure would be counterproductive to the movement against segregation. He recalled that James Shepard refused to attend segregated theaters or sit in Jim Crow railroad cars. Instead he would pay for a Pullman berth. Austin concluded, "Segregation must and will be destroyed."[269] The following week, Austin congratulated the Baltimore NAACP on its victory in desegregating Ford's Theatre in Baltimore after years of picketing and boycotting the theater. Austin did not call for similar action in Durham, although he did counsel self-respecting blacks to steer clear of segregated theaters.[270]

When black Korean War hero Ellison Wynn returned home to Durham, Austin pointed out the horrific treatment doled out to him because of his race: no white hotel in Durham would rent him a room or serve him a meal in its dining room, UNC was fighting to the hilt to deny his children admission to its programs, white churches would shun him if he tried to worship at one, and bus drivers and train conductors would have him arrested and perhaps beaten if he refused to sit in segregated seating. Meanwhile a white Communist from the Soviet Union or a North Korean or Chinese Communist "who blew half of Lt. Wynn's face away with mortar fire while he was fighting for 'his country'" would not be subjected to the indignities of segregation. Austin concluded, "Sometimes we think our white folks in the South are inhuman."[271]

Austin also criticized the failure of Fort Bragg in Fayetteville, North Carolina, to enforce President Truman's executive order integrating the armed forces. The *Times* reported in June 1951 that Fort Bragg continued "to be a cesspool of rank discrimination, jim crow and race phobia." While other southern military installations like Fort Jackson in South Carolina and the Aberdeen Proving Ground in Maryland had integrated, the *Times* reported that at Fort Bragg, black soldiers were relegated to an overcrowded segregated section of the camp, with a dilapidated recreation facility, which caused terrible morale problems among black troops.[272] In August 1951, Austin, noting that the air force and navy had integrated their forces, criticized the army for failing to do so. He wrote, "Segregation is rampant in Army units."[273]

Following the landmark May 1954 U.S. Supreme Court decision in *Brown v. Board of Education* declaring public school segregation unconstitutional, the *Times* proclaimed that the decision meant "the dawn of a new era." But Austin counseled "patience, forbearance and understanding on the part of Negroes and an honest attempt on the part of white citizens to comply with the verdict of the court within the limits of a reasonable time." He also condemned the antagonistic reactions of Georgia governor Herman Talmadge and Georgia senator Richard Russell. Austin called the court's decision "a new birth of freedom for all the people of this great state."[274] After the *Brown* decision, civil rights activist and attorney Pauli Murray, who had grown up in Durham and worked for the *Carolina Times* as a youth, paid tribute to Austin, calling him "a stubborn unsung hero of this triumph." She declared, "Mr. Austin symbolizes that rare brand of fighters throughout history whose dedication to a principal is so great, they endure personal sacrifices, reprisals against their families, public vilification and peril of life and limb, but remain steadfast to the end. We can now appreciate more than ever Mr. Austin's relentless, and sometime heartbreakingly desolate, fight against segregation and discrimination."[275] While the *Brown* decision was an important victory in the civil rights struggle, Austin knew that the struggle was far from over and would continue to require the relentless efforts of thousands of black freedom fighters in the years ahead.

CHAPTER FIVE

We Want Equality Now

Challenging Segregation after Brown

As the *Brown* decision ushered in the era of the modern civil rights movement, black newspapers continued to play an important role in the freedom
struggle. The black press's employment of advocacy journalism had played a
crucial role in the battle for civil rights during the preceding decades.[1] And in
North Carolina, for almost three decades, Louis Austin and the *Carolina
Times* had helped build the foundation for the black freedom movement of
the 1950s and 1960s.

During the late 1950s, Austin continued to be an important leader of black
North Carolinians. Although many whites outside Durham may have dis-
counted his leadership, black Carolinians extolled him and the *Carolina
Times*. In 1959, a study of black leadership in North Carolina found that while
whites did not rank Austin among the top ten black leaders in the state, blacks
ranked Austin the sixth most important leader in the state. While whites
ranked black business and education leaders, like NC Mutual president Asa
Spaulding (#1) and North Carolina College at Durham (NCC) president Alfonso Elder (#2), high, blacks favored leaders in the forefront of social change,
like activists Kelly Alexander, head of the North Carolina NAACP (#1), and
John Wheeler, DCNA head (#2). Among the leaders who appeared on the
list chosen by blacks but not on the list chosen by whites, Austin was the second highest ranked. Indeed, Austin ranked higher among blacks than Asa
Spaulding (#10), Alfonso Elder (#11), the educator Charlotte Hawkins Brown
(#12), the attorney Conrad Pearson (#16), and Durham school board member Rencher N. Harris (#26).[2] Moreover, Austin exerted an important influence on other black leaders in the state. While Austin regularly consulted
Kelly Alexander and Conrad Pearson on important social and political issues,
R. N. Harris, Conrad Pearson, Asa Spaulding, James T. Taylor, and John
Wheeler regularly sought counsel from Austin.[3]

The success of black newspapers in agitating for racial integration and racial equality impelled white newspapers to increase their coverage of black
communities, which gave black newspapers increased competition. Many
black newspapers lost subscribers and readers as a significant number of African Americans switched to reading white newspapers. Austin recognized this

dynamic. In 1962, at a panel at NCC during National Negro Newspaper Week, Austin observed "that the 'constant bombardment' of the general public by Negro newspapers with the facts of progress among Negroes and 'injustices suffered' has 'forced' a change in the attitude of daily newspapers toward news about Negroes." As a result, white newspapers were now competing with black newspapers because both now reported news about African Americans.[4]

To retain his readers, Austin consistently sought to increase circulation. By the mid-1950s, the circulation and influence of the *Carolina Times* had grown dramatically. During the late 1950s, the *Times* boasted the largest circulation of any black paper in the state, with many loyal readers throughout the state, not just in Durham.[5] In March 1960, the *Times* reported that its circulation had reached its highest total ever. Further evidence of growth occurred in 1965, when the *Times* expanded to sixteen pages, and raised the yearly subscription price from $4.00 to $5.00.[6] Thus, the *Times* effectively confronted competition from white newspapers from the mid-1950s to the mid-1960s.

Meanwhile, Austin coped with personal challenges. In October 1961, Austin's mother, Carrie Johnson Austin, died at age eighty-five, following a long illness. Carrie had lived with her son Louis and his family since her husband's death in 1922. Two years before her death, she had moved into a nursing home to gain the medical and custodial care she required. Carrie was survived by her four children: Louis; Maude, a teacher at John Chaloner School in Roanoke Rapids, not far from where the Austins grew up in Enfield; Jesse, who lived in Jamaica, New York; and Lodius, who worked as a linotype operator for the *Carolina Times*. Carrie Austin was also survived by three grandchildren and one great-grandchild.[7]

During the late 1950s, Austin regularly worked with other black leaders in civic, business, and religious organizations to pursue opportunities to move toward racial equality. In addition to his involvement in the Durham Committee on Negro Affairs, Austin strengthened his working relationships with other black leaders through their church work. He served with black businessman, lawyer, and DCNA chairman John Wheeler in the late 1950s as a member of the General Board of the African Methodist Episcopal (AME) Church. Austin, who by 1960 had taught the Men's Bible Class at St. Joseph's for twenty years, also served with Wheeler as a trustee of St. Joseph's AME Church in Durham.[8]

During the mid-1950s and 1960s, Austin continued to employ Cold War rhetoric to highlight American hypocrisy in condemning Soviet tyranny while sustaining anti-black racism and segregation in the United States. By doing this, he hoped to use Cold War ideology in service to the civil rights struggle, dulling the tactic whereby segregationists attempted to demonize racial liberals as Communists. In 1954, Austin denounced the persecution of an African American woman, Annie Lee Moss, by the U.S. Senate Permanent Subcommittee on Investigations led by Joseph McCarthy, the junior senator from Wisconsin. Moss, a Pentagon employee and a former Durham resident, was accused of being a Communist Party member and was investigated several times and suffered three job suspensions before she was restored to her job by the secretary of defense. Austin excoriated McCarthy for victimizing an innocent woman and contrasted the senator's aggressive prosecution of Moss with his failure to condemn such virulent segregationist politicians as Georgia governor Herman Talmadge and South Carolina governor James Byrnes, who upheld white supremacy and in doing so were truly enemies of democracy. Austin asserted that "as long as men like Talmadge and Byrnes are allowed to roam at large and spit defiance in the face of the Constitution and the Supreme Court," the United States would continue to lose international support in the Cold War battle against the Soviet Union.[9]

In 1955, Austin compared American Communists like Junius Scales, who had been arrested the previous year for allegedly violating the 1941 Smith Act—under which Communist Party members were prosecuted for allegedly advocating the overthrow of the U.S. government—with North Carolina legislators, who publicly declared their intention to subvert the U.S. Constitution by blocking enforcement of the *Brown v. Board of Education* decision. Austin declared, "The legislators in North Carolina and other southern states who are passing laws to overthrow a ruling of the U.S. Supreme Court should be arrested and sent to prison." He insisted that Americans who encouraged "others to disobey" the high court were more of a threat to American democracy than were "those who in the name of communism seek its overthrow."[10]

In 1959, during Soviet leader Nikita Khrushchev's visit to the United States, Austin admonished the South on its hypocrisy in rhetorically demonizing Communists while treating white Communists with more respect than they did black Carolinians. Had the Soviet leader visited the South, unlike black Americans, he would have been served in white restaurants and other public facilities. Austin declared, "After all, Khrushchev is white and that makes him right, irrespective of Russia's stockpile of nuclear weapons which he has rattled again and again at this country and in defiance of its president's bid for peace. . . . Khrushchev's white skin entitles him to eat, sleep and get the best in any restaurant or hotel in . . . any . . . southern state, where to be a

Negro is considered worse than being a communist—we mean a white communist."[11]

In 1955, Austin joined other black journalists in condemning the lynching of fourteen-year-old Emmett Till in Mississippi. Till's murder provoked a massive outcry from African Americans, which helped stimulate black protest in the ensuing years. The publication in *Jet* magazine of the photograph of Till's brutalized body was particularly horrifying.[12] By contrast, most white magazines provided limited coverage of the murder of Till.[13] Austin called the lynching "the most revolting offense against decent society all over the world."[14] After an all-white jury acquitted the suspected murderers of Till, Austin called the result "one of the greatest miscarriages of justice ever to occur in a civilized nation." Further, he wrote of whites in Mississippi, "You are so blind with the rage of race hatred you cannot see that you have plunged a dagger into the back of your own country." Austin noted that in the context of the Cold War, this event severely damaged the United States' international reputation and influence.[15] Austin's use of Cold War rhetoric to shame the U.S. government into action proved effective and enduring. The Cold War era, which paralleled the years of major civil rights protests, was also an era when African and Asian colonies were fighting for independence. In this context, if the U.S. government ignored racial injustices that reverberated around the world, it risked losing the battle with the Soviet Union for international influence among the newly emerging nations of Africa and Asia.

In October 1958, a kissing game played by black and white children in Monroe, North Carolina, reignited white fears of interracial sex, and within weeks erupted into an international Cold War controversy. One of the white girls, Sissy Sutton, told her mother about the game, and that she had kissed a black boy, James Hanover Thompson. Mrs. Sutton was "furious. . . . I would have killed Hanover myself if I had the chance." She told her husband about the kiss and he and his friends armed themselves and started looking for Thompson, age ten, and the other black boy, David Simpson, age eight, who had been part of the game. The police arrested Thompson and Simpson and proceeded to brutally beat them, telling the boys, "We'll teach you little niggers not to kiss white girls."[16] When a judge claimed that the boys "were being held only for their protection," Austin commented in the *Times*, "It takes no sage to determine how much help a juvenile judge would be to two little Negro boys to whom he referred to twice in his testimony as 'niggers.'"[17] One week later, the two boys were judged "guilty of molestation" and were confined indefinitely at the Morrison Training School for Negroes in Hoffman, North Carolina. In December, with no help forthcoming from the national or statewide NAACP, Monroe NAACP leader Robert F. Williams and several allies decided to meet with Austin in Durham, where they established the Committee to Combat Racial Injustice (CCRI). The CCRI publicized the story of the incarceration of the two black boys for playing a kissing game, which yielded international attention and in the context of the Cold War, incredible pressure on North Carolina governor Luther Hodges and the U.S. government to release the children. In December, Austin wrote, "The national and world attention which this . . . incident has attracted only serve this country right. No one but a bunch of numbsculls [sic] with hearts full of the filthiest kind of dirt would attach any significance and raise so much hell over what children of six to ten years of age do at play."[18] After almost four months in custody, Simpson and Thompson were released to their families in February 1959.[19]

ALTHOUGH THE *BROWN* DECISION was a great victory for the forces of racial equality, obstacles constructed by white officials throughout the South, including in North Carolina, meant that the struggle for integrated public schools would be long and protracted. Austin persistently challenged those who sought to perpetuate unequal and segregated schools. He also helped motivate and mobilize African Americans to continue the fight. Although there was strong support for racial integration among black Carolinians, black teachers feared that integration could lead to job losses. On the eve of the *Brown* decision, Austin advised black teachers that they "need not fear loss of jobs" with school integration. He claimed that some black teachers who thought they could not do as good a job as white teachers were suffering from an inferiority complex caused by years of white supremacists' "indoctrination." Austin asserted that black teachers had "graduated from some of the best colleges and universities in the United States" and were well prepared for their jobs.[20] In his advice to black teachers, Austin would prove to be less than prescient. When public schools were finally integrated more than ten years later, many black teachers and principals would lose their jobs, not because of their lack of skills, but because many white officials preferred to employ white educators.[21]

Meanwhile, hoping to disarm critics of integration, Austin publicized the words and actions of the few white officials who supported integrated schools, and he shined a light on successful examples of public school integration to prove that integration was possible and workable. Less than two weeks after the *Brown* decision, Austin praised Greensboro officials for advocating compliance with the Supreme Court's desegregation decision. At the same time, he reproved Durham officials for failing to do likewise.[22] In June 1955, Austin lauded the Asheville Board of Education for articulating its plans to comply with the *Brown* decision.[23] In July 1954, he cited the experience of the first black teacher at a previously all-white Camp Lejeune school in Jacksonville, North Carolina, as proof that integration did not necessarily lead to disruption and violence, as white segregationists claimed. The teacher, Winfred Daves, noted that although she initially encountered resistance from white teachers, within a month the other teachers warmed to her. She received cooperation from the parents of her students, and by Mother's Day, she had received gifts from parents and students.[24]

The *Times* also reported on racial segregation in Catholic schools in North Carolina. Although the Catholic diocese in Raleigh declared in June 1953 that racial segregation would not be permitted in Catholic schools, Durham's Catholic Church school continued to exclude black students in 1954. Austin denounced the racist treatment of blacks in Durham by the Catholic Church, noting that it was reminiscent of how Mississippi plantation owners treated blacks. He also denounced Father John A. Risacher, the white priest of the all-black Holy Cross Catholic Church in Durham, who opposed the integration of the Durham Catholic school.[25] Austin's criticism of Catholic officials who resisted integration of Catholic schools may have contributed to the admission of three black students to Durham's Catholic school in the fall of 1955, which made it the first desegregated school in the city.[26]

In 1954, Austin advised Governor William Umstead to convene black and white leaders in order to prepare to integrate schools in North Carolina. Several months before the *Brown* decision, Austin had suggested that the governor appoint an interracial commission of 400 black and white leaders "to prepare for integration in the public schools." Soon after the court's decision, Austin repeated this suggestion, emphasizing that the members of the commission should not be exclusively state employees, who would feel constrained from speaking freely because of their employment with the state.[27] After Umstead appointed three black state employees (and sixteen whites) to his advisory committee on public education, Austin criticized the governor's "lack of statesmanship," noting that the failure to appoint blacks who were independent of government pressure showed that the governor's committee was designed to rubber-stamp his plan to circumvent the *Brown* decision.[28]

When southern white conservatives cried out for states' rights in denouncing the *Brown* decision, Austin pointed out that this cry of states' rights was not about rights, but about retaining the power to oppress African Americans. He explained that states' rights meant "the right . . . to compel Negroes to go to inferior schools, to do the same work for less wages. . . . It means the right to attack and rape Negro women, to shoot down in the streets and even in prison helpless Negroes. . . . It means the right to tax Negroes and deny them representation in government. . . . It even means the right to lynch, to force Negroes to enlist in the armed service, fight for democracy and then deny them the fruits of their sacrifices."[29]

Meanwhile, Austin attacked southern white newspapers that upheld segregated public schools. When the *Winston-Salem Journal* rebuked the NAACP for demanding compliance with the *Brown* decision, Austin declared that change would not occur without constant pressure, to wit, "There is no where in history where the oppressor has voluntarily taken his heel off the necks of the oppressed."[30]

Austin could not contain his outrage after southern governors, including North Carolina governor Umstead, met in Richmond, Virginia, to declare their resistance to the Supreme Court's desegregation decision. Austin proclaimed, "Southern governors deliberately feloniously, with malice and forethought, met . . . for the expressed, avowed and unholy purpose of defying the Supreme Court of their country and its Constitution." He added that they acted "in defiance of God Almighty," and that in doing so, "no scheme of the lowest traitor was ever more despicable and no act was ever more contemptible." Austin contended that a meeting to defy the court was treasonous and if any other group had met for a similar purpose, Congress and the FBI would surely have closely investigated them. Austin insisted, "For less than this men have been hanged or stood up before firing squads and mowed down like common grass."[31]

In the fall of 1954, North Carolina filed a brief largely penned by the assistant attorney general, I. Beverly Lake, that sought to persuade the Supreme Court that public school integration was unworkable and would lead to violence.[32] Austin retorted that it would have been more truthful for state officials to forthrightly state that they wanted to perpetuate their centuries-long tradition of oppressing African Americans. Austin termed North Carolina's brief "fiendish," "unchristian," and "undemocratic."[33]

In December 1954, Governor Umstead's advisory committee on public education concluded, "The mixing of the races forthwith in the public schools throughout the state cannot be accomplished and should not be attempted."[34] Luther Hodges, who had succeeded Umstead as governor after the latter man's death in November, praised the committee's conclusion.[35] Furthermore, to block desegregation of the schools, the committee recommended that the North Carolina General Assembly pass a pupil assignment bill that would "give local school boards control of enrollment and assign-ment of children in the state's public schools." This bill was designed to create a legal obstacle to stop civil rights attorneys from suing the state of North Carolina to force it to integrate its schools. Instead, numerous lawsuits would have to be filed against individual school districts.[36]

Meanwhile, in recognition of the fact that African Americans lacked repre-sentation on most North Carolina school boards, Austin fought to increase the number of black school board members to expand black influence over the question of school integration. Austin repeatedly demanded the appoint-ment of an African American to the Durham city school board when vacan-cies occurred. In August 1954, Austin noted that blacks represented one-third of the city's population and over 40 percent of the city's public school stu-dents, making it a travesty that no African Americans served on the school board.[37]

Austin also advocated financial penalties for public school districts that re-fused to integrate their schools. He backed an NAACP proposal to require that proposed federal legislation that would aid public education include the proviso that no federal funds would be spent on segregated public schools. Furthermore, federal funds for education would be excluded from states that continued to segregate their schools.[38]

In February 1955, Austin joined about 300 of North Carolina's black lead-ers to oppose legislation that would block or delay the integration of the state's public schools. The group "marched on the 1955 session of the General Assembly" in Raleigh. Then a smaller group of about twenty black leaders, including Austin, met with Governor Hodges. The spokesman for the group, the banker and attorney John H. Wheeler, advised the governor that if the state's leaders supported the Supreme Court decision, integration of the schools could be accomplished without significant disruption.[39] Wheeler testified against the proposed pupil assignment plan, which was being con-sidered by the General Assembly's Joint Committee on Education. He ar-gued that the plan was designed to "avoid the execution of the Supreme Court's decision and to slow down or retard the process of integration."[40] Cheered on by hundreds of black supporters, he rejected the notion that white Carolinians would never send their children to integrated schools, not-ing that since 1951 the U.S. Army had operated integrated schools, including at Fort Bragg in Fayetteville, North Carolina. Wheeler insisted that school integration had worked in other cities and would work in North Carolina if the state's leaders took forthright action to enforce federal law.[41] And evi-dence supports Wheeler's statement on both counts. Hundreds of school districts in Washington, D.C.; Delaware; Maryland; Missouri; and other border states had "quickly and peacefully integrated their classrooms."[42] Furthermore, public opinion polls in North Carolina showed that while a minority of white voters was vociferously opposed to school integration, most whites were neither actively in favor of nor actively opposed to integration.[43]

Nonetheless, the pupil assignment law was passed in April 1955, making it much more difficult for civil rights lawyers to challenge public school segregation because instead of suing the state, they would have to sue each of North Carolina's 173 school districts, slowing the process immeasurably.[44] The act proved very effective at bogging down lawsuits for desegregation, as the federal courts required that "plaintiffs exhaust their administrative remedies provided by the act and that rights must be asserted as individuals, not as a class before applying to a Federal court for relief."[45] Ten states passed pupil placement laws in the mid- to late1950s.[46]

When the North Carolina General Assembly passed a resolution in April 1955 that affirmed the governor's committee's claim that racial integration "cannot be accomplished and should not be attempted," Austin passionately denounced the resolution. He called it "an affront to God, a blatant contradiction of a professed democracy, . . . and a sin against the Holy Ghost." He called the assemblymen "craven-hearted bigots, enslaved by the forces of race hatred." Austin concluded that "in the midst of the Easter Season," the assembly had "crucified Christ afresh upon the cross of racial bigotry even while celebrating his resurrection in pageant, sermon, song."[47]

Meanwhile, Governor Hodges and the General Assembly took further action to stop school integration. In April 1955, the legislature appointed an all-white committee, headed by Thomas Pearsall, a former North Carolina Speaker of the House, to act in defiance of *Brown*. This committee, known as the Pearsall Committee, proposed a constitutional amendment that would authorize the state to pay for a student to go to a private school if the student's parents refused to send their child to an integrated school. It would also permit the state to close a school if it determined that integration would lead to "intolerable" conditions.[48] Hodges campaigned for legislative passage of this Pearsall Plan. Calling the *Brown* decision "an unlawful seizure of power . . . in derogation of the Constitution of the United States," he vowed that the North Carolina government would "use every legal means . . . to insure that the effects" of the court's decision were "not forced on our state."[49]

Then, in May 1955, the U.S. Supreme Court aided the segregationists' cause by issuing its implementation decision calling for desegregation "with all deliberate speed" and failing to set a timetable for integration.[50] NAACP lawyer Robert L. Carter noted that during the April 1955 arguments before the court, North Carolina's attorney general made the "most vicious argument . . . for the perpetuation of segregation."[51] Furthermore, according to the federal courts' interpretation, the *Brown* decision did not require "integration in the schools, but only prohibited enforced segregation."[52]

In August 1955, Governor Hodges strengthened the anti-integration movement when he attacked the NAACP and claimed that a black push for school integration would lead to strong white resistance and less education for everyone. Austin compared Hodges's speech to those of Hitler and Mussolini during the 1930s and 1940s for its vitriolic quality. He also noted that Hodges's words essentially encouraged defiance of the Constitution and violent opposition to the *Brown* decision.[53] Seven black leaders in Durham, including DCNA leader John S. Stewart, joined Austin in denouncing Hodges's speech. They characterized his speech as "shockingly paternalistic, inflammatory and utterly devoid of the quality of statesmanship expected of the head of our State."[54] Meanwhile, Austin asserted that Hodges's August 8, 1955, "inflammatory attack" on the NAACP had ironically encouraged membership in the organization: "North Carolina . . . made the greatest gain in membership during 1955 of any state in the nation."[55]

Despite the growing opposition to integration of the schools, Austin declared that blacks would not be discouraged from continuing to struggle for enforcement of racial integration. He wrote, "In this struggle toward human dignity and the right to live as free men in this land . . . God, the author of right and justice, is on our side."[56] A week later, Austin called for the governor's impeachment.[57] In September 1955, Austin praised the North Carolina Teachers Association (NCTA) for rejecting Governor Hodges's suggestion that black teachers support his plan for "voluntary segregation." Instead the NCTA reiterated its support for the *Brown* decision and encouraged the state's public officials to comply with the high court's ruling.[58]

Austin continued to shine a bright light on the machinations of the state's top government officials as they plotted to block implementation of the *Brown* decision. In October 1955, Austin called Governor Hodges; the attorney general, William B. Rodman; and Thomas Pearsall "These Terrible Three," after the Pearsall Committee reported that it was "studying abolition of the public schools and the organization of private schools, perhaps by local option in specially troubled communities."[59]

In November 1955, black college students and faculty at A&T College voiced their displeasure with the governor's policies. Prior to Hodges's speech to an assembly at the Greensboro college, some of the school's students and teachers had planned to demonstrate against the governor's segregationist policies by walking out on the speech. However, college president Ferdinand D. Bluford persuaded them not to take such an action. When Hodges addressed the students, he pronounced the term "Negro" more like "Nigra," a common practice among southern white politicians, which led the audience to protest this insult by loudly "shuffling their feet." Austin defended the students' actions, while condemning Hodges for lacking any understanding or empathy for the plight of blacks in his state. He called Hodges "a symbol of forces dedicated to deny rights and privileges" to African Americans.[60]

In February 1956, the *Times* urged Governor Hodges to "appoint a committee of at least 400 white and Negro leaders to work on the matter of obeying the court's order [in *Brown*]."[61] When Hodges acted instead to delay integration, Austin encouraged "Mayor [Emanuel J.] Evans of Durham and the Mayors of other cities and towns in this state to formulate a committee of Negro and white leaders in their communities whose members have the courage and vision to sit down and talk over the question of ending segregation in our public schools as well as in every other walk of life."[62]

Austin objected to the Pearsall Committee's plans to block implementation of the *Brown* decision in North Carolina. In April 1956, he denounced the Pearsall Committee's threats to close North Carolina schools in order to preserve segregation.[63] Four months later, Austin attacked legislators who backed the Pearsall Plan for resorting "to the lowest and most insulting tactics." Legislative support of the plan convinced Austin that "this state is . . . being run by the most ignorant and vicious element of its citizens," as he decried state legislators' vicious anti-black rhetoric.[64]

John Wheeler testified on behalf of the Negro Committee of 100 Counties, which Austin chaired, at the special session of the General Assembly on the Pearsall Plan. Wheeler argued that the plan would "undermine and destroy the public school system." He called the proposed bills "anti-democratic" and "evidence of bad faith and defiance of the supreme law of the land." He charged the Pearsall Committee with ignoring one-fourth of the state's population—African Americans—as they were excluded from committee membership. He also insisted that the plan would hurt the state's economy because the negative "publicity given racial conflict in the school controversy was driving prospective industry away from North Carolina." Wheeler argued that the dual system squandered precious public funds, and noted that in 1955 North Carolina ranked forty-four out of forty-eight states in education spending, which showed that the state did not have enough money to run two school systems. How could the state run three school systems, white, black, and private?[65]

In September 1956, with the referendum on the Pearsall Plan imminent, Austin recommended rejection of the "plan concocted by its author and backed by the Governor of this state for one expressed purpose, and that is defiance of the U.S. Supreme Court's ruling on segregation."[66] Despite a large black vote against the Pearsall Plan, the constitutional amendments were passed by a four-to-one margin.[67] A large-scale radio and television campaign orchestrated by the governor and his supporters in favor of the Pearsall amendments helped ensure passage.[68] In addition, the continued disfranchisement of most African Americans in eastern North Carolina was a significant factor in suppressing the anti–Pearsall Plan vote. In fact, the largest margin in favor of the amendments was in North Carolina's eastern counties, where few blacks were permitted to vote.[69] The only major city to reject the education amendments was Winston-Salem, where the black vote was crucial. In three large black precincts in that city, the amendments were defeated by a thirty-to-one margin.[70] In implementing the pupil assignment act and the Pearsall Plan, North Carolina acted like other southern states that sought to block implementation of the *Brown* decision.

After the Pearsall Plan was approved by an overwhelming vote of white voters and became part of the state Constitution, Austin stressed the hypocrisy of whites' fear of "mongrelization" of the white race if blacks and whites went to school together. Austin cited the long history of white men satisfying their "bestial lust" on black women with the resulting mixed-race offspring.[71]

Austin's disgust with southern Democrats, including North Carolina's governors, Umstead and Hodges, as well as other southern segregationist politicians, led him to reject the Democratic Party in 1956. In March 1956, Austin remarked, "I have never whole heartedly been connected with the Democratic Party because I could not swallow men like [segregationist Mississippi] Sen. [James] Eastland and numerous other bigots in the Democratic Party." He said he was "now a Republican 'lock, stock and barrel.'"[72] For similar reasons, other black southern newspaper editors, including Carl Murphy of the *Baltimore Afro-American*, Thomas C. Jervay of the *Wilmington Journal*, P. B. Young of the *Norfolk Journal and Guide*, and Roscoe Dunjee of the *Oklahoma City Black Dispatch* backed Dwight D. Eisenhower for president in 1956.[73] Indeed, Austin's action mirrored those of a growing segment of the black electorate that had become increasingly dissatisfied with the Democratic Party. In his bid for reelection in the 1956 presidential election, Eisenhower won about 39 percent of the black vote, an impressive increase from 1952, when he received only 21 percent of the black vote.[74] Black voters' shift to Eisenhower had more to do with their growing distaste for the Democratic Party than with any great attraction to the president or his policies. In the wake of the *Brown* decision, southern elected officials, almost all of whom were Democrats, mounted increasingly virulent campaigns against racial integration, which alienated black voters. And many black voters in North Carolina, who listened to Austin's denunciations of Governor Hodges's segregationist policies, rejected the Democratic Party's nominee for president, Adlai Stevenson, who accommodated southern white Democrats' views in order to avoid losing their votes.[75]

Throughout the 1956 campaign, Austin distanced himself from the Democratic Party. In February 1956, Austin suggested that the Democrats find a challenger to Hodges or black voters would vote Republican or not at all.[76] The following month, Austin suggested that the black vote could have a large impact on the 1956 gubernatorial election. He hoped for a liberal challenge to Hodges, but none emerged. Consequently, Hodges won a huge victory in the May 1956 gubernatorial primary.[77]

Austin believed that his embrace of the Republican Party influenced many blacks to vote Republican. He recalled a few years later that his influence was strong because blacks trusted him because they respected his integrity.[78] Indeed, Austin's influence may be seen in the results of the 1956 presidential election. In 1952, in the predominantly black Pearson election district of Durham, Stevenson defeated Eisenhower with over 91 percent of the vote. Four years later, Eisenhower defeated Stevenson, increasing his proportion of the precinct's vote from less than 9 percent to over 61 percent. In a newly created predominantly black election precinct in Durham, Eisenhower defeated Stevenson with almost 55 percent of the vote. The black election precincts in Durham also gave the majority of their votes to Kyle Hayes, the Republican candidate for governor, a rejection of Governor Hodges's pro-segregation policies.[79] Nonetheless, Hodges defeated Hayes statewide by more than two to-one.[80] In acknowledgment of their support for the president's reelection campaign, Stella and Louis Austin attended Eisenhower's second inauguration in 1957, as the guests of NCC history professor Helen Edmonds, who had seconded Eisenhower's nomination for the presidency at the Republican national convention the previous year.[81]

Although Austin identified as a Republican during the 1950s and early 1960s, he continued to work closely with the Durham Committee on Negro Affairs, which typically supported Democrats, in large part because the winner of almost any election in North Carolina was likely to be the winner of the Democratic primary. In 1957, Austin worked with the Durham Committee, which backed the winners, including black businessman John S. Stewart, in all the city council races in Durham, and helped elect Mayor Emanuel Evans to another term as mayor of the city.[82] Nonetheless, in 1958, as a Republican, Austin ran unsuccessfully for a seat on the Durham County school board.[83]

Austin's support for the Republicans and his influence in persuading other black voters to do likewise helped bring substantive changes for some black workers in Durham. During the mid-1950s, African Americans, who had been shut out of postal work in Durham, gained access to postal jobs, with more than a dozen blacks hired by the post office because of pressure from the Eisenhower administration.[84] The *Carolina Times* used the Republicans' desire to win the black vote to gain Republican backing for hiring black postal workers in Durham.[85] According to the historian Philip Rubio, by 1956, the recently formed Durham chapter of the black National Alliance of Postal Employees numbered thirty-five members.[86] Rubio recounts the story of George Booth Smith, who became "Durham's first black letter carrier and among the first black postal workers." When Smith, who graduated from NCC with undergraduate and graduate degrees, first applied for a postal job, Durham postmaster Allen told Smith, "These jobs weren't for niggers, these jobs were for white high school graduates, why you want to come up here with a master's degree?" An acquaintance of Smith who was a member of the National Alliance knew Postmaster General Arthur Summerfield and arranged for Smith to meet with Summerfield in Washington, D.C. According to Smith, Summerfield called the Durham postmaster and "told him that he was 'sending Mr. Smith back to Durham: if he doesn't have a job when he gets back there, we'll have a new postmaster [in Durham].'" Smith was hired by the Durham post office when he returned from Washington.[87]

Meanwhile, Austin continued to attack Hodges's obstructionist stance on public school integration. He said of Hodges, "There is no bigger apostle of segregation in America," with his 1956 victory showing the strength of segregationists in the state. Austin continued, "Hodges has satisfied them that he will bow down and worship the god of all gods of southern white folks— the god of segregation."[88] By contrast, the *Raleigh News and Observer* claimed that Hodges's election demonstrated the moderation of North Carolina's white voters, noting that it "was an indication that a majority of voters in North Carolina 'are not ready to be made the dupes of those who are desperately ready to sow the furies for the sake of votes.'"[89]

Austin praised North Carolina congressmen who refused to sign the Southern Manifesto, a document signed by 79 percent of all southern congressmen who pledged to block implementation of the *Brown* decision. In March 1956, Austin lauded Congressman Harold D. Cooley of eastern North Carolina for refusing to sign the Southern Manifesto even though he opposed integration of public schools. Austin noted that if Cooley was reelected it would be because of black voters and liberal white voters.[90] In April 1956, Austin praised North Carolina congressman Thurmond Chatham of Washington, North Carolina, who attacked the white supremacist Patriots of North Carolina as "obstructionists, blocking the path to the solution of the race question." Chatham also responded to questions about school integration by stating, "The Supreme Court has ruled and for going on two years it has been the final law of the land."[91] In addition to Cooley and Chatham, North Carolina congressman Charles B. Deane refused to sign the Southern Manifesto against the *Brown* decision.[92] Deane told his pastor, "I shall not sign my name to any document which will make any man anywhere a second class citizen."[93]

While Cooley survived the 1956 primary and served another ten years in Congress, Chatham and Deane's refusal to sign the Southern Manifesto led to their defeats in the 1956 primary, confirming Austin's pessimistic view about most white voters. After the election, Austin pronounced that North Carolina had "taken its place beside other backward and benighted states like Mississippi, Georgia, Alabama and South Carolina."[94] This view was confirmed by the subsequent voting record of North Carolina's congressional delegation. Only Mississippi and South Carolina's delegations had more conservative voting records from 1965 to 1974.[95]

Meanwhile, Hodges urged the North Carolina General Assembly to pass legislation to suppress the NAACP. State NAACP leader Kelly Alexander testified against the anti-NAACP bills, and Louis Austin condemned the legislation.[96] Despite Hodges's support, the state Senate rejected a bill twenty-six to fourteen that would have required the NAACP to divulge its membership and financial records to the legislature.[97] Austin urged black voters to punish state senators who voted for the bill, and to vote for those who opposed the anti-NAACP bill.[98]

When Hodges's attempt to suppress the NAACP brought pressure on black college presidents to do likewise, Austin encouraged black administrators to hold firm. In December 1957, Austin criticized A&T College president Warmoth T. Gibbs for banning the NAACP from the Greensboro campus, while 700 students sought to participate in a college chapter of the NAACP. Gibbs also fired Edwin Edmonds, former president of the Greensboro NAACP, who had served as a part-time campus minister at A&T.[99] Edmonds believed that the state legislature had pressured Gibbs to fire him because of his NAACP activism. After Edmonds was fired, his wife could not get a job (she was a teacher) because the segregationist White Citizens Council "systematically kept my wife from working." The couple was forced to leave Greensboro.[100]

In October 1958, Austin addressed the Chapel Hill Fellowship for School Integration, and dismissed the claim of white segregationists that many blacks opposed integration. Austin explained that in order to avoid retribution, blacks "learned to say what they thought the white man wanted them to say—and some are still doing it," noting that "deception was developed as a technique for survival." Following Austin's speech, a white man proposed gradual movement toward racial integration and equality, to which Austin responded, "Put yourself in the Negro's place for a moment. . . . Think of the indignities he lives with, and see whether you would want to go slow." He concluded, "We want equality now and not in some future generation."[101]

In fall 1959, black legal action and protest finally cracked the walls of segregation in Durham public schools. Backed by petitions by hundreds of black Durhamites and 225 transfer requests by black students and their parents, lawsuits filed by local and NAACP attorneys compelled the Durham city board of education to admit six black students to white schools.[102] Two years earlier, black legal pressure had convinced several school boards to admit twelve black students to previously all-white public schools in Greensboro, Charlotte, and Winston-Salem.[103] White officials agreed to desegregate these schools to preclude federal court orders to integrate schools on a larger scale. Thomas Pearsall recalled, "After the [1956] election we knew we had to move on integration or the court would come in."[104] The attorney William T. Joyner, vice-chairman of the Pearsall Committee, explained to the (all-white) North Carolina Bar Association that token desegregation was "a small price to pay" for keeping most schools segregated. He "said he had nightmares about ending up in a federal court trying to defend a school board that had rejected transfers by Negro students in a state that had never had a single Negro student admitted to any one of the approximately 2,000 white schools in North Carolina."[105] As the historian Davison Douglas has shown, in North Carolina, "token integration, unaccompanied by defiant rhetoric, enabled the state to escape judicial intervention in a manner that other, more defiant southern states did not."[106] This token desegregation reinforced North Carolina's claim that its pupil assignment law and Pearsall Plan were constitutional because the state had permitted some black students to attend white schools.[107] In desegregating schools in three cities, North Carolina joined the border states and three other southern states, Arkansas, Texas and Tennessee, that had desegregated at least some of their schools.[108]

Austin was a key supporter of the first African American students who were admitted to previously all-white schools in Durham. Joycelyn McKissick, daughter of attorney and activist Floyd McKissick, was one of the first blacks to attend Durham High School, in 1959. Joycelyn and the other black students endured terrible harassment from white students, which was regularly ignored by white teachers and administrators. The white students' attitude toward her was "overtly negative." She suffered frightful indignities; she was locked in her locker and dunked in a toilet bowl, and the school's principal and teachers offered little or no protection. She recalled that I. Beverly Lake, an avowed segregationist running for governor in 1960, visited one of her classes, and when her teacher called her name during the roll, Lake said, "I don't want to hear that damn nigra's name."[109] Osha Davidson reported, "Despite her personal strength, Joycelyn relied on her whole community, including Louis Austin, a close friend of her father's. Austin gave Joycelyn her first job, sweeping the floor at the *Carolina Times*. . . . She drew strength from the older man's steadfast support and intellectual nourishment from his commanding intelligence, which grappled with a wide range of issues."[110] By April 1960, Austin had hired Joycelyn McKissick to write a column for the *Times*, called "Mack's Quack." In one column, she compared and condemned both segregation in the United States and apartheid in South Africa.[111]

In September 1961, after two other black students, Charlotte Brame and Maxine Bledsoe, who helped to desegregate Durham High School, were admitted to North Carolina College, Austin urged local black organizations and individuals to help fund these courageous students' educations. The *Times* reported that these young women might be unable to attend college for lack of funds, but had they stayed at Hillside High School, and not gone to Durham High School, they would likely have earned scholarships given to top students at Hillside.[112]

Recognizing that token desegregation of schools in a few North Carolina cities was intended to perpetuate segregation in most of the state's schools, Austin backed litigation to uphold the *Brown* decision and fully integrate public schools in North Carolina. In 1959, Austin praised a longtime ally, the attorney Conrad Pearson, who sued on behalf of black students from Durham and Chapel Hill who had been denied their requests to enter white schools. Austin observed, "The struggle toward the goal of full integration is going to be long, hard and expensive, but we think whatever the price, it is well worth the sacrifice. . . . Our cause is right and just and . . . in the end we will be victorious."[113] Austin applauded Thurgood Marshall's 1960 attack on black leaders in much of North Carolina for not pursuing public school integration with the vigor of Durham, where over 200 black students had applied for reassignment to historically white schools.[114]

Austin regularly reported on the court case to integrate Durham's public schools. Local attorneys Pearson, M. Hugh Thompson, and William Marsh Jr., joined by NAACP attorney Jack Greenberg, represented the plaintiffs. In December 1960, the *Times* reported that Rencher N. Harris, the sole black school board member, testified that if Durham students were assigned to schools without regard to race, 40 percent of the students in historically white schools would be black.[115] In August 1961, the *Times* reported that Harris criticized the school board for flagrantly violating federal law by discriminating against black applicants to white schools by rejecting 129 transfer requests in Durham.[116] After a judge ordered that the Durham school board reconsider the applications, six black students were assigned to white schools in August 1961.[117]

Meanwhile, the *Times* publicized the heroic school integration efforts by blacks in other counties, who braved intimidation and violence by white segregationists. In 1957, in Caswell County, about forty miles northwest of Durham, black farmer Jasper Brown and over forty other parents applied to transfer their children to all-white schools. After the names of the applicants were printed in the local newspaper, the white supremacist Caswell County Patriots of North Carolina sent a threatening letter to the home of every applicant. When the applications for transfer were rejected by the school board, the parents, represented by Durham attorneys Conrad Pearson and William Marsh Jr., filed suit in 1958. That year, Brown also ran unsuccessfully for the Caswell County school board, which was all white. In succeeding years, the *Caswell Messenger* regularly published the names of black parents and their children who applied for transfers to historically white schools, leading to harassment by white segregationists.[118]

In January 1963, under a U.S. district court order, sixteen black students, including the four children of Jasper and Odessa Brown, enrolled in previously all-white schools.[119] After Jasper Brown dropped his children off at school for the first day of class at their new schools, his car was "followed by a carload of whites who cursed at him and called him nigger." Brown stopped at the sheriff's office to ask for protection, but the sheriff told him to "get lost."[120] Before leaving for the six-mile drive home to his farm, he stopped to pick up a suit from the dry cleaners. When he went into the cleaners, he saw several whites search his car. When the African American owner of the cleaners gave Brown his suit, he surreptitiously placed a gun in the bag, as the owner knew that Brown was in danger. On the drive home, several cars with white men followed Brown, and one car "swerved in front of him, and immediately slammed on brakes. Jasper [Brown] was forced off the road, into a ditch. . . . Four white men proceeded . . . towards Jasper. They carried clubs, baseball bats. One carried a rope."[121] As the white men pounded on Brown's car with the bats and clubs, Brown, fearing for his life, took out the hand gun and fired at the men, wounding two, and they all fled the scene. Meanwhile, the black students in the white schools were harassed terribly, the Browns' house was bombed, and one of the Browns' sons was shot while stepping off the school bus. He survived. Then Jasper Brown was arrested for shooting the white men who had threatened to kill him. To avoid a jury trial, which he believed would have resulted in a severe prison sentence, he pleaded no contest. The judge sentenced Brown to ninety days in jail, after which he and his family fled North Carolina.[122]

In March 1963, Austin voiced his disgust with the "cowardly acts" and "depravity" of whites, who attacked, threatened, and yelled nasty epithets at black students who were attending desegregated schools in Caswell County. He praised the moral strength of the black students. Austin also derided the silence of the white church, indicting white Christian pastors and congregations for their moral bankruptcy. He predicted that the reprehensible actions of white southerners would compel federal protection of black students in southern schools.[123]

Back in Durham, in November 1959, Austin had advised black voters to turn down a proposed multimillion-dollar Durham County school bond issue because there was no evidence that it would be used to implement integration.[124] Three months later, Austin backed black school board member R. N. Harris's statement that he would oppose the bond issue if it "would perpetuate segregation."[125] In April 1960, just before the vote, Austin wrote, "Both the city and county boards of education have followed such a rigid pattern of segregation in administering the affairs of the city and county schools that no self-respecting Negro can find it possible to cast his ballot in favor of the $6 million school bond issue."[126] Following Austin's lead, most black voters opposed the bond issue. The four largest black precincts rejected the bond issue by a margin of almost eight to one. However, black hostility to the bond issue, according to the *Durham Morning Herald*, spurred white support, and a very large white voter turnout, ensuring passage of the bond issue.[127]

In 1959, Austin criticized the sole black Atlanta school board member Rufus Clement, former president of the Atlanta University system, who voted in favor of a plan that would keep Atlanta public schools segregated. Austin wrote that Clement "may have increased his stature with the white people, but as a leader of his own race he has shrunk to a size that is less than a pygmy in the estimation of Negroes in Georgia and the rest of the nation."[128] According to historian Tomiko Brown-Nagin, Clement "disavowed involvement with the NAACP and its push to desegregate Atlanta's schools," and endorsed the otherwise all-white school board's disingenuous statements that it had no formal segregation policy.[129] Austin stressed that Clement's actions showed the necessity of having more than token black representation in public office.[130]

Although Terry Sanford, Hodges's successor as governor, enjoyed a more liberal reputation than did his predecessor, his policies were not appreciably different with respect to integration of the state's public schools. In March 1962, Austin showed his contempt for Governor Sanford's lip service for "quality education" for blacks, when he did little to integrate public schools. Austin called Sanford's "perfunctory visit to several Negro schools . . . nauseating if not disgusting," noting that "it is utterly impossible to obtain the maximum of quality education for all the people under a segregated school system." Austin asserted that as "long as the damnable Pearsall Plan remains in force in North Carolina," Sanford and other white leaders should keep quiet about providing quality education for blacks. Instead, Sanford should repeal the Pearsall Plan.[131] In October 1962, after Sanford's statewide tour trumpeting his campaign for "quality education" in the state, Austin reminded the governor that there could be no quality education in a segregated system.[132]

Austin's attacks on Sanford were right on the mark. As governor, Sanford did little to speed up the integration of schools in North Carolina. In 1962, eight years after the *Brown* decision, the U.S. Commission on Civil Rights revealed that only eleven of 173 North Carolina school districts had any black students in desegregated classes, and in those districts, less "than one-tenth of 1 percent of the" black students were in desegregated schools.[133] By early 1963, only 901 black students in fifty-two schools in seventeen school districts in North Carolina, with a total student enrollment of 1.1 million in the state, were enrolled in historically white public schools. While this total was incredibly low, it represented a fourfold increase over the total for 1962.[134] In the fall of 1964, at the end of Sanford's term as governor, the state's superintendent of public instruction reported that less than 1 percent of all black students were attending previously all-white schools and less than 0.2 percent of all white students were attending previously all-black schools.[135] Despite North Carolina's claims of progressivism, it operated one of the least integrated school systems in the South, ranking "behind Florida, Tennessee, Texas and Virginia by 1965."[136]

Meanwhile, Austin continued to press for public school integration in Durham. In June 1962, he attacked the Durham school board for failing to integrate its schools, encouraging black parents and the black community to protest this inaction with lawsuits, picketing, and sit-ins.[137] By early 1963, Durham had the second most black students in desegregated schools in the state with 152, behind Charlotte with 427 black students in desegregated schools. In Durham, the relatively high numbers were due to the constant pressure exerted by the lawsuit and the black community, including leaders like Austin.[138] The fact that so few black students attended desegregated schools in the state was an indication of the formidable obstacles devised by white segregationists.

While he devoted tremendous energy to integrating the city school system in Durham, Austin also shined a light on Durham County's failure to desegregate its public schools. In February 1963, he denounced county school officials for failing to desegregate even one school, while most of the city schools were at least minimally desegregated. He further noted the gross inequities between the facilities at the county's black and white schools. He urged blacks in the county to demand integration of the segregated schools, which he termed "unchristian and unlawful."[139]

After the Durham city school district won approval of a $7.5 million bond issue in May 1964, Austin illuminated the gross inequities in the distribution of the proceeds. The *Times* published statistics that demonstrated the inequitable spending on white schools compared with black schools. While $1.25 million was allocated for two white Durham schools, only $175,000 was allocated for a black school, Pearsontown.[140] Austin commented, "Until integration becomes a two-way street affair, with white pupils being transferred to Negro schools on an equal or lesser degree, as the transfer of Negro pupils to heretofore white schools, we will continue to view with suspicion such inequitable allocation as that announced by the Durham County Board of Education last week." Austin called on the DCNA to protest the inequitable allocation of funds.[141]

The passage of the Civil Rights Act in 1964, in response to widespread civil rights protests, provided advocates of integration with strong federal government support. The inclusion of Title VI in that legislation marked a turning point in the integration of public schools, as it empowered the U.S. attorney general to file lawsuits to integrate public schools and authorized the federal government to withdraw funds from districts that violated integration orders. In April 1965, Congress passed the Elementary and Secondary Education Act, sending more than $1 billion in aid to schools, which reinforced Title VI because school systems now risked losing substantial federal funding if they refused to integrate.[142] In response to the Civil Rights Act, the North Carolina attorney general announced in February 1965 that each of the state's school districts was required to issue a desegregation plan.[143] According to Gary Orfield, "Enforcement of the new law by the Johnson administration and the Warren Court turned a region in which school segregation was almost total into the nation's most integrated within five years of the issuance of the first desegregation guidelines."[144]

Austin used the Civil Rights Act to increase pressure on local white officials to integrate schools. In January 1965, he suggested that if states continued to stall on school integration, then the federal government should place all U.S. schools "under federal supervision." Indeed, the federal government was threatening to cut off federal education funds to Georgia and Mississippi if they did not fully comply with school integration.[145]

As black activists and federal government pressure compelled school districts to increase the pace of integration, white-dominated school boards used their power to punish black interests to the benefit of whites. One manifestation of this dynamic was the firing of hundreds of black teachers. In May 1965, the North Carolina Teachers Association (NCTA), representing black teachers, protested the firing of black teachers, leading Austin to demand investigations of each case. Nonetheless, by the end of the 1965 school year, about 500 black teachers had been fired in North Carolina.[146] In August 1965, NCTA president Elliot B. Palmer said that the firing of black teachers was out of control.[147] So although the black struggle for integration of public schools was finally making some headway, powerful whites in North Carolina and throughout the South continued to employ their authority to the detriment of African Americans. Nonetheless, black activists and their allies refused to give up as they fought for equal opportunity in all facets of American life.

Contemporaneous with black activists' fight to integrate public schools in Durham and throughout the state, an overlapping group of black freedom fighters took to the streets to challenge Jim Crow in public facilities. In April 1957, when the Carolina League's Durham Bulls minor league baseball team finally employed black ballplayers, a full six years after the league's Danville, Virginia, team had done so, twenty blacks attempted to integrate seating at Durham Athletic Park. Austin denounced the team's irrational and cowardly action in upholding segregated seating, and predicted that many black spectators would steer clear of Bulls games due to the team's misguided policy. He also pointed out that the continued segregation of seating was absurd, especially given the fact that when black baseball and football teams played games at the same Durham Athletic Park, no segregated seating policy was enforced.[148]

Two months later, in June 1957, seven young men and women, led by Rev. Douglas Moore, pastor of Asbury Temple Methodist Church, staged what was likely the first sit-in to challenge racially segregated seating at a restaurant in North Carolina. These bold, young African Americans defied segregated seating at the Royal Ice Cream Parlor, located in a black section of Durham. Although traditional accounts of the sit-in movement start with the Greensboro sit-ins, this Durham sit-in occurred almost three years before the more heralded protests of February 1960. Moore was part of a group called ACTION that had been planning to challenge segregation of public facilities in Durham. In response to the protest, the police were called and arrested the young activists. Unlike many of Durham's black leaders who opposed this type of direct action, Austin was a key supporter.[149]

Even before the Royal Ice Cream sit-in, Moore, who had gone to school with Martin Luther King Jr. when both attended Boston University's School of Theology, had challenged Jim Crow in Virginia and North Carolina. In October 1956, Moore wrote King, then in the eleventh month of the Montgomery Bus Boycott, of his own personal resistance to segregation on buses. He described refusing to move to the back of local buses in Newport News, Virginia, and Asheboro and Durham, North Carolina. On an interstate bus ride from Richmond, Virginia, to Greensboro, North Carolina, Moore again refused to sit in the black section of the bus. After the driver ordered Moore to move toward the back of the bus, the pastor replied that he "would die praying for him before I would move. Each time that he stopped he gave me a mean look but he only received a smile from me. We arrived in Greensboro with no difficulty." Moore told King, "I would have died in that seat. Whenever a person threatens us with brutality and even death he is assuming that we value our lives more than eternal principles. I feel that my philosophical and theological belief in immortality comes to my aid in this situation as well as my Christian faith. . . . When a man is afraid to die for what he believes to be true his concept of what is ultimately real is shallow."[150] Given Moore's philosophy of resistance, it is not surprising that Austin was an unequivocal supporter.

In the month before the Royal Ice Cream sit-in, Moore continued to challenge racial segregation in Durham. In May, he urged the city council to desegregate the Carolina movie theater and the Durham County Library.[151] In mid-June, Moore and his family sought entrance to the Long Meadow Park swimming pool, but they were turned away.[152]

The Royal Ice Cream sit-in did not enjoy the support of the traditional black leadership in the city. During the late 1950s, Durham's black leaders, mostly businessmen, who dominated the DCNA, opposed direct challenges to racial segregation. They preferred behind-the-scenes negotiations with white power brokers. In 1958, Richard K. Barksdale, dean of the North Carolina College Graduate School, told historian August Meier that Moore "wanted to imitate Martin Luther King, has come down and agitated things, but gets nowhere, as [he] lacks endorsement of [the Durham] Committee."[153] The DCNA feared that the 1957 sit-in would upset the traditional method that black leaders employed to deal with problems whereby they met secretly with white leaders with, in Osha Gray Davidson's words, change coming "graciously and slowly."[154] In the 1970s, black businessman and DCNA leader John S. Stewart recalled, "Moore was ahead of his times and was too outspoken for the N.A.A.C.P. and the Durham Committee on Negro Affairs." William Marsh Jr., who defended the seven protesters, called Moore "an outsider . . . who moved fast—too fast for Durham, North Carolina."[155] According to Virginia Williams, one of the participants in the Royal Ice Cream sit-in, "It caught the black leaders completely by surprise, the attorneys and all of them."[156]

However, Austin was one leader who was not caught by surprise, and he backed the protest group from the start. While black leaders "called a meeting" to consider what action to take, Austin, according to Williams, "immediately came down to the jailhouse because he wanted to be the one to bail us out." By the time Austin arrived at the jail, however, the protesters had already been bailed out. Williams recalled that Austin "was upset because he did not get there in time to actually bail us out. He wanted to do that."[157]

As he had for decades, Austin opposed the gradualism of the city's more moderate black businessmen. In fact, less than two weeks before the sit-in, Austin had published an editorial that chastised Durham's black leadership for failing to take bold action to challenge racial segregation. He wrote,

This newspaper senses a stagnation that is beginning to creep over the
Durham Committee on Negro Affairs which, if allowed to continue, is
certain to spell its doom. . . . The Durham [black] Ministerial Alliance . . .
is dragging its feet on these same vital issues. . . . The old guard of the
Alliance appears to have smothered efforts of the younger and progressive members to push the segregation question to the front. Thus the two
most influential organizations among Negroes of the city have become
practically "dead ducks" on the all-important question of civil rights. . . .
There comes a time in the life of an organization when it needs new
blood, new faces and some new ideas. . . . Certainly, this is no hour to be
at ease but an hour for positive action. The struggle for freedom and
human dignity for all must go on. It must not be sacrificed on the altar of
greed and power merely to obtain a few crumbs for the few. What we do
now will determine the destiny of thousands who come after us. God
forbid that we falter or recoil from performing our solemn duty.[158]

Austin's unsparing criticism of older black leaders, many of whom were exec-
utives with NC Mutual or the Mechanics and Farmers Bank, likely cost the
paper advertising. Indeed, in 1964, Austin noted that 95 percent of the paper's
advertising came from white-owned businesses.[159]

When the Royal Ice Cream case went to trial, the black attorneys William
Marsh Jr. and M. Hugh Thompson defended the seven defendants before a
packed courtroom. The defendants were convicted of trespassing, and on appeal, with the attorneys Floyd McKissick and Conrad Pearson joining the defense team, the state supreme court affirmed the ruling of the lower court; the
NAACP paid the defendants' fines.[160]

One month after the sit-in, DCNA's economic committee, led by the
attorney Floyd McKissick and the businessman Nathan White, met with
Moore to discuss the possibility of mounting a direct action campaign against
segregation in Durham. While several participants in the meeting supported
direct action, the committee ultimately decided not to take action, thus miss-
ing an opportunity to mount a strong challenge to the status quo.[161]

Nonetheless, blacks continued to challenge racial segregation of public facilities in Durham. One month after the Royal Ice Cream sit-in, NCC student
Joseph G. Riley and Hillside High School tennis star Joe Williams attempted
to desegregate the all-white Forest Hills tennis court. Riley and Williams
were arrested and charged with trespassing and violating the racial segregation rules of the city's recreation department. As Williams was only fifteen
years old, his case was handled by the juvenile court, which placed him on

probation. John Wheeler and William Marsh employed traditional DCNA tactics by lobbying the Durham city manager to convince the city to drop the case against Riley and to negotiate an end to the whites-only policy at the Forest Hills tennis court.[162] Initial talks failed with the city mounting a perfunctory prosecution, with the case being dropped when the arresting officer, by design, failed to appear at the trial. The city did not want to put its discriminatory policies on trial. Austin blasted the city's leadership for refusing to negotiate. He declared that this was just one more piece of evidence that "exposed the façade of deceit behind which southern whites operate as advocates of moderation."[163] It also showed the ineffectiveness of behind-the-scenes meetings between black and white leaders. Direct action was needed to truly challenge Jim Crow law. In the 1960s, this tactic would bear fruit.

CHAPTER SIX

The Gospel of the Sit-In

Direct Action, 1960–1965

On February 1, 1960, three years after the Royal Ice Cream sit-in, four black first-year students from historically black A&T College in Greensboro staged a sit-in at the lunch counter of the downtown Woolworth's, an action that transformed the civil rights movement. Austin was quick to support the A&T students, as in Osha Gray Davidson's words, he "preached the gospel of the sit-in that Saturday."[1] Austin pronounced the student protest "the most encouraging incident that has occurred within the past five years." He praised the students' "courage and independence." He also called for boycotts of Woolworth's in Greensboro, Durham, and elsewhere, to support the students in Greensboro. Austin knew that one sit-in does not make a movement, so it was incredibly important that African Americans in Durham and other cities join Greensboro's black college students in taking direct action. The long-time activist's hope that the students' action would "awaken members of the race, in North Carolina, if not the entire South, to the vicious practice of 'for whites only,'" was more than redeemed as the movement quickly spread to Durham, and within weeks to many cities throughout North Carolina and the South.[2]

It is worth noting that the Greensboro sit-in's impact on the movement was predicated on other communities following its lead, and the first to do so was Durham. One week after the Greensboro protest began, black students from North Carolina College (NCC) initiated a sit-in at the Woolworth's lunch counter in Durham. NCC student Callis Brown "first heard of the [Greensboro] lunch-counter protest [on February 1, 1960] ... while watching the nightly news at his parents' home in Durham. His reaction was immediate: 'We ought to do that here.' ... Brown telephoned a few of his college friends and asked what they thought. The unanimous response was, 'Let's do it.'" But before taking action, the following morning, Brown "went to see the man he had long considered his mentor, Louis Austin. Should NCC students take up the sit-in? The publisher smiled at Brown and nodded."[3]

On Saturday night, February 6, NCC students Lacy Streeter, president of the NAACP chapter at NCC; Callis Brown; and Robert Kornegay, student government president, convened a meeting of 200 students to plan the Durham protests.[4] In order to ensure the continued development of the movement, "NCC student leaders contacted their counterparts at Shaw University in Raleigh and urged them to orchestrate their own sit-in and to pass the word along to other black schools."[5] On Monday, February 8, twenty students, seventeen from NCC and three from Duke University, staged a sit-in at Woolworth's in downtown Durham.[6] The *Times* provided extensive coverage of the sit-ins. In the second issue following the beginning of the Greensboro sit-ins, the front page of the *Times* included several photos of sit-ins and several articles. Stories focused on Greensboro and Durham but also discussed the spread of the sit-in movement to Winston-Salem, Raleigh, Fayetteville, and Charlotte.[7] Austin criticized the *Durham Morning Herald* for denouncing the sit-in tactic. When the white daily said there had to be a "better way" than the sit-ins, Austin replied the better way would be if whites would follow the golden rule, to treat others as they would like to be treated. But since whites refused to do so, blacks had no alternative but to file lawsuits and pursue direct action.[8] Quinton Baker, an NCC student and a local movement leader in the early 1960s, recalled, "Louis Austin was the only black businessman consistently on their [students'] side. . . . [and Floyd] McKissick . . . was our leader."[9]

While the *Carolina Times* was a consistent and outspoken supporter of the sit-ins, Raleigh's black newspaper, the *Carolinian*, was less so. The editor of the *Carolinian* criticized the participation of high school students in the protests. He argued that high school students were too immature and their parents should not allow them to participate in the protests.[10]

In contrast with its reaction to the 1957 Royal Ice Cream sit-in, the DCNA quickly backed the 1960 sit-ins, rejecting calls by white leaders that black leaders stop the student protests. The DCNA declared, "We have an obligation to support any peaceful movement which seeks to remove from the customs of our beloved Southland those unfair practices based upon race and color which have for so long a time been recognized as a stigma on our way of life and stumbling block to social and economic progress of the region."[11]

The week after the Durham sit-ins began, Southern Christian Leadership Conference leader Martin Luther King Jr. came to Durham to speak in support of the protests. Appropriately, Louis Austin, who by this time had been a leader in the black freedom struggle for three decades, introduced King to the overflow crowd of 1,500 at White Rock Baptist Church.[12] King's February 16 speech became known as the "Fill up the Jails" speech. He told the crowd, "Let us not fear going to jail. If officials threaten to arrest us for standing up for our rights, we must answer by saying that we are willing and prepared to fill up the jails of the South."[13]

Unlike many other older black leaders, Austin recognized that the students who had started the sit-in movement should retain leadership. When he heard that some "school officials" in Durham were trying to take control of the sit-in movement, he denounced them, asserting that the students who began and continued the sit-ins should be the key participants in any negotiations with store officials.[14] Austin also advised sit-in critics that the black community was united in support of the student movement. Moreover, he asserted that the students would not back down, which was demonstrated by the willingness of eleven black students from Raleigh's Shaw University and Saint Augustine's College to go to jail for the cause. Austin also suggested that a boycott of stores was a likely next tactic. Steeled by decades of struggle, he counseled African Americans "to gird themselves for a long, hard and bitter struggle before the goal of human dignity is achieved."[15]

On February 27, 1960, Austin praised white student protesters for their willingness to risk arrest in serving the cause of equal access to lunch counters. That week, black and white protesters were arrested in Winston-Salem, the white protesters from Wake Forest College and the black protesters from Winston-Salem Teachers College.[16]

The sit-ins received strong support from the faculty at NCC. In April 1960, 103 members of the college's faculty signed an American Association of University Professors (AAUP) petition supporting the student sit-in movement. Mathematics professor C. Elwood Boulware, president of the NCC chapter of the AAUP, organized faculty support.[17]

In May 1960, Austin praised black student protesters for their bravery and reprimanded white students who had viciously attacked some of the protesters in Durham. Austin wrote, "The Negro youths are to be saluted for their courage, manhood and fortitude, from which they are daily growing morally stronger while the white youths who attack them are to be pitied for the lack of control and cowardice they have exhibited."[18]

A devout Christian who served as president of the Interdenominational Ushers Association of North Carolina, Austin was quick to criticize white Christians for their hypocrisy in opposing equality for all God's children.[19] In April 1960, Austin criticized students at Winston-Salem's Wake Forest College, a Baptist school, for voting overwhelmingly 1,346 to 282 against the admission of black students.[20] Austin was not surprised by the vote: "We have long since learned that the last place to look for Christianity is in a so-called [white] Christian church or [white] Christian church-related institution. Especially is this true when it is a matter of the members of such an institution accepting Negroes as members."[21] In March 1962, Austin reported that several

NCC students had been refused entrance to three white churches in Durham, while some white churches had admitted NCC students. He condemned the churches that excluded the NCC students for attempting "to justify their dastardly act by taking refuge behind the ungodly iron curtain of race hatred."[22]

While Austin generally did not participate in direct action protests, on at least one occasion he joined the lunch counter sit-in at Woolworth's in downtown Durham. Photographer and journalist Alex Rivera, an old friend, recalled that Austin said to Rivera, "Let's go down to the Woolworth's store and sit in and see how they're getting along." So Rivera and Austin walked over to Woolworth's. According to Rivera, "there was a vacant seat at the counter. So lo and behold Louis Austin just had to sit in this vacant seat. Somebody poured something hot on him. It was coffee or soup or something. He jumped up and started screaming and carrying on and he said, 'Now listen.' Says, 'Those down at that end and that end, those are the non-violent ones.' He said, 'I'm violent as hell.'" Rivera and Austin "left there with him and his suit messed up and came out. We didn't do much with it."[23] So that was an occasion when Austin's oft-voiced opposition to violence did not extend to the case of self-defense.

While many sit-ins occurred in the larger North Carolina cities, which received the lion's share of news coverage, there were also protests in smaller towns, and Austin made sure that these events were covered in the *Times*. For example, on April 9, 1960, Austin reported that eleven black "students were arrested and jailed" in Statesville, in western North Carolina, for "participating in a sit-down demonstration at a local F. W. Woolworth store lunch counter."[24]

As the summer dragged on, it became clear that the determination of black protesters was greater than the resistance of white-owned businesses. On August 1, 1960, Durham's lunch counters were integrated after six months of protests.[25] White businesses feared that the movement might expand its boycott to all white businesses in downtown Durham if they did not integrate downtown lunch counters.[26] By early August, nine North Carolina cities had integrated their lunch counters, and over sixty cities throughout the South had done so.[27]

Having succeeded in integrating lunch counters, student protesters sought to broaden their attack on racially segregated public facilities in North Carolina, and the *Times* provided extensive coverage. In January 1961, the *Times* publicized early efforts to desegregate movie theaters in Durham and Chapel Hill. In Durham, NAACP Youth Council members Billie Thorpe and Bruce

Baines tried to purchase tickets at the ticket window for whites at the Center Theater and the Carolina Theater in Durham but were refused tickets. In Chapel Hill, over 100 blacks and whites, including students from NCC, the University of North Carolina at Chapel Hill, and Chapel Hill high schools, picketed the Carolina Theater in Chapel Hill when management refused to permit integrated seating during showings of *Porgy and Bess*. Charles Jones, white pastor of the Community Church in Chapel Hill, led the protest effort.[28]

Austin spoke out in support of the movie theater protests, which by late January were occurring regularly in several North Carolina cities, including Durham. After the Durham theaters' management defended themselves by saying they charged less money for blacks to sit in the balconies, Austin called their comments "weak, stupid and about as asinine as any we have ever heard by so-called intelligent persons." He added, "It is not the pocketbook . . . of the Negro that is being injured, but his soul when he is asked to accept facilities or accommodations different than those given other American citizens." Austin predicted that the anti-segregation protests would spread until they put an end to racial injustice.[29] The theater protests in Durham were led by John Edwards, a Durham Business College student and Durham NAACP youth leader; Claude Daniels, a graduate of Durham Business College; Billie Thorpe and Bruce Baines, NAACP youth chapter members; and Dave Opton, a Duke student.[30] Protests against segregated theaters in Greensboro and Winston-Salem also began in January 1961.[31] Austin singled out white student protesters for special praise in early February 1961, commending them for their willingness to stand up against the views of most whites, including members of their own families.[32] When several NCC and Duke University professors joined the movie theater protests in Durham, Austin noted that they were apparently the first college faculty members in the state to picket against segregation.[33]

In March 1962, with the Carolina Theater in Durham still segregated, and negotiations between the NAACP youth council, the theater management, and the city at a standstill, Austin encouraged the theater to integrate, but if it did not, he insisted that a lawsuit should be a last, but perhaps necessary, resort.[34] In Chapel Hill, two movie theaters, the Carolina and the Varsity, had integrated seating by March 1962, under pressure from protests by hundreds of students, while management of the Carolina Theater in Durham refused to do so, despite continued protests. The Durham City Council refused to back the integration of the Carolina Theater.[35] In July 1962, eight black Durham students, ages twenty to twenty-two, sued the Carolina Theater in federal court to integrate the theater.[36]

Meanwhile, the 1960s protests led by students from Duke, NCC, and Durham's Hillside High School inspired renewed efforts to integrate the Royal Ice Cream parlor.[37] In November 1962, Austin commended the students who continued to picket and boycott the ice cream parlor, which refused to integrate its seating.[38] Four months later, the *Times* reported that a boycott of the company's products sold to the public schools as well as picketing convinced the company's owner to remove the barriers between separate dining areas for blacks and whites.[39] However, this concession did not mean that the facility had truly integrated its seating, as black customers were not permitted "to sit down and be seated at a table with white people or even located in a room that is serving white people." Austin urged a continued boycott of wholesale and retail sales of Royal.[40] Eventually, the pressure from the boycotts and the protests forced the ice cream parlor to cease operations. One of the original participants in the 1957 sit-in, Virginia Williams, remarked, "The Royal Ice Cream parlor was shut down. We did force him out of business."[41]

Like other black activists, Austin realized that access to public facilities would be of limited value if blacks' economic opportunities remained severely restricted because of widespread racial discrimination. In fact, in Durham, during the 1950s, African Americans' economic status declined when compared with that of whites. While blacks in Durham earned about 60 percent of whites' median income in 1949, they earned only about 51 percent of whites' median income a decade later.[42] Consequently, Austin agitated against private-sector and public-sector employment discrimination. He also regularly backed labor unions' efforts to win wage increases and improved conditions for workers but criticized the widespread racial discrimination practiced by many unions, which diminished economic opportunities for African Americans.

During the late 1950s and early 1960s, Austin had a complicated relationship with the labor movement. While he was ideologically in support of strong labor unions because they could advance the rights and goals of workers, he had no patience for the marginalization of black workers by whites in the labor movement. In 1959, Austin reproved George Meany, head of the AFL-CIO, for attacking black labor and civil rights activist A. Philip Randolph, who had criticized racism in the nation's largest labor confederation. Meany reportedly challenged Randolph, "Who in the hell gave you the authority to speak for [the] whole Negro race?" Austin countered by insisting that most blacks would be pleased to have Randolph speak for them. He supported Randolph's position, asserting that "there are some segments of the AFL-CIO that stink to high heaven with discrimination[,] a fact of which every Negro of average intelligence in this country is fully aware."[43] Austin observed that Meany had "lost stature as a labor leader by defending Jim Crow locals within the ranks of labor."[44] In 1962, Austin resumed his attack on Meany, this time for his criticism of the NAACP, which had denounced the labor movement for racial discrimination against black workers.[45]

In June 1962, Austin indicted Liggett and Myers and American Tobacco Company for their discriminatory training, hiring, promotion, and pay practices, which were grossly unfair to black tobacco workers.[46] In January 1963, the *Times* reported that North Carolina's factory workers were tied with those in Mississippi with the lowest average wages in the nation. Austin urged labor unions to integrate and fight for higher wages for black workers.[47]

Six years earlier, Austin had raised the hackles of labor leaders when he praised R. J. Reynolds Tobacco Company for its treatment of its workers, who were not unionized. In 1957, Austin applauded the Winston-Salem-based firm for providing its workers, many of whom were black, paid vacations, a pension plan, and a stock purchase plan. Austin contrasted Reynolds' policies with those of Holly Farms Poultry Co., in the same city, whose "foremen . . . used vile language in the presence of women and felt free to enter the dressing room at any time."[48] Durham labor leader Wilbur Hobby took exception to Austin's praise of Reynolds. To his credit, Austin published Hobby's critical letter in the *Times*. Hobby, who worked for the American Tobacco Company and had spoken to many Reynolds employees, reported, "The fear that the company has instilled in many of its employees is not what I call a fine example of management employee relationship." Hobby emphasized that Reynolds was the only nonunion cigarette company in the country and that the company employed paternalism to keep the union out.[49]

Nonetheless, Austin regularly voiced his appreciation for labor unions' support for the rights and opportunities of working people. In December 1957, Austin praised the president of the International Union of Electrical Workers and vice president of the nation's largest labor confederation, the AFL-CIO, James B. Carey, who opposed anti-union efforts, including right-to-work laws, taxes on union members, laws that charged exorbitant fees for union organizer licenses, and racist tactics to destroy unions. Austin encouraged black leaders to "identify themselves with the working man."[50]

After Terry Sanford's election in 1960, Austin urged the governor-elect to call a statewide conference to address the lack of employment opportunity for African Americans in both the private and the public sectors.[51] Following the late November 1960 television broadcast of CBS newsman Edward Murrow's *Harvest of Shame*, detailing the oppressive conditions faced by American migrant farm workers, Austin demanded that North Carolina officials ensure that these workers were protected by worker compensation and child labor laws, that the children were provided access to public education, and that these workers were paid a living wage.[52]

In April 1961, Austin reaffirmed his support for the labor movement, but also emphasized his opposition to segregated labor unions: "As long as segregated unions exist, the labor movement will continue to operate at a disadvantage, not only to the Negro worker but to the white worker as well."[53] In May 1961, Austin urged President John F. Kennedy to back up his recommendation that labor union leaders stop excluding black workers from skilled work.[54]

Meanwhile, black activists, including Austin, attorney Floyd McKissick, and many others, staged protests for equal employment opportunity for black workers in Durham. The editor played a key role in backing local campaigns to compel white Durham businesses to hire black workers. In February 1961, Austin publicized the campaign by the DCNA to persuade white-owned retail businesses to hire blacks as sales clerks. That month, a downtown Durham store agreed to hire two black clerks in response to DCNA pressure. Unlike in other southern cities, the DCNA had not employed a boycott, but the *Times* suggested that a boycott would persuade more white retailers to hire blacks.[55]

Austin's suggestion became reality when in March 1961, black students in Durham's NAACP youth chapter rejected the DCNA campaign of gentle persuasion, instead orchestrating a boycott of stores that maintained segregated facilities and refused to hire black clerks. The *Carolina Times* played a critical role in the boycott by publishing the names of the stores targeted by the boycott in each edition of the paper. This made it easy for black supporters to know which stores to avoid, and proved quite effective.[56] As stores hired black clerks, they were removed from the *Times'* boycott list.[57] In July 1961, Austin castigated Carolina Power and Light for failing to comply "with President Kennedy's executive order which bans discrimination in employment for firms which receive government contracts."[58] That same month, five Durham stores were still being boycotted by the local Durham youth chapter of the NAACP.[59] In October 1961, the A&P grocery store was removed from the boycott list after it promoted a black employee to "cash register checker."[60] The same month, Austin gave his editorial support for a statewide NAACP boycott of Winn-Dixie grocery stores because they refused to hire blacks.[61]

In August 1961, Austin backed a strike by Durham's black sanitation workers. He reported that black sanitation workers were excluded from driving sanitation trucks, with those higher-paid jobs restricted to white workers. Truck drivers were paid about 70 percent more than the $1.00 per hour that many of the black workers received. In fact, black workers' wages had been cut in the last few years. Austin advised the workers to join a union, which could better fight for their interests.[62] He criticized black business leaders for failing to help the sanitation workers, noting that only a white labor leader had come to their aid.[63]

In late July and early August 1962, the direct action movement in Durham expanded with the Congress of Racial Equality (CORE) and the NAACP joining forces to mount a picketing campaign against retail businesses with segregated facilities and those that refused to hire black workers in all but menial positions.[64] After four students, including Joycelyn McKissick, were arrested and sentenced to thirty-day jail terms for staging a sit-in at Durham's Howard Johnson's restaurant, a massive protest with over 1,000 persons was held at that restaurant in August 1962.[65] Austin praised the demonstration and called for continued protests until the movement's goals were achieved.[66]

Later that month, prior to another mass protest at Howard Johnson's, Austin addressed an "overflow" crowd at a protest meeting at "steaming hot" St. Mark's African Methodist Episcopal (AME) Zion Church in Durham. According to the *Amsterdam News*, Austin encouraged protesters to persevere with "courage and determination." He told his audience, "If they spit in our faces we can take it; if they hit us we can take it." He concluded, "We have suffered so long under the weight of segregation that a few more white man's slaps won't hurt us." Meanwhile, U.S. senator from North Carolina B. Everett Jordan, the owner of Durham's Howard Johnson's franchise, made no public comment.[67]

In December 1962, during the Christmas season, integrated groups of protesters sought service and were turned away at several downtown restaurants in Durham and Greensboro. NCC student leader Quinton Baker said that the protests were designed to "reaffirm the belief that 'brotherhood is an inseparable part of the Christmas message.'"[68]

In April 1963, Durham mayor Emanuel J. Evans created a Good Neighbor Council at the urging of Governor Sanford, to encourage employment opportunities for blacks. As was typical in that era, white officials made sure that they dominated government councils or committees that concerned African Americans. Mayor Evans appointed seven whites but just three blacks, NC Mutual vice president Noah H. Bennett, Service Printing Company manager Nathaniel White, and NCC professor Theodore R. Speigner.[69] The previous month, Austin had urged the Durham mayor to appoint a Good Neighbor

Council to negotiate with black protesters about employment discrimination and other issues.[70]

In 1963, the *Carolina Times* continued to publish the list of white-owned businesses on the boycott list. In late February 1963, the NAACP Youth Chapter and the Durham chapter of CORE boycotted sixteen downtown Durham stores for employment discrimination, and discrimination against black customers.[71] Within a week, the boycott enjoyed some success as five stores hired black workers in sales and other customer relations positions.[72] In March 1963, Austin urged blacks in Durham to donate to the NAACP-CORE Students Protest Group, to help them sustain their movement for equal employment opportunity in Durham.[73] In April 1963, he praised black ministers for joining the picket lines and backing the boycott of six Durham stores that discriminated against black workers. The names of the six stores were printed on the front page of the *Times* to remind readers to boycott those stores.[74]

The movement to integrate downtown Durham restaurants yielded fruit in May 1963 as a result of the pressure of massive protests and the efforts of newly elected Durham mayor R. Wensell Grabarek, who "had actively campaigned for black votes and had run on a platform of moderation in race relations."[75] On the day that Grabarek was elected mayor, Durham's CORE and NAACP chapters started a wide-ranging effort to integrate the city's public facilities. The police arrested and jailed hundreds of protesters. Meanwhile, "each day ever-larger crowds of angry whites gathered to jeer the civil rights demonstrations." In order to defuse this volatile situation and prevent the outbreak of violence, Grabarek convinced several white businessmen to integrate their restaurants, which helped him persuade black leaders to call a temporary halt to the demonstrations. The mayor then "appointed an interracial committee to work toward voluntary desegregation." But resistance to integration from "Durham's white restaurant owners association" led to the resumption of demonstrations.[76] After three more days of protests, including huge demonstrations at Howard Johnson's, Grabarek helped negotiate another truce. About 1,400 students, mostly from NCC and Hillside High School, had been arrested. The huge protests produced results. That month, seven "restaurants, mostly drive-ins, . . . lifted racial barriers."[77] By late June 1963, fifty-seven Durham businesses had desegregated.[78]

In May 1963, the *Times* reported on protests in other North Carolina cities. In Raleigh, "mass demonstrations staged by hundreds of students" convinced "a group of prominent businessmen" to support the integration "of the city's downtown restaurants and theaters." This breakthrough was preceded by a demonstration at the governor's mansion "during a formal ball for the North Carolina symphony. The Governor left the ball and came outside in his white tie and tails to address the group."[79] A week later, the *Times* reported, "A wave of racial unrest over segregation that started in Birmingham broke-out anew throughout cities in North Carolina," including student protests in Fayetteville, Wilmington, Charlotte, Greensboro, and Raleigh.[80] In an editorial, Austin reiterated his support for peaceful demonstrations, but was "opposed to any and all forms of violence."[81]

After Governor Sanford, at a speech before a segregated audience, criticized black protests in June 1963, including "sit-downs in streets, theaters, and stores where customers are blocked," Austin condemned Sanford's statements and his decision to address a segregated group.[82] Austin supported black leaders' decision to continue protests.[83]

Meanwhile, the *Carolina Times* covered protests in smaller North Carolina towns, where black protesters often faced more violent opposition than they did in the state's larger cities. In May 1961, Austin denounced a Rutherford County sheriff as a "gangster" after the sheriff told a group of white bystanders to a sit-in, "Now ain't these the blackest niggers you've ever seen?" and then threatened to pummel the protesters with his blackjack. The sheriff's comments helped provoke a brutal beating of three demonstrators by a white man.[84]

In December 1962, Austin praised the boycott of white-owned businesses in Elizabeth City that refused to hire black workers. This boycott succeeded in persuading several white businesses to hire black workers. Austin argued that increasing job opportunities for black workers would lead to economic growth, which would benefit all Carolinians, regardless of race.[85]

In November 1963, Austin commended the protest movement in Williamston, North Carolina, for its tenacity in standing up to the particularly racially oppressive white populace in eastern North Carolina. Several Boston ministers joined with local blacks and Southern Christian Leadership Conference field secretary Golden Frinks in marching to desegregate public facilities in the town.[86]

The *Times* publicized the actions of black college presidents, who faced tremendous pressure from top state officials, including Governor Sanford, to punish students who took part in civil rights protests. For example, in May 1963, the *Times* disclosed that in Greensboro, "Acting A. and T. College President L. C. Dowdy has been reported under extreme pressure from high state officials to take action to halt A. and T. students from taking part in racial demonstrations." Dowdy's office announced that students who continued to demonstrate would be expelled. In contrast, NCC president Alfonso Elder refused to force students to remain on campus. He told students "that they should exercise their duties as students and as citizens of a democracy."[87] One year earlier, Elder had defended the right of students and teachers to participate in sit-ins and other civil rights protests, a position that brought him praise from Austin.[88]

Meanwhile, Austin censured blacks who opposed civil rights protests. In August 1963, the determined editor denounced two black educators, Walter Ridley, Elizabeth City State Teachers College president, and Joseph Taylor, NCC Summer School director and history professor, for urging students to terminate civil rights demonstrations and instead engage in negotiations. Austin indicated that he was not surprised by Ridley's statement because according to Austin, Ridley had a long history of employing " 'Uncle Tom' antics," but he was surprised by Taylor's agreement with Ridley. Austin noted that as a historian Taylor should understand that oppressors do not voluntarily end oppression. Struggle was required. Austin advised Ridley and Taylor to keep their mouths shut if they were unwilling to participate in the struggle for equality.[89] Austin's characterization of Ridley may have been based on incomplete information. The historian William Chafe has described an occasion when Ridley became quite concerned about the safety of Elizabeth City College students after he was advised that rural whites were "pouring into the city to confront student demonstrators." At one point, to protect his students, the college president provided "official college vehicles" to transport them to and from the protest location, even after an aide to Governor Sanford lambasted him.[90]

In July 1963, the *Times* had announced an important civil rights victory, when all Durham movie theaters except one had agreed to fully integrate their seating, following many months of protests and two months of negotiations with the Durham Interim Committee, which had been created by Durham mayor Grabarek.[91] The desegregation of the theaters began with a trial period in which several of the theaters permitted a limited number of black customers.[92]

In the weeks leading up to the August 1963 March on Washington for Jobs and Freedom, the *Times* promoted the event with front-page articles and provided useful information about making bus transportation arrangements from Durham. The *Times* advised its readers that the Durham chapters of the NAACP and CORE had arranged bus transportation at $8 for the round-trip bus ride. Rev. Melvin C. Swann, pastor of St. Joseph's AME Church (Austin's church); NCC librarian Sadie Hughley; businessman I. O. Funderburg; and

NCC student Joyce Ware served as Durham coordinators for the march.[93] After the march, Austin declared it a great success.[94] Furthermore, he praised those who participated, and he hoped that the goals of the march, including congressional passage of the civil rights bill, which would mandate equal employment opportunity and integration of public facilities, would be achieved. At the same time, Austin castigated "some of Durham's so-called Negro leaders whose absence from Washington on last Wednesday made them entirely too conspicuous to the Negro masses of this city." He added, "The leadership of an oppressed people cannot forever remain the recipients of favors from the oppressors without becoming puppets."[95]

After the march, Austin noted that despite the accomplishments of the movement in Durham, there was still much to be done. Many white businesses refused to hire blacks, city government limited blacks' economic opportunities to janitorial positions, black police had no opportunity for promotions, and blacks were denied overnight accommodations at the YWCA (most of Durham's hotels did admit blacks at that time), so this was no time for the movement to rest.[96]

In October 1963, the movement won an important victory, when the Durham City Council and Durham County commissioners passed resolutions opposing racial discrimination. These actions were in response to a recommendation by the Durham Interim Committee.[97]

In November 1963, Austin spoke at a meeting in Rocky Mount of the North Carolina NAACP Youth Council and College Chapter, along with Quinton E. Baker, president of the organization. Austin in "his own inimitable Methodist manner, delivered his down-to-earth address based on thriftiness, frugality and all-out registration and voting instead of shiftlessness, [and] needless spending on the part of impoverished Negroes." He further "struck out unflinchingly at the Cadillac preachers who seek so-called prestige rather than the amount of good they could do for the people."[98]

After the assassination of President Kennedy in November 1963, Austin linked this tragic event with the nation's long history of failing to punish whites, who lynched, raped, or killed African Americans. Austin proclaimed that Americans had created the "climate in which this horrible crime was committed." He concluded, "So the nation has been called on to drink from the cup of retribution and to the last drop, the bitter dregs contained in the backwash of its own slimy sins."[99] Austin's comments evoke those made by Nation of Islam spokesperson Malcolm X, which were uttered the day after Austin's published statement. Malcolm famously connected the Kennedy assassination to the killings of foreign leaders like Patrice Lumumba of the

Congo and Ngo Dinh Diem of South Vietnam, and the murders of African Americans like Mississippi NAACP leader Medgar Evers and the four black girls who died in a bombed-out Birmingham church. Malcolm declared the violent murder of Kennedy a case of "the chickens coming home to roost."[100]

In January 1964, the NAACP recognized the important role played by black newspapers, like the *Carolina Times*, in helping advance the civil rights struggle. The *Times* published a letter from the executive secretary of the NAACP, Roy Wilkins, who praised the *Times* and other black papers for their role in recent civil rights victories. Wilkins wrote, "We of the NAACP salute you and your fellow editors for the vital role you played in awakening the American conscience to the urgency of the civil rights crisis. . . . Certainly the banner year that the NAACP achieved in 1963 has been due measurably to the generous support your newspaper gave to our efforts."[101]

Although Chapel Hill enjoyed a reputation as one of the most liberal towns in the South, in 1964, several of its restaurants remained segregated, while several North Carolina cities had integrated many of their public facilities. Accordingly, Austin backed protests in Chapel Hill. In January, as protesters marched and picketed in Chapel Hill to end segregation in restaurants and other public facilities, Austin declared that the home of the University of North Carolina no longer deserved its progressive image. He also shined a light on the violence perpetrated by white segregationists against white and black civil rights workers in Chapel Hill. The *Times* reported on a notably crude and despicable action by a segregationist: the co-owner of a Chapel Hill restaurant "stood over the prostrate body of a white demonstrator on the floor of the Watts Restaurant [lifted her skirt] and urinated in his face."[102]

Meanwhile, when Governor Sanford again called for an end to civil rights demonstrations, Austin denounced the governor. Austin argued that moderate politicians like Sanford had done little to support racial equality. Progress in the fight for racial justice had come from sit-ins and other street protests, not moderate rhetoric by the likes of Sanford. Therefore, Austin did not hesitate to underscore his continued support for protest.[103] In January 1964, after Governor Sanford castigated CORE, which advocated massive civil rights protests to force Chapel Hill to integrate all public facilities, Austin fought back. Indeed, Sanford gave his full support to Chapel Hill authorities, and uttered, in Austin's words, a "threat to use all the force at his command against the Congress of Racial Equality." Austin characterized the governor's policy as a "corrupt abuse of power by a public official." He concluded that "all the talk of the governor and others about 'voluntary integration' is purely and solely 'softsoap.'"[104]

In addition to advocating integration of lunch counters, restaurants, and movie theaters, Austin challenged other segregated institutions. In 1955, he had condemned the harsh treatment of black women patients at the state's black mental hospital in Goldsboro. With many of the hospital's patients forced to work for private farmers picking cotton, Austin characterized the conditions faced by these women as "little better than slavery." He demanded an investigation by black and white Carolinians of the conditions at the state hospital. Failing that, he proposed desegregation of state hospitals because at integrated institutions, blacks would have a much better opportunity to be treated fairly.[105]

In April 1960, Austin demanded the termination of inequitable federal funding of segregated hospitals in the South. Under the Hill-Burton Act of 1946, which provided billions of dollars in federal government funding for private hospitals, segregation was permitted, but facilities for blacks and whites were required to be equal. As was the case in other public facilities, separation was enforced, but equality was a fiction. Austin reported that "the Wesley Long Community Hospital of Greensboro which admits no Negroes has been allocated $1½ million of federal funds under the Hill-Burton Act." In addition, "the Moses Cone Memorial Hospital which admits only a few Negroes as patients and bars Negro physicians from practicing there has been allocated $807,950 from the same source."[106] Austin voiced the frustration felt by many African Americans because of denial of access to public facilities: "When one is constantly faced with a system of you can't eat here, you can't sit here, you can't be treated here, you can't worship here, you can't ride here, you can't buy here and hundreds of other can'ts and don'ts, one reaches the point when he is willing to resort to any method or go to any extent to remove such barriers."[107]

Austin's call for action to challenge racially segregated hospitals was answered by a group of African Americans led by dentist and civil rights activist George Simkins, who sued two Greensboro hospitals in April 1960 for violating the Hill-Burton Act.[108] Simkins was not new to the civil rights struggle; he and several friends had previously challenged a racially segregated, whites-only public golf course, in Greensboro, in 1955, just days after Rosa Parks's arrest in Montgomery, Alabama, for refusing to move to the back of the bus. After playing several holes on the golf course, which had been leased by the city to a private operator for one dollar, the black golfers were removed from the golf course, arrested, and jailed. They appealed and won the case in federal court, but their victory was short-lived. Simkins recalled, "Two days before integration was supposed to take effect, the clubhouse mysteriously burned down." The course was closed for the next seven years. Simkins later served as head of the Greensboro NAACP.[109]

The hospital case began when a patient with an infected jaw and a raging fever came in to see Simkins, who sought to find a hospital room for him. With no rooms available at the overcrowded and underfunded local black hospital, Simkins contacted Wesley Long and Moses Cone hospitals, but neither hospital would admit a black patient. After a local black attorney refused to file a lawsuit because he feared reprisals, Simkins contacted Jack Greenberg, head of the NAACP Legal Defense Fund. Greenberg told Simpkins to contact Conrad Pearson of Durham, head of the statewide NAACP legal team, who filed the case. After Simkins lost in the district court, U.S. attorney general Robert Kennedy filed a friend of the court brief in support of Simkins and they won at the court of appeals. The Supreme Court refused to accept an appeal by Moses Cone.[110] In March 1964, Austin praised the U.S. Supreme Court decision that sustained the appeals court decision in *Simkins v. Cone*, which ruled that it was unconstitutional for racially segregated hospitals to receive federal funds.[111]

Meanwhile, Austin continued to shine a bright light on inequities in medical care at other institutions in the state. In July 1962, he illuminated the indignities experienced by black patients at a Lexington hospital that segregated black and white patients. Black men, women, and children were permitted to use just one toilet in the hospital. Austin praised the NAACP for attacking this blatant case of racial discrimination. He also condemned those blacks who failed to protest these conditions: "Those who tolerate certain conditions should rightfully be placed in the category of a jackass."[112] In February 1963, Austin reported on the financial problems of Durham's black facility, Lincoln Hospital, observing that they were caused by employment discrimination against blacks, which left them unable to pay for hospitalization. He urged the Durham County commissioners to ensure that the hospital received adequate funding to pay for indigent patients.[113] Moreover, Austin recognized that black political power was fundamental to the fight for racial justice, so he persisted in voter registration efforts.

Austin's efforts and those of his allies led to consistent growth in black voter registration in North Carolina during this era: 24 percent in 1956, 32 percent in 1958, 38 percent in 1960, and 47 percent in 1964. While North Carolina ranked eighth among southern states in 1956, it rose to fourth in 1964. Black voter registration in the state varied widely by region, with piedmont cities recording much higher registration rates than did the rural eastern part of the state, where white registrars regularly blocked black voter registration. Over half of North Carolina's counties had black voter registration rates below 30 percent in 1958.[114] While blacks in Durham County succeeded in regularly registering large numbers of black voters, black registration rates still lagged behind that for white voters. In 1960, 98 percent of voting-age whites were registered to vote in Durham, but only 68 percent of voting-age blacks were registered to vote. Nonetheless, black voter registration in Durham jumped from 61 percent in 1958 to 68 percent in 1960, thanks to the efforts of Austin and other black activists.[115]

One of the biggest obstacles to black voter registration in North Carolina, particularly in the rural east, was the literacy test. According to a 1961 study conducted by the North Carolina Advisory Committee to the U.S. Commission on Civil Rights, the state's registrars inconsistently applied the literacy test. The study indicated that county registrars "administered literacy tests which included such requirements as the taking of oral diction, extensive reading aloud, and answering questions on the meaning of words and phrases; others settled for an ability to fill out an application form properly and to sign one's name." While several registrars from the mountain counties with small black populations claimed that they did not administer literacy tests, northeastern counties like Bertie, Halifax, and Warren, with large black populations, "reported literacy tests that appeared to be unusually difficult or arbitrary."[116]

In eastern North Carolina, white registrars regularly refused to register black voters. Austin publicized and encouraged legal efforts to stop voter suppression. In May 1956, when four black candidates ran for office in two counties in the Enfield area, they hired the attorney James R. Walker Jr. of Weldon, who demanded "the resignation of a registrar for using an 'improper' examination which disqualified a Negro seeking to register."[117] Walker, one of the first black graduates of the law school at the University of North Carolina, was the only black attorney in the six counties surrounding Weldon.[118] He and Charles A. McLean of Winston-Salem, an NAACP field secretary, charged that qualified African Americans were regularly denied voter registration in many eastern North Carolina counties, including Halifax, Northampton, Franklin, Nash, Bertie, Tyrell, Bladen, Jones, Camden, Pamlico, Currituck, Pitt, Hertford, Person, Hoke, and Hyde.[119] Austin attacked these voter suppression tactics, stressing the "ignorance and beastly attitude among a majority" of whites in the east. He suggested the formation of "a state-wide committee . . . to raise funds for the prosecution of these and other cases arising out of the denial of registration and voting rights to qualified Negroes."[120]

In 1956, Walker demanded the dismissal of Seaboard, North Carolina, registrar Helen Taylor, who denied registration to qualified blacks. Not only was Taylor not dismissed, but local police intervened to stop the black voter registration movement by arresting Walker "on charges of trespassing in the Taylor store." He was convicted, "fined and given a suspended sentence . . . in a trial at Northampton County Recorder's Court."[121] According to the socialist newspaper *The Militant*, "Walker was arrested for allegedly shaking his finger at Mrs. Taylor. He was first convicted of disorderly conduct . . . and then convicted of the charge of assaulting a female." He served jail time and was fined a total of $650.[122] Moreover, the black man and black woman who were denied registration suffered reprisals. The man was "threatened with prosecution for a check he" wrote five months earlier and the woman had her "permit to practice as a midwife" revoked after practicing in the county for twenty years.[123]

The attorney Walker, with two Raleigh attorneys, had also filed suit in 1956 on behalf of Louise Lassiter, a Northampton County woman, after the registrar, Taylor, had refused her application to register to vote, claiming she had failed the literacy test. Lassiter challenged the state's literacy test. After a prolonged legal battle, in 1959, the U.S. Supreme Court ruled that the state's literacy test did not violate the U.S. Constitution.[124] By 1960, little had changed; Walker was still reporting violations of blacks' right to register to vote in eastern North Carolina.[125]

While Austin had backed the Republicans in the 1956 presidential and gubernatorial elections, he took a more complex approach to the 1960 campaigns. In August 1960, Austin leaned toward the Republican Party's Richard Nixon in the presidential campaign based on the vice-president's rhetoric in favor of civil rights.[126] However, in an editorial right before the election, Austin did not endorse either candidate but urged voters to seriously consider both.[127] Although Austin did not overtly support either candidate, he emphasized the racist politics of southern white Democrats, who had long played a central role in oppressing blacks in politics, workplace opportunity, education, and the justice system. He also stressed white supremacist Mississippi senator James Eastland's support for vice presidential candidate Lyndon Johnson, which would diminish black support for the Democrats, who had nominated Massachusetts senator John F. Kennedy for president. Austin wrote, "It is also our firm belief that if the 12 million or more Negroes of the South are ever freed from its vicious one-party system they, and they alone, must strike the first blow. They must strike it by voting against nominees of a party that from all evidence has abandoned them to the wolves of white supremacy." Thus Austin indirectly supported the Republicans in the national election.[128] By contrast, John Wheeler and John Stewart, prominent business leaders and DCNA officials, supported the Democrats, while black pastors E. T. Browne and F. L. Tyson wrote columns in the *Carolina Times* backing the Republicans right before the election.[129]

In the 1960 Democratic primary campaign for governor in North Carolina, Austin backed the racial moderate Terry Sanford over the virulent advocate of racial segregation I. Beverly Lake. Austin predicted that most blacks would vote for Sanford, in part because of his service as campaign manager for Senator W. Kerr Scott, who had strong black support.[130] In the issue of the *Times* right before the election, Austin implored his readers to vote against Lake. Austin predicted that if Lake was elected, he would "throw this state into a vicious period of arraying race against race." Austin did not mention Sanford's name in his editorial in order to limit the Lake campaign's ability to use a black newspaper's endorsement of Sanford to increase the white vote for Lake.[131]

Following the Democratic primary runoff for governor in June 1960, Austin reported that the black vote against Lake was the margin of victory for Sanford. Austin estimated that about 150,000 blacks were registered to vote in the state and about 90,000 cast ballots. Sanford won by a 77,000-vote margin, with blacks voting overwhelmingly for Sanford because of Lake's "vicious attack" on integration, blacks, and the NAACP.[132] A recent study of the 1960 election concurred with Austin's analysis.[133]

The *Times* reported that black voters also played a key role in the Democrats' victory in the presidential election. About 72 percent of blacks in Durham County voted for Kennedy.[134] A measure of the strength of black voting in Durham was that by 1961, while Durham's population was about 25 percent black, black voters generally counted for 30 percent of the city's voters, meaning that black voter turnout percentage exceeded that for whites.[135]

While the DCNA generally could count on over 80 percent of the black vote choosing its preferred candidate, that did not occur in the 1961 mayoral race. The DCNA supported J. Leslie Atkins Jr., former Durham County Democratic Party leader, who had been a key leader in the black-labor-liberal Voters for Better Government coalition in the late 1940s and early 1950s. About 66 percent of African Americans voted for Atkins, who also enjoyed labor support. Nonetheless, despite DCNA support for Atkins, incumbent mayor Emanuel J. Evans, who had enjoyed DCNA support in previous elections, was reelected mayor. Only a little over 20 percent of registered voters cast ballots.[136] Austin tried to put a positive spin on the split in the black vote, as he called both candidates "proven friends of the race" and said that divisions in this race would not detract from the impact of DCNA choices in future elections.[137]

In 1962, Austin reissued his call for blacks to leave the Democratic Party and register as Republicans because of the Democrats' failure to provide anything close to equal employment opportunity for blacks in state government jobs.[138] The previous September, Austin had highlighted the persistent lack of economic opportunity for blacks in North Carolina, noting that the white press had finally discovered that this was an issue, likely in response to the "forthright efforts of the North Carolina Advisory Committee to the United States Commission on Civil Rights." Austin demanded action, not just talk, on this issue.[139] In April 1961, he had denounced Governor Sanford for failing to appoint even one African American to public office, while praising President Kennedy for adding John Wheeler, DCNA leader and businessman, to the president's committee on equal employment opportunity.[140] After Sanford appointed two black educators, James Seabrook and Samuel Duncan, in the summer of 1961, to nonsalaried state boards, Austin urged the governor to elevate blacks to more powerful positions, especially given that the black vote was so important to Sanford's electoral victory.[141] In July 1961, the *Times* published an article detailing NAACP leader Kelly Alexander's demand that the governor appoint blacks to salaried state government positions to signal that he would reject racial discrimination in state government jobs.[142] While Sanford did not act quickly in response to Alexander's demand, he did increase black membership on the trustee boards of several of the state's black colleges, including North Carolina A&T and Winston-Salem Teachers College.[143] In August 1961, Sanford also increased the number of black members of NCC's board of trustees from three to five, including the appointment of Durham attorney M. Hugh Thompson.[144]

Austin grew tired of Sanford's rhetorical support for black economic opportunity, when he refused to take action to eliminate racial discrimination in employment. For example, Sanford suggested voluntary action by businesses but refused to back a government agency to ensure economic opportunity for blacks.[145] In March 1962, Austin reported that the state's National Guard and Highway Patrol did not employ any African Americans. While the state government employed 7,000 workers, fewer than twenty-five blacks were employed in Raleigh in any state job besides janitor or messenger.[146] In October 1962, Austin advised black voters not to blindly vote for Democratic Party candidates, noting Sanford's failure to appoint blacks to positions of significant influence in his administration. Austin claimed that when Sanford was "approached by one of the state's leading Negroes for an appointment of a Negro to a position with a $10,000 per year salary," the governor "replied that a position with such a salary belongs to a white man."[147] In January 1963, when Sanford called for more employment opportunity in the state for black workers, Austin praised his words but again encouraged him to back up his words with action.[148]

In December 1964, Austin criticized Governor Sanford for his disingenuous claim in a *Look Magazine* article that "North Carolina, without court order and on its own initiative, repealed the color ban of the National Guard." Austin corrected Sanford, noting that the General Assembly acted to include blacks only in response to a planned lawsuit to integrate the state's National Guard. And despite "phone advertisements asking for new recruits," the National Guard in North Carolina was still all-white.[149] When a state government report claimed that there was no racial discrimination in hiring for government positions, Austin was apoplectic in his disbelief, as were other black leaders, notably John Wheeler. Austin called the report's conclusions perhaps "the biggest lie that has been told within the last 50 years."[150]

While Austin publicly embraced the Republican Party during the early 1960s, he also worked with the DCNA in supporting progressive black and white Democrats who sought local office. In 1962, Austin and the DCNA backed C. Elwood Boulware's run for Durham County commissioner. Boulware, a mathematics professor at NCC, placed fifth in the first primary, which put him in the runoff election.[151] Austin urged black voters to turn out for Boulware in the runoff election, but Dewey Scarboro, the white incumbent, defeated Boulware by about 2,800 votes.[152] After the election, Austin criticized the Democratic Party for failing to back Boulware in the runoff, or in the initial primary election, and once again advised black voters to reconsider their loyalty to the Democrats.[153]

Occasionally, the DCNA joined Austin in backing black Republican candidates for local office. In the 1962 general election, the DCNA backed Rev. E. T. Browne for Durham County commissioner. Running as a Republican, Browne received 5,000 votes, but lost by over 3,000 votes. Alexander Barnes, running as a Republican, without DCNA backing, for the state assembly from Durham, lost by over 6,000 votes. With DCNA support, Austin was elected justice of the peace, also running as a Republican. About 6,000 black Durhamites voted in the election, with a slightly higher turnout rate than that of white voters.[154]

Austin regularly pushed for increased black voter registration, with editorials and articles. In April 1964, in advance of the primary that month, the

Carolina Times placed a large banner on the bottom of the front page with the words, "You Cannot Vote in the May Primary Unless You Register. A VOTE-LESS PEOPLE IS A HOPELESS PEOPLE."[155] Austin encouraged blacks to increase their statewide voter registration numbers from about 200,000 to 260,000 for the primary on May 30, 1964.[156] When voter registration was about to open again in fall 1964, Austin again publicized it with a boldface banner on the bottom of the front page of the paper.[157]

Austin also encouraged more African Americans to seek public office. He backed longtime friend H. M. "Mickey" Michaux Jr., a law student at North Carolina College and the son of businessman H. M. Michaux Sr., in his run for the state legislature in 1964. Michaux, who had gone to school with Martin Luther King Jr.'s younger brother A. D. King, later recalled that Dr. King had urged him to run for public office. Black candidates, Austin argued, would stimulate a larger black vote.[158]

Several black candidates won election to southern state legislatures in 1964. In November, the *Times* reported on gains for black elected officials, including the election of two African Americans to the Georgia state legislature, and one each to the Oklahoma and Tennessee legislatures. In Durham, Michaux was defeated and no blacks won seats in the North Carolina legislature that year, leaving the state legislature without any black members, which had been the case for over six decades.[159]

Meanwhile, Austin continued to promote black voter registration in the eastern counties, where white registrars made it incredibly difficult for blacks to register. In February 1963, Austin urged blacks in Warren County to register to vote, noting that because the county had a black majority, black voters had the potential to defeat North Carolina assemblyman John Kerr Jr., a vocal opponent of civil rights protest. Kerr had pressured Lewis Dowdy, acting president of A&T College in Greensboro (Samuel D. Proctor was on leave with the Peace Corps), to punish students involved in civil rights protests. After noting that A&T students were involved in anti-segregation sit-ins in Greensboro, Kerr told Dowdy, "And you come down here begging the white folks to give more money to your school. . . . Some of us are getting tired of it."[160]

In Halifax County in 1964, where blacks outnumbered whites 32,000 to 26,000, black activists mounted a major voter registration campaign. Moreover, eleven blacks ran for public office, including state senate, state house, county commission, county coroner, and the school board, in the county's May 30 primary.[161] According to Willa Cofield Johnson, an Enfield teacher, "the 'social revolution of the '60s' came to the region in the spring of 1963, when her husband, Reed Johnson, director of one of the Cofield family's funeral homes, ran for a seat on the town council in . . . Enfield."[162] Austin encouraged the movement—Enfield was his birthplace—noting the travesty of having no black elected officials in a majority-black county.[163] In early May, Freedom Day was held in Halifax County with 500 new black registrants, bringing total black voter registration to more than 2,000. These totals were impressive, especially with the continued intimidation tactics employed by white officials. The *Times* reported that registrants faced "delaying tactics by registrars and harassment by police," including the "setting off of a stench bomb" at the registration location. John R. Salter Jr., field organizer for the Southern Conference Educational Fund, who had participated in sit-ins in Jackson, Mississippi, in 1963, reported that white resistance to black voter registration in parts of eastern North Carolina "was as bad as anything in Mississippi." Salter observed that "in some places registrars took half an hour to register one applicant. One registrar took three hours for lunch. In another place, the registrar refused to tell applicants whether they were registered or not." These tactics were very similar to those used in Mississippi, according to Salter.[164] Austin denounced these delaying tactics in Warren and Halifax County, and praised blacks for their persistence in registering to vote despite the obstacles. He also urged legal action against county officials who violated blacks' voting rights.[165]

The *Times* regularly illuminated the struggles of the Halifax Voter Movement. In May 1964, after two white registrars resigned, black activists urged the appointment of a black registrar. The movement succeeded in obtaining a restraining order from U.S. district court judge John D. Larkins to stop the stalling tactics by the Halifax County registrars. Nonetheless, white registrars ignored the court orders. Led by A. C. Cofield of Weldon, the movement persuaded the U.S. Justice Department to intercede, sending FBI agents to investigate. The *Times* featured this information on the front page, along with photographs from Warren County showing black voter registration applicants waiting in line at a voter registration office in Warren County, as irrefutable evidence of the antidemocratic tactics used by white supremacists in eastern North Carolina.[166] Austin was not sanguine about the FBI investigation leading to justice. He noted that the photographs "published on the front page" of the *Times* "speak louder than it is possible for any words can about the sorry and low type of whites that are in control of Halifax and Warren counties. If there are conditions to be found any worse in the most depraved sections of Alabama and Mississippi God help the United States in its efforts to promote democracy among other nations of the world and its fight against communism."[167]

During late spring and summer 1964, the Halifax Voter Movement faced increasing intimidation and violence from white supremacists. On May 29, 1964, a "cross was burned" while a voter registration meeting was held at Weldon's First Baptist Church, whose pastor, Clyde Johnson, was running for county commissioner.[168] On July 4, 1964, the KKK burned a seventeen-foot-tall cross near the home of thirty-six-year-old Enfield civil rights leader Willa Cofield Johnson, after she was fired from her high school teaching job in retaliation for her civil rights advocacy. She sued the school district for $250,000.[169] Two days before the cross burning, "carloads of robed KKK members several of them seen to be masked and carrying guns—staged a motorcade and rally in Enfield and traveled into Negro neighborhoods in that community in an obvious attempt to spread fear and terror." Johnson's lawsuit targeted several local white officials, including Joe Branch, the Halifax County school board attorney who also managed Dan K. Moore's 1964 campaign for governor.[170] Austin urged black churches, businesses, and individuals to back Johnson with funds for her lawsuit and to replace her salary. In June 1965, the U.S. district court ruled against Johnson in her suit. Austin encouraged civil rights organizations to back an appeal of the adverse court ruling.[171]

In response to the KKK terror campaign and the firing of Johnson, as well as the generally oppressive conditions of blacks in Enfield, Austin initiated a boycott of the town by black motorists: "So we declare here and now the town of Enfield to be on the BLACK LIST. Until further notice, we would urge Negro motorists to buy what they need, while traveling, before they get to Enfield or after they have passed through it."[172]

In December 1964, Austin praised the Halifax County Voters Movement for its tenacious battle for racial justice and equality in the face of harassment by white segregationists. Movement activists demanded that the county board of commissioners end segregation throughout the county, hire black workers for city and county government, include blacks on juries, and adopt a fair employment practices law to ensure equal employment opportunity. Austin urged black freedom fighters to "stand steadfast and immovable in their quest for first-class citizenship."[173]

Prior to the May 1964 Democratic primary for governor, Austin made no public endorsement, but he did denounce candidate I. Beverly Lake. The other candidates, Dan K. Moore and L. Richardson Preyer, both appealed for black support in advertisements in the *Times*.[174] Austin rebuked those who criticized blacks for bloc voting. He noted that whites engaged in bloc voting all the time, but only when blacks voted for a black candidate did white commentators raise an objection. Blacks, of course, often voted for white candidates, because in most cases there was no black candidate for many offices.[175] In the first primary for the Democratic nomination for governor, Preyer, backed by Governor Sanford, led with 37 percent, followed by Moore with 34 percent and Lake with 28 percent.[176]

In June 1964, Austin told black voters that both gubernatorial candidates in the runoff, Preyer and Moore, were opposed to the civil rights bill then being debated in the U.S. Congress, which would ban racially segregated public facilities and job discrimination based on race and sex. Apparently, blacks had been more supportive of Preyer, but after he spoke against federal involvement in civil rights, Austin opined that until there was a viable Republican Party in the state, voters had little to choose from among Democratic candidates. But he also concluded that North Carolina's white Republican and Democratic candidates were often equally opposed to civil rights for African Americans.[177]

Although Austin did not publicly support either gubernatorial candidate, there is evidence of his preference for Preyer over Moore. Preyer's advertisements appeared in the *Times* right before the runoff primary, while Moore's did not. Indeed, one Preyer ad appeared on the bottom of the front page, and attacked Moore: "Moore Snakes in the Lake! Warning! Moore Snakes in the Lake! . . . No Moore Vboating. Just Say a Preyer June 27."[178] Austin encouraged progressive white and black voters to support "the candidate who at least appears to be the better of the two now running for governor of North Carolina," a thinly veiled preference for Preyer, the more progressive of the two candidates.[179] Austin was likely following the *Times*' usual practice of disguising its endorsement to avoid a white backlash against the black newspaper's favorite. In the June 27, 1964 issue, Preyer placed a half-page ad, comparing his position on various issues to those of Moore. Preyer supported the Good Neighbor Councils created by Sanford, while Moore did not. Both opposed the civil rights bill, but Preyer backed an increase in the minimum wage, while Moore did not.[180]

With I. Beverly Lake's endorsement, as well as the support of big business because of his anti–government regulation stance, Moore defeated Preyer in the runoff 62 percent to 38 percent. Jesse Helms, a conservative television commentator for TV station WRAL at the time, also opposed Preyer. To increase white support for Moore, Helms publicized the large black vote for Preyer in the first primary.[181]

Austin called the results of the Democratic primary a major setback for the cause of civil rights. The victor in the gubernatorial primary, Moore, was backed by the White Citizens Council and the KKK. In addition, staunch segregationist governor of Alabama George Wallace easily "secured the 10,000 names, necessary to place his name on the ballot [in North Carolina] in his campaign for the presidency."[182] In July 1964, Austin noted Moore's anti–civil rights bill and "anti-Negro" statements, and said that black voters should reject Moore in the general election and value "self-respect and race pride" over "party loyalty."[183]

Although he had been lukewarm at best toward the Democratic Party in recent years, in the 1964 presidential campaign, Austin made it crystal clear that he backed President Lyndon Johnson over his Republican opponent, Senator Barry Goldwater of Arizona. On civil rights issues, the difference between the two candidates was undeniable, with President Johnson signing the Civil Rights Act in July 1964, while Goldwater had opposed it. A couple of weeks after the Civil Rights Act became law, Austin urged black voters to choose Johnson over Goldwater.[184] In October 1964, Austin again encouraged black voters to help LBJ defeat Goldwater, terming the election "the most crucial election in history."[185]

Austin's strong backing of Johnson likely contributed to his decision in late October to publish a half-page advertisement from the Democratic Party that urged readers to vote for Democratic candidates. This advertisement was balanced by a long letter to the editor by John R. Dungee of Henderson, North Carolina, which urged blacks to reject Moore and either sit out the governor's race or support the Republican candidate, Robert Gavin, who said that although he had opposed the Civil Rights Act, he would enforce it. Governor Sanford had also opposed the act but counseled North Carolinians to obey it once it became law.[186]

In the 1964 election, about 12,000 of 14,000 registered black voters in Durham County cast ballots. Durham County had a total of 49,000 registered voters with about 40,000 voting in the 1964 general election. In North Carolina, about 260,000 blacks were registered to vote and 200,000 voted, the large majority supporting Moore for governor and Johnson for president. Led by John Wheeler, the DCNA backed the Democratic ticket and supported Moore and Johnson. Johnson carried the state by 176,000 votes over Goldwater, so the black vote likely made the difference. Johnson won Durham County by 7,000 votes, so without the black vote, Goldwater would have easily carried the county.[187] Moore defeated the Republican candidate Gavin by 184,000 votes, so if the black vote had gone entirely for Gavin, Gavin might have prevailed. Moore's margin of victory exceeded that of Sanford in 1960, when Sanford defeated Gavin by 122,000 votes.[188]

Following the election, Austin called for a renewed effort to increase black voter registration in the state and the nation. He encouraged unrelenting action to register voters in eastern North Carolina, where blacks were regularly "barred from registering by intimidation or denied the right to vote through other unlawful means."[189] The Halifax movement had succeeded in registering 4,000 blacks out of a total of 15,000 eligible blacks in the county. Austin sought to shame Halifax County whites by comparing the ongoing intimidation of black voters there to similarly nefarious tactics in Mississippi. The intimidation included widespread "threats of economic reprisals." Austin also noted the role of several "unscrupulous" black preachers who told "members of their race that it was 'unChristian' to register and vote."[190]

In early 1965, Austin supported boycotts of goods produced in the most racially oppressive regions of the South. He backed the NAACP's boycott of Mississippi products because of the state's denial of voting rights to blacks. Austin suggested that given the similarly oppressive situation in eastern North Carolina, products from eastern counties, like Halifax, should also be boycotted.[191] In mid-March 1965, Austin encouraged an international boycott of Alabama products in response to police brutality against voting rights activists there, after the Selma police brutally beat black demonstrators on the Edmund Pettus Bridge on what became known as Bloody Sunday.[192] The following month, Austin backed away from this boycott, although it was supported by Martin Luther King Jr., because he feared that it would hurt innocent black Alabamans too much.[193] King had proposed an international boycott of Alabama goods on March 28, 1965. The NAACP had begun a boycott of Mississippi goods in summer 1964 and extended that boycott to Alabama goods in spring 1965.[194]

Despite the successes of the civil rights movement, most notably the passage of the Civil Rights Act of 1964, many African Americans, especially in the North and the West, had seen little improvement in their lives as they continued to suffer from economic oppression. When massive frustration over police brutality and economic oppression sparked violence in numerous cities, Austin reacted as he had during similar disturbances during World War II. Although he noted the justified frustrations over the killing of a black teenager by a white policeman, Austin was very critical of black rioters in Harlem in July 1964. He described the rioters' actions as cowardly and condemned those blacks who demonized all whites, noting that many white members of Congress had voted for the Civil Rights Act of 1964.[195]

Similarly, in August 1965, Austin criticized rioters in Chicago and Watts, calling the events "senseless rioting." He continued, "Whatever the cause or excuse, we draw our sword against every single Negro participant in the riots or any sympathizer of their participants."[196] Nonetheless, the following week, the *Times* published a lengthy letter to the editor that blamed city governments headed by white mayors in Los Angeles, Chicago, and other cities, including Durham, for the high level of black frustration over continued racial segregation and inequities that erupted in violence. Austin now sympathized with the letter writer's analysis that unresponsive city governments to racial inequities were largely responsible for the riots.[197]

In September 1965, Austin reiterated this position, asserting, "Let there be no mistake about it[;] the general pattern that only 'White is right,' and must be respected, is partly to blame for much of the racial strife that now besets North Carolina and other southern states." Austin also denounced Governor Moore's poor treatment of black leaders at a recent meeting. He called for voter registration to increase black political power.[198]

In March 1965, civil rights advocates in North Carolina voiced their support for voting rights activists in Alabama, who were suffering from brutal police attacks. That month about 1,200 blacks and whites, half from North Carolina College (NCC), marched from NCC to the main post office in Durham in response to the murder of white civil rights activist Rev. James Reeb in Selma.[199] When President Johnson was inspired by the Alabama movement to speak out for voting rights, Austin praised the president's speech as "the most forthright any president of the United States has made since Abraham Lincoln's Emancipation Proclamation. History is sure to accord it a high place among the greatest of all time."[200] Recently, Johnson biographer Robert Dallek affirmed Austin's judgment, when he called it "Johnson's greatest speech and one of the most moving and memorable presidential addresses in the country's history." At the end of that speech, the president "embraced the anthem of black protest," when he declared, "It is all of us, who must overcome the crippling legacy of bigotry and injustices. And . . . we shall overcome."[201]

The *Carolina Times* regularly publicized violent attacks by white segregationists against civil rights activists, which were particularly prevalent in eastern North Carolina. In February 1965, the *Times* reported on Ku Klux Klan violence in the region. On January 29, 1965, the FBI arrested suspected perpetrators of bombings in New Bern that "damaged two automobiles and a mortuary during a civil rights meeting in a church January 24." Alabama civil rights leader Fred Shuttlesworth called on U.S. attorney general Nicholas

Katzenbach to initiate "a vigorous investigation of Ku Klux Klan terrorism in all parts of North Carolina." John Salter of the Southern Conference Educational Fund (SCEF) reported that the KKK had 10,000 members in the state. Salter wrote to Governor Moore that "there had been numerous incidents such as cross-burnings, threats, . . . arson and shootings for which no one has been apprehended." Most of these events were not reported in the mainstream press.[202] Salter later recalled that a "typical Klan rally" in November 1964 in Halifax County "drew almost a thousand hooded, sheeted figures." Some KKK rallies, according to Salter, included "national KKK leaders and sometimes numbered several thousand. There were armed Klan motorcades, shootings, burnings. The FBI was no help; indeed, it was an enemy. In Enfield, Klan dues were collected in the local police station and, across the region, many 'lawmen' were Klansmen." Nonetheless, Salter and local activists "kept right on going—dead ahead—and, as we were increasingly successful, we eventually forced the Klan and comparable groups out of the Black Belt."[203]

In addition to trying to terrorize the eastern part of the state, the KKK was also active in the piedmont. The *Times* reported that on April 24, 1965, the KKK, led by Imperial Wizard Robert Shelton, marched in downtown Durham. Opposition protesters, including NAACP members and college students, "greatly outnumbering the KKK members displayed no violence but much disapproval." The KKK then held a rally of over 7,000 people at a "field about five miles northeast of Durham."[204]

After President Johnson signed the Voting Rights Act, outlawing literacy tests and providing federal registrars to enforce voting rights in the South, in August 1965, two of North Carolina's top civil rights leaders, Floyd McKissick and Charlotte activist Reginald Hawkins, urged the U.S. Justice Department "to immediately dispatch registrars" to eastern North Carolina. The *Times* noted that this "action was prompted by the 30 or more counties, principally in the eastern section . . . of the state, where Negroes have been barred outright from voting, intimidated, delayed or subjected to other tactics."[205] Austin recommended a boycott of goods sold by white merchants in the state's eastern counties like Bertie and Halifax, because blacks were regularly denied the right to vote.[206]

In June 1965, Austin noted that while black voters should support the Democratic Party in national elections, in state elections, they should consider both parties. Austin suspected conservative pro-segregationist attorney I. Beverly Lake of secretly calling the shots for the Democrats at the state level. Austin also criticized white Democrats for blocking black candidates for the state legislature. He noted that while Georgia had ten black state representatives, North Carolina had none.[207] In August 1965, Governor Moore rewarded Lake for his support in the gubernatorial runoff primary the previous year by appointing him to the North Carolina Supreme Court.[208]

Thus, despite the passage of the Civil Rights Act of 1964 and the Voting Rights Act of 1965, Austin realized that there was still much work to be done in the long struggle for equal rights in North Carolina and throughout the nation. Over a decade after the *Brown* decision, most of the state's students still attended segregated schools. Employment discrimination was still the rule, rather than the exception. And the state legislature remained an all-white institution. Louis Austin would devote the last five years of his life to continuing the long struggle for racial equality.

CHAPTER SEVEN

It Was a Wonder I Wasn't Lynched

A Freedom Fighter till the End, 1966–1971

While the passage of landmark civil rights legislation had partially redeemed the long years of struggle, Louis Austin knew that African Americans' fight for racial justice was far from over. As he began his fifth decade publishing the *Carolina Times*, Austin continued to attack racial oppression, which remained pervasive, despite the victories won by the efforts of thousands of black freedom fighters. In March 1966, Austin gave voice to the frustration felt by many African Americans with the failure of the justice system to deal with police brutality. He showed his disgust after two particularly egregious cases. In one case, a state trooper was found not guilty of raping a black nurse in her home. In the second case, no charges, not even a reprimand, were brought against two Durham County deputy sheriffs who "brutally" beat a black man "with a club." Austin reacted to these injustices by noting that "you will get some conception of the reason why Negroes riot, why the new generation of the race has lost respect, not only for white leaders but their own adult leaders." He asserted that these types of racial injustices increased the likelihood that Durham was headed for violence like the riots that erupted in Watts, Chicago, and elsewhere.[1]

THE LATE 1960S presented business challenges for the *Carolina Times*, as it did for many black newspapers. According to Larry Muhammad, "By the Black Power era, the formerly cutting-edge medium [referring to black newspapers] was considered powerless. The black press was considered, at best, a farm team for major [white-owned] dailies, which recruited top black journalists to cover the civil rights movement and eventually attracted readers and advertisers once considered the black press's captive market. Conventional wisdom by the 1980's was that the black press, by doing such a bang-up job promoting racial equality, had made itself obsolete."[2] Similarly, Ronald Jacobs reports that black newspapers' circulation declined between 50 and 75 percent from 1950 to 1969.[3] However, in 1965, there were still 150 black newspapers that combined for an average total circulation of about three million.[4]

As the civil rights struggle made important advances in integrating American society, some black activists argued that there was a declining need for black institutions like the black press. Indeed, Jacobs notes that "a significant minority of African American intellectuals during the 1950s and early 1960s were beginning to believe that racial integration would remove the need for a separate black newspaper, and began arguing that the black press should fight for its own disappearance."[5] However, as Jacobs points out, "the power of something like the black press is not tied directly to the number of people who read it. Rather, its potential power resides in the fact that people know it is there, available to be read should the need be perceived. One important reason for this is that interest in the black press tends to increase during periods of racial crisis." For instance, after the Watts riot in 1965, circulation of the *Los Angeles Sentinel* grew by about 20 percent from 1966 to 1971.[6]

The *Carolina Times* was not immune to the pressures felt by other black newspapers, with circulation declining dramatically from 22,000 in 1957 to about 11,000 in 1970. The paper's circulation had peaked in March 1960.[7] Although circulation had declined by 1970, the number of pages in each issue continued to increase, an indication of financial health. While the *Times* had been eight pages long in 1957, it grew steadily to twelve by 1960, fourteen by 1965, and eighteen by 1971. Thus, the *Times* enjoyed some success in confronting the competition from white newspapers during the 1960s and 1970s.

While the business of running the paper was important, for Austin the fight for racial equality and justice remained his first priority, and he continued to shine a bright light on racial injustice and to advocate for civil rights gains. During the late 1960s, the movement in Durham sought to address housing inequities, with Austin backing this crusade. One of the main targets of Durham housing activists was white landlord Abe Greenberg, who was known for the abysmal conditions of his rental property. Greenberg had purchased many houses in East Durham to profit off of the housing shortage caused by the razing of housing, during urban renewal. He raised rents, but did nothing to bring the houses up to code. These actions brought a quick response from the tenants, who formed the Edgemont Community Council, "one of the most militant neighborhood councils" in Durham.[8] The head of the Edgemont Community Council wrote to Greenberg in September 1965, demanding rent reductions and improvements in conditions of the housing, while criticizing his actions as "morally reprehensible and without justification."[9]

After months of petitioning the city council and the mayor to force Greenberg to bring the housing up to code proved futile, the Edgemont council employed direct action. It picketed Greenberg's office, city hall, and the home of David Stith, a Greenberg associate. Stith, an African American who presided over the Southeastern Business College in Durham, had been backed by Greenberg in his 1965 failed candidacy for local office, and had defended Greenberg against community criticism. In 1966, one local citizen observed, "Greenberg financed Stith's unsuccessful campaign for local office . . . and [Stith] acts as his Uncle Tom."[10] During that campaign, Stith had opposed DCNA candidate John Stewart for the city council in the Democratic primary. Austin supported Stewart and suspected that Stith's candidacy was a "sinister move to destroy the work of" the DCNA.[11] Stewart, with 4,543 votes, defeated retired white textile executive William J. Lee (1,786 votes), and Stith came in last with 1,486 votes. After the election, Stith claimed irregularities in the four predominantly black precincts, although Stewart would have won the election even without those districts' votes. Stewart defeated Lee in the runoff primary, running well in some of the largely white precincts.[12]

One day in June 1966, when Stith returned home to find his house being picketed, he drove his car directly into the picket line, "all of whom escaped by jumping out of the way" except for seventeen-year-old John Lee Garner, who was hospitalized with minor injuries. Stith told police that he did not hit Garner and that Garner faked his injuries.[13]

While the *Carolina Times* shined a bright light on Greenberg's housing code violations, Mayor Wense Grabarek and the *Durham Morning Herald* demonized the Edgemont Community Council for taking to the streets to demand action by the city government to force Greenberg to repair substandard housing. In June 1966, the editor of the *Durham Morning Herald* disingenuously scolded the Edgemont council for not bringing its grievances to the appropriate city officials. In fact the council had done precisely that for months. When the city failed to take action, the council resorted to picketing.[14]

In July 1966, the *Times* reported that the investigation of Durham rental housing owned by Greenberg revealed numerous housing code violations, including the lack of indoor toilets.[15] Austin praised the Edgemont Community Council for "exposing" the horrendous conditions endured by Greenberg's tenants and called for substandard housing to be brought up to code within ninety days.[16] While Greenberg did not bring his housing up to code, he did make some improvements, and the protests convinced other local landlords to make repairs to avoid protests against them.[17]

Austin also pressured the city to make the Durham Housing Authority (DHA) more responsive to the black community by increasing black influence in that agency. In February 1966, he criticized the DHA for failing to promote its vice-chairman, NC Mutual treasurer James J. Henderson, "the best qualified member" with the most seniority, to be chairman. Austin characterized the

DHA's perpetuation of white domination as sinking "to the lowest depths to preserve their sadistic notions of white supremacy."[18] Austin noted that Henderson was "continuously by-passed . . . for no other reason than he is a Negro."[19] Fed up after being bypassed three times, Henderson resigned from the DHA in late 1968.[20]

The *Carolina Times* also reported on the struggle by residents of McDougald Terrace, a low-income housing project in east Durham, for decent housing conditions. In March 1967, the *Times* reported that the NAACP Legal Defense Fund represented Joyce Thorpe of Durham as she appealed her eviction from McDougald Terrace in August 1965, "the day after she was elected president of the Parents' Club, a tenant organization."[21] In April 1967, the U.S. Supreme Court ordered the reversal of Thorpe's eviction, "declaring that landlords in public housing projects must provide cause and adequate notice for evictions."[22]

Meanwhile, Austin spoke out for integrated and upgraded health care for blacks in Durham. In January 1966, he called for the complete, not token, integration of historically white Watts Hospital.[23] In doing so, however, he refused to abandon historically black Lincoln Hospital, which had served Durham's black community for over six decades, since its founding in 1901. As hospitals were integrated in the mid-to-late 1960s, Austin sought to protect historically black institutions, notably Lincoln Hospital. In April 1966, the *Times* reported that a "so-called special study committee of the Health Planning Council for Central North Carolina, was designed [to close] . . . Lincoln Hospital." John Wheeler, chairman of the Lincoln Hospital board, objected, arguing that Watts Hospital did not provide equal treatment and access for black patients and black doctors, and therefore, Lincoln should remain open.[24]

In May 1966, Austin urged support for bond issues of $14.1 million for Watts Hospital and $3.5 million for Lincoln Hospital, instead of a competing proposal wherein almost all the bond money would go to Watts Hospital, with little or none for Lincoln.[25] In July 1966, Austin echoed Wheeler's comment that the proposed bond issue of $13.5 million for Watts Hospital and only $1.1 million for Lincoln Hospital was "a fraud on the [black] community."[26] The referendum on the bond issue, designed to fund an integrated Watts Hospital, was defeated by African Americans, who opposed the loss of Lincoln Hospital and suspected that they would continue to be treated poorly at the historically white hospital. Many segregationist whites also helped defeat the bond issue.[27]

Similarly, in April 1967, Austin opposed the takeover of Watts and Lincoln Hospitals by the all-white Durham County Commission because he did not trust that body to provide fair treatment to the historically black Lincoln Hospital.[28] The opposition of the black community helped ensure significant black input in developing a plan that was more amenable to blacks and whites in Durham. Consequently, a 1968 plan formulated by a biracial committee for a brand new integrated hospital in Durham, replacing both Lincoln and Watts Hospitals, led to the passage of a bond issue with substantial black support.[29]

Black schools, black teachers, and black students continued to be a key concern for Austin and the black freedom struggle during the late 1960s. In April 1966, the *Times* reported encouraging news for the integration of schools. A federal court had declared the Pearsall Plan unconstitutional, in a case brought in Charlotte by the attorney Julius Chambers, on behalf of three black families: Dr. and Mrs. Reginald Hawkins and their two children, Rev. and Mrs. Darius Swann and their children, and Rev. and Mrs. E. J. Moore.[30] The court endorsed Chambers's argument that the Pearsall Plan's authorization of private school vouchers was illegal.[31]

While Austin continued to press for integration, he, along with other black activists, sought to ensure that the black community would not bear the entire burden of integrating the schools. The *Times* continued to publicize the lawsuits to reinstate black teachers who were fired by white officials as public schools integrated. In June 1966, the *Times* reported that Willa Cofield Johnson, who had sued the Halifax County school board for damages of $250,000, "was one of 17 Negro teachers ordered reinstated to their jobs Monday by the 4th [U.S.] Circuit Court of Appeals." Johnson had been fired from her teaching job at T. S. Inborden High School in Enfield in retaliation for her civil rights activism. The *Times* reported that "the other 16 teachers, of Hendersonville" had been fired when schools integrated in the 1965–66 school year.[32] The U.S. Supreme Court rejected an appeal by Enfield school officials, thereby affirming the appeals court decision, which had awarded Johnson damages.[33] The North Carolina Teachers Association (NCTA), led by executive secretary Elliot B. Palmer, and the National Education Association backed Johnson with crucial funding for her legal expenses and her living expenses from 1964 to 1967.[34] In an editorial, Austin voiced his disgust with racist white officials in eastern North Carolina: "One has to live in that God forsaken section of the state to know of the ignorance and viciousness of its white people in high places against any Negro who dares raise his finger or head in protest against the brutal exploitation suffered by the race."[35]

Austin regularly backed black activists' efforts to combat the firing of black teachers. In June 1969, the *Times* reported that white principals had fired black teachers in Warren County. One white principal who sought to protect black teachers' jobs and praised the work of a black teacher was himself fired. Similarly, in Franklin County, thirteen black teachers and one black principal were fired.[36] In June 1969, NCTA leader Palmer urged black teachers to stand together to fight the removal of black teachers and administrators by white officials. Palmer reported that the percentage of teachers in Charlotte who were black had declined from 44 percent in 1966 to 22 percent in 1969. Further, Charlotte schools hired only seventeen black teachers of a total of 722 new teachers for the 1968–69 school year. As black students were moved to white schools, black teachers were regularly fired instead of being assigned to historically white schools.[37]

In March 1971, as the state's schools integrated, Austin encouraged the NCTA to take legal action to protect black principals from being replaced by whites, who were "not as qualified or prepared."[38] Despite these and other efforts to protect black principals in North Carolina, their numbers declined dramatically from 226 in the early 1960s to only fifteen by the early 1970s.[39]

Austin joined with other black leaders in speaking out to protect black schools from being shut down by white-majority school boards as public schools were integrated throughout the state. In February 1969, black leaders protested plans to shut down Merrick-Moore County School on Cheek Road at a Durham County school board meeting.[40] In March 1969, Austin exhorted black leaders to mobilize to stop white-dominated school boards from closing black schools and terminating black principals and teachers.[41]

Austin also criticized national policies that hindered school integration. In August 1969, he denounced President Richard Nixon for "abolishing the timetables previously established [by the Johnson administration] in the matter of desegregation in the public schools of the South." Austin correctly concluded that Nixon had sold out to southern white segregationists. The president's embrace of anti-integration tactics was part of his southern strategy to move conservative southern white voters from the Democratic Party to the Republican Party. Austin responded to Nixon's tactics by advising black Republicans to reject the Grand Old Party, which had adopted a strategy of buying "the vote of the white South at the expense of the gains in the matter of desegregation."[42]

While Austin recognized that white-controlled integration was hurting black institutions and black educators, he remained a staunch integrationist. For example, in February 1969, he argued that "the time is now for every black and white citizen who believes in Christianity and democracy to take up the cudgel to rid our nation of the hypocrisy of token integration now being maintained in public offices of our states, counties, and cities." Austin included in this attack the token hiring of only a few blacks in government offices.[43] Nonetheless, 1969 brought an important step forward for black power in public education in Durham. In that year, Theodore R. Speigner, chairman of the Department of Geography at North Carolina Central University (formerly North Carolina College at Durham), became the first black chair of the Durham City Board of Education and the first African American to head any Durham government board.[44]

Just as he fought to protect black elementary and secondary schools, Austin also sought to protect black colleges. Therefore, he denounced white politicians' plan to use racial integration as a pretext for eviscerating black colleges. When, in 1967, Governor Dan Moore called for the closing of the NCC law school because it was now "outmoded," Austin came to its defense. He praised the NCC law school because it successfully trained "competent legal talent for a significant segment of the State's population." If it was terminated, black students' opportunities for legal training would be severely circumscribed. Austin noted that although the law schools at Duke and the University of North Carolina (UNC) had desegregated, they still admitted very few black students. Further, he noted that closing the NCC law school would save the state very little money, as the school operated on a small operating budget of $85,000 annually. Austin also criticized the governor's administration for failing to hire any black attorneys to work in the state's attorney general's office, the state supreme court, administrative offices of the courts, or even the tax research department.[45]

After the governor's call for the closing of the NCC law school, Austin publicized a report by NCC School of Law dean Daniel G. Sampson that provided ample evidence of the need for the law school. Sampson reported that in North Carolina there was only one black attorney for every 13,000 blacks, while there was one white attorney for every 768 whites. In fact, there were only eighty-six black attorneys in the entire state in 1966, forty-six of whom had gone to the NCC law school, while only nine had graduated from one of the state's historically white law schools, UNC–Chapel Hill, Duke, or Wake Forest. During the 1965–66 academic year, these three historically white schools combined to enroll only five black law students. UNC's law school had just one black student out of a total of 509 law students. Clearly, the historically white institutions offered very few opportunities for African Americans to earn a law degree. Meanwhile, NCC had graduated a total of 107 lawyers in its history.[46]

In December 1968, when the North Carolina Board of Higher Education recommended phasing out the NCC law school, Austin again came to its defense. He noted, "There are probably sinister and determined efforts in certain corners of the state to abolish the NCC Law School." While the board claimed that the UNC law school could absorb black law school students who attended NCC, UNC's record of admitting very few black students undercut the board's claim.[47] Ultimately, the work of Austin, other black leaders, and the wider black community helped save the NCC law school.

DURING THE MID- TO LATE 1960S, Austin continued to be a strong supporter of the younger generation of black activists, notably Howard Fuller, who came to Durham in 1965.[48] An employment specialist for the Chicago branch of the Urban League, Fuller was hired to direct community organizing efforts for Operation Breakthrough, an anti-poverty organization in Durham created under the auspices of the North Carolina Fund in 1964. The North Carolina Fund was an anti-poverty initiative started by Governor Sanford in 1963 with Ford Foundation funding. Operation Breakthrough later received federal funding from the Office of Economic Opportunity (OEO), part of President Lyndon Johnson's War on Poverty.[49] The OEO required that all community action programs have "maximum feasible participation" of local people, and "demanded that one-third of Operation Breakthrough's board come from Durham's low-income communities and that the board be thoroughly integrated."[50]

An outspoken advocate for the rights and opportunities of African Americans, Fuller regularly looked to Austin for advice. Fuller's office was located above the Scarborough Funeral Home on 522 East Pettigrew Street (which had housed the Rex Theater in earlier times), just down the block from the office of the *Carolina Times*, which was at 436 East Pettigrew Street. Fuller recently recalled that he "often stopped by his [Austin's] office to chat and seek advice."[51] When Fuller was under attack from various quarters, Austin told him, "Howard, don't listen to these people." Instead, he advised Fuller to continue to do what he thought was right, and not to be deterred by criticism. Austin regularly encouraged Fuller to confront a recalcitrant black upper class while battling powerful white leaders. Austin's support was important to Fuller, who praised the older man's fighting spirit. Fuller recalled that Austin was "like a bulldog at the ankles of the black bourgeoisie." He continued, "I loved Mr. Austin," who was "crazier than me." Fuller admired Austin's courage in speaking out for justice regardless of the consequences, which was a trait that the young activist cultivated for himself.[52]

In 1967, Austin told an interviewer working with the North Carolina Fund, "Fuller and his movement embarrass other Negro leaders, especially us older men, who don't stand up the way he does. Most of today's adult Negro leadership is hopeless. The future is in these young people." Despite Austin's harsh criticism of older black leaders, James Cunningham of the North Carolina Fund reported that "behind the scenes, [DCNA leader John] Wheeler did much to protect Fuller's freedom to operate." Wheeler told Cunningham that "he and the old-time Durham Committee on Negro Affairs had" supported young black activists; "they furnished sage advice and legal assistance,... and had put Fuller on their political sub-committee."[53]

In July 1967, after Howard Fuller was suspended by the OEO, Austin and a group of prominent blacks supported Fuller's reinstatement. The group included black educators, like James Brewer, NCC history professor, and C. E. Boulware, Durham city councilman and NCC mathematics professor; and businessmen like J. C. Scarborough II, funeral home director; F. V. Allison Jr., NC Mutual executive; the attorney and realtor Mickey Michaux; and Asa Spaulding, NC Mutual president.[54] The suspension of Fuller was a response to the growing criticism of black OEO activists by conservative Democrats and Republicans. In North Carolina, Republican congressman Jim Gardner was a key critic of Fuller and black activist involvement in the OEO in Durham. Nonetheless, boosted by black community support, as well as that of North Carolina Fund director George Esser, Fuller regained his position, with his salary now paid directly by the fund.[55]

During the late 1960s, Austin backed the anti-poverty initiatives of Fuller and other young black activists in Durham. In October 1967, Austin embraced Fuller's call for middle-class blacks to work with poor blacks to fight for better housing and improved economic opportunities for all African Americans. Austin wrote, "The black man must take pride in himself, and consider his fellow Negro to be a brother whatever his lot. In the struggle of our times, Negroes must be united."[56] He urged the Durham City Council to respond to the needs of the city's poor. He suggested that if the council did not "allow the words of the people to influence their decisions" on housing and other issues of importance to the poor, then they would "have to be pressured by every means the inventive minds of such men as Howard Fuller and Ben Ruffin can come up with."[57] A native of Durham who worked closely with Fuller in Operation Breakthrough, Ruffin, like other young activists, greatly admired Austin as they fought for racial equality. In 1968, Ruffin expressed his pride in being "one of Mr. Austin's younger soul brothers."[58]

During these years, many black activists, including Fuller, employed rhetoric that rejected the strategy of nonviolent resistance to racial oppression. While Fuller had been an integrationist advocate of nonviolent protest when he arrived in Durham in 1965, he soon embraced Black Power, black nationalism, and the use of violence in self-defense.[59] In an October 1967 speech at North Carolina College, Fuller told students that he "did not come to NCC to start a riot," but at the same time, he had "turned the last cheek. The next time I turn a cheek, I'll follow it with a right cross."[60] In November 1968, Fuller declared, "I see the control of schools and their curricula as being more important than the integration of many schools. . . . I am not an integrationist."[61]

While he did not publicly criticize Fuller's rejection of nonviolence or his advocacy of Black Power, Austin had harsh words for black nationalist organizations. In 1963, Austin told an interviewer that he refused to include information about Durham's Muslim Temple, which was just a few blocks from the *Carolina Times* offices, because he hoped that lack of attention would lead to the temple's demise. He noted that most of Durham's black leaders rejected the Muslim Temple's "separatist views."[62] At a meeting of the Black Panther Party of New York in Harlem, in August 1966, Maxwell Stanford, a founder of the Revolutionary Action Movement (RAM), suggested the use of Molotov cocktails to help end white oppression in the United States. The following month, Austin rejected the Panthers' promotion of violent tactics as a way of resolving the problems of African Americans. Instead, Austin reaffirmed his support for Martin Luther King Jr.'s "philosophy of nonviolence."[63]

In April 1967, Austin opposed Adam Clayton Powell Jr.'s call for the creation of a black political party, reiterating his rejection of separatism. Austin argued that "no Negro who has opposed segregated schools, churches, employment and other such public accommodations can honestly be an advocate of a third party movement composed entirely of Negroes or whites."[64] Austin pledged that "this newspaper will continue to oppose with all its might . . . any individual, group of individuals or organization that sets themselves up for operation in this country on the grounds of race or color."[65] After the July 1967 Black Power conference in Newark, New Jersey, Austin condemned black separatism as "an objective" that would "come to no good end." He also contended that black nationalism was no better than white nationalism, as symbolized by the Ku Klux Klan.[66] In August 1967, the editor, who had long praised the Student Nonviolent Coordinating Committee (SNCC), which had recently rejected nonviolence, took exception to its "stand in favor of violence" and its "recent violent attack . . . on Israel and the Jewish people in general."[67] Austin denounced SNCC's opposition to Israel and support for Palestinian nationalism in the aftermath of the June 1967 Arab-Israeli War. The mainstream press also condemned SNCC's embrace of the Palestinians, which coincided with the civil rights organization's support for nationalist movements in Africa and Asia.[68]

Notwithstanding his militant rhetoric, Howard Fuller often acted to prevent violent outbursts by the black community because he believed that violence would do more harm than good for the cause of the black freedom struggle. Indeed, Fuller's efforts to keep the peace did not go unnoticed. In July 1967, Watts Hill Jr., a prominent white Durham businessman and member of the state board of education, said that Fuller was "the single person most responsible for there not being riots in Durham."[69] Austin made a similar point in defending Fuller from his enemies. In July 1967, Austin observed, "Facing a street lined with white hecklers who were endeavoring to inflame Negro marchers to the City Hall, it was Fuller who stood in the path and held back those of his own race and the white hecklers from engaging in a free for all."[70]

Nine months later, after the assassination of Martin Luther King Jr., in April 1968, Austin stood with the NAACP in its opposition to the use of violence, even in the face of violence committed by reactionary whites against blacks. Austin referred to scripture to support his position, quoting Jesus's admonition from the Bible, "For all they that take the sword shall perish with the sword."[71]

Although he distanced himself from Black Power organizations, Austin continued to be a fierce advocate for black political power during the late 1960s. As he had done for over three decades, he regularly played a leading role in voter registration drives. Before the primary on May 28, 1966, the *Carolina Times* reminded its readers to register to vote. It ran a boldface banner at the bottom of the front page of two editions announcing, "Registration Books Are Now Open . . . Register Now! A Voteless People Is a Hopeless People."[72]

With the North Carolina General Assembly still all white, as it had been for over six decades, Austin pressed for the election of at least one African American legislator. In May 1966, Austin contrasted North Carolina with other southern states that had recently elected black legislators, including Georgia, with nine blacks in its legislature, and Texas, which had just elected three blacks to its legislature. Austin noted that North Carolina's white supremacist legislature was backed up, in part, by the fact that the state had more Ku Klux Klan members than any other state.[73] Austin's friend and businessman Mickey Michaux of Durham ran for a seat in the General Assembly that year.[74] After Michaux's defeat in the primary, Austin blamed low black voter turnout for his defeat and that of other black candidates, including the attorney M. Hugh Thompson, who would have been elected district court judge if he had gotten ninety-four more votes.[75]

Although the DCNA and Austin had backed Mayor Wense Grabarek, who ran "on a liberal platform," in his first two runs for mayor in 1963 and 1965, they opposed him in 1967, as Grabarek showed declining sympathy for the needs of the black community. In 1968, a North Carolina Fund official described Grabarek as "a rather pompous man who is also a clever politician. He is not a racist, but neither is he sympathetic to the problems of poor people—black or white." Grabarek, who had initially supported the North Carolina Fund, was increasingly hostile to it and was "allied with the city's major white economic interest."[76]

During the 1967 mayoral campaign, Austin and the DCNA backed Grabarek's Democratic Party opponent in the primary, Duke University law professor Paul Hardin.[77] In May 1967, Austin denounced white politicians, a not-so-veiled attack on Grabarek, who railed against the "bloc vote." Austin characterized Grabarek's tactic as "a sinister attempt to arouse the unintelligent white voters" to vote "to offset the Negro vote." While conservative white politicians censured blacks for bloc voting, Austin countered that in fact, whites regularly voted as a bloc against black candidates and rejected policies and bills that challenged racist policies and actions. He added that white southern congressmen regularly voted as a bloc to oppose civil rights legislation. Austin urged black voters to cast ballots in the May 13 primary.[78] Nonetheless, as Christina Greene observed, the mayor's "race-baiting tactics worked, and Grabarek roused enough white support, [including the segregationist Citizens Council] to win" another term as mayor.[79]

After the election, Austin thanked letter writers to the *Durham Morning Herald* who chided Grabarek for his cynical tactics. The editor praised the letter writers "for their analysis and comment on the lowbrow or win-at-any-cost type of campaign" run by the mayor. With Grabarek's reelection, Austin expected "another do-nothing term about raising the status of Negro citizens." Consequently, he called for renewed efforts by blacks to increase their voter registration to ensure a different result in the next campaign.[80]

The May 1967 primary did yield an important victory for the black community, with NCC mathematics professor C. Elwood Boulware's success in his campaign to become the second African American serving on the Durham City Council. In March and April 1967, Austin had urged black voters to help elect Boulware to add another black voice to that of John S. Stewart. With DCNA backing, Boulware won the primary, according to Austin, thanks to a coalition of "progressive white" and black voters.[81]

Following the 1967 election, Austin became increasingly critical of the mayor. In August 1967, he attacked Grabarek for his failure to address substandard housing and poverty in the black community. He noted that since 1965, the mayor had employed "political trickery" in his attempt to undermine the anti-poverty efforts of the United Organizations for Community Improvement (UOCI). Austin criticized Grabarek's "unholy alliance with [Republican Congressman] Jim Gardner" in their attacks on UOCI and anti-poverty activists like Fuller, and Grabarek's "unnecessary" call for the National Guard to patrol Durham's streets, which the editor characterized as "anti-Negro antics." Austin urged Durham citizens to take action to end employment discrimination and address inadequate housing for whites and blacks.[82]

In 1968, rising black political consciousness and voter registration in Durham and throughout the state helped increase the number of black candidacies and black electoral victories. Throughout the campaign season, the *Carolina Times* implored its readers to vote, with banners regularly displayed on the bottom of page one, which read, "A Voteless People Is a Hopeless People" and "Don't Be a Traitor to Your Race by Failing to Register and Vote in All Elections."[83] The *Carolina Times* also worked closely with the Durham Committee on Negro Affairs to increase black voter participation. Both organizations arranged for volunteers, including Duke University students, to drive voters to the polls on Election Day. Drivers would meet at the office of the *Carolina Times* on Pettigrew Street, which served as campaign headquarters.[84]

Austin publicized black candidacies, including the attorney Mickey Michaux's run for the state House of Representatives in Durham and the attorney Henry Frye's run for the state House of Representatives in Greensboro.[85] Black dentist and activist Reginald Hawkins of Charlotte ran in the Democratic primary for governor. In April 1968, Austin praised Hawkins for his deft analysis of Governor Moore's race-based reaction to events. Hawkins explained that Moore called out the National Guard when blacks marched for justice and equality, but when black homes were bombed, the governor did nothing but "study" the issue.[86]

David Stith's 1968 run for Congress from Durham proved particularly controversial. Stith, a black businessman who had defended slumlord Abe Greenberg, had made many enemies in the black community. But as a black candidate, Stith gained some black support, especially given the fact that no black North Carolinian had served in Congress since 1901. In March 1968, Austin condemned the factions in the black community warring and dividing over Stith's candidacy.[87]

Black voter registration and turnout efforts yielded some fruit in 1968. Two black candidates, funeral director J. C. Scarborough III and former NC

Mutual president Asa Spaulding, won Democratic primaries for seats on the Durham County Board of Commissioners. While Scarborough was defeated in the general election, Spaulding was elected the first black Durham County commissioner. Greensboro voters elected the attorney Henry Frye to the North Carolina General Assembly, making him the first African American to serve in that body in over six decades.[88]

In January 1969, Austin renewed his attacks on Durham mayor Grabarek, chastising the mayor for his failure to open up city government to more black influence. Austin contrasted the selection of Rev. Philip R. Cousin, pastor of St. Joseph's African Methodist Episcopal (AME) Church, as the third black president in five years of the interracial Durham Ministerial Association, with the mayor's failure to end the white domination of the Durham Housing Authority. According to Austin, the actions of the Ministerial Association put "to shame Durham's mayor and its city council for by-passing three times within 19 years the promotion of [black businessman] J. J. Henderson as chairman of the Durham Housing Authority."[89]

In March 1969, Austin called for the election of a new mayor of Durham but said he preferred a "worthy" white candidate because he did not think a black candidate could get enough white votes to be elected.[90] Austin also urged white and black voters to elect three African Americans, John S. Stewart, Eugene Hampton, and Harris Johnson, to the city council, so that blacks would have more equitable representation in Durham politics.[91] Austin took an active role in the campaign by participating in a forum for the candidates for mayor and city council. On April 30, 1969, a few days before the Democratic primary, Austin asked questions of candidates alongside several other local journalists from the *Durham Morning Herald*, the *North Carolina Anvil*, and the *Durham Sun*.[92]

As in previous elections, the *Carolina Times* worked with the DCNA to increase black voter registration and black voter turnout. Once again, the *Times* offices served as an informal campaign headquarters for black voter registration efforts, with volunteer drivers meeting there to provide black citizens transportation to register to vote.[93]

After the May 17 runoff primary, Austin reported that low black voter turnout damaged the candidacies of progressive politicians, like Jack Preiss, who was defeated for city council.[94] The previous month, Austin had criticized black Durham leaders for apathy and failing to mount a vigorous voter registration campaign to increase black political power. He suggested that a change in DCNA leadership might be necessary.[95] While Grabarek was reelected in Durham in 1969, a few miles away, Howard Lee was elected the first black mayor of Chapel Hill, and he was the first African American to be elected in a majority-white town or city in the state.[96]

Following Grabarek's primary victory, Austin continued to criticize the mayor for his failure to govern fairly. In September 1969, Austin denounced Grabarek and other white officials for failing to silence "a representative of the Ku Klux Klan, armed with a pistol" who threw "his weight around in a threatening and menacing manner" at a city council meeting. Austin reported that the mayor and police officers did nothing to stop Klan leader Claiborne P. Ellis, who, for two hours, insulted black citizens, employing nasty epithets. Councilman John Stewart urged the mayor to terminate Ellis's speech; when the mayor refused to do so, Stewart left the meeting in protest. Austin noted that if a black militant addressed the council in the way the Klansman did, white officials would have immediately silenced him.[97]

Following the 1969 election, Austin sought to reinvigorate the old progressive-labor-black political alliance of the late 1940s and early 1950s. He endorsed "a coalition of liberals, labor and Negroes in North Carolina" as articulated by Wilbur Hobby, president of the North Carolina AFL-CIO. Austin noted that Hobby had reported that the average industrial worker in North Carolina earned only "87 cents an hour 'less than the average for industrial workers in this country.'" Austin urged black and white workers to unite in the fight to raise workers' wages in the state.[98]

In March 1971, the *Carolina Times* supported Asa T. Spaulding Jr. in his candidacy for Durham mayor.[99] Spaulding was defeated by James R. Hawkins, but C. E. Boulware and John Stewart were reelected to the city council. Stewart also served as mayor pro tem.[100]

During the late 1960s, Austin's statements on national politics showed that he was more sympathetic to the Democrats than he had been during the second half of the 1950s, when he had endorsed Eisenhower in his campaign for reelection. However, he regularly criticized Democratic officeholders when they opposed civil rights legislation. In addition, Austin became an outspoken critic of President Johnson's conduct of the Vietnam War. While Austin was a strong supporter of the president's domestic policies, notably his support for civil rights legislation and the War on Poverty, like many black journalists, he broke with the president on Vietnam. Historian Lawrence Eldridge has observed, "During the Johnson administration the pillars of the black press found themselves increasingly torn between a desire to support a president who had displayed a theretofore unprecedented level of presidential commitment to black goals and African American concerns about the diversion of scarce national resources to a far-off war."[101]

By 1966, Austin's editorials were decidedly critical of U.S. foreign policy and supportive of anti-war activists. The sixty-eight-year-old editor predicted that more and more people would embrace Senate Foreign Relations Committee chair William Fulbright's critique of Johnson's policies in Vietnam. In February 1966, Austin anticipated that more people would soon realize "the futility of modern warfare. . . . After all is said and done, who will be the winner of a war in which every human being on earth is left a corpse?"[102]

Austin also revealed the disproportionate impact of the war on African Americans. In September 1966, Austin contrasted the large sacrifice made by black soldiers in Vietnam—they represented 40 percent of American soldiers in Vietnam—with the limited black representation in political office. He noted that there was still only one black member of the Durham City Council and no blacks served on the Durham County Board of Commissioners.[103] In April 1967, Austin discussed the disproportionate number of blacks fighting and dying in Vietnam. He reported that blacks suspected that there was "a deliberate policy on the part of the armed service of the nation to use members of their race for cannon fodder, in a war which it now appears neither side can win."[104] Austin's view that blacks were disproportionately affected by the war is backed up by statistical evidence. From 1961 to 1966, when blacks represented 11 percent of all Americans, 20 percent of "Army combat deaths were" African American. By the end of the war, blacks represented 13.7 percent of total American casualties.[105]

In April 1967, Austin highlighted the financial and social costs of the Vietnam War, quoting a CORE statement that "eight hours of the war in Viet Nam costs more than the [federal] government will spend for the combined budget for education, child care, sanitation and housing of 400,000 families of migrant workers this year." The CORE statement also stressed the terrible human cost of the war in American lives, disproportionately black men.[106]

By 1969, Austin was becoming increasingly militant in his opposition to the war. Earlier, he was less willing to directly attack Johnson because of that president's pro–civil rights record. In the case of Nixon, Johnson's Republican successor, who had less sympathy for the plight of black Americans, Austin had no compunction about mounting a direct attack. In September 1969, the editor advocated massive marches and protests in Washington, D.C., to "bring the stupid war in Vietnam to an end." He noted that "military might" was not enough to win a war, as shown by the "futility of modern warfare" in Vietnam.[107] In December 1969, Austin again supported mass demonstrations against Nixon's conduct of the Vietnam War. He called Nixon's policies "foolhardy . . . in a war of which there appears to be no end and no hope for victory" with "endless sacrifice of American lives" and "senseless carnage" at great financial cost and damage to the United States' reputation.[108]

Unlike in the late 1950s and early 1960s, Austin was not sympathetic to Republican efforts to win black votes, especially as the GOP increasingly endorsed policies antithetical to the interests of African Americans. In April 1966, Austin criticized the Republican Party's attempt to attract black voters after the Republican congressional candidate for the Fourth District, Jim Gardner, who was the former head of the state's Republican Party, endorsed Senator Strom Thurmond of South Carolina, who had joined the Republican Party after LBJ and other northern Democrats backed civil rights legislation. Still distrustful of many southern white Democrats, Austin observed that black southern voters would have a hard time choosing between Democrats and Republicans "were it not for President Johnson, Vice President [Hubert] Humphrey and a few other liberal democrats."[109]

Nonetheless, Austin did not hesitate to attack conservative white Democrats. In October 1966, Austin encouraged blacks in the Second Congressional District, in eastern North Carolina, to mount an effective voter registration campaign to defeat Congressman Lawrence H. Fountain, a Democrat, who had opposed the Civil Rights Act of 1964 and other civil rights legislation. Austin noted that Fountain was from "Tarboro, located in a section of North Carolina where the economy—agricultural—enjoyed by whites, has for years been maintained off the labor, sweat and blood of Negroes."[110] Nonetheless, Fountain would continue to represent North Carolina in the House of Representatives until his retirement in 1983.[111]

After the Republicans nominated Nixon for president and Maryland governor Spiro Agnew for vice president at their convention in 1968, and South Carolina senator Strom Thurmond escorted Nixon to the podium, Austin urged blacks to back any Democratic candidate to run against Nixon.[112] In November 1968, Austin advised African Americans to vote for Democratic Party nominee Hubert Humphrey for president. Austin reminded his readers of Humphrey's 1948 speech at the Democratic National Convention in support of civil rights, and in opposition to the Dixiecrats, then led by the same Strom Thurmond, who was now allied with Nixon and the Republicans.[113]

ONE OF THE MOST controversial issues in Durham during the late 1960s was urban renewal. At first, African Americans supported urban renewal because they believed that federal and local funding would dramatically improve housing and roads, much of which was substandard, in the Hayti community. After congressional housing legislation, passed in 1949 and 1954, authorized federal funding for urban slum clearance and new construction, Durham officials sought to capitalize on the opportunity to revitalize the city, which suffered from deteriorating housing, loss of industrial employment, and inadequate roads. In 1958, the city established the Durham Redevelopment Commission, to pursue federal housing and transportation subsidies, and authorized a study by UNC's Department of City and Regional Planning. The study recommended "that two hundred acres of Hayti 'be made an attractively clean and modern residential section,'" but the chief goal of the project was to improve "the city's tax base" and make "room for the planned expressway," which could be built with federal highway funds.[114] The federal government required that localities contribute funding for urban renewal projects, so in 1962, Durham voters narrowly approved an $8.6 million bond issue to finance water, sewer, and street improvements in the Hayti section. The bond issue also supported the construction of the East-West Expressway, which would connect Interstate 85 in northwestern Durham with the Research Triangle Park, an industrial park southeast of the city. Part of the expressway's path went right through the section of Hayti slated for clearance. While many whites opposed the bond issue because they frowned on programs that benefited the black community, African Americans were almost unanimously in favor of it. The bonds enjoyed strong support from the city's major black and white civic and business organizations and newspapers, including the Durham Chamber of Commerce, the Durham Business and Professional Chain, the Durham Committee on Negro Affairs, the Central Labor Union, the Durham Board of Realtors, the *Carolina Times,* and the *Durham Morning Herald.*[115] White proponents of the bond issue supported urban renewal based on their belief that by improving Hayti, they would increase property values in the white sections of Durham. Indeed, Durham's planners argued that Hayti was an "'economic and esthetic drag' on the city, and a detriment to 'public health, safety, morals, and welfare.'"[116]

In contrast, many blacks viewed Hayti as a vibrant, though poor, African American community, which suffered because of overcrowding and inadequate housing. The black community favored the 1962 referendum because it expected that urban renewal would bring funding to improve black people's lives. Austin and other black leaders maintained that the Hayti community needed the promised infusion of federal and local funds to clear away substandard housing and build proper homes for the city's African Americans.

While Austin backed the bond issue, he was not sanguine about white support. Several weeks before the referendum, he feared that the bond issue would be defeated by white voters who would "take delight in keeping a

Negro section of the city a blighted area where they will have the delight of looking down or turning up their noses at Negroes."[117] Nonetheless, Austin encouraged the city's voters to back the bond issue because "the future growth and development of Durham will be at stake."[118] While Austin correctly predicted that most white voters would oppose the bond issue, tremendous black voter support provided the margin of victory in the 1962 referendum.[119]

While in 1963 and 1964 the project appeared to be going well, with some black families expressing satisfaction with their move to better homes, by the mid-1960s, blacks who lived in Hayti were becoming increasingly skeptical about how the program was being carried out. As parts of Hayti were razed, residents found that little or no provision had been made for them to move into low-income housing, which had been promised by the Redevelopment Commission. In addition, there was increasing trepidation about the plans to build the East-West Expressway, with the route planned right through the heart of Hayti.[120]

In April 1967, the *Carolina Times* reported on the growing tensions surrounding these issues: "Residents living in the East-West Expressway right-of-way this week petitioned the Redevelopment Commission of the City of Durham for a hearing to air problems relating to their relocation." The United Organizations for Community Improvement (UOCI) backed up the residents and called on the commission's chairman, the white attorney Robinson Everett, to halt the removal of residents to substandard housing. Ann Atwater, chair of the housing commission of UOCI, noted that the city of Durham had "known for years that this area would have to be cleared," but had not made any effort to ensure that low-income citizens who were displaced would be moved into decent, not substandard housing.[121]

Later in April 1967, Atwater told the redevelopment commission that the UOCI would not take legal action to stop the "letting of the expressway contract." She noted, "We feel that the expressway is important to all of the citizens of Durham, though we feel at the same time that low income people are making most of the sacrifices." But Atwater demanded that the commission and the community find suitable homes for people who were displaced because they lived inside the expressway's planned route.[122]

Despite its promising beginnings, urban renewal proved to be a disaster for Hayti. After urban renewal and the building of the East-West Expressway, Hayti was virtually unrecognizable. As historian Fitz Brundage observed, "Where once hundreds of homes and businesses had stood, an expressway and weed-infested lots stood."[123] Many Hayti residents bitterly declared that "urban removal" was a more apt name for what had been done to their community.[124]

Meanwhile, in July 1967, black citizens protested the city's plans to build a segregated housing project on Bacon Street. While the black community had been pushing for low-income housing to replace housing razed in Hayti as part of urban renewal, it refused to accept the expansion of segregated housing projects. Instead black activists demanded the construction of an integrated housing project elsewhere.[125] At the protest, "more than 150 black citizens, most of them members of UOCI, appeared before the city council to demand that the housing authority drop its plans for Bacon Street and actively promote residential desegregation." In addition, they insisted that the housing authority enforce its housing code and crack down on slumlords.[126] Toward the end of the meeting, Howard Fuller said, "I didn't come to beg, and I didn't come . . . with my hat in my hand. . . . We're tired of you white folks turning down everything that will benefit Negroes. . . . You all better wake up, you all better lean back on those chairs and listen to what these folks are talking about. And you all better start doing something to benefit these black people. Cause they're tired, and they're frustrated, and people who get tired and frustrated do things they wouldn't ordinarily do." Fuller's point was clear; frustrated blacks in Durham might turn to violence. This point was heard loud and clear by the city council, especially because Fuller's words were spoken on July 17, 1967, the last day of riots in Newark, New Jersey, that resulted in the deaths of twenty-six people.[127] Two days later, inspired by Ann Atwater's speech at St. Joseph's AME Church, about 200 blacks marched to city hall. In what the *Durham Sun* called a "ruckus" on the return from the march, a few young African Americans threw "rocks, breaking windows, and slightly injuring one policeman." Though there was minimal violence, the mayor, without conferring with the city council, asked the governor to send in the National Guard.[128]

In the fall of 1967, Austin renewed his attack on Mayor Grabarek for supporting housing policies that perpetuated racial segregation. Austin praised businessman Mickey Michaux for opposing construction of the Bacon Street "housing project in the already overcrowded section of the city." Michaux told the mayor, "If you do not wish to aid us in the perpetuation of progress, then we will not aid you in the perpetuation of peace."[129] Austin noted that "Negroes of all classes" were "opposing the Bacon Street Housing Project."[130] Ultimately, the movement against the Bacon Street project succeeded as the Durham Planning and Zoning Commission refused to approve a zoning variance, the developer withdrew, and the city council affirmed the Planning and Zoning Commission decision.[131]

In April 1968, the civil rights movement was dealt a terrible blow with the assassination of Martin Luther King Jr. Austin wrote, "The assassination of Dr. King, intended by its perpetrator to put an end to one of the greatest leaders against the practice of racial discrimination, has instead brought to their knees the consciences of every respectable and just citizen of this nation." The *Times* printed King's 1963 "I Have a Dream" speech, because Austin believed that the civil rights leader's own words best expressed his legacy.[132]

In Durham and throughout the nation, the black freedom struggle moved forward, inspired to make sure that an assassin's bullet would not end the movement. Following the assassination, nonacademic Duke University workers, mostly black female cafeteria workers and housekeepers, who were members of union Local 77 of the American Federation of State, County, and Municipal Employees (AFSCME), struck for increased wages and collective bargaining rights. Thousands of students and some faculty supported the workers by boycotting classes and joining the workers in massive demonstrations and vigils on campus. The 1968 strike was the culmination of two years of organizing and protests by Duke workers for improved working conditions and higher wages. Austin praised the workers and students for their actions. He also related the workers' fight for fair wages and decent working conditions to the long history of exploitation by Duke-owned American Tobacco Company and its history of low pay for black workers. Making a larger point, Austin argued that the "very foundation of the American economy has been built on the blood, sweat and labor of Negroes," many of whom resented "their white neighbors who dare to assume the attitude that this country belongs to them and them alone." Six days after the King assassination, the Duke protests succeeded in forcing the university board of trustees to approve the workers' demand that their minimum wage be raised to $1.60/hour.[133]

Three months later, Durham activists organized a boycott of white-owned stores to address multiple forms of racial discrimination in the city. Historian Christina Greene has characterized this protest, which lasted from July 1968 to February 1969, as "the longest, most successful, and broadest-based protest ever waged by Durham blacks."[134] With strong support from Austin and the *Carolina Times*, the boycott began in response to Watts Hospital's firing of thirty-one black employees who had joined Local 77 of AFSCME. After the firing, middle- and working-class blacks formed the Black Solidarity Committee for Community Improvement (BSC). In July 1968, the BSC "delivered a ... memorandum to the Durham Chamber of Commerce and the Merchants Association that outlined eighty-eight 'essential' demands covering employment, education, representation of blacks on local boards, and relations between the police and the black community."[135] Austin declared, "The Negro wants his full share of citizenship in this country, nothing more and nothing less, and he wants it now."[136]

The *Times* reported regularly on the boycott, and by publicizing statements by black boycott leaders, helped contribute to the boycott's success. For example, in August 1968, the *Times* reported that BSC leader A. J. (Howard) Clement III encouraged blacks to continue the boycott of downtown stores "until grievances in public housing, recreation, employment, education, administration of justice, equitable representation on public boards and agencies, welfare, building code enforcement and passage of open housing and human relations commission ordinances have been resolved."[137] In November 1968, the *Times* noted that Howard Fuller, now director of training for the Foundation for Community Development, urged continuation of the black boycott of downtown stores.[138] In December 1968, the *Times* reported that NC Mutual executive R. Kelly Bryant Jr. challenged all black Durhamites to join the boycott and attend weekly Sunday night meetings at local churches and the Saturday meetings at Durham Business College.[139] In late January 1969, the *Carolina Times* published the appeal by Nathaniel B. White, president of Service Printing Co., Inc., for black unity in the boycott. White "warned . . . that the current Black Solidarity boycott 'may be . . . the last attempt to settle the racial problems in our city peacefully.'"[140]

Austin also backed the boycott by speaking out at public meetings meant to increase community support. In October 1968, he addressed a boycott meeting at Mount Vernon Baptist Church in Durham. Meetings such as this one were crucial to promoting widespread participation in the boycott by blacks and liberal whites. Indeed, Duke University's student newspaper backed the boycott and promoted Austin's speech on its editorial page.[141] Austin implored the mostly black audience of 300 to remain united in the struggle for "the advancement of the race." He also emphasized the importance of the political process and urged blacks to register to vote and elect candidates supportive of the black freedom struggle.[142]

In February 1969, the boycott ended, with BSC leader Ben Ruffin's announcement that sufficient progress had been made so that continued negotiations with the Durham Merchants Association and the Durham Chamber of Commerce would proceed without the continuation of the boycott.[143] Although the boycott did not achieve all its goals, it did force white businesses and government agencies to make some important concessions. Black employment opportunities increased, the Housing Authority added two African

Americans to its board, and housing projects adjusted utility bills to benefit tenants. The city also created a Human Relations Commission headed by an African American.[144] Austin declared that Sunday, February 16, 1969, would "long be remembered as a high day in this city" because of agreements between Duke University and black students, and the agreement to end the BSC boycott of Durham merchants.[145]

Other cities in North Carolina also employed selective buying campaigns to push for equal treatment for African Americans. In Rocky Mount, blacks boycotted four white stores that restricted black employment opportunities. In November 1968, the *Times* reported that the Rocky Mount boycott was suspended after the local chamber of commerce agreed to address issues of concern to the black community. For example, the chamber of commerce "adopted a policy calling for a personal and business creed of non-discrimination and equal opportunity."[146]

While advocating for equal job opportunities for blacks in white businesses, Austin also advocated on behalf of local black businesses. In May 1969, he supported a "$900,000 grant for Black business in Durham" given to the Foundation for Community Development (FCD), noting that this organization was controlled by low-income African Americans. Created in 1967 by former North Carolina Fund workers, the FCD had initially received most of its budget from the fund, but this $900,000 grant came from the U.S. Office of Economic Opportunity, created during President Johnson's administration as part of his War on Poverty. Black businessman Nathan Garrett, who had previously served as deputy director of the North Carolina Fund, was executive director of FCD, which funded "eleven poor people's corporations" in North Carolina, including the United Organizations for Community Improvement (UOCI) in Durham. Howard Fuller directed the FCD Department of Training. Austin supported black control, and he argued that the grant would boost black employment and provide "increased self-reliance for Durham's Black citizens."[147]

Meanwhile, 1969 saw the opening of Malcolm X Liberation University (MXLU), an expression of the increasing black nationalist consciousness, particularly among young African Americans. It was created by black Duke University students and other activists, notably Howard Fuller, who wanted a curriculum that was "meaningful and relevant" to black students.[148] MXLU was housed in "an abandoned warehouse" at 426–428 East Pettigrew Street, which was just a few doors down from the office of the *Carolina Times* at 436 East Pettigrew Street.[149] So Austin had a front row seat to the development of MXLU.

Although the new university was founded on nationalist principles, which Austin, an avowed integrationist, generally disparaged, he was sympathetic to MXLU. This sympathy was likely influenced by Austin's great respect for the university's leader, Howard Fuller. In November 1969, Austin praised Fuller and MXLU for their success in gaining $45,000 in grants from the national Episcopal Church Urban Crisis Program, to help begin operations in Durham. Although Austin did not agree with every aspect of "Fuller's program," he said, "We support with all our hearts the overall conception of the Malcolm X University." Austin continued, "Not until you have been on the receiving end of their [whites] contemptible stares is it possible to understand that there is a serious need for some movement [like Malcolm X University] . . . to convince members of its black power structure that they have not yet been accepted as equals by the white power structure."[150] A week later, however, Austin criticized the new school's budget for appropriating too much money for salaries and administration. The editor opined, "Are we witnessing the birth of another facet of the Negro 'cadillac set,' this time masquerading under the honorable term Black?" He noted that too often, money had corrupted activists with good intentions. He concluded, "Are Black people . . . to be disappointed again? . . . Is this grand dream of a new order to dissolve into the old familiar nightmare of hypocrisy?"[151]

The school opened in late October 1969, with Betty Shabazz, Malcolm X's widow, giving a speech at the dedication ceremony.[152] Fuller explained that the purpose of the university, which planned a two-year program, was "to provide a framework within which Black Education can become relevant to the needs of the black community and the struggle for Black Liberation."[153] Fuller later recalled that 3,000 people attended the opening ceremonies.[154]

As Austin ended his seventh decade and began his eighth, he received deserving recognition for his life of service to the black community. In May 1967, he was awarded an honorary doctor of laws degree by NCC.[155] In 1970, he became trustee emeritus on the board of St. Joseph's AME Church.[156] In March of that year, the DCNA and the Durham chapter of the NAACP paid tribute to Austin for his contributions to the black freedom struggle with a testimonial dinner held in the cafeteria at North Carolina Central University.[157] Public officials, educators, and friends, including business and civic leaders John S. Stewart, Asa Spaulding, and John Wheeler, praised Austin's sacrifices for the black community. Younger leaders like Ben Ruffin, executive director of UOCI, were equally effusive in their praise. Ruffin said, "Mr. Austin came along 30 or 40 years before his time. Some of the things we are doing and people think are radical, he was doing years ago. He is the type of black man the young look up to and the type of man who had the courage to stick with the struggle. . . . He could have been a rich man and sold his soul to the white and black establishment. Instead he chose to stick with the people. Since Howard (Fuller) is out of town, I am sure that I speak his sentiments in saying Mr. Austin has been an inspiration for both of us." On the occasion of this program, a *Durham Morning Herald* reporter interviewed Austin, who commented with his usual candor, "I've been into every type of scrap you can think of. When I was young I was a nuisance to white folks. It was a wonder I wasn't lynched." He continued, "This paper is not for sale. I was brought into this world to fight for my people. I don't see why we have to bow and scrape and I am not going to do it."[158]

Just a few months after the testimonial dinner in his honor, Austin was diagnosed with pancreatic cancer. Although he continued to work after the diagnosis, by March 1971, his illness was taking its toll and Austin increasingly missed work and then stopped going to the office at all. John Myers, who was hired by Austin as a reporter and columnist in February 1971, observed that the old editor's eyes appeared to be "looking straight through you as he had done to so many people and causes of the past decades." Austin told Myers, "When I get well, my daughter and I are going to make the paper into a giant."[159] Myers described Austin as this "small, slender gentleman who wore plain dark suits, white shirts, and narrow ties, but rebel is a term Austin could wear proudly, with dignity."[160] In his last days, his friends and neighbors in Hayti learned "that he needed a blood transfusion." Almost immediately, over five dozen people showed up at Lincoln Hospital to offer their blood to the man who had given his life to make their lives better.[161]

Louis Ernest Austin died on Saturday evening, June 12, 1971, at Lincoln Hospital.[162] His funeral was held on Tuesday, June 15, at St. Joseph's AME Church, with Rev. Philip R. Cousin delivering the eulogy. Austin's obituary confirmed that "his religious philosophy was a dominant force in his life to the very end."[163] His survivors included his wife, Stella; his daughter, Vivian; his grandson, Kenneth; his sister Maude; and his two brothers, Jesse and Lodius.[164] He was also survived by thousands of freedom fighters who had worked with him and been inspired by him. Though Louis Austin had taken his last breath, his survivors would carry on the "fight for my people."

Epilogue

I don't know any single individual . . . who meant more to change in this city and elsewhere than L. E. Austin.

—T. R. Speight, a member of the NAACP's Durham branch for over fifty years

Austin's death dealt a huge blow to his immediate family, to his *Carolina Times* family, to African Americans, and to freedom fighters in Durham and throughout the state. But Austin's wife, Stella Austin, and their daughter, Vivian Edmonds, with the support of the employees at the newspaper as well as the paper's subscribers, would not let the paper die with its publisher. They were committed to see the *Times* sustain Louis Austin's legacy of speaking truth to power.[1] Stella Austin, who had retired four years earlier from Lakewood Elementary School in Durham after a long career as a public school teacher, succeeded her husband as president of the *Carolina Times* Publishing Company. Vivian Edmonds became the publisher, and Austin's younger brother Lodius, who had worked as a linotype operator at the *Times* since 1959, became managing editor. Lodius had also set type for the *Times* during the 1930s before doing similar work during the 1940s and 1950s in Wilmington, Raleigh, Washington, D.C., and Richmond.[2]

Edmonds's elevation to publisher of the *Carolina Times* was a logical step given her varied experience with the paper and her unwavering commitment to its purpose. A graduate of Hillside High School (1944) and North Carolina College (1948), she had performed several jobs for the paper, including serving as the city editor from 1949 to 1950. After her marriage in 1950, she and her husband, Woodrow Edmonds, raised their son, Kenneth, born in 1953, and she taught school and then worked as a guidance counselor at Lincoln High School in Chapel Hill in the 1970s. After her father's death, Vivian Edmonds continued her work as a guidance counselor, and tried to keep an eye on the paper as an absentee owner.[3]

During the 1970s, the *Carolina Times* continued to play a vital role in the life of the city. Valerie Whitted, who received the paper by "mail on Monday or Tuesday each week," recalled, "If you wanted to know what was going on in OUR Durham and beyond, you needed to get a copy of *The Carolina Times* . . . period!"[4] Eight months after Austin's death, the paper employed seventeen part-time and full-time workers, including two full-time reporters. Acting city editor James Vaughn penned most of the editorials. The paper had about 10,000 subscribers; many were Durhamites who had moved out of state and wanted to keep in touch with the community. Moreover, overall circulation was considerably more than 10,000 because of the additional sales of single issues.[5]

As in the past, the *Times* reported on the black community in Durham and throughout North Carolina, while covering national and international news of interest to its readers. It also extended Austin's legacy of promoting black political influence and advocating for the rights and opportunities of African Americans. In February 1973, the *Times* criticized President Nixon's domestic and foreign policies, including his conduct of the Vietnam War and his cuts in domestic programs that benefited the poor and needy, including veteran's benefits, welfare, health, housing, and public education programs. The *Times* called these cuts "inhumane and socially dangerous."[6] The *Times* also opposed a ban on the use of Medicaid funds for abortions, calling this proposal "openly racial and discriminatory" because it would limit access to abortions for poor and minority women. The *Times* concluded that regardless of one's views on abortion, women receiving Medicaid "should be allowed to make up their own minds, just like anyone else."[7]

The *Times* reported on the May 1973 bombing of the offices of the *Wilmington Journal*, the black news weekly published by Thomas C. Jervay. The *Times* denounced this "dastardly" attempt to silence the *Journal*, which "has been in the forefront in fighting for oppressed blacks as well as backing civil rights activists," like Ben Chavis and others, who were charged with firebombing a white-owned grocery store in Wilmington.[8] Lawrence Little, a member of the white supremacist organization, the Rights of White People, that had terrorized black activists in Wilmington during the early 1970s, was convicted of bombing the *Journal* offices.[9]

During the 1970s, the *Carolina Times* continued to play a pivotal role in the election of black candidates for public office. In a 1974 interview, Louis Austin's old friend Mickey Michaux, who had been elected the first African American state legislator from Durham in 1972, reported, "Everybody knows now that the *Carolina Times* office is central headquarters on election day. . . . Sometimes we [the DCNA] will send out leaflets about a week before stating that the campaign headquarters are at [the] *Carolina Times*." When voters needed a ride to the polls, they were told to call the *Carolina Times*'s phone number, and rides were arranged for them.[10] The *Times* promoted the 1974 campaigns of three black candidates for Durham County commissioner: William (Bill) Bell and Nathan Garrett, who were running for reelection, and

Elna Spaulding, a first-time candidate, who had founded Women-in-Action for the Prevention of Violence and Its Causes.[11] Bell and Spaulding ran successful campaigns, but Garrett was defeated by a small margin.[12]

In 1975, due to suspected financial improprieties at the *Times*, Vivian Edmonds decided to take early retirement from the public schools and returned to run the paper full-time.[13] Meanwhile, Louis Austin's brother Lodius retired, and his grandson, Kenneth Edmonds (Vivian's son), joined the paper in 1976. Kenneth, who had been very close to his grandfather, did some writing for the paper, but he preferred the business end, which has been his main focus ever since.[14]

The *Times* was a strong supporter of Soul City, a project developed by civil rights leader Floyd McKissick with federal government subsidies to create a planned city in Warren County, North Carolina.[15] In 1976, after an audit by the U.S. General Accounting Office cleared Soul City of accusations of financial improprieties, the *Times* demanded an apology from Senator Jesse Helms and Congressman Lawrence H. Fountain, who had called for a federal investigation of supposed financial misdeeds by McKissick and his associates. The *Times* declared that "Helms got elected by, and still relies upon the ignorance and racism of racist people."[16]

The *Times* consistently backed the attempts of Ben Chavis and nine other young freedom fighters, who became known as the Wilmington Ten, to obtain justice from the courts. In the context of a black protest movement in Wilmington during the early 1970s, the Wilmington Ten had been convicted of burning down a white-owned grocery store. In March 1976, the *Times* provided an outlet for Chavis by publishing a letter he wrote from prison titled "The Dialectics of Incarceration," in which he enumerated the many injustices in North Carolina's prison system. Chavis recounted attempts to create an inmate council at Caledonia Prison, in Halifax County, where he was held. Prison officials retaliated against Chavis by putting him on "administrative lock up" and refusing to allow him to leave his cell, with a prison guard stationed at his cell door at all times.[17] In June 1976, the *Times* printed a two-part analysis enumerating the ways in which the Wilmington Ten had been denied justice in the courts. *Times* reporter Ray Jenkins pointed to the prosecution witnesses' lack of credibility and the mistrial that was declared when the prosecuting attorney claimed illness because, in the opinion of many observers, the prosecution did not like the fact that there were ten blacks and only two whites on the jury. During the subsequent trial that resulted in the convictions of the ten defendants, the jury included ten whites and only two blacks.[18] Kenneth Janken's recent study of the Wilmington Ten case confirmed Jenkins's analysis: "In September 2012 the *Wilmington Journal* published newly discovered documents that definitively show that State solicitor [Jay] Stroud feigned illness in order to get a mistrial and a second chance at a favorable jury."[19]

The *Carolina Times* suffered a severe setback in January 1979 when a fire, eerily reminiscent of the attack on the *Wilmington Journal* six years earlier, destroyed the newspaper's offices housed in a building at 436 East Pettigrew Street, which Austin had purchased in 1954. The Durham Fire Department indicated that the fire was caused by arson. Vivian Edmonds said, "Everything was lost." She believed the newspaper had been targeted because of its civil rights advocacy, noting that the paper had "been under attack by racists here because of its fight on discrimination and police brutality." Indeed, during the latter part of 1978, the *Times* had published numerous articles about police brutality against African Americans in Durham. Edmonds also believed that the *Times* may have been targeted because of its dispute with the land redevelopment agency that was trying to complete the urban renewal project started many years earlier. The *Carolina Times* and the business in the building next door, E. N. Toole & Sons, "the largest Black electrical contractors in the state," were the last holdouts that refused to sell their buildings. They had refused to sell because they believed that the prices offered were inadequate and unfair. The Toole building was also destroyed in the fire.[20] A few days after the fire, Vivian Edmonds overheard a conversation that bolstered her view that the fire was intentionally set to destroy the newspaper. She was looking around the rubble when she heard three firefighters, who were unaware of her presence, laughing about the fire. One firefighter said, "The boys down at the police station gonna be mighty happy now the *Carolina Times* is out of business."[21]

After the fire, many people thought that the *Carolina Times* would be unable to continue. The fire had destroyed most of the paper's equipment and files, and the building had been destroyed. But Vivian Edmonds refused to quit in the face of this disaster. She "thought about my parents' struggle and the fact that this paper was their lives and a living monument to their commitment to Black people." So, she, her husband, and her son brought the paper back to life.[22] The *Times* did not miss an issue, thanks in part to the generosity of Alex Rivera, an old friend of Louis Austin and Vivian Edmonds, who offered his photography shop as a temporary office for the newspaper.[23] After the fire, the *Times* received tremendous support from the Durham community and from sympathetic friends around the country. Many supporters renewed their subscriptions, took out new subscriptions, or paid their arrears. Edmonds also received many expressions of support and sympathy.[24]

Moreover, the *Times* continued to report on the growing movement against police brutality in Durham.[25] In fact, soon after the fire, in late January 1979, a mass meeting, promoted on the front page of the *Times*, was called to discuss police brutality, a beating of a black man by a white store employee, and the fire that burned down the *Carolina Times* building.[26]

Meanwhile, the *Times* provided important opportunities for black journalists to gain valuable experience. While a student at the University of North Carolina School of Journalism, Valerie Whitted did her internship with the *Carolina Times*. Phyllis Coley, publisher of *Spectacular Magazine* of Durham, recalled, "Mrs. Edmonds gave me my first job as a journalist. I had a column that covered the local organizations. She taught about caring for your community. She stressed to me that every group, no matter how big or little, was important. I have carried that with me." Milton Jordan, who worked for the *Times* during the 1970s and 1980s, "spoke about her eye for detail and distaste for 'dangling participles.'" *Durham Herald-Sun* reporter John McCann said, "Ms. Edmonds allowed me to get some writing experience at *The Carolina Times*. And the money she paid wasn't bad at all, either!"[27]

AUSTIN'S WIDOW AND VIVIAN EDMONDS'S mother, Stella Walker Austin, died at age eighty on October 6, 1981, of chronic renal failure caused by congestive heart disease. The veteran public school teacher had been active in the civic, social, and religious life of her community. She was a member of many local organizations, including the Year Round Garden Club and the Pearsontown Community Club. A devoted member of St. Joseph's African Methodist Episcopal Church, she had served on the church's stewardess board number one, and taught Sunday school for many years. Like her husband, Stella Austin was laid to rest in Durham's Beechwood Cemetery.[28]

Despite increasing competition from historically white daily newspapers, which now provided more coverage of the black community than they had in previous years, the *Times* was able to expand the paper during the early 1980s. At the end of the 1970s, issues of the *Times* generally ran sixteen pages, but by 1981, the *Times* ran thirty-two pages, with no shortage of advertisements. One important change was that the *Times* no longer published weekly editorials, although it still included opinion columns as it had in previous years. Hard news coverage focused on national news, with local coverage of black business, religion, education, and social events.

In 2002, after thirty-one years as publisher, Vivian Edmonds, age seventy-four, turned the reins of the *Carolina Times* over to her son, Kenneth Edmonds.[29] Six years later, Vivian Edmonds died in May 2008, at age eighty.[30] At this writing, nine decades after his grandfather purchased the newspaper, Kenneth Edmonds continues to publish the *Carolina Times*. Recently, Carl Kenney II said that the *Carolina Times* expressed "a communal perspective. They tell the untold stories of countless black men and women. Stories locked out of the majority press due to the stroke of an editor's pen. Those words, in the *Carolina Times*, connect proud people to the lives and events of others who share a common purpose."[31] The *Carolina Times* continues to provide an important voice for the black community of Durham, North Carolina.

AS EDITOR AND PUBLISHER, Louis Austin created a document titled "Our Creed" to guide the operations of the newspaper. The creed contains five paragraphs, but perhaps the last one best sums up the essence of the *Carolina Times*: "These pages constitute a battleground across which the struggle for justice must never cease until every underprivileged human being in the world has the opportunity to rise to the fullest capacity with which God has endowed him."[32]

For over four decades, Austin played an essential role in African Americans' struggle for freedom. He helped lay the foundation for the important victories produced by the postwar civil rights movement. And then he worked with a new generation of activists to produce those very victories. He fought against economic injustice, police brutality, racial segregation, and white supremacy. He agitated for economic opportunity, voting rights, equal education, and the right of blacks to be safe from vicious racist violence. He fought for African American inclusion in all aspects of American society.

Austin helped to win a place for African Americans in the political system in North Carolina. When he first came to Durham in 1917, only a few dozen blacks were registered to vote, if that many. The notion that a black man could be elected to serve as a justice of the peace, let alone a member of the city council or the state legislature, was preposterous. Yet seventeen years after his arrival in Durham, Austin was elected justice of the peace, and as a Democrat, which would have been hard to fathom just a few years earlier.

Over the years, Austin used many different tactics in the pursuit of racial justice. As early as 1929, he called for a boycott of segregated movie theaters. In 1933, he helped initiate the first legal challenge to racial segregation in public education in the South. A year later, he was elected justice of the peace. In

1935, he helped create the Durham Committee on Negro Affairs, a key organization in the fight for African Americans' rights and opportunities. In 1941, he backed A. Philip Randolph's March on Washington Movement. Twenty-two years later, he supported the 1963 March on Washington, organized by Randolph and Bayard Rustin, among others. In 1932, he helped move many African Americans into the Democratic Party, a strategy that would eventually increase black political representation and power. A notable victory was the 1953 election of Rencher N. Harris to the Durham City Council. In 1956, disgusted by southern white Democrats' massive resistance to the *Brown v. Board of Education* decision, he advocated for the Republican Party. During the 1960s, Austin supported sit-ins, boycotts, marches, and lawsuits that succeeded in ending legal segregation of public facilities, including restaurants, movie theaters, hotels, hospitals, sports venues, and schools. His advocacy helped lead to the passage of the Civil Rights Act of 1964 and the Voting Rights Act of 1965.

As a freedom fighter, Austin worked with many like-minded Americans who looked to a day when, as Martin Luther King Jr. so eloquently stated, African Americans would "not be judged by the color of their skin but by the content of their character."[33] Austin worked with anyone who fought for blacks' rights and opportunities, regardless of race or party. He worked with Communists, socialists, Democrats, and Republicans. His closest collaborators included courageous activists in Durham like R. McCants Andrews, Cecil McCoy, Conrad Pearson, Dan Martin, John Wheeler, Floyd McKissick, Howard Fuller, and Ben Ruffin. But he also worked with activists outside Durham and outside North Carolina, including Pauli Murray, Ella Baker, Walter White, William Hastie, A. Philip Randolph, Bayard Rustin, and Martin Luther King Jr. Working with organizations like the Durham Committee on Negro Affairs, the North Carolina Committee on Negro Affairs, and the NAACP, Louis Austin stood for the principle that all people were entitled to equal rights regardless of race. For fighting the good fight, Louis Austin was threatened, had crosses burned on his lawn, and suffered harassment by the FBI and the IRS. But he refused to be intimidated. Because he would not compromise his principles, he was a hero to many African Americans.

DESPITE MANY IMPORTANT VICTORIES, over four decades after Austin's death, racial discrimination still pervades the state of North Carolina, as well as the nation. Police departments racially profile African Americans. Blacks suffer from police brutality. Mass incarceration disproportionately affects African Americans. The disfranchisement of felons denies many blacks the right to vote. Voter identification laws in many states disproportionately suppress the black vote. Prosecutors regularly strike blacks from juries because of their race. The death penalty is applied to blacks in a discriminatory manner. Black job applicants are less likely than whites to be granted interviews, and black employees in some job sectors are paid less than white employees.[34]

Just as Louis Austin challenged white supremacy and racial inequities in his time, so today, many activists are challenging racial inequities in North Carolina and around the nation. Today's activists follow in the large footsteps of earlier activists like Austin, who recognized that, in the immortal words of Frederick Douglass, "If there is no struggle there is no progress."[35]

Notes

Introduction

1. Weare, *Black Business*, 232.

2. This study relies heavily on the *Carolina Times* newspapers, with many years' issues now digitized and available online. Unfortunately, the microfilm edition, upon which the digitized version is based, is incomplete. A 1979 fire at the offices of the *Carolina Times* destroyed many of the newspapers. Austin published the paper from 1927 to 1971, but the newspapers from 1927 to 1936 and from 1944 to 1948 are unavailable. Another obstacle in researching Austin's life is that there is no collection of Austin's personal papers. Nonetheless, I have located information about Austin and the *Carolina Times* in other black newspapers, notably the *Norfolk Journal and Guide* (Virginia), which reported extensively on blacks in North Carolina. I have also consulted many manuscript collections, which contain information related to Austin's activism. I also use Austin's FBI file, which covers the 1940s and includes copies of his editorials during 1944 and 1945, which is fortuitous because those are two of the years for which there are no extant copies of the *Carolina Times*. I also rely on interviews conducted with Louis Austin by several historians as well as interviews with friends, relatives, and colleagues of Austin. I interviewed Austin's daughter, Vivian Edmonds, and grandson, Kenneth Edmonds, as well as several other individuals who knew him or worked with him.

3. For southern black journalists, see Alexander, *Race Man*; Suggs, *P. B. Young, Newspaperman*; Sullins and Parsons, "Roscoe Dunjee"; Odum-Hinmon, "Cautious Crusader"; Roefs, "Leading the Civil Rights Vanguard"; Griffin, "Courier of Crisis"; Suggs, *Black Press in the South*.

4. While a comprehensive history of the role of southern black journalists in the long black freedom struggle has yet to be written, numerous studies provide us with a sense of the terrain, with journalists responding in a variety of ways to racial segregation and oppression. For examples, see the following notes.

5. Dittmer, *Local People*, 74; Irons, *Reconstituting Whiteness*, 66–67.

6. Brown-Nagin, *Courage to Dissent*, 99, 228, 232.

7. Douglas, *Reading, Writing, and Race*, 63–64; Bloom, *Class, Race, and the Civil Rights Movement*, 164.

8. Washburn, *African American Newspaper*, 8.

9. Felder, *Civil Rights in South Carolina*, 27–31, 40–43.

10. Stockley, *Daisy Bates*, 24–29.

11. Thompson, "Little Caesar of Civil Rights," 172.

12. While this study does not amount to a comprehensive study of the black freedom struggle in North Carolina, it does provide an important window into the movement

in many parts of the state, especially in towns and cities in the piedmont and the east, which were regularly covered in the *Carolina Times*. There are a number of excellent studies of the black freedom struggle in North Carolina. Most of these studies mention Louis Austin and the *Carolina Times* but do not center the black press in the story of the freedom struggle. In addition, most of them do not provide an in-depth discussion of the 1930s and 1940s. The best study of the civil rights movement in Durham, Christina Greene's *Our Separate Ways: Women and the Black Freedom Movement in Durham, North Carolina*, focuses largely on the 1960s and 1970s and in particular the role of women in the movement. While Greene does mention Austin several times, he is a peripheral figure in her narrative. There are several other fine studies of blacks in Durham, but they say little about Austin and the *Carolina Times*, and they do not encompass the four decades of the long black freedom struggle. Leslie Brown's study, *Upbuilding Black Durham: Gender, Class, and Black Community Development in the Jim Crow South*, takes the story of blacks in Durham up to 1930. Walter Weare's *Black Business in the New South: A Social History of the North Carolina Mutual Life Insurance Company* focuses on moderate business leaders like North Carolina Mutual president C. C. Spaulding, and Weare's narrative ends in the 1950s. Furthermore, there are no book-length biographies of black leaders from Durham, home to a celebrated black community with many successful financial institutions, which by 1949 had given Parrish Street, the locus of these businesses, the moniker "Wall Street of Negro America." "The Wall Street of Negro America," *Ebony*, September 1949, 19. For an excellent dissertation on Durham businessman, attorney, and civic leader John H. Wheeler, see Winford, "'Battle for Freedom.'"

While there have been many studies of black newspapers and black editors, relatively few book-length studies focus on the southern black press. Moreover, there is no book-length study of the role of southern black journalists in the black freedom struggle. The only published work on Austin is by the present author and consists of two journal articles: Gershenhorn, "Courageous Voice for Black Freedom"; Gershenhorn, "Double V in North Carolina." Most studies of the black press and the civil rights struggle ignore the southern black press, and the *Carolina Times*, the most important black newspaper in North Carolina, is rarely mentioned, despite the key role played by Austin in the struggle in North Carolina. There are several fine studies of the black freedom struggle in North Carolina that focus on cities and towns outside of Durham or on significant leaders: Chafe, *Civilities and Civil Rights*; McKinney, *Greater Freedom*; Tyson, *Radio Free Dixie*; Barksdale, "Indigenous Civil Rights Movement"; Janken, *Wilmington Ten*; Cecelski, *Along Freedom Road*.

13. Charles Payne has demonstrated that "the well-publicized activism of the sixties depended upon the efforts of older activists who worked in obscurity." Payne, *I've Got the Light of Freedom*, 29. Patricia Sullivan argued, "By 1938 a loose political network had developed around the labor movement, local branches of the National Association for the Advancement of Colored People (NAACP), voter leagues, Communist Party initiatives, and New Deal programs." Sullivan, *Days of Hope*, 70.

14. Hall, "Long Civil Rights Movement," 1233–63. For a critique of Hall's article, see Cha-Jua and Lang, "'Long Movement' as Vampire." Movement scholars, like Hall and

Glenda Gilmore, who have studied civil rights activism in the 1930s and 1940s tend to emphasize leftists and communists, but they were not the only radical activists of the 1930s and 1940s. In order to understand the long black freedom struggle, we must know more about southern black activists, including black journalists and lawyers, who had few connections with the radical left. Men like Louis Austin and attorney Conrad Pearson fought for racial justice in North Carolina and played key roles in the struggle for racial equality during the 1930s and 1940s.

15. On the modern civil rights movement as a social movement, see Morris, *Origins of the Civil Rights Movement*.

16. Walker, "Changes in Race Accommodation," 168.

17. "What Is It Worth?," *Carolina Times*, May 9, 1942, 2.

18. "Where Is Great Britain's Army?," *Carolina Times*, June 15, 1940, 4.

19. Annie McClennon, "Winston-Salem Citizens Hold Emancipation Day," *Norfolk Journal and Guide*, January 13, 1951, E4.

20. "Senator Hoey Comes to Town," *Carolina Times*, October 22, 1949, 2.

21. "Why the Theaters Are Being Picketed," *Carolina Times*, January 28, 1961, 2.

22. "State Rights—Southern Style," *Carolina Times*, June 12, 1954, 2.

23. Martin Luther King Jr., "Remarks of Dr. Martin Luther King, Jr." (web source).

Chapter One

1. Walker, "Changes in Race Accommodation," 166.

2. Kenneth Edmonds interview, May 23, 2011.

3. Louis Austin, interview by August Meier, 1958, notes, August Meier Papers, Schomburg Center for Research in Black Culture, New York, NY (hereafter cited as Meier Papers); North Carolina State Board of Health, Office of Vital Statistics, Louis Austin, Certificate of Death, copy in author's possession.

4. "Lewis [*sic*] Austin," 1920 U.S. Census; Austin, 1910 U.S. Census; Lodius Austin and DeNina Austin interview.

5. Louis Austin, interview by August Meier, 1958; "Lewis [*sic*] Austin," 1920 U.S. Census; William L. Alston [*sic*], Death Certificate #1922000251, May 3, 1922, Durham County (NC) Register of Deeds.

6. Louis Austin, interview by August Meier, 1958; Austin, 1910 U.S. Census.

7. Kenneth Edmonds interview, May 23, 2011; Louis Austin, interview by August Meier, 1958.

8. Kenneth Edmonds interview, May 23, 2011.

9. Walker, "Changes in Race Accommodation," 166.

10. Louis Austin, interview by August Meier, 1958; William L. Alston [*sic*], Death Certificate #1922000251.

11. "Lewis [*sic*] Austin," 1920 U.S. Census; Louis Ernest Austin, Death Certificate, June 17, 1971. Census records put Carrie's birth at approximately 1876, but North Carolina death records indicate that she was born approximately 1879. "North Carolina, Deaths,

1931–1994," Carrie J. Austin, 1961, index, FamilySearch, https://familysearch.org/pal:/MM9.1.1/FGYZ-LX8, accessed June 28, 2012.

12. Louis Austin, interview by August Meier, 1958.

13. Kenneth Edmonds interview, May 23, 2011.

14. "North Carolina, Deaths, 1931–1994," index, Carrie J. Austin, 1961.

15. Kenneth Edmonds interview, May 23, 2011. The 1920 and 1930 censuses indicate Carrie Austin was born about 1876. According to Carrie's obituary, she was born in Edgecombe County to Mr. and Mrs. Calvin Johnson. "Mother of TIMES Publisher Dies," *Carolina Times*, October 14, 1961, 1.

16. Anderson, *Race and Politics in North Carolina*, 25.

17. Ibid., 10, 24. Between 1880 and 1900 the black population declined from 69.8 percent (21,162) to 64.1 percent (19,733) of the county's population.

18. Anderson, *Race and Politics in North Carolina*, 25, 31; Taves, Black, and Black, *Historic Architecture of Halifax County*, 75.

19. Crow, Escott, and Hatley, *History of African Americans in North Carolina*, 109; Anderson, *Race and Politics in North Carolina*, 12; Justesen, *George Henry White*, 212–14.

20. Anderson, *Race and Politics in North Carolina*, 160.

21. On the Wilmington Racial Massacre, see Prather, *We Have Taken a City*.

22. Weare, *Black Business*, 21. The lynching was reported in the *Durham Sun*, October 29, November 5, 7, 1898.

23. Taves, Black, and Black, *Historic Architecture of Halifax County*, 467.

24. Ibid., 467–68.

25. There were also white politicians from the region who enjoyed national political influence, notably Claude Kitchin of Halifax County, who was chair of the U.S. House Ways and Means Committee in 1917. Allen, *History of Halifax County*, 133–34.

26. Kousser, "Progressivism—For Middle-Class Whites Only," 178.

27. Jones, *Negro Education*, 387.

28. Taves, Black, and Black, *Historic Architecture of Halifax County*, 89.

29. Crow, Escott, and Hatley, *History of African Americans in North Carolina*, 156.

30. *Public Education in North Carolina: A Report*, 33. Although there were many white high schools, few of them provided a program that truly could be considered a four-year high school education. A small number of black elementary schools provided a limited amount of instruction that could be considered high school level.

31. Louis E. Austin, interview by Anne Braden, ca. 1957, notes, box 49, folder 11, Carl and Anne Braden Papers, Wisconsin Historical Society, Madison, WI (hereafter cited as Braden Papers).

32. Austin, interview by Anne Braden, ca. 1957.

33. Department of the Interior, U.S. Board of Education, *Negro Education*, 403; Warlick, "Practical Education and the Negro College," 309–17; Inborden, *History of Brick School*, 46; Greene, *Biography*, 46, 241, 247–48.

34. "Reunion Set at Bricks [sic] School in Late August," *Norfolk Journal and Guide*, August 19, 1950, 5.

35. Austin, interview by August Meier, 1958.

36. Jones, *Negro Education*, 440–41.

37. Caldwell, *History of the American Negro*, 762–65.

38. Warlick, "Practical Education and the Negro College," 191–92.

39. Ibid., 309.

40. Jones, *Negro Education*, 440–41.

41. "Kittrell College to Celebrate 79th Founders Day February 17," *Carolina Times*, February 20, 1965, 1.

42. Austin, interview by August Meier, 1958. O'Kelly served as vice president of Durham's National Religious Training School and Chautauqua (NRTS) from 1911 to 1912. He then returned to Kittrell College, serving as president from 1912 to 1917. He left Kittrell in 1917 to return to the NRTS, now called the National Training School. Caldwell, *History of the American Negro*, 762–65.

43. Jones, *Negro Education*, 401–2.

44. Louis Ernest Austin, "Registration Card," September 12, 1918, copy in the author's possession.

45. Shenk, *"Work or Fight!,"* 4–5.

46. Asa Spaulding, "School Days in Durham, 1918–1923," ca. 1981, box AWS-2, Asa and Elna Spaulding Papers, David M. Rubenstein Rare Book & Manuscript Library, Duke University, Durham, NC (hereafter cited as Spaulding Papers); Weare, *Black Business*, 163. Asa Spaulding later served as president of the North Carolina Mutual Life Insurance Company.

47. "Lewis [*sic*] Austin," 1920 U.S. Census. William Austin moved to Durham in early 1920, then briefly returned to Enfield that same year, before moving permanently to Durham. "Local and Personal Items of General Interest," *The Progress* (Enfield, NC), June 25, 1920.

48. Austin, interview by August Meier, 1958.

49. Ibid.; *Bulletin: The National Training School*.

50. Vivian Edmonds interview, August 30, 2004.

51. *Bulletin: The National Training School*. Austin served as vice president of the school's alumni association in 1929, while H. McKinley Michaux Sr. was treasurer of the alumni association. James T. Taylor was general secretary of the alumni association. *1929–1939 Catalogue, 1930–1931 Announcements, the North Carolina College for Negroes*.

52. *Educational Publications of the Superintendent of Public Instruction of North Carolina*, nos. 31–60, 1921–1922, 40.

53. *Standardization and Classification of Public High Schools in North Carolina, 1921–1922, Educational Publication* no. 60, 16.

54. Austin, interview by August Meier, 1958; Boyd, "Louis Austin," 9–10.

55. *Baltimore Afro-American*, March 4, 1933; Weare, *Black Business*, 29, 119–24, 247.

56. Anderson, *Durham County*, 257.

57. Ibid., 257–58.

58. Ibid., 260.

59. Ibid., 260.

60. *Hill's Durham Directory, 1925*, 80 (web source).

61. Boyd, "Louis Austin," 32.

62. Warlick, "Practical Education and the Negro College," 431.

63. Weare, *Black Business*, 27.

64. Ibid., 13–14.

65. Ibid., 78. Weare located only one copy of the *Reformer*.

66. Ibid., 78.

67. Charles Arrant Death Certificate, December 6, 1922 (web source).

68. "Negro Editor Killed in Gun Duel; Dave M'Neil Injured," *Durham Morning Herald*, December 4, 1922; "Negro Editor's Funeral Today," *Durham Morning Herald*, December 6, 1922.

69. "Two Killed in Dispute over Vice Probe: Editor and Gambler in Gun Battle," *Chicago Defender*, January 6, 1923, 1. Thanks to Bob Healy for bringing this article to my attention.

70. J. A. Jackson, "No 'Bull' in Durham, N.C. Business Men," *Baltimore Afro-American*, November 25, 1921, 11.

71. "Negroes Met and Organized League," *Durham Morning Herald*, April 25, 1922, 6.

72. "Negro Voters to Hold a Meeting," *Durham Morning Herald*, October 16, 1922.

73. Brown, *Upbuilding Black Durham*, 282.

74. "Two Killed in Dispute over Vice Probe," 1; "Negro Editor Killed in Gun Duel."

75. "Two Killed in Dispute over Vice Probe," 1.

76. Ibid.

77. "Negro Editor Killed in Gun Duel."

78. "Two Killed in Dispute over Vice Probe," 1.

79. "Negro Editor Killed in Gun Duel."

80. "Negro Editor's Funeral Today."

81. "Spirit of the Press: Prosperous Negroes," *Norfolk Journal & Guide*, December 15, 1923, 12. This is a reprint of an article published in the *Durham Morning Herald*.

82. "Queen Street Baptist Church: Our History"; "Black History Month."

83. "First Baptist Church: History" (web source).

84. "Fine Progress by Negroes of Durham," *Durham Morning Herald*, December 31, 1922, 1.

85. "106 West Parrish Street." The 1915–16 Durham Directory listed the *Durham Reformer* at 206½ West Parrish and the NC Mutual at 212½ West Parrish. *Hill's Durham Directory 1915–16* (web source).

86. Rev. R. Spiller Death Certificate (web source).

87. Boyd, "Louis Austin," 9–10, 32; *Hill's Durham Directory, 1923*, listed Spiller as editor and Harris as general manager of the *Standard Advertiser*, with the office at 106½ West Parrish. *Hill's Durham Directory, 1923*, p. 479 (web source).

88. *Hill's Durham Directory, 1926*, 47 (web source). The *Carolina Times* was not listed in either the 1924 or the 1925 *Durham Directory*.

89. "N.C. Negro Historical Asso.," *Norfolk Journal and Guide*, September 24, 1921, 7.

90. *Hill's Durham Directory, 1925,* 80 (web source); Louis Austin, interview by August Meier, 1958, notes, August Meier Papers, Schomburg Center; "Local and Personal Items of General Interest," *Enfield, NC, Progress,* May 6, 1922; "Mother of TIMES Publisher Dies," *Carolina Times,* October 14, 1961, 1; William L. Alston [*sic*], Death Certificate #1922000251.

91. Lodius Austin and DeNina Austin interview.

92. "In Memoriam: Mrs. Stella Walker Austin, November 22, 1900—October 6, 1981," box 3, Clydie F. Scarborough Papers, David M. Rubenstein Rare Book & Manuscript Library, Duke University, Durham, NC (hereafter cited as Scarborough Papers); Kenneth Edmonds interview.

93. Lawrence V. Lutes, FBI report on Louis Austin, April 6, 1944, FOIPA no. 1129984-000; "In Memoriam: Mrs. Stella Walker Austin, November 22, 1900—October 6, 1981," box 3, Scarborough Papers; "Final Rites Held for Mrs. Stella W. Austin," *Carolina Times,* October 10, 1981, 1; Vivian Louise Austin, Birth Certificate #1927001163, August 21, 1927, Durham County (NC) Register of Deeds.

94. Boyd, "Louis Austin," 9–10; Austin, interview by August Meier, 1958.

95. The 1927 *Durham Directory* listed Louis Austin as editor of the *Carolina Times,* with office at 203½ East Chapel Hill Street. *Hill's Durham Directory, 1927,* 128, online, accessed June 24, 2012. According to one biographer, Austin bought the *Times* with Alexander Barnes in 1928. But there is no other evidence that Austin was not the sole owner of the paper. Boyd, "Louis Austin," 32. In 1928 Austin moved the newspaper to Fayetteville Street from Chapel Hill Street. Boyd, "Louis Austin," 9–10.

Chapter Two

1. "Durham Ready for Fact-Finding Confab," *Pittsburgh Courier,* March 23, 1929, 1.

2. Boyd, "Louis Austin," 31, 42.

3. Ibid.; Cone, *Martin & Malcolm & America,* 123–24. Austin was also active in the Interdenominational Ushers' Association of North Carolina. He served as its president from 1937 to 1968. "The Interdenominational Ushers' Association of North Carolina, Inc. Presents Louis E. Austin Day," July 31, 1983, program copy in the author's possession.

4. Finkle, *Forum for Protest,* 18.

5. Edmonds quoted in Suggs, *Black Press in the South,* xi.

6. Richard Davis has defined advocacy journalism as "the practice of using news stories to support issue positions advocated by the journalist." This type of advocacy was associated with the rise of the "new journalism" in the 1960s. Davis, *Press and American Politics,* 101. By contrast, Richard Digby-Junger applies a broader definition of advocacy journalism, including papers that support one political party, and muckrakers and reform journalists of the Progressive Era. Digby-Junger, *Journalist as Reformer,* 4–7. Everette E. Dennis and William L. Rivers define advocacy journalists as those who "write with an unabashed commitment to particular points of view, casting their reporting of events along the lines of their beliefs." Dennis and Rivers, *Other Voices,* 8.

7. Leonard, *Power of the Press*, 33–53, 167, 173; Davis, *Press and American Politics*, 47–48, 72–73.

8. Cooper Jr., *Pivotal Decades*, 83–88.

9. Landers, "National Observer, 1962–77," 15.

10. Ibid., 15.

11. Newkirk, *Within the Veil*, 54–55, 71.

12. Lodius and DeNina Austin interview.

13. Austin to Claude Barnett, March 5, 1948, pt. 2, reel 20 (microfilm), Claude A. Barnett Papers, North Carolina State University, Original Collection at the Chicago Historical Society (hereafter cited as Barnett Papers).

14. Louis Austin, Interview notes, no date, ca. 1957, box 49, folder 11, Carl and Anne Braden Papers, Wisconsin Historical Society, Madison, WI (hereafter cited as Braden Papers).

15. Boyd, "Louis Austin," 51–52.

16. Pearson interview.

17. Weare, *Black Business*, 111, 225–26.

18. "Survey Indicates Need for Concrete Appreciation of Little Business Man," *Chicago Defender*, July 9, 1938, 6.

19. "1938 Durham Business and Professional Chain Inc. 1972, Building Better Business," *Carolina Times*, August 19, 1972, 3.

20. Barnett to Austin, July 25, 1932, Austin to Barnett, September 5, 1932, pt. 2, reel 20, Barnett Papers.

21. Claude Barnett to J. H. Avery, N.C. Mutual, October 2, 1928, pt. 3, ser. 3, reel 5, Barnett Papers.

22. Austin to Barnett, May 24, 1929, pt. 2, reel 20, Barnett Papers; Barnett to *Carolina Times*, October 18, 1929, pt. 3, ser. 3, reel 5, Barnett Papers.

23. Austin to Claude Barnett, October 4, 1932; Barnett to Austin, October 8, 1932, both in pt. 3, ser. H, reel 2, Barnett Papers.

24. Harlan, *Booker T. Washington*, 28.

25. Hogan, *Black National News Service*, 28, 166.

26. Austin to National Features Services, Chicago, Illinois, September 27, 1932, pt. 3, ser. H, reel 2, Barnett Papers.

27. Walker, "Changes in Race Accommodation," 168.

28. Lodius and DeNina Austin interview.

29. Guy Johnson to Louis Austin, November 12, 1932, box 34, Guy B. Johnson Papers, Southern Historical Collection, Wilson Library, University of North Carolina at Chapel Hill (hereafter cited as Johnson Papers); Guy B. Johnson, "Depression and Race Relations: Conference with Louis Austin, editor of *Carolina Times*, Durham, and with Mr. Foushee, mger. of *Carolina Times*, Durham," ca. 1932, ser. 5.6, folder 1144, Johnson Papers. Johnson wrote Austin asking for an update on the campaign to get black clerks hired. Johnson noted that "Lerner's store in Atlanta has employed a Negro saleswoman." Johnson to Austin, November 12, 1932. It is not known if the 1932 protest succeeded.

30. Walker, "Changes in Race Accommodation," 171–72; "Negro Pickets Regain Jobs for Members of Own Race," *Durham Morning Herald*, February 16, 1936, 1; "Negroes Boycott Durham Stores with White Help," *Daily Tar Heel* (Chapel Hill), February 20, 1936; Bill Levitt, "Boycott," *Daily Tar Heel* (Chapel Hill), February 22, 1936; Kiser, "Occupational Change," 44. Similar boycotts took place in black sections of cities like Baltimore, Washington, D.C., Chicago, and New York during the Great Depression. Moreno, "Fair Employment," 29–63.

31. Walker, "Changes in Race Accommodation," 171–72.

32. "Durham Memorandum," ca. 1939, box 85, Ralph J. Bunche Papers (Collection 2051), Special Collections, Charles E. Young Research Library, University of California at Los Angeles (hereafter cited as Bunche Papers).

33. Lodius and DeNina Austin interview.

34. Floyd J. Calvin, "Calvin's Digest," *Pittsburgh Courier*, March 19, 1932, 2.

35. Chafe, *Civilities and Civil Rights*, 8–9.

36. Douglass quoted ibid., 2.

37. Walker, "Changes in Race Accommodation," 167; John Dolan Myers, "In Memory of Louis E. Austin," *New York Times*, July 26, 1971, 25. DeNina Austin, Lodius Austin's wife, also recalled a cross burning on Louis Austin's lawn. Lodius and DeNina Austin interview.

38. Floyd J. Calvin, "Calvin's Digest," *Pittsburgh Courier*, March 19, 1932, 2.

39. William Conklin Brown, "In North Carolina," *Baltimore Afro-American*, July 22, 1933, 14.

40. Sitkoff, *New Deal for Blacks*, 23. In 1923, the Durham interracial committee was chaired by W. F. Carr and included five white men and five black men, C. C. Spaulding, secretary; Stanford L. Warren; Aaron M. Moore; W. G. Pearson; and John M. Avery. The North Carolina interracial committee was headed by William L. Poteat, president of Wake Forest College, and included Aaron M. Moore; R. McCants Andrews, secretary; James Shepard; and W. G. Pearson. "Dr. Poteat Addresses the Colored Citizens," *Norfolk Journal and Guide*, March 24, 1923, 6.

41. Dillard et al., *Twenty Year Report of the Phelps-Stokes Fund*, 70; Gilmore, *Defying Dixie*, 252.

42. L. R. Reynolds, Director, North Carolina Commission on Interracial Cooperation, to N. C. Newbold, Howard Jenson, C. C. Spaulding, J. W. Seabrook, William Stuart Nelson, and Mrs. Kemp Neal, October 11, 1934, box 6, Howard W. Odum Papers, Southern Historical Collection, University of North Carolina at Chapel Hill (hereafter cited as Odum Papers); Johnson interview.

43. L. R. Reynolds to Clyde R. Hoey, December 13, 1938, box 1, folder 3, North Carolina Commission on Interracial Cooperation Papers, Southern Historical Collection, University of North Carolina at Chapel Hill (hereafter cited as NCCIC Papers).

44. "Does Some Good," *Norfolk Journal and Guide*, January 13, 1934, 6.

45. Weare, *Black Business*, 254.

46. "Does Some Good," 6.

47. "Durham Memorandum," ca. 1939, box 85, Bunche Papers.

48. Johnson interview.

49. Rosen, *Terror in the Heart of Freedom*, 136.

50. Guy Johnson to Louis Austin, January 17, 1934, box 14, Johnson Papers.

51. Haley, "Carolina Chameleon," 610–12.

52. Reed, *Simple Decency & Common Sense*, 25.

53. "Life Membership in Advancement Asso'n Becoming Popular," *Carolina Times*, July 28, 1928; "Free and Accepted Masons Aid N.A.A.C.P.," *Carolina Times*, July 28, 1928; both in NAACP Branch Files, Durham, NC, 1927–30, NAACP Papers, Proquest History Vault (database), Duke University (hereafter cited as NAACP Papers, Proquest); J. M. Avery to John R. Shillady, March 27, 1919, NAACP Branch Files, Durham, NC, 1919–26, NAACP Papers, Proquest; J. M. Avery to William T. Andrews, September 12, 1930; "Money Talks," *Carolina Times*, November 23, 1929, NAACP Branch Files, Durham, NC, 1927–30, NAACP Papers, Proquest. James T. Taylor, dean at North Carolina College for Negroes, became branch president in 1930.

54. Parker quoted in "Fight over Parker Laid before Hoover," *New York Times*, April 12, 1930, 3.

55. "Pushes Fight on Parker," *New York Times*, April 13, 1930, 4; "Committee Gets 36 Protests against Parker, Only Three Boosts," *Baltimore Afro-American*, April 26, 1930, 3; Maltese, *Selling of Supreme Court Nominees*, 66.

56. "Committee Gets 36 Protests against Parker," 3.

57. "Other Papers Say: A Wise and Fair Attitude," *Chicago Defender*, July 12, 1930, 14. The article is a reprint of an editorial from the *Winston-Salem Journal and Standard*.

58. Maltese, *Selling of Supreme Court Nominees*, 66.

59. Floyd J. Calvin, "James E. Shepard's Friends Deplore Stand on Parker, but Refuse to Forsake Educator's Leadership," *Pittsburgh Courier*, June 28, 1930, 3.

60. "Extra Paper Is Issued after De Priest Speaks in Durham," *Baltimore Afro-American*, June 6, 1931, 9.

61. "Jobless Denied Relief; Negroes Barred from Soup Kitchen in Western N.C.," *Carolina Times*, September 26, 1931, box 81, Johnson Papers.

62. Johnson, "Depression and Race Relations," ca. 1932, ser. 5.6, Johnson Papers.

63. "Crop Control," *Carolina Times*, September 30, 1939, 4.

64. Dries, "Into the Lion's Den," 15–16.

65. Ibid., 18; Janiewski, *Sisterhood Denied*, 158. See also Rice, "Negro Tobacco Worker."

66. Dries, "Into the Lion's Den," 18; D. S. Upchurch to E. Lewis Evans, March 31, 1934, box 61, Tobacco Workers International Union Papers, Special Collections, Hornbake Library, University of Maryland, College Park; Janiewski, "Seeking 'a New Day,'" 170; Irons, *Testing the New Deal*.

67. Dries, "Into the Lion's Den," 14, 19.

68. Ibid., 21.

69. Korstad, *Civil Rights Unionism*, 131–32.

70. Dries, "Into the Lion's Den," 22–25; "L&M Strike Settled," *Carolina Times*, April 29, 1939, 1.

71. "The Tobacco Strike," *Carolina Times*, April 29, 1939, 4.

72. Dries, "Into the Lion's Den," 25–26.

73. "Duke University," *Carolina Times*, May 6, 1939, 4.

74. Rice, "Negro Tobacco Worker," 65; Korstad, *Civil Rights Unionism*, 181, 185.

75. "A Negro State," *Carolina Times*, March 10, 1934, box 81, Johnson Papers; "The National Movement for the Establishment of a 49th State," in Aptheker, *Documentary History of the Negro People*, 84–90; Nuruddin, "Promises and Pitfalls," 384.

76. Thurgood Marshall to Luther Jackson, April 12, 1939, box 148, August Meier Papers, Schomburg Center for Research in Black Culture, New York, NY (hereafter cited as Meier Papers).

77. Pearson interview; *Greensboro Daily News*, February 13, 16, 1933; *Durham Morning Herald*, February 14, 1933.

78. James E. Shepard to J. C. B. Ehringhaus, February 16, 1933, folder 13, ser. 1, Personal Correspondence, James E. Shepard Papers, University Archives, James E. Shepard Memorial Library, North Carolina Central University, Durham (hereafter cited as Shepard Papers).

79. J. C. B. Ehringhaus to James E. Shepard, February 17, 1933, folder 13, ser. 1, Personal Correspondence, Shepard Papers.

80. Newbold to Spaulding, March 14, 1933, Odum Papers; Sosna, *Silent South*, ix.

81. Shepard to Newbold, February 17, 1933; Shepard to Newbold, March 1, 1933; Department of Public Instruction, Division of Negro Education Papers, North Carolina Division of Archives and History, State Archives, Raleigh (hereafter cited as Division of Negro Education Papers).

82. James E. Shepard to J. C. B. Ehringhaus, March 17, 1933, folder 13, ser. 1, Personal Correspondence, Shepard Papers.

83. Louis Austin, interview by August Meier, no date, ca. 1958, notes, box 139, Meier Papers.

84. Pearson interview; Malone, "Divine Discontent," 229–30.

85. Walker, "Changes in Race Accommodation," 158; Weare, *Black Business*, 153; Austin quoted in Boyd, "Louis Austin," 50–51.

86. Austin, interview by August Meier, no date, ca. 1958, notes, box 139, Meier Papers.

87. "Presidents and Soda Jerker," *Carolina Times*, August 22, 1931, box 81, Johnson Papers; "Clerk Attacks C. C. Spaulding," *Durham Sun*, August 4, 1931, 2.

88. "Clerk Fined for Assault on Spaulding," *Durham Sun*, August 7, 1931, 5. See also "Fine White Clerk $15.00 for Attack on Negro Banker," n.d., ca. 1931, "C. C. Spaulding Assaulted by Soda Fountain Clerk," n.d., ca. 1931, both in pt. 3C, reel 6, Barnett Papers.

89. C. A. McCoy to Walter White, March 21, 1933, box 147, Meier Papers; "Letter to the Members of the Durham Branch NAACP and Other Negro Citizens, Durham, NC," March 20, 1933, Division of Negro Education Papers. Shepard sent a copy of this letter to Newbold. Shepard to Newbold, March 23, 1933, Division of Negro Education Papers.

90. McCoy to White, March 21, 1933, NAACP Papers (microfilm); Shepard to Newbold, March 23, 1933, Division of Negro Education Papers.

91. George Streator to Walter White, September 6, 1933, reel 33, William Hastie Papers (microfilm).

92. Walter White to Charles H. Houston, March 20, 1933, NAACP Papers (microfilm).

93. Austin quoted in Weare, *Black Business*, 232.

94. *Thomas R. Hocutt v. Thomas J. Wilson, Jr., Dean of Admissions and Registrar, and the University of North Carolina*, Superior Court, Durham County, 1933, NAACP Papers (microfilm); McCoy, Pearson to White, February 6, 1933, NAACP Papers (microfilm); Murray, *States' Laws on Race and Color*, 329–33.

95. Shepard to Newbold, March 19, 1933; Newbold to Shepard, March 22, 1933; Division of Negro Education Papers.

96. Shepard to Newbold, March 18, 1933, Division of Negro Education Papers.

97. M. T. Van Hecke, Dean of UNC School of Law, to Frank Porter Graham, February 16, 1933, Frank Porter Graham Papers, Southern Historical Collection, Wilson Library, University of North Carolina at Chapel Hill (hereafter cited as Graham Papers); Robert H. Wettach, "Memorandum on Admissions of Negroes to the University," n.d., Graham Papers.

98. Odum to Graham, March 20, 1933; NAACP press release, March 31, 1933, Graham Papers.

99. Pearson interview; Pearson to White, March 31, 1933; White to McCoy, Pearson, March 22, 1933; Hastie to White, March 24, 1933, NAACP Papers (microfilm); Ware, *William Hastie*, 49; "Wilson Ordered to Explain Negro Ban," *Durham Morning Herald*, March 19, 1933, 1.

100. *Baltimore Afro-American*, April 8, 1933; Pearson to White, March 31, 1933, NAACP Papers (microfilm); "Hocutt's Suit to Enter Carolina Again Continued," *Durham Morning Herald*, March 26, 1933, 5; "Hocutt Loses Opening Round in Legal Fight to Enter University," *Durham Morning Herald*, March 29, 1933, 1, 2.

101. Turner interview; Spaulding interview.

102. *Thomas R. Hocutt v. Thomas J. Wilson, Jr., Dean of Admissions and Registrar, and the University of North Carolina*, Judgement, March 28, 1933, Superior Court, Durham County, NAACP Papers (microfilm); Pearson interview; "State Laws Forbid Mingling of Races, Asserts University," *Durham Sun*, March 28, 1933; Resolution, "adopted by a mass meeting of the colored people," March 20, 1933, enclosed in letter from Shepard to Newbold, March 23, 1933, Division of Negro Education Papers; *University of North Carolina Record, Catalogue Issue 1932–1933*, 37, 38–39, 42, 259; Snider, *Light on the Hill*, 145; Noble, *School of Pharmacy*, 55, 78–79.

103. "Men of Courage," *Carolina Times*, April (date illegible), 1933, Hastie Papers (microfilm).

104. Gershenhorn, "*Hocutt v. Wilson* and Race Relations," 275–308. Austin later recalled the impact of the case on Pearson and McCoy: "Pressure was put on them; McCoy left town. Pearson suffered. Others would not give him business." Louis Austin, interview by August Meier, n.d., ca. 1958, notes, box 139, Meier Papers.

105. "Walter White to Make Tour," *Baltimore Afro-American*, May 6, 1933, 8.

106. Walter White to J. N. Mills, president of Durham branch of NAACP, May 29, 1933, NAACP Papers, box 147, Meier Papers.

107. "University of North Carolina Discrimination Case," June 7, 1933, box 147, Meier Papers.

108. "Walter White Finds a New Spirit in North Carolinians," *Baltimore Afro-American,* June 3, 1933, 2.

109. "University of North Carolina Discrimination Case." Indicative of the importance the white press assigned to the NAACP's efforts in the state, the *Raleigh News and Observer* reported White's speech on its front page on May 23, 1933.

110. "N.A.A.C.P. Durham Campaign Wins 500 Members," February 2, 1934, NAACP Branch Files, Durham, NC, 1934, NAACP Papers, Proquest.

111. James E. Shepard to J. C. B. Ehringhaus, February 2, 1934, folder 15, ser. 1, Personal Correspondence, Shepard Papers.

112. J. C. B. Ehringhaus to James E. Shepard, February 3, 1934, folder 15, ser. 1, Personal Correspondence, Shepard Papers.

113. James E. Shepard to J. C. B. Ehringhaus, February 16, 1934, folder 15, ser. 1, Personal Correspondence, Shepard Papers.

114. James E. Shepard to J. C. B. Ehringhaus, May 31, 1934, folder 15, ser. 1, Personal Correspondence, Shepard Papers.

115. James E. Shepard to J. C. B. Ehringhaus, June 27, 1934, folder 15, ser. 1, Personal Correspondence, Shepard Papers.

116. James E. Shepard to J. C. B. Ehringhaus, May 28, 1934, folder 15, ser. 1, Personal Correspondence, Shepard Papers.

117. James E. Shepard to J. C. B. Ehringhaus, June 27, 1934, folder 15, ser. 1, Personal Correspondence, Shepard Papers.

118. Ibid.

119. Weare, *Black Business,* 226.

120. Richard L. McDougald to Walter White, July 21, 1936, pt. 12, ser. A, reel 18, NAACP Papers (microfilm).

121. "North Carolina Committee on Negro Affairs," *Carolina Times,* December 4, 1937, 4.

122. William A. Tuck, "Gov. Urges Law, Pharmacy and Medicine at NCC," *Carolina Times* January 14, 1939, 1; Gilmore, "Admitting Pauli Murray," 62–67.

123. Murray, *The Autobiography of a Black Activist, Feminist, Lawyer, Priest, and Poet,* 8, 12, 22–23, 92–93, 100, 109–10; Lin Holloway, "Around the Town," *Carolina Times,* February 23, 1946, box 4, Pauli Murray Papers, Schlesinger Library, Radcliffe Institute, Harvard University, Cambridge, MA (hereafter cited as Murray Papers).

124. Murray, *Autobiography of a Black Activist,* 110–12.

125. Ibid., 119–20.

126. Pauli Murray, Interview by Robert Martin, New York, NY, August 15, 17, 1968, box 1, Murray Papers.

127. Murray, *Song in a Weary Throat,* 127.

128. Ibid., 124.

129. Pauli Murray to Editor, *Durham Morning Herald*, January 14, 1939, box 15, Murray Papers.

130. "A Momentous Decision," *Carolina Times*, December 17, 1938, 4; "Missouri Loses Law School Suit," *Carolina Times*, December 17, 1938, 1; "Graduate Schools for Negroes," *Carolina Times*, December 17, 1938, 4. Other black newspapers responded with "guarded optimism," similar to Austin's reaction. Weaver and Page, "Black Press," 20.

131. Glenn Hutchinson, "Jim Crow Challenged in Southern Universities," *Crisis*, April 1939: 103; Pauli Murray to Editor, *Durham Morning Herald*, January 14, 1939, box 15, Murray Papers.

132. "A Momentous Decision," *Carolina Times*, December 17, 1938, 4; "Missouri Loses Law School Suit," *Carolina Times*, December 17, 1938, 1; "Graduate Schools for Negroes," *Carolina Times*, December 17, 1938, 4.

133. "Graduate Courses for Negroes, *Carolina Times*, January 14, 1939, 4.

134. "Editorially Speaking: The Proper Course to Pursue," *Carolina Times*, February 25, 1939, 1, 4. Austin published statistics indicating that in 1935–36, white public colleges received about eight times as much funding from the state as did black public colleges. "The Educational Rape of Negroes in North Carolina," *Carolina Times*, May 15, 1937, 4, 8.

135. "Equal Educational Opportunities," *Atlanta Daily World*, December 19, 1938, 6.

136. "Doctor Shepard's Request," *Carolina Times*, August 6, 1938, 4.

137. "Should Meet the Emergencies," *Carolina Times*, August 27, 1938, 4; Public Works Administration, Press Release, ca. 1938, pt. 3, ser. A, reel 5, NAACP Papers (microfilm). On the Public Works Administration, see Smith, *Building New Deal Liberalism*, 54–134.

138. "Graduate Courses for Negroes," *Carolina Times*, January 14, 1939, 4; "The Negro Graduate School," *Carolina Times*, July 1, 1939, 4. Austin believed that if a separate law school was going to be set up at NCCN, black professors should staff the school. Consequently, in September 1939, Austin decried the fact that while the new law school at NCCN was created to "thwart integration," "the first dean of the Black law school was Maurice Van Hecke," dean of UNC School of Law, and the "entire initial faculty of NCC[N] Law School were whites." Thorpe, *History of North Carolina Central University*, 19–20.

139. "Editorially Speaking: North Carolina's Disgrace," *Carolina Times*, October 3, 1931, box 81, Johnson Papers.

140. "Minutes of the Board of Education of the City of Durham, North Carolina, July 17, 1933" (microfilm), North Carolina State Archives, Raleigh, NC.

141. "Minutes of the Board of Education of the City of Durham, North Carolina, August 21, 1933" (microfilm), North Carolina State Archives, Raleigh, NC. Lyda Moore Merrick was married to businessman Edward Merrick and was the daughter of Aaron Moore, one of the founders of NC Mutual. Edward Merrick was the son of NC Mutual founder John Merrick. "Lyda Moore Merrick," (web source). Julia Warren was the wife of Stanford Warren, a prominent physician in Durham.

142. "Durham White Schools Get $155,000 from County but Negro Schools Get $21,000," *Carolina Times*, May 8, 1937, 1, 8; "Educational Rape of Negroes," 4, 8; Thorpe, *History of North Carolina Central University*, 20. In June 1939, Austin reported that official state statistics showed that during the 1936–37 school year North Carolina spent about $29 per white student, but only $19 per black student. "The Educational Differential," *Carolina Times*, June 10, 1939, 4.

143. "Educational Differential," 4.

144. "Durham White Schools Get $155,000," 1, 8; "Educational Rape of Negroes," 4, 8. In December 1937, Austin demanded that Durham blacks sue to force the city to remedy the horrific conditions at the East Durham School. "The Fuller School Cafeteria and East Durham School," *Carolina Times*, December 11, 1937, 4.

145. Walker, "Changes in Race Accommodation," 270. The quote is from the July 18, 1936 *Carolina Times*.

146. "Negroes Again Seek to Serve on Durham's Juries," *Durham Morning Herald*, December 18, 1936, sec. 2, p. 8.

147. Thuesen, "Classes of Citizenship," 260; "Another Victory Won," *Carolina Times*, August 28, 1937, 8. Austin also advocated more black influence in staffing decisions in education. He criticized the Durham schools superintendent for failing to consider the choice of local blacks and refusing to meet with the DCNA before choosing a principal for East Durham Negro School. "The East Durham School Appointment," *Carolina Times*, June 25, 1938, 4; "Negroes Again Seek to Serve."

148. Clyde Hoey, "Preparatory Education: Address Delivered at the Dedication of the New High School Building, Shelby, February 11, 1938," in Corbitt, *Addresses, Letters and Papers of Clyde Roarke Hoey*, 177–78.

149. Gavins, "Within the Shadow of Jim Crow," 77. In 1930, Austin attacked the Durham school system "for paying a local black principal only $75 per month," observing that the principal must be "either a 'philanthropist or a martyr' to work at such low pay." Thuesen, "Classes of Citizenship," 220; Brinton, "Negro in Durham," 381.

150. Austin to Walter White, September 11, 1933, box 147, Meier Papers; William Hastie to Walter White, September 22, 1933, reel 33, William Hastie Papers (microfilm); White to Austin, September 27, 1933, box 147, Meier Papers.

151. White to Austin, September 27, 1933, box 147, Meier Papers.

152. George Streator, "The Colored South Speaks for Itself," in Aptheker, *Documentary History of the Negro People*, 40–45; Walter White to W. E. B. Du Bois, October 30, 1933, box 147, Meier Papers.

153. Walter White to W. E. B. Du Bois, October 30, 1933, box 147, Meier Papers.

154. Hastie to White, September 22, 1933, reel 33, Hastie Papers. In November 1933, James Shepard told Walter White, "I am more inclined to the remedy of the ballot than I am to the resort of the courts." Shepard to White, November 13, 1933, box 147, Meier Papers.

155. Walter White to W. E. B. Du Bois, October 30, 1933, box 147, Meier Papers.

156. Ibid.

157. "Report—Committee on Race Relations, North Carolina Conference for Social Service," April 30, 1934, Raleigh, NC, box 24, Johnson Papers.

158. Gavins, "Within the Shadow of Jim Crow," 78.

159. Austin to White, March 2, 1934, box 147, Meier Papers.

160. White to Austin, March 6, 1934, box 147, Meier Papers.

161. James E. Shepard to J. C. B. Ehringhaus, October 31, 1933, folder 13, ser. 1, Personal Correspondence, Shepard Papers.

162. "North Carolina Committee on Negro Affairs," *Carolina Times*, December 4, 1937, 4; "The NCCNA Met Last Sunday," *Carolina Times*, December 18, 1937, 4; "Welcome Teachers, the Hour Has Come!," *Carolina Times*, April 16, 1938, 4.

163. R. N. Harris, Letter to Editor, *Carolina Times*, December 25, 1937. Harris, of course, was well known to Austin. In fact, Harris's wife, Plassie Harris, had been Austin's secretary back in 1929. "Secretary to Editor," *Pittsburgh Courier*, June 29, 1929, 6.

164. Fairclough, *Class of Their Own*, 309.

165. Shepard quoted in Thuesen, "Classes of Citizenship," 238. In 1933, Shepard wrote a letter of protest to Secretary of Labor Frances Perkins against the "reported effort of some employers to secure exemption from the minimum wage" under the National Industrial Recovery Act, with respect to jobs held by blacks. "No Place for Prejudice," *Raleigh News and Observer*, August 8, 1933, box 81, Johnson Papers. In November 1933, a group of black educators, including Shepard, "who are regarded as conservative," met in Durham and "adopted a strong statement embodying most of the N.A.A.C.P. philosophy. . . . The only difference . . . is that the" black conservative educators urged "appeal to the fairness of the white people and the state officials," while the NAACP advocated legal action if white officials failed to act. "North Carolina Factions Uniting behind Program," November 24, 1933, box 147, Meier Papers.

166. White to P. B. Young, April 24, 1939, box 147, Meier Papers.

167. "Editorially Speaking: Teachers Aroused," *Carolina Times*, September 11, 1937, 1, 8. Austin called Charles M. Eppes, a black Greenville leader, an "Uncle Tom" for stopping action on teacher salary equalization. "The NCCNA Met Last Sunday," *Carolina Times*, December 18, 1937, 4.

168. Beezer, "Black Teachers' Salaries," 208. In 1939, the U.S. district court "in Baltimore granted an injunction to a black teacher restraining the Anne Arundel County Board of Education from discriminating in the payment of teachers," based on the Fourteenth Amendment. In 1940, Circuit Court of Appeals judge John J. Parker ruled that unequal teacher salaries in Norfolk, Virginia, violated the Fourteenth Amendment. The U.S. Supreme Court rejected an appeal by the Norfolk school board, so Parker's decision bound the states. Sitkoff, *New Deal for Blacks*, 238–39. Mark Tushnet reports, "In 1942, the legislature appropriated $242,000 to narrow the differential, and the N.C. School Commission indicated its desire to eliminate all differences within two or three years." Tushnet, *NAACP's Legal Strategy*, 199. See also Burns, "North Carolina and the Negro Dilemma," 77–80; *Greensboro Daily News*, June 12, 1942, 12. Many southern states introduced the National Teacher Examination (NTE) in the 1940s and 1950s in order to increase salary differentials between black and white teachers. The

NTE was also used in the 1960s "to demote and dismiss thousands of African American teachers in desegregated school systems." Baker, "Testing Equality," 64.

169. On black voting drives in the South in the 1930s, see Sullivan, *Days of Hope*, 143.

170. Weare, *Black Business*, 242; Walker, "Changes in Race Accommodation," 184. In piedmont cities where whites outnumbered blacks, voting restrictions were less rigid than in eastern North Carolina, where there were black majorities in certain areas. Walker, "Changes in Race Accommodation," 184. During the 1920s and early 1930s, whites would pay black "ward heelers" to get blacks to vote for them. Asa Spaulding recalled that during those years, "the new generation coming along saw that as retarding the progress of blacks instead of improving it." Spaulding interview.

171. Floyd J. Calvin, "Durham Editor Says Hoover Will Win," *Pittsburgh Courier*, October 27, 1928, 2. In a listing of black editors prepared by the Colored Voters Division of the Republican National Party, Austin was termed a loyal Republican. By contrast, Robert L. Vann of the *Pittsburgh Courier* was termed "Disloyal and Bitter," Robert S. Abbott of the *Chicago Defender*, leaning Democrat; and P. B. Young of the *Norfolk Journal and Guide*, nonpartisan and anti-Hoover. M. Hawkins, "Publicity Committee Colored Voters Division, 1928 Campaign, Confidential Comments on Loyalty," pt. 3, ser. H, reel 2, Barnett Papers.

172. Weare, *Black Business*, 242, 244.

173. "Publisher Named Head of Vote Body," *Chicago Defender*, February 17, 1940, 4.

174. Floyd J. Calvin, "Durham Editor Says Hoover Will Win," *Pittsburgh Courier*, October 27, 1928, 2. In 1932, *Pittsburgh Courier* editor Robert L. Vann pronounced, "I see millions of Negroes turning the pictures of Abraham Lincoln to the wall. This year I see Negroes voting a Democratic ticket." Vann, "This Year I See Millions of Negroes Turning the Picture of Abraham Lincoln to the Wall," *Pittsburgh Courier*, September 17, 1932, 12. Although more African Americans voted Democratic in 1932 than they had in previous years, most black voters still supported Hoover. Black support for Democratic candidates increased in the congressional election of 1934, and in 1936, most blacks voters supported Franklin Roosevelt for president. Tindall, *Emergence of the New South*, 555–57.

175. It is worth noting that black Democrats met in Washington, D.C., in March 1932, led by North Carolina–born F. O. Williston, head of the National Democratic Negro Voters League, to organize nationally to aid various states in increasing black voter registration in the Democratic Party. "Negro Democrats Confer in Capital," *Washington Post*, March 7, 1932, 5.

176. The court's ruling allowed Texas Democrats to exclude blacks if the state legislature played no part in that exclusion, and if the Democratic Party was deemed to be a private organization. Edward T. Folliard, "Texas Ban on Negro Vote Ruled Illegal," *Washington Post*, May 3, 1932, 2; Bell, *Race, Racism and American Law*, 191–92. While the Supreme Court invalidated the white primary in Texas in 1932, subsequent changes in the primary led to a drawn-out series of cases as Texas's white Democrats changed their primary in form in hopes of sidestepping the court's rulings. In 1944, in *Smith v. Allright*, the Supreme Court again ruled the Texas Democratic white primary unconstitutional,

ruling that the party's action was a state action and not a private action, which would have been beyond the court's jurisdiction.

177. Guy B. Johnson, "Depression and Race Relations," ca. 1932, ser. 5.6, Johnson Papers.

178. "North Carolinians Hold State-Wide Political Confab," *Pittsburgh Courier*, April 2, 1932, 3; "Negroes Band for Political Crusade," *Durham Morning Herald*, April 1, 1932, 1, 8.

179. "Negroes Band for Political Crusade," 1, 8; Albert L. Hinton, "Durham, Thriving Southern Metropolis of 17,000 Negro Inhabitants, a City of Big Business, Fine Homes and Churches," *Norfolk Journal and Guide*, April 16, 1932, 7.

180. Austin to National Features Services, Chicago, Illinois, September 27, 1932, pt. 3, ser. H, reel 2, Barnett Papers.

181. "Negroes Band for Political Crusade," 1, 8; "North Carolina Election Official Fined $300," *Crisis*, July 1936, 216.

182. "Former Publisher Nanton, Dead at 81" (web source). Nanton edited and published the *Carolina Tribune* from 1932 to 1940, when the name of the newspaper was changed to the *Carolinian*, under the leadership of editor-publisher Paul R. Jervay Sr. Jervay's father published the *Cape Fear Journal* in Wilmington, North Carolina. "The CAROLINIAN Has Rich Traditions" (web source).

183. "Give Statements on Registration," *Raleigh News and Observer*, May 30, 1932, 3. White attorney A. B. Breece noted that blacks' voter registration campaign sought to register 5,000 black voters in Raleigh.

184. "More Talk about Negro Situation," *Raleigh News and Observer*, June 1, 1932, 1, 14.

185. "A Dagger at the Heart," *Raleigh News and Observer*, May 25, 1932, 4.

186. "Sowing Dragon's Teeth," *Raleigh News and Observer*, May 29, 1932, 4. The *Atlanta Daily World* reported that "white alarmists" condemned the *Carolina Times* for having the audacity to "question a white man of the standing of the Hon. Josephus [Daniels]." White opposition claimed that several white officials had instigated black voter registration, but one accused official said that he had nothing to do with black voter registration, which was the consequence of a black "educational campaign on citizenship." The Negro Voters League of Raleigh had organized the voter registration campaign and hired four black attorneys to defend black voters against attempts to deny them their voter registration. "Carolina Whites Horrified as Negro Democrats Vote: Everything Is Done to Bar Them," *Atlanta Daily World*, June 6, 1932, 1. One white supremacist Democratic candidate for state senator attacked the *Times*: "It is a disgrace when a Negro paper openly comes out with such language against such a man as Mr. Daniels."

187. "Disqualified Negro Voters Restored Suffrage Rights," *Carolina Times*, July 2, 1932, copy of clipping in the author's possession. Andrews, born in Sumter, South Carolina, in 1891, earned an A.B. degree from Howard University in 1915, and went to Harvard Law School. "Howard University Commencement," *New York Age*, June 10, 1915; Robert McCants Andrews, "Registration Card," June 6, 1917, (web source). In 1917, Andrews, who was the son of Johnson Andrews, a railway mail clerk, "enlisted in

the reserve officers' training corps at Harvard." He had just completed his second year of law school. "R. McCants Andrews," *The Watchman and Southron* (Sumter, SC), May 30, 1917. Andrews moved to Durham in 1919, after graduating from Harvard Law School, "to take up special work in the field service of the Department of Labor as the assistant of Dr. A. M. Moore, director of the division in charge of colored interests in the State of North Carolina." Andrews had worked as a journalist for the *Baltimore Herald*, the *Boston Chronicle*, and the *Washington Eagle*. Jeannette Carter, "Washington Letter," *New York Age*, February 8, 1919. According to the *Raleigh News and Observer*, Andrews was the "assistant supervisor of Negro Economics Department of Labor" in Raleigh. "Negroes to Organize a YMCA," *Raleigh News and Observer*, February 16, 1919. Andrews received his law license to practice in North Carolina in February 1921. "Two New Lawyers," *Durham Morning Herald*, February 6, 1921.

188. Standard Certificate of Death, North Carolina State Board of Health, R. Mc-Cants Andrews, July 5, 1932. Andrews was buried in Sumter, South Carolina, his birthplace. Floyd J. Calvin, "Lawyer Andrews Dies," *Pittsburgh Courier*, July 23, 1932.

189. According to one report, "Polk was openly antagonistic toward the protest of the Negroes and had M. Hugh Thompson, a Negro attorney who was protesting the registration procedure, forcibly ejected from the precinct." Bunche referred to the registrar as Polk while the *Durham Morning Herald* called him Pope. Bunche, *Political Status of the Negro*, 316; "Many Sign Pope Ouster Petition," *Durham Morning Herald*, April 14, 1933, 3. In 1933, T. D. Parham was president of the Independent League of Negro Voters. "Many Sign Pope Ouster Petition," 3.

190. "Negroes Deny Opposition to Hill, Smith and Isaacs," *Durham Morning Herald*, April 12, 1933, 5.

191. "Negro Vote Saves City Supplement," *Carolina Times*, August 12, 1933, box 81, Johnson Papers.

192. John A. Fouchee, "Elect Magistrates on Democratic Ticket in North Carolina," *Pittsburgh Courier*, November 24, 1934, 3; Regester, "From the Buzzard's Roost," 118–19. In 1921, Watkins was president of the National Colored Exhibitors Association, and owned the Wonderland Theater, which showed movies and newsreels, and the Rex Theatre, which staged vaudeville shows. Watkins also owned movie theaters in Petersburg, VA; South Boston, VA; Chapel Hill, NC; and Apex, NC. He was building a theater in Hot Springs, AR. J. A. Jackson, "No 'Bull' in Durham, N.C. Business Men," *Baltimore Afro-American*, November 21, 1921, 11.

193. "1218 Fayetteville St.—F. K. Watkins House," "Open Durham" (web source).

194. Walker, "Changes in Race Accommodation," 246–47; Bunche, *Political Status of the Negro*, 177; "New County Officers Are Sworn In by Clerk Young," *Durham Sun*, December 3, 1934, 1.

195. Fouchee, "Elect Magistrates on Democratic Ticket," 3; "Tar Heelia's Surprise," *Norfolk Journal and Guide*, November 17, 1934, 8. According to the *New York Amsterdam News*, "No Negro had been elected to a judicial post in Durham for fifty years, and the last one was a Republican." "N.C. Gets Negro Democrats as Judges—St. Louis Ditto," *New York Amsterdam News*, November 17, 1934, 5.

196. "Durham Memorandum," ca. 1939, box 85, Bunche Papers. In 1939, there were still two black justices of the peace in Durham. O'Kelly and Watkins were the two justices serving in 1939 in Durham. Ibid.

197. Walker, "Changes in Race Accommodation," 247, 249. In 1934, a black candidate for justice of the peace in Raleigh lost to a white candidate. Fouchee, "Elect Magistrates on Democratic Ticket," 3.

198. Louis Austin, interview by August Meier, n.d., ca. 1958, notes, box 139, Meier Papers.

199. Walker, "Changes in Race Accommodation," 246–47; Bunche, *Political Status of the Negro*, 177; "New County Officers Are Sworn In by Clerk Young," *Durham Sun*, December 3, 1934, 1.

200. Walker, "Changes in Race Accommodation," 246–47.

201. Rencher Harris to Austin, June 29, 1962, box 3, Rencher N. Harris Papers, David M. Rubenstein Rare Book & Manuscript Library, Duke University, Durham, NC (hereafter cited as Harris Papers); Bell, *Hard Times*, 78; Weare, *Black Business*, 225, 240, 244; Bunche, *Political Status of the Negro*, 317. See Walker, "Changes in Race Accommodation"; Carver, "Role of the Durham Committee," 33–34.

202. Carver, "Role of the Durham Committee," 32–33.

203. Weare, *Black Business*, 241.

204. Winford, "'Battle for Freedom,'" 134.

205. "Civic Affairs Discussed by Negroes at Mass Meeting," *Durham Morning Herald*, November 18, 1935, 3.

206. Weare, *Black Business*, 244; Tindall, *Emergence of the New South*, 557.

207. "For Mayor," *Carolina Times*, April 29, 1939, 8.

208. "North Carolina Committee on Negro Affairs," *Carolina Times*, December 4, 1937, 4. In June 1936, as a sign of the increasing importance of the black vote and its potential for controversy, charges were made that Clyde Hoey, candidate for governor, had placed advertisements in the *Carolina Times* to get black support. In response to the charge, Hoey's campaign manager claimed that Hoey's opponent, Ralph W. McDonald, had also placed campaign ads in the *Carolina Times*. "Race Issue Flares in N.C. Politics," June 30, 1936, box 81, Johnson Papers.

209. Tindall, *Emergence of the New South*, 557.

210. "North Carolina Committee on Negro Affairs," 4.

211. "The June Primaries," *Carolina Times*, March 19, 1938, 4. In April, Austin renewed his call for black voter registration before the June 1938 primary to support candidates favorable to black opportunities. "Prepare to Register and Vote," *Carolina Times*, April 23, 1938, 4.

212. "The Present Political Campaign," *Carolina Times*, April 2, 1938, 4. The NCCNA was headed by Winston-Salem attorney Hosea V. Price.

213. "Negro Democrats to Convene Today in Unusual Rally," *Durham Morning Herald*, May 28, 1938, 12.

214. "Taylor Reelected Precinct Chairman; Martin Secretary," *Carolina Times*, May 14, 1938, 1.

215. Walker, "Changes in Race Accommodation," 249; "Negro Democrats to Convene Today," 12.

216. "Durham Memorandum," ca. 1939, box 85, Bunche Papers. Curiously, the *Times* reported that Austin was "automatically nominated and his appointment will more than likely be confirmed by the legislature if the proper pressure is brought to bear by those who are interested in the progress of the race in this section." "1,600 Vote for Race Candidate," *Carolina Times*, June 11, 1938, 1.

217. "Large Crowd Expected Here for District's Political Meeting," *Carolina Times*, May 28, 1938, 1; "1,600 Vote for Race Candidate," 1; "How Durham Voted in Local and District Contests," *Durham Morning Herald*, June 6, 1938, 3.

218. Walker, "Changes in Race Accommodation," 251.

219. "The Flying Field Referendum," *Carolina Times*, January 8, 1938, 4; "First Things First," *Carolina Times*, January 29, 1938, 4.

220. *Carolina Times*, February 5, 1938, 8.

221. L. E. Austin, "Race Vote Helps Defeat Airport: Negro Citizens Refuse to Be Herded to Polls by Political Crooks," *Carolina Times*, March 5, 1938, 1. Austin credited R. N. Harris with getting the black vote out to defeat the bond issue. Ibid. R. N. Harris told Wilhelmina Jackson, who was assisting Ralph Bunche in his study of black politics for the Carnegie Corporation's study of African Americans, that 2,400 blacks were registered. Jackson concluded that the campaign by the Durham Committee, the *Carolina Times* editorials and advertisements against the bond issue, and the voter registration campaign were important factors in defeating the bond issue. "Durham Memorandum," ca. 1939, box 85, Bunche Papers.

222. "The Airport Election," *Carolina Times*, March 5, 1938, 4. During the election, some white opponents of the airport challenged black voters' right to vote, thereby breaking federal law, according to Austin. He called on the DCNA to investigate. "The Right to Vote," *Carolina Times*, March 5, 1938, 4.

223. "The City Election," *Carolina Times*, April 1, 1939, 4.

224. "Organize Now," *Carolina Times*, August 5, 1939, 4. The same month, he praised a voter registration campaign in South Carolina, condemned the arrest of a black youth for disorderly conduct while helping blacks register for the Greenville primary, and reported that in North Carolina "there are many sections in which Negroes are not allowed to register and vote not only in city elections, but in national elections.... There can be no freedom without the ballot and no ballot without freedom." "Freedom and the Ballot," *Carolina Times* August 19, 1939, 4.

225. "Freedom and the Ballot," 4.

226. Bell, *Hard Times*, 78; Weare, *Black Business*, 240, 244; Bunche, *Political Status of the Negro*, 317. See Harry J. Walker, "Changes in Race Accommodation."

227. "Bus Case Hotly Contested in Randolph Court," *Carolina Times*, August 12, 1939, 6; Williams, "History of Strieby Congregational Church."

228. "Bus Case Hotly Contested in Randolph Court," *Carolina Times*, August 12, 1939, 6.

229. "Wins Important Case," *Carolina Times*, August 12, 1939, 3; Williams, "History of Strieby Congregational Church and School."

230. "Sympathy for Whom?," *Carolina Times*, April 9, 1938, 4.

231. "Jim-Crow Bus Case Take[n] to State Supreme Court," *Carolina Times*, May 14, 1938, 1, 8.

232. "Sympathy for Whom?," 4. Even the *Durham Morning Herald* believed that the charges would be dropped.

233. "Jim-Crow Bus Case Take[n] to State Supreme Court," *Carolina Times*, May 14, 1938, 1, 8; "Supreme Court Reverses Bus Case: High Court Says Miss Harris Did Not Violate Jim Crow Law on Bus," *Carolina Times*, June 11, 1938, 1; Walker, "Changes in Race Accommodation," 280. Austin criticized the local branch of the NAACP for failing to aid in Harris's defense. "The Jim Crow Bus Case," *Carolina Times*, May 21, 1938, 4.

234. "The Bus Case Reversal," *Carolina Times*, June 25, 1938, 4.

235. McGuire, *At the Dark End of the Street*, xix.

236. Walker, "Changes in Race Accommodation," 167; "White Hayti Merchant Beats Sightless Negro," *Carolina Times*, September 25, 1937, 1.

237. "Housewives League Rally Song," n.d., ca. 1930s, "Unite and Support Negro Business! The Durham Housewives League," n.d., ca. 1930s, box 81, Johnson Papers.

238. "Support That Is More Than Lip Service," *Carolina Times*, March 18, 1961, 2.

239. "White Theatres Face Boycott in Greensboro," *Norfolk Journal and Guide*, January 22, 1938, 16. See also Henry Cross, "Carolina Won't Have 'Mixed Movies,'" *Chicago Defender*, January 29, 1938, 18; "Smart Theatre Owners," *Carolina Times*, December 18, 1937, 4.

240. "Southern Students Fight Movie Mixing Resolution," *New York Amsterdam News*, February 19, 1938, 17; Slab Singleton, "Movies 'About Face' after Boycott," *Chicago Defender*, February 26, 1938, 3.

241. "The Voice of Youth," *Carolina Times*, January 15, 1938, 4; "Greensboro Theatre Boycotted by A&T and Bennett Students," *Carolina Times*, January 15, 1938, 1.

242. "What about It Students?" *Carolina Times*, February 12, 1938, 4. According to UNC journalism doctoral student Lorraine Ahearn, Bennett students "proposed the boycott in a meeting with their professors." Lorraine Ahearn to author, email communication, August 12, 2012.

243. "Hospital Discrimination," *Carolina Times*, May 14, 1938, 4.

244. "Little Men in Big Places," *Carolina Times*, May 28, 1938, 4.

245. "Table II: Disposition of 821 Homicide Indictments in Ten Counties in North Carolina, 1930–1940," in Guy B. Johnson to Cyrus M. Johnson, January 15, 1947, box 1, folder 16, NCCIC Papers.

246. "Senator Bailey Raves Again," *Carolina Times*, July 17, 1937, 2; "The Anti-Lynching Bill," *Carolina Times*, November 13, 1937, 8; "Political Jackasses," *Carolina Times*, January 22, 1938, 4.

247. "Senator Bailey Speaks," *Carolina Times*, September 24, 1938, 4. White newspapers, including the *Johnston County Record*, criticized Bailey's insular analysis and attack on outsiders, but not his white supremacy. "Senator Bailey Speaks," 4.

248. "Seven Out [of] Ten in Favor of Anti-Lynching Bill," *Carolina Times*, November 20, 1937, 5.

249. "What Our Senators Fought For," *Carolina Times*, February 5, 1938, 4.

250. Boyd, "Louis Austin," 36, 41.

251. Walker, "Changes in Race Accommodation," 171–72.

252. "Vernon Farrington Victim of Willful Attack for Sitting with Officer," *Carolina Times*, May 29, 1937, 1; "Policeman Convicted and Suspended for Attacking Young Negro; Appeals Case," *Carolina Times*, June 5, 1937, 1; "Justice Has Been Satisfied," *Carolina Times*, June 5, 1937, 2; "Officer to Appeal $5 Fine Put on Him for Hitting Negro," *Durham Morning Herald*, May 30, 1937, sec. 2, p. 1. Whitfield said he hit Farrington to "teach a nigger his place." Walker, "Changes in Race Accommodation," 281.

253. "Vernon Farrington Victim," 1.

254. Walker, "Changes in Race Accommodation," 283, 306.

255. "Vernon Farrington Victim," 1; "Policeman Convicted and Suspended for Attacking Young Negro; Appeals Case," *Carolina Times*, June 5, 1937, 1; "Justice Has Been Satisfied," *Carolina Times*, June 5, 1937, 2; "Officer to Appeal $5 Fine Put on Him for Hitting Negro," *Durham Morning Herald*, May 30, 1937, sec. 2, p. 1. While some called for Whitfield's firing, Austin demurred. Instead, he said that the policeman needed "sympathy," as his racist attitude and action stemmed from his lack of education and limited cultural development, which limited his "self-control [to] . . . that of a six or eight year old child." "Justice Has Been Satisfied," 2.

256. "Charlotte Negroes Fight Police Double Slaying," *Carolina Times*, November 27, 1937, 1.

257. "Charlotte Police Guilty of Murdering Negro," *Carolina Times*, December 11, 1937, 1.

258. "Shot by an Unidentified Policeman," *Carolina Times*, February 19, 1938, 4.

259. "Local Cop Assaults Boy: Slaps Lad for Sitting on Fender," *Carolina Times*, May 6, 1939, 1.

260. "Should Be Expelled," *Carolina Times*, May 13, 1939, 4. In June 1939, a Charlotte police officer choked and beat a black woman he had arrested for suspicion of operating an illegal liquor house, but the cop was found not guilty.

261. "North Wilkesboro Police Kills 13 Year-Old Boy; Set Free by Coroners Jury," *Carolina Times*, May 7, 1938, 1.

262. "James McNeal Shot to Death and Badly Beaten by Policeman Wilkie," *Carolina Times*, June 4, 1938, 1.

263. "Should Be Investigated," *Carolina Times*, June 4, 1938, 4. While the *Times* claimed that McNeil had no criminal record, the *People's Rights Bulletin* reported the charge "against McNeill [*sic*] that he had a police record of three or four arrests . . . charges of petty liquor-selling—he was in the habit of giving parties to his friends" and he was also once arrested for "being caught with a pistol in his pocket when on an automobile trip." "Shot by A.B.C. Officer: Questions Raised by Death and Alleged Slugging of James McNeill [*sic*] in Own Home at Durham," *People's Rights Bulletin*, July 1938, 1–2, 4, in box 85, Bunche Papers. See also "ABC Officer Kills Negro Who Hit Him," *Durham Morning Herald*, May 28, 1938, 1; "The ABC Shooting," *Durham Sunday Herald-Sun*, May 29, 1938, 4.

264. "Shot by A.B.C. Officer," 1–2, 4. Members of the Southern Committee for People's Rights included playwright Paul Green, Gertrude Weil, William T. Couch, Josiah Bailey, and Virginius Dabney. Ibid. On the Southern Committee for People's Rights, see also Gilmore, *Defying Dixie*, 221–26.

265. "Shot by A.B.C. Officer," 1–2, 4.

266. "Charge of Murder to Be Brought against Officer T. D. Wilkie," *Carolina Times*, June 11, 1938, 1; "Killer Cop Bound Over on Manslaughter Charge; Bond Is Set at $1,000," *Carolina Times*, June 18, 1938, 1.

267. "Durham Memorandum," ca. 1939, box 85, Bunche Papers; "Warrant Accuses Whisky Raid-Chief of Manslaughter," *Durham Morning Herald*, May 31, 1938, 3.

268. "Killer Cop Bound Over," 1.

269. "Shot by A.B.C. Officer," 1–2, 4.

270. Ibid.

271. "Killer Policeman to Be Tried by Judge Spears," *Carolina Times*, July 16, 1938, 1.

272. "The Wilkie Case Closed Issue," *Carolina Times*, July 30, 1938, 4. According to one account, Wilkie was "removed from the ABC squad." "Durham Memorandum," ca. 1939, box 85, Bunche Papers.

273. "White Cop Freed on Charge of Beating and Abusing Race Woman," *Carolina Times*, August 5, 1939, 1.

274. "Harry Morgan on Rampage Again: Durham Negro Brutally Beaten by ABC Officer," *Carolina Times*, August 26, 1939, 1.

275. "Negro Policemen and Crime," *Carolina Times*, February 19, 1938, 4; "Police Shooting," *Carolina Times*, February 26, 1938, 4.

276. "Negro Policemen," *Carolina Times*, February 1, 1941, box 81, Johnson Papers.

277. "Negroes Seek Place in Jury Box in Durham: L. E. Austin Appears before County Board in Interest of His Race," *Durham Sun*, January 6, 1936, box 81, Johnson Papers.

278. "Welcome Lawyers," *Carolina Times*, August 6, 1938, 4.

279. "Negro Jurymen," *Carolina Times*, June 17, 1939, 4.

280. "Grand Jury Won't Indict White Who Burned Negro to Death," *Carolina Times*, June 25, 1938, 3.

281. Conrad O. Pearson to Charles H. Houston, NAACP Special Counsel, September 15, 1936, NAACP Branch Files, Durham, NC, April–October 1936, NAACP (Proquest); "White Man Rapes 13-Year-Old Colored Girl," September 11, 1936, *Washington Tribune*, NAACP Branch Files, Durham, NC, April–October 1936, NAACP (Proquest).

282. "Attackers of Negro Women and the Law," *Carolina Times*, April 15, 1938, 4; "White Attacker Freed: Negro Woman Victim," *Carolina Times*, April 8, 1938, 1.

283. "Borland Continues Assault Case 25th Time," *Carolina Times*, July 15, 1939, 1.

284. "Breeds No Respect for the Law," *Carolina Times*, July 22, 1939, 4. In a rare case, in September 1938, the *Times* reported that a white woman "was convicted in Wake County Superior Court of whipping [with a hickory switch] . . . a seven year old Negro girl." "White Woman Beats Child," *Carolina Times*, September 24, 1938, 1.

Chapter Three

1. Washburn, *"Pittsburgh Courier's* Double V Campaign," 73–75; Lawson, *Running for Freedom,* 7.

2. Myrdal, *American Dilemma,* 924.

3. Sitkoff, "Racial Militancy and Interracial Violence," 662; Kruse and Tuck, "Introduction," 4–12.

4. Suggs, *P. B. Young,* 119–28; White, "Economic and Social Development of Negroes," 202; Myrdal, *American Dilemma,* 910. For another example of a southern black journalist who consistently attacked racial injustice locally and nationally during the war, see Roefs, "Leading the Civil Rights Vanguard."

5. Du Bois, "Close Ranks," in Lewis, *W. E. B. Du Bois,* 697. Similarly, in May 1918, Robert S. Abbott told his *Chicago Defender* readers to set aside "grievances at home" until "after the greater task of winning this war is over." Jones, "Editorial Policy of Negro Newspapers," 26.

6. Sitkoff, *New Deal for Blacks,* 22; Tuttle, *Race Riot,* 221.

7. Sullivan, *Days of Hope,* 135.

8. Austin quoted in Kiser, "Occupational Change," 35.

9. Lawrence V. Lutes, FBI report on Louis Austin, April 6, 1944, FOIPA no. 112 9984-000.

10. Lawrence V. Lutes, FBI report on Louis Austin, May 26, 1944, FOIPA no. 112-9984-000.

11. Lawrence V. Lutes, FBI report on Louis Austin, April 9, 1945, FOIPA no. 1129984-000.

12. Washburn, *African American Newspaper,* 177, 190; Farrar, *Baltimore Afro-American,* 19.

13. Washburn, *African American Newspaper,* 181.

14. Griffin, "Courier of Crisis, Messenger of Hope," 149–50.

15. In 1945, the *Charlotte Post,* at 4,200, had the second largest circulation. In comparison, the *Norfolk Journal and Guide* had a circulation of 85,000 during World War II. Suggs, *P. B. Young,* 119. In April 1944, the FBI claimed that the *Carolina Times* circulation was about 2,000 based on information from the printers. Lawrence V. Lutes, FBI report on Louis Austin, April 6, 1944, FOIPA no. 1129984-000.

16. Suggs, *Black Press in the South,* x.

17. Columns in the *Pittsburgh Courier* by George Schuyler and P. L. Prattis and editorials in the *Chicago Defender* observed the similarities between German occupation of Poland and British imperialism in Africa. Dalfiume, " 'Forgotten Years,' " 93–94.

18. "Hands of America," *Carolina Times,* September 23, 1939, 4.

19. "Hitlerism vs. the British Lion," *Carolina Times,* April 13, 1940, 4; "Henry Ford Speaks," *Carolina Times,* February 22, 1941, 2.

20. Lawrence V. Lutes, FBI report on Louis Austin, October 9, 1944, FOIPA no. 1129984-000.

21. Lawrence V. Lutes, FBI report on Louis Austin, January 6, 1945, FOIPA no. 1129984-000.

22. "America Will Be Drawn into War Says Shepard," *Carolina Times*, September 30, 1939, 1.

23. Myrdal, *American Dilemma*, 1006.

24. "College Leader Reviews War Situation; Asks Daily Newspaper to Use Influence to Right Minority Wrongs," press release, April 1942, pt. 3, ser. B, reel 5, Barnett Papers.

25. Shapiro, *White Violence and Black Response*, 341.

26. Dalfiume, " 'Forgotten Years,' " 96.

27. Clifford Jenkins, "Carolina Readers Speak," *Carolina Times*, August 8, 1942, 2.

28. Stanley Winborne to Governor J. Melville Broughton, June 17, 1943, box 82, Governor J. Melville Broughton Papers, North Carolina Division of Archives and History, State Archives, Raleigh, NC (hereafter cited as Broughton Papers).

29. "Keep the Faith . . . Buy Bonds," *Carolina Times*, April 17, 1943, 4.

30. "While the Governor Speaks," *Carolina Times*, July 24, 1943, 4.

31. Broughton to H. Shelton Smith, August 2, 1943, box 82, Broughton Papers. The "judge in the case apologized to Mrs. Williamson and her attorneys for the [guilty] verdict with the explanation that he was 'on the spot.' " She received a thirty-day suspended sentence after being convicted of violating the Jim Crow law, assaulting the bus driver, and resisting arrest.

32. "Bus Accommodations for Negroes," *Carolina Times*, April 6, 1940, 4; Murray, *Autobiography of a Black Activist*, 138–42.

33. Pauli Murray to Jean and Pan, April 2, 1940, box 4, Murray Papers.

34. Ellsworth, *The Secret Game*, 240–41, 268–73, 277–80. Ellsworth provides a fine account of the "secret game" but makes an erroneous claim about Austin. Ellsworth claims that "Austin . . . didn't give a plugged nickel about sports," when in fact he had played baseball as a youth and a young man, and later played a key role in integrating sports in North Carolina, as recounted in chapter 4. Austin also served as president of the Carolina Semi-Professional Baseball League, which included four teams and a sixty-two-game schedule. "Carolina League Announces 62-Game Baseball Schedule," *Norfolk Journal and Guide*, April 20, 1946, 10.

35. Junot, " 'Huc': The Story of Henry Hucles," (web source); "Post Season Basketball Records," (web source); "L.I.U. Prevails, 57 to 40," *New York Times*, March 25, 1938, 26; "Eagles Win from Brooklyn College," *Carolina Times*, February 7, 1942, 4; "Colored N.C. Five Wins Here," *Washington Post*, February 1, 1942, SP3.

36. Tyson, "Wars for Democracy," 256–57.

37. Finkle, "Conservative Aims of Militant Rhetoric," 697.

38. "Negro Soldiers," *Carolina Times*, August 10, 1940, 4.

39. "Federal Discrimination," *Carolina Times*, April 6, 1940, 4.

40. "Credit to Whom Credit Is Due," *Carolina Times*, September 21, 1940, 4.

41. "Where Is Great Britain's Army?," *Carolina Times*, June 15, 1940, 4.

42. McGuire, "Desegregation of the Armed Forces," 147–48.

43. James R. Hennessey, FBI report on Louis Austin, March 18, 1943, FOIPA no. 1129984-000; LaRossa, *Of War and Men*, 31.

44. Bertram D. Hulen, "Draft Stops at 38," *New York Times*, December 6, 1942, 1.

45. A 1935 study reported that the average black family in Durham earned less than 70 percent of the average earnings for a white family in Durham. Janiewski, *Sisterhood Denied*, 223.

46. "Our National Defense," *Carolina Times*, March 15, 1941, 2; Korstad, *Civil Rights Unionism*, 132.

47. Suggs, *P. B. Young*, 102; "Spaulding Takes Stand against Proposed Negro March on Washington," *Durham Herald-Sun*, June 22, 1941, 7.

48. Janken, *Rayford W. Logan*, 128.

49. Suggs, *P. B. Young*, 121.

50. "Suggests Protests Be Tempered with Judgment: Prefers 'Long Visional Planning to Purposeless Clamor,' Tells How North Carolinians Do It," press release, July, ca. 1942–43, pt. 3, ser. C, Barnett Papers.

51. James Shepard to Claude Barnett, November 26, 1944, pt. 3, ser. B, reel 5, Barnett Papers.

52. Shepard quoted in Dalfiume, "'Forgotten Years,'" 101.

53. Shepard, "Racial Relationships in North Carolina," Radio Broadcast, March 7, 1944, box 82, Broughton Papers.

54. Frazier to Shepard, February 17, 1944, box 82, Broughton Papers; Leach, *Langston Hughes*, 115–16.

55. "As We Expected," *Atlanta Daily World*, March 15, 1944, 6.

56. "No Solution," *Carolina Times*, June 21, 1941, 2.

57. "The March on Washington," *Carolina Times*, July 5, 1941, 2.

58. "The Platform of the *Carolina Times*," *Carolina Times*, June 20, 1942, 2; "The Platform of the *Carolina Times*," *Carolina Times*, February 20, 1943, 4; James R. Hennessey, FBI report on Louis Austin, March 18, 1943, FOIPA no. 1129984-000; Lawrence V. Lutes, FBI report on Louis Austin, May 26, 1944, FOIPA no. 1129984-000.

59. "The Texarkana Lynching," *Carolina Times*, July 18, 1942, 2.

60. "We Think the Time Has Arrived . . ." *Carolina Times*, February 28, 1942, 2; Shapiro, *White Violence and Black Response*, 341;

61. "We Think the Time Has Arrived . . . ," 2; Shapiro, *White Violence and Black Response*, 341; Murray, *History of the North Carolina Teachers Association*, 47.

62. McGuire, "Desegregation of the Armed Forces," 155. In 1944, the navy began to commission black officers. Franklin and Moss, *From Slavery to Freedom*, 390–91.

63. Finkle, "Conservative Aims," 695. Virginius Dabney leveled the charge.

64. Ibid., 696.

65. Finkle, *Forum for Protest*, 65.

66. Washburn, *Question of Sedition*, 8–9, 147–48, 206; Simmons, *African American Press*, 88.

67. Washburn, *Question of Sedition*, 8, 82–85; Simmons, *African American Press*, 80–84. The Office of Facts and Figures, the Office of War Information, the Justice Department, the White House, the Office of Censorship, and the army also investigated the black press during the war.

68. Vivian Edmonds interview, August 30, 2004.

69. James R. Hennessey, FBI report on Louis Austin, March 18, 1943, FOIPA no. 1129984-000.

70. Ibid.

71. Kenneth Edmonds interview, May 23, 2011. According to Austin's daughter, an FBI agent once came to the offices of the *Carolina Times*, where Austin promptly told him off, and the FBI never returned. Vivian Edmonds interview, August 30, 2004.

72. SAC, Charlotte, to Director, FBI, October 12, 1945, FOIPA no. 1129984-000; SAC, Charlotte, to Director, FBI, February 11, 1946, FOIPA no. 1129984-000.

73. Lawrence V. Lutes, FBI report on Louis Austin, July 8, 1943, FOIPA no. 1129984-000.

74. Lawrence V. Lutes, FBI report on Louis Austin, September 16, 1943, FOIPA no. 1129984-000.

75. Lawrence V. Lutes, FBI report on Louis Austin, January 25, 1944, FOIPA no. 1129984-000.

76. James R. Hennessey, FBI report on Louis Austin, March 18, 1943, FOIPA no. 1129984-000.

77. Lawrence V. Lutes, FBI report on Louis Austin, April 6, 1944, FOIPA no. 1129984-000. Rhodes was born in 1909 in Highlands, North Carolina, and lived at 619 Price Street in Durham. He earned $25 per week.

78. SAC, Charlotte, to Director, FBI, October 12, 1945, FOIPA no. 1129984-000; SAC, Charlotte, to Director, FBI, February 11, 1946, FOIPA no. 1129984-000.

79. Washburn, *Question of Sedition*, 146–47.

80. Finkle, *Forum for Protest*, 64–65; Washburn, "Pittsburgh *Courier's* Double V Campaign," 80.

81. Washburn, *African American Newspaper*, 161.

82. Simmons, *African American Press*, 82.

83. Finkle, "Conservative Aims," 696–97.

84. Washburn, *Question of Sedition*, 8–9, 147–48, 206; Simmons, *African American Press*, 88.

85. "We Think the Time Has Arrived . . . ," 2.

86. "Freedom for India," *Carolina Times*, March 14, 1942, 2.

87. "Fifth Columnists in Durham," *Carolina Times*, March 28, 1942, 2.

88. "What Is It Worth?," *Carolina Times*, May 9, 1942, 2.

89. Korstad, *Civil Rights Unionism*, 181, 185.

90. Lawrence V. Lutes, FBI report on Louis Austin, September 16, 1943, FOIPA no. 1129984-000.

91. For example, on July 31, 1943, the CIO placed two advertisements on page 3 of the *Carolina Times* that covered about half the page. *Carolina Times*, July 31, 1943, 3.

92. Lawrence V. Lutes, FBI report on Louis Austin, May 26, 1944, FOIPA no. 112 9984-000.

93. Lawrence V. Lutes, FBI report on Louis Austin, July 18, 1945, FOIPA no. 112 9984-000.

94. Broughton speech, July 11, 1943, box 82, Broughton Papers.

95. "Threads of Nazism," *Carolina Times*, July 23, 1943.

96. Broughton to Forney Johnston, December 31, 1942, Broughton to Walter Davenport, June 30, 1943, box 82, Broughton Papers.

97. Shepard to Broughton, June 19, 1944, box 82, Broughton Papers.

98. Finkle, "Conservative Aims," 709.

99. "They Have Found the Secret," *Carolina Times*, April 4, 1942, 2. The tablet was placed in front of Durham County's courthouse. Some African Americans, however, like Lewis Jones, refused to accept induction into a Jim Crow army and went to jail. While the Baltimore newspaper, the *Afro-American*, condemned Jones, forty Howard University students announced their support for Jones and claimed that "he was considered a hero by thousands of blacks." Finkle, "Conservative Aims," 709.

100. "Race Relations Day," *Carolina Times*, March 6, 1943, 4.

101. "Conference on Race Relations, July 10, 11, 12, 1944, North Carolina College for Negroes, Durham, North Carolina," North Carolina Room, Durham County Library, Durham, North Carolina.

102. Gavins, *Perils and Prospects*, 123–26.

103. Ibid.

104. Suggs, *P. B. Young*, 122.

105. Gavins, *Perils and Prospects*, 125–26.

106. "The Southern Conference on Race Relations," *Carolina Times*, November 21, 1942, 4.

107. "Let Them Rave," *Carolina Times*, January 2, 1943, 4.

108. Lawrence V. Lutes, FBI report on Louis Austin, May 26, 1944, FOIPA no. 1129984-000.

109. Sitkoff, "Racial Militancy," 671.

110. Tyson, "Wars for Democracy," 264–65; "Police Use Tear Gas to Rescue Officer from Angered Soldiers," *Carolina Times*, April 10, 1943, 1–2; George A. Lankes, FBI report on Louis Austin, April 23, 1943, FOIPA no. 1129984-000.

111. "The Right Solution," *Carolina Times*, April 10, 1943, 4.

112. "Thomas Allen Arrested and Brutally Beaten in Courthouse by Police," *Carolina Times*, April 17, 1943, 1–2.

113. "Fundamentally Wrong," *Carolina Times*, June 26, 1943, 4.

114. "CPU Slates First Panel of Summer School," *Daily Tar Heel* (Chapel Hill, NC), July 7, 1943.

115. Tyson, "Wars for Democracy," 259–60.

116. Ibid., 259–61.

117. "Editorially Thinking," *Carolina Times*, June 26, 1943, 1, 4; Shapiro, *White Violence and Black Response*, 330.

118. Shapiro, *White Violence and Black Response*, 311; "Hoodlums in Harlem," *Carolina Times*, August 14, 1943, 4.

119. Claude Barnett to C. C. Spaulding, August 7, 1943, pt. 3, ser. C, reel 5, Barnett Papers.

120. Shapiro, *White Violence and Black Response*, 337.

121. Ibid., 327.

122. Ibid., 326, 333.

123. Kenneth Edmonds, interview by the author, May 23, 2011, Durham, NC, notes in the author's possession.

124. Lawrence V. Lutes, FBI report on Louis Austin, November 6, 1943, FOIPA no. 1129984-000.

125. Ibid.

126. Sitkoff, "African American Militancy," 80–81.

127. "Where It Should Be Settled," *Carolina Times*, September 11, 1943, 4.

128. Crow, Escott, and Hatley, *History of African Americans in North Carolina*, 148, 201.

129. The number of Durham's black registered voters rose from about 1,000 in 1935 to over 3,000 in 1939, which represented 13 percent of the total voter registration for the county. Weare, *Black Business*, 240.

130. "Publisher Named Head of Vote Body," *Chicago Defender*, February 17, 1940, 4.

131. Mathews and Prothro, *Negroes and the New Southern Politics*, 148.

132. C. D. Halliburton, "Tarheel Week," *Norfolk Journal and Guide*, May 5, 1945, A16; Lawrence V. Lutes, FBI report on Louis Austin, July 18, 1945, FOIPA no. 1129984-000; Burns III, "North Carolina and the Negro Dilemma," 210.

133. "First Winner Says It Was 'Durham Victory,'" *Carolina Times*, May 9, 1953, 1; Cannon, "Organization and Growth of Black Political Participation," 62.

134. Louis Austin to Asa T. Spaulding, May 17, 1945, box AC-1, Asa and Elna Spaulding Papers, Rare Book, Manuscript, and Special Collections Library, Duke University, Durham, NC (hereafter cited as Spaulding Papers).

135. Cannon, "Organization and Growth of Black Political Participation," 62.

136. Tyson, "Wars for Democracy," 265–67; "Bus Driver Only Required to Post $2,500 in Brutal Slaying of Soldier," *Carolina Times*, July 15, 1944, http://nuweb9.neu.edu/civilrights/north-carolina/booker-t-spicely/, accessed May 27, 2014; "Council Case Gets Under Way with Nine Witnesses Heard," *Durham Morning Herald*, September 14, 1944; "Confidential War Department Memo, July 10, 1944."

137. "Statement of Pfc. Robert C. Martin" (web source). This statement was given about thirty minutes after the shooting.

138. Lawrence V. Lutes, FBI report on Louis Austin, May 26, 1944, FOIPA no. 1129984-000.

139. McCaffrey, "Memorandum for the Officer in Charge" (web source).

140. McCaffrey, "Memorandum for the Officer in Charge."

141. "Scene at Durham's $250,000 Fire," *Raleigh News and Observer*, July 9, 1944, 1.

142. "Fire Wipes Out Block," *Durham Morning Herald*, July 9, 1944, 1, 8.

143. "Scene at Durham's $250,000 Fire," 1.

144. "Fire Wipes Out Block," 1, 8; "Durham Fire Damage May Exceed $250,000," *Durham Morning Herald*, July 10, 1944, 1–2. There were fewer than fifty firemen in Durham.

145. Tyson, "Wars for Democracy," 265–67; Greene, *Our Separate Ways*, 19.

146. "Copy of Letter from Mr. C. C. Spaulding," n.d., ca. July 1944, pt. 9, ser. B, reel 14, NAACP Papers (microfilm); Robert Spicely to Charles Houston, July 20, 1944, pt. 9, ser. B, reel 14, NAACP Papers (microfilm).

147. Edward R. Dudley to Carolyn D. Moore, August 31, 1944, pt. 9, ser. B, reel 14, NAACP Papers (microfilm).

148. R. A. Spicely to Hugh Thompson, July 26, 1944, pt. 9, ser. B, reel 14, NAACP Papers (microfilm).

149. Hastie to Edward R. Dudley, August 18, 1944, pt. 9, ser. B, reel 14, NAACP Papers (microfilm).

150. Dudley to Thurgood Marshall, September 10, 1944, pt. 9, ser. B, reel 14, NAACP Papers (microfilm); "Biographical Note" (web source).

151. Harry McAlpin, "Criminals Go Free; Justice on Holiday," *New York Amsterdam News*, August 5, 1944, 1.

152. Thurgood Marshall to Carolyn D. Moore, September 7, 1944, pt. 9, ser. B, reel 14, NAACP Papers (microfilm).

153. Dudley to Thurgood Marshall, September 10, 1944, pt. 9, ser. B, reel 14, NAACP Papers (microfilm); "Council Case Gets Under Way with Nine Witnesses Heard," *Durham Morning Herald*, September 14, 1944, sec. 2, p. 8. This was reported on the last page of the paper.

154. "Decision Is Expected Today in Case against H. L. Council," *Durham Morning Herald*, September 15, 1944, sec. 2, p. 8. Once again the case was reported on the absolute last page of the paper.

155. Dudley to Thurgood Marshall, September 10, 1944, pt. 9, ser. B, reel 14, NAACP Papers (microfilm); "Council Case Gets Under Way," 8.

156. "Driver Acquitted in Bus Shooting," *Durham Morning Herald*, September 16, 1944, 1.

157. "Bus Driver Freed in Soldier's Death," *Baltimore Afro-American*, September 23, 1944, 1.

158. Charles Houston to Walter White, November 3, 1944, pt. 9, ser. B, reel 14, NAACP Papers (microfilm); Thurgood Marshall to Robert A. Spicely, November 7, 1944, pt. 9, ser. B, reel 14, NAACP Papers (microfilm).

159. Greene, *Our Separate Ways*, 19–22; Thurgood Marshall to Carolyn D. Moore, September 7, 1944, pt. 9, ser. B, reel 14, NAACP Papers (microfilm); Robert A. Spicely to Thurgood Marshall, November 14, 1944, pt. 9, ser. B, reel 14, NAACP Papers (microfilm).

160. Greene, *Our Separate Ways*, 19–22; Thurgood Marshall to Carolyn D. Moore, September 7, 1944, pt. 9, ser. B, reel 14, NAACP Papers (microfilm); Robert A. Spicely to Thurgood Marshall, November 14, 1944, pt. 9, ser. B, reel 14, NAACP Papers.

161. "North Carolina Branches," February 15, 1944, pt. 26, ser. A, reel 16, NAACP Papers (microfilm).

162. Lawrence V. Lutes, FBI report on Louis Austin, October 9, 1944, FOIPA no. 1129984-000; Greene, *Our Separate Ways*, 19–22; R. A. Young to Walter White, September 28, 1944, box C135, ser. 2, NAACP Papers, Library of Congress, Washington,

D.C.; Thurgood Marshall to Carolyn D. Moore, September 7, 1944, pt. 9, ser. B, reel 14, NAACP Papers (microfilm); Robert A. Spicely to Thurgood Marshall, November 14, 1944, pt. 9, ser. B, reel 14, NAACP Papers; "Spicely Family at Memorial Services," box 10, Murray. For Young, see Díaz, "'A Racial Trust.'"

163. Lawrence V. Lutes, FBI report on Louis Austin, October 9, 1944, FOIPA no. 1129984-000.

164. Lawrence V. Lutes, FBI report on Louis Austin, January 6, 1945, FOIPA no. 1129984-000.

165. Robert A. Spicely to Thurgood Marshall, November 13, 1944, pt. 9, ser. B, reel 14, NAACP Papers.

166. Edward Scheidt, SAC, to Director, FBI, August 7, 1944, FOIPA no. 1129984-000.

167. SAC, Charlotte, NC, to Director, FBI, September 1, 1944, FOIPA no. 1129984-000.

168. Lawrence V. Lutes, FBI report on Louis Austin, October 9, 1944, FOIPA no. 1129984-000.

169. Louis E. Austin, Interview by Anne Braden, notes, box 49, folder 11, n.d., ca. 1957, Carl and Anne Braden Papers, Wisconsin Historical Society, Madison, WI.

170. Lawrence V. Lutes, FBI report on Louis Austin, April 9, 1945, FOIPA no. 1129984-000.

171. C. D. Halliburton, "Tarheel Week," *Norfolk Journal and Guide*, May 5, 1945, 4.

172. Lawrence V. Lutes, FBI report on Louis Austin, October 9, 1944, FOIPA no. 1129984-000.

173. Lawrence V. Lutes, FBI report on Louis Austin, January 6, 1945, FOIPA no. 1129984-000.

174. Ibid.

175. Lawrence V. Lutes, FBI report on Louis Austin, October 9, 1944, FOIPA no. 1129984-000.

176. Shapiro, *White Violence and Black Response*, 325.

177. "Threads of Nazism," *Carolina Times*, July 17, 1943, 4.

178. "The Spirit of Sacrifice," *Carolina Times*, September 25, 1943, 4.

179. "America's Greatest Soldier," *Carolina Times*, October 2, 1943, 4.

180. Lawrence V. Lutes, FBI report on Louis Austin, October 9, 1944, FOIPA no. 1129984-000; Reed, "Black Workers, Defense Industries," 368.

181. Lawrence V. Lutes, FBI report on Louis Austin, July 18, 1945, FOIPA no. 1129984-000.

182. "Proceedings of Conference on Race Relations, North Carolina College for Negroes, Durham, NC, July 11–13, 1945," North Carolina Room, Durham County Library, Durham, NC.

183. After Roosevelt issued Executive Order 8802, Walter White began to retreat from supporting Randolph's March on Washington Movement because of differences over the use of mass protest tactics and fears that the movement would undercut NAACP membership and organizational growth. Janken, *White*, 258–59.

184. Finkle, "Conservative Aims," 711; Sitkoff, *Struggle for Black Equality*, 13.

185. Tyson, "Wars for Democracy," 257.

186. Stanley Winborne, Chairman, North Carolina Utilities Commission, to Broughton, June 27, 1943, box 82, Broughton Papers.

187. Tyson, "Wars for Democracy," 257.

188. "Calling All Negroes of Chicago to Storm the Coliseum, Friday, June 26, at 7 P.M.," pt. 13, ser. B, reel 2, NAACP Papers; Janken, *White*, 258.

189. "Handpicked Leaders," *Carolina Times*, August 29, 1942, 2; Burns, "North Carolina and the Negro Dilemma," 137.

190. "We Haven't Mentioned It—Yet," *Carolina Times*, May 23, 1942, 2.

191. "A Definite Understanding," *Carolina Times*, September 26, 1942, 2.

192. "Dr. Shepard's Letter," *Carolina Times*, August 15, 1942, 2; Joseph D. Bibb, "Shepard Speaks: Declares Negro Leaders Misguided, and We Should Forget Our Lawful Rights," *Pittsburgh Courier*, August 8, 1942, 13. Consequently, Austin pronounced that "the time has come to throw off the yoke placed on the shoulders of the Negro masses by this type of Negro leadership." "Handpicked Leaders," *Carolina Times*, August 29, 1942, 2.

193. "Where It Should Be Settled," *Carolina Times*, September 11, 1943, 4.

194. Lawrence V. Lutes, FBI report on Louis Austin, July 8, 1943, FOIPA no. 1129984-000.

195. Ibid.

196. Lawrence V. Lutes, FBI report on Louis Austin, July 18, 1945, FOIPA no. 1129984-000.

197. Crow, Escott, and Hatley, *History of African Americans in North Carolina*, 151.

Chapter Four

1. Pauli Murray, "Pauli Murray Reminisces in Letter to Friends in City," *Carolina Times*, March 23, 1946, box 4, Murray Papers.

2. Washburn, *African American Newspaper*, 190; Farrar, *Baltimore Afro-American*, 19.

3. Washburn, *African American Newspaper*, 185. Washburn attributes the *Courier's* declining circulation to mismanagement.

4. In 1945, the *Charlotte Post*, at 4,200, had the second largest circulation. In 1957, the Raleigh *Carolinian*, founded in 1941, had a circulation of 7,800. In comparison, the *Norfolk Journal and Guide* had a circulation of 85,000 during World War II. Suggs, *P. B. Young, Newspaperman*, 119.

5. Austin to Claude Barnett, March 5, 1948, Barnett to Austin, May 5, 1951, pt. 2, ser. B, reel 20, Barnett Papers.

6. "Home Ceremony Is Setting for Austin-Edmonds Nuptials," *Carolina Times*, July 1, 1950, 5, 8.

7. "Techniques of Sabotage," *Carolina Times*, August 6, 1949, 2. On the impact of the Cold War on the civil rights struggle, see Dudziak, *Cold War Civil Rights*. While Dudziak's work provides a complex and compelling analysis of its subject, it largely omits the role of the black press in the black freedom struggle.

8. "Grapes of Wrath," *Carolina Times*, November 11, 1950, 2.

9. "Defenders of Democracy," *Carolina Times*, August 12, 1950, 2. The police failed to arrest any members of the white mob but did arrest one African American.

10. Daniel, *Lost Revolutions*, 30–31.

11. "Double Taxation," *Carolina Times*, February 17, 1951, 2; "Fund Raising Programs in Negro Schools," *Carolina Times*, October 27, 1951, 2.

12. Durham City School Board Meeting Minutes, March 10, 1947. The principal would later kill his child and himself. Wilkinson, "Patterns of Negro Segregation," 17–22.

13. The attorneys on the case were John Wheeler and M. Hugh Thompson. "Seek to Hold School Funds in Bias Case," *Carolina Times*, October 22, 1949, 1; "State Education Officials Denied Dismissal from School Suit by Ruling," *Carolina Times*, November 5, 1949, 1. The suit was filed on "behalf of 26 of the city's Negro children alleging inequalities in school facilities for whites and Negroes in Durham Schools." "Judge Hayes Postpones Durham Equalization School Suit," *Carolina Times*, April 29, 1950, 1.

14. "$$$Taken from Negro School Pupils," *Carolina Times*, July 1, 1950, 1.

15. "The Equalization School Suit," *Carolina Times*, July 8, 1950, 2.

16. "Judge Hayes Rules Discrimination in Durham Schools," *Carolina Times*, February 3, 1951, 1, 8; "Judge Hayes' Decision," *Carolina Times*, February 3, 1951, 2.

17. "Conditions in Negro Schools Demand Equalization or Integration," *Carolina Times* September 15, 1951, 2.

18. "Many Cities Planning Legal Action for Equal School Rights," *Carolina Times*, March 3, 1951, 1; Crow, Escott, and Hatley, *History of African Americans in North Carolina*, 165.

19. "Plymouth, Wilson to Sue as Negro Unrest Mounts," *Carolina Times*, January 7, 1950, 1; "The Hour of True Leadership," *Carolina Times*, February 4, 1950, 2. In September 1951, a federal court rejected a motion filed by Durham lawyer M. Hugh Thompson to integrate Washington County schools. The *Carolina Times* reported, "Washington County school board admitted that the school facilities for Negroes are inferior to those offered white students." School board officials planned to address this inequity by building a black high school in Roper. Thompson planned to appeal the case. "Judge Rules against Integration Move in Plymouth School Equality Case," *Carolina Times*, September 8, 1951, 1.

20. "McDowell Man Says Race Schools Inferior," *Carolina Times*, August 22, 1953, 1.

21. "Equal Education Suits," *Carolina Times*, January 14, 1950, 2. In 1953, Austin wrote that the state was "one of the most backward of all southern states on the matter of the race question." "North Carolina's Pretense at Liberality," *Carolina Times*, April 25, 1953, 2.

22. The Wilson Citizens Committee was represented by Durham lawyer M. Hugh Thompson. "Wilson Citizens Sue in Equal Education Fight; Law Students Refused," *Carolina Times*, January 28, 1950, 1.

23. "Equal Education Suits," *Carolina Times*, January 14, 1950, 2; "Destroyers of Democracy," *Carolina Times*, January 14, 1950, 2. Austin asserted that the Northampton

County school board had "deliberately disobeyed law and provided schools within the county for one race at the detriment of the other." "Do Figures Lie?," *Carolina Times*, January 21, 1950, 2.

24. "School Disturbances in Sanford," *Carolina Times*, February 24, 1951, 2; "White People in Sanford Have Strange Conception of Equal Schools for Negro Citizens of City," *Carolina Times*, March 3, 1951, 1, 8.

25. "What Price Popularity?," *Carolina Times*, August 25, 1951, 2.

26. "Equal Education Suits," 2.

27. "The County School Bond Issue," *Carolina Times*, September 22, 1951, 2.

28. "The School Bond Issue," *Carolina Times*, October 18, 1952, 2.

29. "City's Idea of Abiding by Court Order Rejected," *Carolina Times*, November 10, 1951, 1, 8.

30. "City Board Is Cold to Objection of Lawyers to Unpaved Location Area," *Carolina Times*, February 16, 1952, 1, 8. See also "New Faces but the Same Policies," *Carolina Times*, February 16, 1952, 2.

31. "The General Attitude of Durham City Officials toward Negro Citizens," *Carolina Times*, November 24, 1951, 2.

32. What Shall It Be Equalization or Integration?," *Carolina Times*, December 1, 1951, 2. See also "Outside Interference!: State to Survey Durham Schools," *Carolina Times*, December 22, 1951, 1. Austin also reported that a white Durham newsweekly, the *Public Appeal*, supported blacks who were fighting for equal schools and opposed the site of the proposed new school. The *Appeal* wrote, "Were a white school proposed on an inaccessible site such as the Pine Street area, the people would rise up so vigorously that the school board would immediately be put to shame!" "In Defense of Durham Negro Schools," *Carolina Times*, December 22, 1951, 2.

33. "Seek Permit for Negro Students to Enter White Pamlico Schools until Equality Gained," *Carolina Times*, September 29, 1951, 1; Thuesen, *Greater than Equal*, 194–95.

34. "Admit Pamlico Schools Are Unequal; Settlement Sought," *Carolina Times*, November 3, 1951, 1. In November 1953, lawyers filed a lawsuit to integrate Stanley County schools because of inequitable white and black school facilities. "Integration Suit in Gaston," *Carolina Times*, November 28, 1953, 1, 8.

35. Thuesen, *Greater than Equal*, 195.

36. "Over 700 Students Walk Out in Protest over Poor Facilities," *Carolina Times*, November 24, 1951, 1; "The Student Strike at Kinston," *Carolina Times*, December 1, 1951, 2.

37. "School Suit at Kinston," *Carolina Times*, March 8, 1952, 1. Austin condemned the white newspaper, the *Kinston Free Press*, for "a tirade of attacks" against one of the plaintiffs in the Kinston case, Mrs. J. J. Hannibal. "The Fight for Equal Schools in Kinston," *Carolina Times*, March 22, 1952, 4.

38. Thuesen, *Greater than Equal*, 196.

39. W. R. Blake, "21 Schools Are Sub-standard," *Carolina Times*, April 5, 1952, 5.

40. "Separate but Unequal Schools in Person County," *Carolina Times*, April 12, 1952, 2. Austin similarly investigated black schools in Caswell County and urged the North

Carolina Teachers Association to file suit for equal facilities. Austin, "23 One Room Schools; Seven Classes in Each," *Carolina Times*, December 13, 1952, 1, 8; "Caswell County Schools and the North Carolina Teachers Association," *Carolina Times*, December 27, 1952, 2.

41. "Person County Citizens Forced to Seek Equal Schools in U.S. Courts," *Carolina Times*, November 8, 1952, 1.

42. "Court Delay Stirs Dixie Muddle," *Carolina Times*, June 20, 1953, 1, 8.

43. "The New Goal of the NAACP," *Carolina Times*, July 4, 1953, 2.

44. "Enemies of Democracy," *Carolina Times*, October 25, 1947, pt. 26, ser. A, reel 16, NAACP Papers (microfilm), Duke University.

45. Gavins, "Within the Shadow of Jim Crow," 80; Crow, Escott, and Hatley, *History of African Americans in North Carolina*, 178; Cheek, "Historical Study of the Administrative Actions," 91–92. According to the *Baltimore Afro-American*, when a state legislator claimed that Austin was behind the demonstration, Austin "denied the charge." "Law Students Picket N.C. Capitol as Solons Meet," *Baltimore Afro-American*, April 9, 1949, 1–2.

46. "Law Students Picket," 1–2.

47. "15 Law Students Stage Picket Protest of 'Inadequacies' at N.C. College," Associated Negro Press Release, April 4, 1949, pt. 3, ser. B, reel 4, Barnett Papers.

48. Ibid.

49. Burns, "Graduate Education for Blacks," 210.

50. Ibid., 212–17; Cheek, "Historical Study," 117.

51. Burns, "Graduate Education for Blacks," 210–12.

52. "UNC Bars Negroes from Law School," *Carolina Times*, January 28, 1950, 1; "Judge Refuses to Grant Jury Trial in City and Law School Suits Here," *Carolina Times*, March 4, 1950, 1, 8.

53. "Father Loses Job after First Try; to Enter as a Freshman," *Carolina Times*, October 23, 1948, Clipping File, North Carolina Collection, Wilson Library, University of North Carolina at Chapel Hill.

54. Burns, "Graduate Education for Blacks," 210–12. By the early 1950s, "the five black public law schools then in operation had a total enrollment of 90 students and were graduating black attorneys at the rate of only 18 per year." These small numbers were mirrored in the other graduate programs. Kujovich, "Public Black Colleges," 74. In 1959, the NCC law school had twenty-eight students, only sixteen from North Carolina. UNC's law school had 220 students. "Gray Will Request U.N.C. Heads to Appeal Decision," *Durham Morning Herald*, March 28, 1951, 1.

55. "An Asinine Statement," *Carolina Times*, March 11, 1950, 2.

56. "Full Equality or No Segregation." *Carolina Times*, September 9, 1950, 2. Austin called Elder perhaps "the most pathetic figure to appear as a witness." Austin, "Hearings End in Law School Cases," *Carolina Times*, September 2, 1950, 1.

57. Link, *William Friday*, 70–75; Snider, *Light on the Hill*, 239–40. Gray's role on the Personnel Security Board of the Atomic Energy Commission in denying security clearance to physicist J. Robert Oppenheimer in 1954 turned many at UNC against

Gray. Many academics perceived the board as executing an "anticommunist witch hunt." Link, *William Friday*, 79.

58. "A Good Selection," *Carolina Times*, January 28, 1950, 2.

59. Nalty, *Strength for the Fight*, 252–53.

60. Gray to Kemp D. Battle, J. Hampton Price, W. Frank Taylor, June 2, 1951, box 2, Gordon Gray Records, University Archives, Wilson Library, University of North Carolina at Chapel Hill (hereafter cited as Gray records).

61. Cheek, "Historical Study," 134.

62. Snider, *Light on the Hill*, 247–48. Julius Chambers later wrote, "It was not until 1979 that Dr. [William] Friday, the Board of Governors, and the Governor publicly conceded that the state's practices had created inferior facilities at the predominantly black institutions." Chambers, "Impact of Supreme Court Decisions," 191.

63. Burns, "Graduate Education for Blacks," 216–17; "NAACP Sees in UNC Victory End of Jim Crow Law Schools," *Carolina Times*, April 7, 1951, 1.

64. Pauli Murray to Louis Austin, March 24, 1951, box 15, Murray Papers.

65. "Trustees Vote to Admit Negroes at Greater University; Appeal Case to U.S. Supreme Court," *Carolina Times*, April 7, 1951, 1.

66. "Three N.C. College Students Win Fight to Enter UNC," *Carolina Times*, June 9, 1951, 1.

67. "Students Get 'Colored' Seats at Grid Game; Contempt Charge Filed," *Carolina Times*, September 29, 1951, 1.

68. "A Clash of the Old and New South," *Carolina Times*, October 6, 1951, 2.

69. "UNC Heads Stick to Policy; Protests Mount; State-Wide Action Pushes Suit," *Carolina Times*, October 13, 1951, 1, 8. The initial attempt to restrict the students to the black section of the stadium was revealed after one of the students, James R. Walker, turned down the offer of a ticket to the segregated section. Ibid.

70. "Editorially Speaking: Dr. Elder Must Take a Stand," *Carolina Times*, May 26, 1951, 1, 2.

71. "Editorially Speaking: Educational Statesmanship Needed," *Carolina Times*, June 2, 1951, 1, 2.

72. "The Problem of Strengthening and Extending Graduate and Professional Work at the North Carolina College at Durham, Presented to the Board of Trustees, June 14, 1951," box 1, Gray Records; UNC Board of Trustees Meeting, minutes, July 16, 1951, box 122, Governor W. Kerr Scott Papers, North Carolina Division of Archives and History, State Archives, Raleigh, NC (hereafter cited as Scott Papers); Alfonso Elder to the Governor and the Council of State of North Carolina, August 3, 1951, box 95, Scott Papers; "North Carolina College's Dr. Elder, U.N.C. and the United States Supreme Court," *Carolina Times*, June 23, 1951, 2.

73. "North Carolina College's Dr. Elder," 2.

74. Burns, "Graduate Education for Blacks," 217.

75. "North Carolina College Blocks Whites' Plans for More Grad Courses," June 18, 1951, pt. 3, ser. B, reel 5, Barnett Papers.

76. UNC Board of Trustees Meeting, minutes, May 22, 1951, box 122, Scott Papers.

77. Arch T. Allen to Governor Kerr Scott, telegram, July 12, 1951, box 122, Scott Papers; UNC Board of Trustees Emergency Meeting, minutes, July 16, 1951, box 122, Scott Papers.

78. "N.C. College Trustees Approve Ph.D. Plan," *Carolina Times,* July 14, 1951, 1; "State Buys Jim Crow Ph.D. Plan at N.C.C. for $271,000," *Carolina Times,* August 11, 1951, 1. The board had three black members: J. M. Hubbard, a Durham dentist; Robert M. Hendrick, an Asheville dentist; and C. C. Spaulding. Spaulding, age seventy-six, did not attend the meeting.

79. Bascom Baynes to Umstead, July 6, 1954, box 46, Governor William B. Umstead Papers, North Carolina Division of Archives and History, State Archives, Raleigh, NC (hereafter cited as Umstead Papers).

80. "Editorially Speaking: Segregation Finds Friend in 'Dean' Alfonso Elder," *Carolina Times,* July 7, 1951, 1.

81. "Editorially Speaking: A Declaration of Policy Needed," *Carolina Times,* July 14, 1951, 1.

82. "State Buys Jim Crow Ph.D. Plan," 1. The *Times* reported that a poll of students by the *Campus Echo* "showed one hundred percent opposition" to the PhD program. Ibid.

83. "Ph.D. Work at North Carolina College," *Carolina Times,* August 2, 1952, 2.

84. "State NAACP Opposes N.C. College Ph.D. Degree," *Carolina Times,* October 25, 1952, 1.

85. "The Eternal Fight for Equality," *Carolina Times,* February 21, 1953, 2.

86. "Request for Ph.D. Funds Branded as an Insult," *Carolina Times,* February 21, 1953, 1, 8.

87. Thorpe, *Mind of the Negro,* 305.

88. "Nurse School Plan Raises Old Doubts," *Carolina Times,* July 11, 1953, 1. See also "No Special Nurse Training for Negroes Needed," *Carolina Times,* July 18, 1953, 2.

89. "Jim Crow Nursing Plan May Get Underway in Fall," *Carolina Times,* July 25, 1953, 1. See also "Editorial: Jim Crow Bad Anywhere," *Carolina Times,* August 1, 1953, 1.

90. "Universities by Appointment," *Carolina Times,* March 20, 1954, 2.

91. Cyrus Johnson to John M. Doe, Chief of Police, Wabash, North Carolina, March 1947, box 1, folder 16, NCCIC Papers.

92. "Report of Special Committee on Principles and Aims," October 17, 1948, box 1, folder 26, NCCIC Papers; "First Durham Citizens New Year Convention," January 11, 1953, box 9, folder 3, Rencher N. Harris Papers, Rare Book, Manuscript, and Special Collections Library, Duke University, Durham, NC (hereafter cited as Harris Papers).

93. Arsenault, *Freedom Riders,* 18–19; "Court Grants Continuance in Jim Crow Action," *Durham Morning Herald,* April 15, 1947, sec. 2, p. 6.

94. Cyrus Johnson to Gov. W. Kerr Scott, March 10, 1949, box 1, folder 28, NCCIC Papers.

95. Arsenault, *Freedom Riders,* 42.

96. Sullivan, *Days of Hope,* 206–7. For Mary Price, see Uesugi, "Gender, Race, and the Cold War," 270–311.

97. "Committee for NC, Durham Chapter Newsletter," ca. February 1947, box 9/9, Southern Conference for Human Welfare Collection, R. D. Woodruff Library, Atlanta University (hereafter cited as SCHW Collection).

98. Mary Price to W. L. Greene, September 24, 1947, box 10/1, SCHW Collection.

99. Lawson, *Running for Freedom*, 81; Lawson, *Black Ballots*, 134. Morgan Kousser estimated black voter registration rates in North Carolina at 15 percent in 1948 and 36 percent in 1962. Georgia's blacks had a higher voter registration percentage than North Carolina did in 1948. Kousser, *Colorblind Justice*, 245. Mathews and Prothro estimated black voter registration at 10 percent in 1940, 14 percent in 1947, 18 percent in 1952, and 24 percent in 1956. Mathews and Prothro, *Negroes and the New Southern Politics*, 148. Steven Lawson reported that 135,000 blacks in North Carolina were registered to vote in 1956. Lawson, *Black Ballots*, 134. Southern black voter registration rates were 3 percent in 1940, 12 percent in 1945, 20 percent in 1952, and about the same in 1962. Morrison, *African American Political Participation*, 56.

100. R. N. Harris, "Annual Report of Branch Activities–1946," ca. May 1947, box C136, ser. 2, NAACP Papers, Library of Congress, Washington, D.C. (hereafter cited as NAACP Papers).

101. Franklin and Moss, *From Slavery to Freedom*, 414. The 63 percent rate was reported by Alex Rivera in a 1952 article in the *Pittsburgh Courier*. Rivera, "Powerful Negro Bloc Vote in Durham, N.C.," *Pittsburgh Courier*, December 27, 1952, 19.

102. "Welcome Iota Phi Lambda Sorority," *Carolina Times*, August 23, 1952, 2.

103. "Taylor Reelected Precinct Chairman; Martin Secretary," *Carolina Times*, May 14, 1938, 1.

104. "Leaf Workers Union Groups Meet in Durham," *Norfolk Journal and Guide*, June 16, 1945, 17. Trice presided over local 208 in 1943, when Ben Morris presided over local 194 in Durham. "War Fund Workers," *Carolina Times*, November 6, 1943, 1.

105. "Program," June 21–22, 1945, pt. 26, ser. A, reel 16, NAACP Papers (microfilm).

106. "Join the NAACP," *Carolina Times*, October 22, 1949, 2. At the time, Durham's membership in its local NAACP branch had dropped below the minimum number required to maintain its charter. Gloster Current, Director of Branches, to Kelly Alexander, President, NC NAACP, October 11, 1949, reel 26-A-16, NAACP Papers (microfilm). In 1952, Austin participated in the Durham NAACP–sponsored "First Durham Citizens New Year Convention," at White Rock Baptist Church. For the discussion, "Evaluating the Standard of the Negro of Our City in 1953," three speakers, Austin, J. S. Stewart, and A. J. Stanley, gave talks, with Austin's titled "By Broadening Our Own Horizons." "First Durham Citizens New Year Convention," January 11, 1953, box 9, folder 3, Harris Papers.

107. "Register and Vote," *Carolina Times*, March 23, 1946, box 58, Fred D. Alexander Papers, Special Collections, J. Murrey Atkins Library, University of North Carolina, Charlotte, NC (hereafter cited as Alexander Papers).

108. Korstad, *Civil Rights Unionism*, 253, 262.

109. Ibid., 262.

110. Ibid.

111. Ibid., 264, 361. Folger did not run for reelection in 1948, and Thurmond Chatham won the seat.

112. "Negro Vote Bloc Worries Politicians in Durham," *Chicago Defender*, June 29, 1946, 4.

113. Enoc P. Waters, "Ballot Key to N.C. Struggle," *Chicago Defender*, May 25, 1946, 1.

114. "Negro Vote Bloc Worries Politicians," 4.

115. Waters, "Ballot Key to N.C. Struggle," 1.

116. "Economic Butchery of Negro Teachers," *Carolina Times*, September 7, 1946, box 2, folder 70, NCCIC Papers; C. D. Halliburton, "Tarheel Week," *Norfolk Journal and Guide*, September 21, 1946, A11.

117. Alfred Smith, "Adventures in Race Relations," *Chicago Defender*, May 17, 1947, 15.

118. Cannon, "Organization and Growth of Black Political Participation," 62. Austin ran for city council to represent the Third Ward in 1945. James T. Taylor, professor of psychology at North Carolina College, ran in 1949, 1951, and 1953. "Negro Enters City Council Contest in North Carolina," *Atlanta Daily World*, March 14, 1953, 5.

119. "First Winner Says It Was 'Durham Victory,'" *Carolina Times*, May 9, 1953, 1; Cannon, "Organization and Growth of Black Political Participation," 62.

120. "Negro Enters City Council Contest in North Carolina," *Atlanta Daily World*, 5.

121. Winford, "'Battle for Freedom,'" 191–93; Hobby interview. Martin headed the political subcommittee of the DCNA until his death in 1956 at age fifty-six. "Insurance Exec Dies," *Pittsburgh Courier*, January 14, 1956, 6.

122. Cole, "Rencher Nicholas Harris," 28–31.

123. "Durham to Have 23 Negroes at State Democratic Confab," *Carolina Times*, May 13, 1950, 1.

124. Bowman, "Negro Politics," 162.

125. Anderson, *Durham County*, 237.

126. Sindler, "Youth and the American Negro Protest Movement"; A. M. Rivera, "Powerful Negro Bloc Vote in Durham, N.C.," *Pittsburgh Courier*, December 27, 1952, 19.

127. Davidson, "Recent Evolution of Voting Rights Law," 25; McKinney, *Greater Freedom*, 59. Butterfield was elected in 1953 by one vote. Ibid.

128. "Interracial Group Formed to Support Henry Wallace," *Norfolk Journal and Guide*, February 7, 1948, 4; "Report of the Nominating Committee, First Convention, Progressive Party of North Carolina," ca. 1948, box 2, folder 13, Junius Scales Papers, Southern Historical Collection, Manuscripts Department, Wilson Library, University of North Carolina (hereafter cited as Scales Papers).

129. Frederickson, *Dixiecrat Revolt*, 76.

130. "Negroes in Fight for Discrimination," *Carolina Times*, February 28, 1948; "Governor Cherry Commits Political Suicide," *Carolina Times*, February 28, 1948, North Carolina Collection Clipping File, North Carolina Collection, Wilson Library, University of North Carolina at Chapel Hill.

131. Covington and Ellis, *Terry Sanford*, 94.

132. "Anti vs. Anti-Anti," *Carolina Alumni Review*, March 1948, 170; "Tonight: Open Meeting against Conscription," *Daily Tar Heel*, March 30, 1948; Taylor, *Every Citizen a Soldier*, xi–xv.

133. "Progressives to Hear Austin," *Daily Tar Heel*, February 25, 1949; Taylor, *History of the North Carolina Communist Party*, 193–94.

134. "Wallace Group Organizes in North Carolina," *Norfolk Journal and Guide*, May 1, 1948, C19; "Report of the Nominating Committee, First Convention, Progressive Party of North Carolina," n.d., ca. 1948, box 2, folder 13, Scales Papers.

135. "Program, Founding Convention, Progressive Party of North Carolina," April 25, 1948, box 2, folder 13, Scales Papers. Participants included Virginia Durr, Mary Price, Don West, and John Myers. Ibid.

136. "Peace, Freedom, and Abundance: The Platform of the Progressive Party as Adopted at the Founding Convention, Philadelphia, Pennsylvania," July 23–25, 1948, box 2, folder 13, Scales Papers.

137. Culver and Hyde, *American Dreamer*, 493.

138. "Wallace Party Names Picks for N.C. Posts," *Norfolk Journal and Guide*, September 4, 1948, D8. Logan owned movie theaters and restaurants, including the Donut Shop in Durham. "Mr. and Mrs. G. W. Logan Honored by Hampton Institute Alumni Club," *Carolina Times*, April 23, 1955, 5.

139. Culver and Hyde, *American Dreamer*, 493.

140. Susie Jones, interview by William H. Chafe (web source).

141. "Wallace Party Names Picks for N.C. Posts," D8.

142. Korstad, *Civil Rights Unionism*, 362–63. See also MacDougall, *Gideon's Army*, 707–19, on Wallace's trip to North Carolina.

143. "Report on the Meeting of Candidates and Staff, State Headquarters, Progressive Party," September 23, 1948, box 2, folder 13, Scales Papers. Austin and C. O. Pearson attended this meeting.

144. "How Durham County Citizens Voted in Four-Party Election," November 3, 1948, box 10, folder 2, Harris Papers.

145. Dudziak, *Cold War Civil Rights*, 25–26.

146. Devine, *Henry Wallace's 1948 Presidential Campaign*, 264.

147. "Communist Repudiation," *Carolina Times*, March 4, 1950, 2.

148. "Approaching Shadows," *Carolina Times*, December 31, 1949, 2.

149. "A Cheap Political Trick?," *Carolina Times*, November 19, 1949, 2; Gardner, *Harry Truman and Civil Rights*, 149–51; "Killers of the Dream," *Carolina Times*, February 11, 1950, 2. In 1952, Austin demanded an end to the practice whereby black colleges named buildings after white supremacist politicians like Clyde Hoey. "Naming Buildings on Negro College Campuses," *Carolina Times*, June 14, 1952, 2.

150. "Senator Hoey Comes to Town," *Carolina Times*, October 22, 1949, 2.

151. *Carolina Times*, November 27, 1948, North Carolina Collection Clipping File, Wilson Library, University of North Carolina at Chapel Hill.

152. "The Civil Rights Meeting," *Carolina Times*, January 21, 1950, 2.

153. "Prepare Now to Register and Vote," *Carolina Times*, January 28, 1950, 2.

154. "Register and Vote," *Carolina Times*, February 11, 1950, 2.

155. "Drive Launched for 250,000 Negro Voters in North Carolina," *Carolina Times*, March 11, 1950, 1; "Drive to Secure 250,000 Voters Launched in Carolina," *Norfolk Journal and Guide*, March 11, 1950, C3. A meeting in Durham on March 4, 1950, focused on voter registration planned for 1,000 attendees, according to NAACP NC state president Kelly Alexander. M. E. Johnson was president of the Durham NAACP branch. "1,000 Expected at NAACP Vote Meeting," *Carolina Times*, February 25, 1950, 1.

156. "Non-Partisan Vote-Registration Committee Organizational Meeting," March 4, 1950, reel 26-A-16, NAACP Papers (microfilm).

157. Kelly M. Alexander, "A Report about the North Carolina NAACP Political Action Program," reel 26-A-16, NAACP Papers (microfilm).

158. "Register and Vote," *Carolina Times*, April 22, 1950, 2.

159. "Still Being Denied the Right to Register," *Carolina Times*, May 13, 1950, 2.

160. "Criminal Action May Be Brought against Obstinate Registrars," *Carolina Times*, May 20, 1950, 1.

161. "North Carolina State Conference of NAACP Branches, Fayetteville, North Carolina, June 1–2, 1950," reel 26-A-16, NAACP Papers (microfilm). From 1946 to 1950, the Durham NAACP branch had the following membership totals: 1946: 304, 1947: 973, 1948: 591, 1949: 230, 1950: 323. Average NAACP branch membership in Winston-Salem and Greensboro for those years was much higher than Durham's. "Comparative Study of North Carolina Branches," n.d., ca. 1950, reel 26-A-16, NAACP Papers (microfilm).

162. "Address of Kelly M. Alexander of Charlotte, N.C., President, North Carolina State Conference of NAACP Branches—June 1, 1950 at 7th Annual North Carolina Conference in Fayetteville, N.C.," reel 26-A-16, NAACP Papers (microfilm); "Wilkins and Alexander Address Meet," *Carolina Times*, June 10, 1950, 1.

163. "The Durham Committee on Negro Affairs," ca. May 1950, box 13, William J. Kennedy Papers, Southern Historical Collection, Manuscripts Department, Wilson Library, University of North Carolina (hereafter cited as Kennedy Papers).

164. "No Race Baiting for Senator Graham," *Carolina Times*, April 29, 1950, 2; "The Durham Committee on Negro Affairs," ca. May 1950, box 13, Kennedy Papers. See also Pleasants and Burns, *Frank Porter Graham.*

165. "The Attack on Senator Graham," *Carolina Times*, May 27, 1950, 2.

166. "En Bloc Voting," *Carolina Times*, June 24, 1950, 2.

167. "Not by Bread Alone," *Carolina Times*, August 26, 1950, 2.

168. "Negroes and the N.C. General Assembly," *Carolina Times*, February 17, 1951, 2.

169. "Registrar Apologizes for Refusing to Register Negro Woman in Winston-Salem Last Week," *Carolina Times* November 1, 1952, 1, 8.

170. "Organize Now for 1952 Elections," *Carolina Times*, November 17, 1951, 2.

171. "On Selecting a Gubernatorial Candidate," *Carolina Times*, April 24, 1952, 2.

172. Claytor, "Negro Councilmanic Office-Holders," 40–41.

173. Lawson, *Black Ballots*, 134.

174. Franklin, *From Slavery to Freedom*, 414.

175. Christensen, *Paradox of Tarheel Politics*, 147–48.

176. "The Negroes Choice for Governor," *Carolina Times*, May 31, 1952, 2.

177. Christensen, *Paradox of Tar Heel Politics*, 148.

178. "Senator Taft Flunked His Examination at North Carolina College," *Carolina Times*, December 1, 1951, 2. In January 1952, Austin noted that white NC newspapers did not uniformly oppose anti-lynching legislation. The *Greensboro Daily News* supported such legislation, while the *Charlotte Observer* opposed it. "No Need of Anti-lynching Legislation," *Carolina Times*, January 12, 1952, 2.

179. "Unacceptable to Negro Voters," *Carolina Times*, June 21, 1952, 2.

180. "An Attack on the U.S. Constitution," *Carolina Times*, September 13, 1952, 2.

181. "On Selecting a Presidential Candidate for 1952," *Carolina Times*, October 4, 1952, 2; Carmines and Stimson, *Race and the Transformation of American Politics*, 35; "Editorial: Problem for Voters," *Crisis*, August–September 1952, 412–13.

182. Lawson, *Running for Freedom*, 38.

183. "Editorially Speaking: The Days of the Negro Beggar Have Passed," *Carolina Times*, August 2, 1952, 1, 2. Austin also recalled James Shepard's appearance before the city council when he urged the appointment of C. C. Spaulding to the school board in the late 1940s. Ibid.

184. "The Approaching City Council Election," *Carolina Times*, January 17, 1953, 2.

185. "A Stronger Committee on Negro Affairs," *Carolina Times*, May 2, 1953, 2; "First Winner Says It Was 'Durham Victory,'" *Carolina Times*, May 9, 1953, 1. See also "Durham's Negro Councilman," *Carolina Times*, May 16, 1953, 2. After Harris took office and was not notified of a meeting, the *Times* reported this. "Durham's Negro Councilman Is Ignored by Body," *Carolina Times*, August 8, 1953, 1; "The City Council Should Be above Suspicion," *Carolina Times*, August 8, 1953, 2. See also John L. Clark, "The Durham Pattern! . . . One of Best," *Pittsburgh Courier*, September 26, 1953, 23.

186. "Prepare Now for the Spring Election," *Carolina Times*, January 9, 1954, 2; "The Lethargy of Negro Voters," *Carolina Times*, June 5, 1954, 2.

187. "Wanted a Democratic Candidate for Governor," *Carolina Times*, March 3, 1956, 2; "'Win at Any Price' (WAAP) Candidates," *Carolina Times*, June 5, 1954, 2; Pleasants, *Political Career of W. Kerr Scott*, 262–67.

188. "The Columbia Riot," *Carolina Times*, March 9, 1946, box 58, Fred Alexander Papers.

189. Tushnet, *Making Civil Rights Law*, 52–53.

190. "The Columbia Riot," *Carolina Times*, March 9, 1946, box 58, Fred Alexander Papers.

191. "ABC Officers Arrested for Tieing Negro Up by Hands," *Carolina Times*, October 29, 1949, 1.

192. "Former N.C. Co-ed: Beaten and Kicked by Greenville Police: Officer Absolved and Young Woman Fined; Case Appealed," *Carolina Times*, October 18, 1952, 1.

193. "Justice Weeps in Pitt County," *Carolina Times*, October 25, 1952, 2.

194. "The Proper Treatment of Persons under Arrest," *Carolina Times*, January 31, 1953, 2.

195. "Charge Cop in Battery," *Carolina Times*, June 6, 1953, 1. On the Apex police chief's brutality and attempted rape, see "Negro Girls Charge Apex Cop Attempted Rape," *Carolina Times*, May 1, 1954, 1, 8.

196. "Jury Takes Only Half Hour; Victim Leaves Four Kids," *Carolina Times*, November 10, 1951, 1.

197. "Justice Is a One-Way Street in North Carolina," *Carolina Times*, November 17, 1951, 2.

198. Freedman, "Milestones in Habeas Corpus," 1558.

199. "N.C. Lawyers—Before U.S. Supreme Court," *Carolina Times*, May 10, 1952, 1.

200. Most of the newspaper articles, including those in the *Carolina Times*, reporting the case called the defendant "Mack" Ingram, but several sources identified the defendant as "Matt" Ingram: Berry, "Matt Ingram Case," 233. The 1940 U.S. Census lists twenty-nine-year-old Matthew, not Mack, Ingram, in Yanceyville, North Carolina. See also "What Happened to Matt Ingram," *Ebony Magazine*, September 1953, 38.

201. Scales and Nickson, *Cause at Heart*, 227, 230.

202. "Orchids for the State NAACP," *Carolina Times*, July 14, 1951, 2. See also "The Issues in the Mack Ingram Case," *Carolina Times*, November 24, 1951, 2.

203. Scales and Nickson, *Cause at Heart*, 230.

204. Ibid.

205. "Ocular 'Rape,'" *Crisis*, February 1952, 99.

206. "NAACP May Fight 6 Months Suspended Sentence Given Caswell Man for 'Leering,'" *Carolina Times*, November 15, 1952, 1, 8.

207. "'Leering' Assault Draws North Carolina Conviction," *Christian Science Monitor*, November 12, 1952, 16; "NAACP May Fight," 1, 8; Berry, "Matt Ingram Case," 228.

208. "NAACP May Fight," 1, 8.

209. "'Assault by Leer' Verdict Voided in North Carolina," *Christian Science Monitor*, February 25, 1953, 5.

210. "Says Death for Rape Is a Negro Penalty," *Carolina Times*, November 25, 1950, 1. In May 1951, Austin made the same point when Willie McGee was executed, inveighing against the fact that only blacks in the South were executed for raping or murdering white women, but white men were never executed for raping or murdering black women. "Death Penalties 'For Negroes Only,'" *Carolina Times*, May 19, 1951, 2.

211. McGuire, *At the Dark End of the Street*, xvii–xviii.

212. "White Man Freed of Negro Rape Charge," *Carolina Times*, December 2, 1950, 1.

213. "Soldiers Attack Woman as She Leaves Church; Young Boy Made to Watch," *Carolina Times*, September 15, 1951, 1.

214. "No Crime to Rape Negro Women in the South," *Carolina Times*, September 22, 1951, 2. See also "3 White G.I.s on Trial for Rape," *Carolina Times*, January 26, 1952, 1.

215. "Three White G.I.'s Get Mild Sentence on Charge of Rape on Negro Wife," *Carolina Times*, February 2, 1952, 1, 8. See also "Lower the Curtain and Pray for Carthage: An Editorial," *Carolina Times*, February 2, 1952, 1. For another editorial on the inequitable treatment of blacks and whites charged with rape, see "The Harvest of Unequal Dispensation of Justice," *Carolina Times*, November 14, 1953, 2; "The Death Penalty for

Rape in North Carolina—'For Negroes Only,'" *Carolina Times*, January 16, 1954, 2; "The Infinite Belongs to God," *Carolina Times*, January 23, 1954, 2.

216. "No Punishment for White Rapists of Negro Women," *Norfolk Journal and Guide*, November 17, 1951, B17.

217. "Convicted for Attack on Negro Woman," *Carolina Times*, June 21, 1952, 1. See also "'Death for Rape' for Negroes Only," *Carolina Times*, February 28, 1953, 2.

218. "A Surprising, but Hopeful Sign," *Carolina Times*, June 27, 1953, 2.

219. P. P. Burford, "High Point Church Has Rites for Bomb Victims," *Norfolk Journal and Guide*, January 26, 1952, B3; Arthur B. Spingarn and Louis T. Wright, "NAACP Letter to President Truman Asking Presidential Action in Christmas Slaying of Harry Moore," *Crisis*, February 1952, 105–6.

220. "Randolph Calls for March on Washington," *Carolina Times*, March 9, 1946, box 58, Alexander Papers.

221. "Set Our White Folks Free," *Carolina Times*, February 25, 1950, 2.

222. "FEPC: A True Test of Democratic Inclinations," *Carolina Times*, June 17, 1950, 2.

223. "The South's Objection to FEPC," *Carolina Times*, January 10, 1953, 2. On employment discrimination, see also "The South Begins to Look at Itself," *Carolina Times*, November 7, 1953, 2.

224. "Party Loyalty for What?," *Carolina Times*, August 19, 1950, 2.

225. "Negro Membership for the Paroles Commission," *Carolina Times*, June 20, 1953, 2.

226. Kiser, "Occupational Change," 79.

227. "Proposal for Race Firemen for City Being Studied," *Carolina Times*, November 26, 1949, 1.

228. "A Tale of Two Cities," *Carolina Times*, April 21, 1951, 2.

229. "Prepare for the May Election Now," *Carolina Times*, February 17, 1951, 2.

230. "Employment of Negroes in City Government," *Carolina Times*, January 19, 1951, 2.

231. "How Long before a Haiti [*sic*] Fire Station," *Carolina Times*, March 7, 1953, 2. See also "The Employment of Negroes in Municipal Government," *Carolina Times*, October 24, 1953, 2. A black firefighter was not hired in Durham until 1958. Thorpe, *Concise History*, 41.

232. "At Long Last a Fire State for Hayti," *Carolina Times*, February 6, 1954, 2.

233. "City Leaders Take Note of Precedent in Briefing of Recruits at New Fire Station to Begin Training Period," *Carolina Times*, October 4, 1958, 1.

234. "Reward for Faithful and Efficient Service," *Carolina Times*, April 8, 1950, 2; "Negro Deputy Sheriffs for Durham," *Carolina Times*, April 22, 1950, 2; "Promotions for Police Officers," *Carolina Times*, November 4, 1950, 2; Austin renewed his call for black policemen to be promoted in Durham in August 1951. "Promotions for Negro Policemen," *Carolina Times*, August 25, 1951, 2.

235. "Creating Interracial Goodwill," *Carolina Times*, December 8, 1951, 2. By 1947, eight North Carolina cities, including High Point and Durham, had black policemen who patrolled black communities. Fayetteville had no black policemen. See letters

from March 1947 from several police chiefs in several cities to John R. Larkins, North Carolina Department of Public Welfare, box 1, folder 16, NCCIC Papers.

236. "Three Cents Worth of Injustice," *Carolina Times*, October 29, 1949, 2.

237. "The Negro's Contribution to the Tobacco Industry," *Carolina Times*, October 13, 1951, 2.

238. "The Negro and Southern Economy," *Carolina Times*, September 27, 1952, 2.

239. "It's Time for Action," *Carolina Times*, July 11, 1953, 2.

240. "Durham: The Complacency of Negro Labor Leaders in Durham," *Carolina Times*, September 19, 1953, 2.

241. "More Jobs for Negroes Greatly Needed," *Carolina Times*, April 11, 1953, 2. See also "The Negro's Eternal Hunt for Jobs," *Carolina Times*, May 16, 1953, 2; "A Voluntary FEPC Needed in Every Community," *Carolina Times*, October 10, 1953, 2.

242. Wilkinson, "Patterns of Negro Segregation," 44–45.

243. "Mixed Crowd Sees Mixed Game in Dixie," *Chicago Defender*, December 6, 1947, 11; "City Sanctions Interrace Game at Durham, N.C.," *Norfolk Journal and Guide*, November 29, 1947, 23.

244. "Mixed Crowd Sees Mixed Game in Dixie," 11. See also "City Sanctions Interrace Game," 23; "Inter-Racial Contest Ends in 6-6 Deadlock," *Durham Morning Herald*, November 24, 1947, 9.

245. "White Team Plays Negro Eleven at Durham," *Charleston News and Courier* (SC), November 24, 1947, 7.

246. "Negroes and Whites Play Football on Southern Field for First Time," *New York Times*, November 24, 1947.

247. Dave McKenna, "Harold Bell's Black History Month" (web source).

248. "A Challenge to the Christian Church," *Carolina Times*, April 15, 1950, 2; "Dodger 'B' Team Is Victor," *New York Times*, April 10, 1950, 31. The Carolina League did not employ a black ballplayer until 1951, when the Danville (Virginia) Leafs signed Perry Miller. Adelson, *Brushing Back Jim Crow*, 1. The Durham Bulls did not employ a black ballplayer until 1957. "Race Players Force Issue of Park Seating," *Carolina Times*, April 20, 1957, 1.

249. "Negroes in White Organized Baseball in the South," *Carolina Times*, April 7, 1951, 2. The following year, Austin played in an old timers game "between the Durham Elites and the players of yesteryear of college, sandlot and pro" at Durham Athletic Park. "Old-Timers Tilt in Durham Aug. 31," *Norfolk Journal and Guide*, August 23, 1952, 20.

250. "What Price Prejudice," *Carolina Times*, April 17, 1954, 2.

251. "No Support for the Bulls Baseball Club," *Carolina Times*, April 24, 1954, 2.

252. "Promoting Interracial Goodwill," *Carolina Times*, April 24, 1954, 2.

253. Scott Ellsworth, "Jim Crow Losses; The Secret Game," *New York Times*, March 31, 1996, http://www.nytimes.com/1996/03/31/magazine/sunday-march-31-1996-jim-crow -losses-the-secret-game.html, accessed June 4, 2014.

254. "The Liberalty [*sic*] We Talk About," *Carolina Times*, July 12, 1952, 2.

255. "Charlotte Negro Golfers Fighting for Right to Play on Municipal Golf Course," *Carolina Times*, November 22, 1952, 1, 8.

256. Wolcott, *Race, Riots, and Roller Coasters*, 121.

257. "Negro Bus Drivers for Durham," *Carolina Times*, September 13, 1952, 2.

258. "Jim Crow Loses in Test Case," *Carolina Times*, July 29, 1950, 1; Crow, Escott, and Hatley, *History of African Americans in North Carolina*, 192.

259. "Man Beats Jim Crow: To Sue Bus Firm," *Carolina Times*, September 16, 1950, 1.

260. "Bus Company Faces Jim Crow Travel Suit," *Carolina Times*, December 29, 1951, 1.

261. "'Dark-Skinned Man' Beats Jim Crow," *Carolina Times*, January 24, 1953, 1.

262. "The Burden of Segregation," *Carolina Times*, October 17, 1953, 2.

263. "Hospital Refuses Dying A&T Student," *Carolina Times*, December 9, 1950, 1.

264. "Hospitals—'For Whites Only,'" *Carolina Times*, March 4, 1950, 2.

265. "No Discrimination at C. P. Hospital," *Carolina Times*, April 1, 1950, 2. A 1962 report indicated that the North Carolina Cerebral Palsy Hospital was the only one in the state where the patients were completely integrated. *Equal Protection of the Laws in North Carolina*, 188.

266. "Human Dignity," *Carolina Times*, August 5, 1950, 2.

267. "NCC Students May Ban Local J C Theatres," *Carolina Times*, February 3, 1950, 1.

268. "A Long Past Due Awakening," *Carolina Times*, February 10, 1951, 2. Although some students may have stayed away from segregated theaters, there is no evidence of a substantial boycott.

269. "Retreat but Never Capitulate on Segregation," *Carolina Times*, February 2, 1952, 2.

270. "Congratulations Baltimore NAACP," *Carolina Times*, February 9, 1952, 2.

271. "A Hero Returns after Fighting for 'His Country,'" *Carolina Times*, May 19, 1951, 2.

272. "Ft. Bragg Still Cesspool of Rank Segregation," *Carolina Times*, June 9, 1951, 1.

273. "The Army Stalling on Integration," *Carolina Times*, September 1, 1951, 2.

274. "Prominent Citizens Hail Supreme Court Decision: Editorially Speaking: The Dawn of a New Era," *Carolina Times*, May 22, 1954, 1.

275. Pauli Murray, "Open Letter to Citizens of Durham, May 21, 1954," *Carolina Times*, June 12, 1954, 2.

Chapter Five

1. Washburn, *African American Newspaper*, 8.

2. Larkins, *Patterns of Leadership*, 8–10. Among those leaders ranked high only by blacks, only Livingstone College president Samuel E. Duncan, third, was more highly ranked than Austin, sixth. The other black leaders whom only blacks ranked highly were NCC historian Helen Edmonds, seventh; P. A. Bishop, eighth; and W. L. Greene, ninth. Ibid.

3. Ibid., 31–32.

4. "Future of Negro Press Foretold by J-G's Young," *Carolina Times*, March 17, 1962, 1, 2.

5. White, "Economic and Social Development," 202; Korstad, *Civil Rights Unionism*, 185.

6. "Thanks to Our Readers," *Carolina Times*, April 2, 1960, 1; "5,000 New TIMES Readers!," *Carolina Times*, October 7, 1961, 1; "Notice a Bigger and Better *Carolina Times*," *Carolina Times*, June 19, 1965, 2.

7. "Mother of TIMES Publisher Dies," *Carolina Times*, October 14, 1961, 1.

8. "Western North Carolina Annual Conference, St. Joseph's A.M.E. Church, Durham, North Carolina, November 18–22, 1959," box 3, Clydie F. Scarborough Papers David M. Rubenstein Rare Book & Manuscript Library, Duke University, Durham, NC (hereafter cited as Scarborough Papers).

9. "Work for McCarthy and His Committee," *Carolina Times*, October 2, 1954, 2; Friedman, "Strange Career of Annie Lee Moss," 445–68.

10. "No Patience for Disloyalty," *Carolina Times*, April 30, 1955, 2; Ari L. Goldman, "Junius Scales, Communist Sent to U.S. Prison, Dies at 82," *New York Times*, August 7, 2002. Scales, a white North Carolinian who had joined the Communist Party in 1939, was active from the 1930s to the 1950s in the struggle for equal rights for African Americans in North Carolina. Scales and Nickson, *Cause at Heart*.

11. "Thank God, Khrushchev Did Not Visit the South," *Carolina Times*, October 3, 1959, 2.

12. Isaac, "Movement of Movement," 55.

13. Thornton, "Murder of Emmett Till," 102–3.

14. "American Negroes Position in World Affairs," *Carolina Times*, September 17, 1955, 2.

15. "The Retribution of Unpunished Murder," *Carolina Times*, October 1, 1955, 2.

16. Tyson, *Radio Free Dixie*, 92–95.

17. Ibid., 100; "Running True to Form," *Carolina Times*, January 17, 1959, 2.

18. "Making Its Impact on World Opinion," *Carolina Times*, December 27, 1958, 2.

19. Tyson, *Radio Free Dixie*, 100–101, 114–15, 130–36.

20. "Teachers Need Not Fear Loss of Jobs Resulting from Integration," *Carolina Times*, May 15, 1954, 2.

21. "NCTA Protests Dismissal of Negro Teachers," *Carolina Times*, May 29, 1965, 1; "Teacher Employment in an Integrated School System," *Carolina Times*, May 29, 1965, 2; "Palmer Charges Black Teachers Being Dismissed Enmasse under Desegregation," *Carolina Times*, June 21, 1969, 1.

22. "Congratulations for Greensboro," *Carolina Times*, May 29, 1954, 2.

23. "Pointing the Way to Good Citizenship," *Carolina Times*, June 18, 1955, 2.

24. "North Carolina's First Negro Teacher in a White School," *Carolina Times*, July 3, 1954, 2.

25. "Catholic Church Segregation in Durham," *Carolina Times*, September 11, 1954, 2; "Refuse Negro Catholics at Immaculata School," *Carolina Times*, September 11, 1954, 1; Shadle, "Black Catholicism and Music," 30; "What Price New Catholic Church?," *Carolina Times*, October 2, 1954, 2.

26. "A Salute to Immaculata School," *Carolina Times*, September 24, 1955, 2.

27. "Editorial Prophecy on Integration in Our Public Schools," *Carolina Times*, June 5, 1954, 2.

28. "The Governor's Advisory Committee," *Carolina Times*, August 14, 1954, 2.

29. "State Rights—Southern Style," *Carolina Times*, June 12, 1954, 2.

30. "Defiance of the United States Supreme Court," *Carolina Times*, October 23, 1954, 2.

31. "Black Thursday in Richmond, Virginia," *Carolina Times*, June 26, 1954, 2.

32. Douglas, "Rhetoric of Moderation."

33. "More Time to Do Wrong," *Carolina Times*, November 20, 1954, 2.

34. Douglas, *Reading, Writing, and Race*, 28–30; Crow, Escott, and Hatley, *History of African Americans in North Carolina*, 167; Day, "North Carolina," 64; Peebles-Wilkins, "Reactions of Segments of the Black Community," 113.

35. "Address by Governor Luther Hodges," 11. For Hodges, see also Walker, "'Legal Means.'"

36. Crow, Escott, and Hatley, *History of African Americans in North Carolina*, 167.

37. "Negro Representation on Policy Making Bodies," *Carolina Times*, August 21, 1954, 2.

38. "Support for the NAACP," *Carolina Times*, February 19, 1955, 2.

39. "300 Protest Segregation Bill," *Carolina Times*, February 26, 1955, 1, 8; "Why Turn Back the Clock in Education," March 5, 1955, 2.

40. Crow, Escott, and Hatley, *History of African Americans in North Carolina*, 168–69.

41. Ray Jenkins, "School Bill Opposed by Negroes," *Raleigh News and Observer*, February 23, 1955, 1, 2; Covington and Ellis, *Terry Sanford*, 159. Black supporters included "representatives of the North Carolina Teachers Association, the General Baptist State Convention, the Free and Accepted Prince Hall Masons, and three black city councilmen." Jenkins, "School Bill Opposed by Negroes," 1, 2.

42. Sitkoff, *Struggle for Black Equality*, 23. See also Moran, "Border State Ebb and Flow"; Drone, "Desegregation and Effective School Leadership," 410–12.

43. Chafe, *Unfinished Journey*, 154. According to a poll of white residents of Guilford County, "18 per cent of the population was ready to resist desegregation at all costs; another 18 per cent wished to push ahead much faster with integration. The vast majority, however, were in the middle." Chafe, *Civilities and Civil Rights*, 59.

44. Crow, Escott, and Hatley, *History of African Americans in North Carolina*, 168; Day, "North Carolina," 65.

45. Day, "North Carolina," 66.

46. Patterson, *Brown v. Board of Education*, 100.

47. "Crucifixion at Easter Time," *Carolina Times*, April 16, 1955, 2.

48. Crow, Escott, and Hatley, *History of African Americans in North Carolina*, 169–70.

49. "Address by Governor Luther Hodges," 8–9.

50. Crow, Escott, and Hatley, *History of African Americans in North Carolina*, 169.

51. Robert L. Carter to Kelly Alexander, April 29, 1955, box 140, ser. I, NAACP Legal Defense and Educational Fund Records, Library of Congress, Washington, D.C. (hereafter cited as NAACP-LDF Records).

52. Day, "North Carolina," 67.

53. "Governor Hodges Report on School Segregation," *Carolina Times*, August 13, 1955, 2; L. E. Austin, "Governor's Speech Nets Big Increase in NAACP Membership in State," *Carolina Times*, August 13, 1955, 1, 8.

54. "Hodges Speech Called Inflammatory by Seven Organization Heads," *Carolina Times*, August 20, 1955, 1.

55. "Governor Hodges for President of NAACP," *Carolina Times*, February 11, 1956, 2.

56. "Governor Hodges Report," 2; Austin, "Governor's Speech Nets Big Increase," 1, 8.

57. "Governor Hodges' Lost Opportunity," *Carolina Times*, August 20, 1955, 2.

58. "New Teachers for a New Day," *Carolina Times*, September 3, 1955, 2.

59. "Rascality in Raleigh," *Carolina Times*, October 15, 1955, 2.

60. "The A. and T. Affair," *Carolina Times*, November 12, 1955, 2; Covington and Ellis, *Terry Sanford*, 157.

61. "Committees for Obedience to the Law," *Carolina Times*, February 11, 1956, 2.

62. Ibid.

63. "A Lack of Leadership and Statesmanship," *Carolina Times*, April 14, 1956, 2.

64. "The Plight of North Carolina," *Carolina Times*, August 4, 1956, 2.

65. A. M. Rivera Jr., "Negro Group Terms School Bills 'Economic Suicide,'" box 3, Reed Sarratt Papers, Southern Historical Collection, Manuscripts Department, Wilson Library, University of North Carolina at Chapel Hill (hereafter cited as Sarratt Papers); 1956 Extra Session, North Carolina General Assembly, Audio-Visual Materials Collection, CD, TR 1-10, 1-11, box 1, North Carolina Division of Archives and History, State Archives, Raleigh, NC. The *Norfolk Journal and Guide* published the complete text of Wheeler's statement. "Citizens' Report to the North Carolina Legislature," *Norfolk Journal and Guide*, August 11, 1956, 9.

66. "Vote against the Pearsall Plan," *Carolina Times*, September 8, 1956, 2.

67. "Voters Approved Pearsall School Plan," *Raleigh News and Observer*, September 9, 1956, 1; "Hodges Pleased by Margin of Victory for School Plan," *Raleigh News and Observer*, September 10, 1956, 1.

68. Numerous letters attest to this point in a folder titled "Segregation," box 130, Governor Luther H. Hodges Papers, North Carolina Division of Archives and History, State Archives, Raleigh, NC (hereafter cited as Hodges Papers).

69. "Hodges Pleased by Margin of Victory," 2. For disfranchisement of blacks in eastern North Carolina through unfair application of the literacy test and "systematic discrimination by eastern county registrars," see Pleasants and Burns III, *Frank Porter Graham*, 84.

70. "Local Vote on Pearsall Plan Suggests Situation Calm Here," September 10, 1956, *Winston-Salem Journal*, box 3, Sarratt Papers.

71. "Mongrelization and Segregation," *Carolina Times*, September 15, 1956, 2; Crow, Escott, and Hatley, *History of African Americans in North Carolina*, 169–70.

72. "Says Negroes Abandoning Democratic Ranks for GOP," *Atlanta Daily World*, March 21, 1956, 1; "You Get What You Pay for—Politically," *Carolina Times*, May 5, 1956, 2.

73. "They're Everybody's President and Vice President," *Indianapolis Recorder*, November 3, 1956, 8.

74. Walton, *Invisible Politics*, 123.

75. Moon, "Negro Vote," 219–20. In the 1956 election, Stevenson won seven states, all in the South, including North Carolina. Woolley and Peters, "Election of 1956" (web source).

76. "North Carolina's Lack of Leadership," *Carolina Times*, February 18, 1956, 2.

77. "Wanted a Democratic Candidate for Governor," *Carolina Times*, March 3, 1956, 2; "'Win at Any Price' (WAAP) Candidates," *Carolina Times*, June 5, 1954, 2; Drescher, *Triumph of Good Will*, 20–21.

78. Louis Austin, interview by August Meier, 1958, notes, Meier Papers.

79. Moon, "Negro Vote," 224, 228; Fleer, *Governors Speak*, 52.

80. Eamon, *Making of a Southern Democracy*, 50.

81. Kenneth Edmonds interview, May 23, 2011; Gelman, *President and Apprentice*, 150.

82. Claytor, "Negro Councilmanic Office-Holders," 48–49; "A High Tribute to the Committee on Negro Affairs," *Carolina Times*, May 25, 1957, 2.

83. Ruben Borr, "Pickin' at Politics," *The Public Appeal* (Durham), June 4, 1958, 1, 3.

84. Louis Austin, interview by August Meier, 1958, notes, Meier Papers.

85. Ibid.

86. Rubio, *There's Always Work at the Post Office*, 358.

87. Rubio, *There's Always Work at the Post Office*, 144. Smith recalled that he got his post office job in 1957, but Rubio believes it was 1955 or 1956 because there were thirty-five National Alliance of Postal Employee members in Durham by that time. Rubio does not mention Austin or the *Carolina Times*. Ibid., 358. Summerfield reported progress in black employment in the post office, with the promotion in 1955 of "more than 300 colored employees to supervisory positions throughout the country." Galambos and Ee, eds., *Papers of Dwight David Eisenhower*, vol. 14–17, 2095.

88. "Worshipping the God of Segregation," *Carolina Times*, June 2, 1956, 2. Austin reported that "over 5,000 of the estimated 10,000 registered Negro voters went to the polls and voted the ticket recommended to them by the Durham Committee on Negro Affairs." "No Rocking Chair Leadership," *Carolina Times*, June 2, 1956, 2.

89. "Worshipping the God of Segregation," 2.

90. "A Courageous Southern Congressman," *Carolina Times*, March 24, 1956, 2; Christensen, *Paradox of Tar Heel Politics*, 164.

91. "The Cost of Being Right," *Carolina Times*, April 7, 1956, 2.

92. "What Price Political Office?," *Carolina Times*, May 5, 1956, 2.

93. Christensen, *Paradox of Tar Heel Politics*, 164.

94. "Worshipping the God of Segregation," 2; Bass and De Vries, *Transformation of Southern Politics*, 221.

95. Bass and De Vries, *Transformation of Southern Politics*, 221–22.

96. "Anti-NAACP Bills Will Not Stop Struggle for Equality Says Kelly M. Alexander," *Carolina Times*, June 1, 1957, 1; "The North Carolina Legislature's Attack on the NAACP," *Carolina Times*, June 1, 1957, 2.

97. "'Hodges-ocracy' Yields to Democracy in N.C. Senate," *Carolina Times*, June 15, 1957, 1.

98. "We Will Remember the State Senate of 1957," *Carolina Times*, June 15, 1957, 2.

99. "A&T President Weighed in the Balance and Found Wanting," *Carolina Times*, December 21, 1957, 2; Covington, *Henry Frye*, 71.

100. Edwin R. Edmonds, interview by William Henry Chafe (web source).

101. "Negroes Who Say They Don't Want Equality 'Crazy' or Practicing Deception," *Daily Tar Heel* (Chapel Hill), October 21, 1958, 3.

102. Greenberg, *Crusaders in the Courts*, 260; "Delegation Presents Request to School Board Asking Elimination of Segregation for Use as Solution to Problem of Crowded Schools Here," *Carolina Times*, April 18, 1959, 1.

103. Crow, Escott, and Hatley, *History of African Americans in North Carolina*, 171.

104. "Rocky Mount Lawyer Parried Blow of '54 Ruling," *Raleigh News and Observer*, November 7, 1976, box 3, Thomas Pearsall Papers, Southern Historical Collection, Manuscripts Department, Wilson Library, University of North Carolina at Chapel Hill (hereafter cited as Pearsall Papers).

105. Reed, *School Segregation in Western North Carolina*, 37; Day, "North Carolina," 72. In Virginia, a federal appeals court overruled Virginia's pupil assignment act in 1957 because "it was backed up by inflexible segregation laws and practices." Day, "North Carolina," 72.

106. Douglas, "Rhetoric of Moderation," 116, 133.

107. Day, "North Carolina," 73.

108. Douglas, "Rhetoric of Moderation," 131.

109. Joycelyn McKissick, Interviewed by Chris D. Howard, March 15, 1983, tape 27a, box 4, Chris D. Howard Papers, David M. Rubenstein Rare Book & Manuscript Library, Duke University, Durham, NC (hereafter cited as Howard Papers).

110. Davidson, *Best of Enemies*, 93.

111. Joycelyn McKissick, "Mack's Quack (Teenage Happenings)," *Carolina Times*, April 16, 1960, 7.

112. "Heroines See Dreams Disappear," *Carolina Times*, September 16, 1961, 1; "Durham Reacts Quickly to B&B," *Carolina Times*, September 23, 1961, 1; "A Scholarship Fund for Freedom Fighters," *Carolina Times*, September 23, 1961, 2.

113. "No Alternative but the Federal Courts," *Carolina Times*, October 17, 1959, 2.

114. "A Timely Blast at Negro Leaders in North Carolina," *Carolina Times*, January 5, 1960, 2.

115. "Policy Stays Integration, Board Member Testifies," *Carolina Times*, December 17, 1960, 1, 6.

116. "City School Board Silent on Harris Blast," *Carolina Times*, August 12, 1961, 1. See also "No Substitute for Integrity of Public Officials," *Carolina Times*, August 12, 1961, 2.

117. "Six Pupils Admitted to White Schools on Review Ordered by Judge Are Identified by Officials," *Carolina Times*, August 26, 1961, 1.

118. Brown, *Dead-End Road*, 27–35, 38.

119. Ibid., 53.

120. Ibid.

121. Ibid., 54–56.

122. Ibid., 57, 77–81, 86–90. See also "Caswell Man Harassed before Shooting," *Carolina Times*, January 26, 1963, 1; "A Mississippi Visit to North Carolina," *Carolina Times*, January 26, 1963, 2; "Justice Dept. Investigating Caswell Case: FBI Probes Shooting by Negro Farmer," *Carolina Times*, February 2, 1963, 1; "Jasper Brown Family Moves to Washington" (web source).

123. "An Invitation to Federal Authorities," *Carolina Times*, March 23, 1963, 2.

124. "The Proposed Durham County School Bond Issue," *Carolina Times*, November 21, 1959, 2.

125. "The Proposed Bond Issue," *Carolina Times*, February 13, 1960, 2.

126. "Day of Destiny for Durham Schools," *Carolina Times*, April 23, 1960, 1.

127. Across the City Desk," ca. May 1960, box 6, folder 5, Harris Papers; "A Political Lesson," ca. May 1960, box 6, folder 5, Harris Papers.

128. "The Danger of Token Representation," *Carolina Times*, December 5, 1959, 2.

129. Brown-Nagin, *Courage to Dissent*, 315. Atlanta began token desegregation of its schools in fall 1961. Ibid., 324.

130. "Danger of Token Representation," 2.

131. "Governor Sanford's Visit to Negro Schools," *Carolina Times*, March 24, 1962, 2.

132. "Quality Education and Segregation," *Carolina Times*, October 13, 1962, 2.

133. Day, "North Carolina," 63.

134. "School Integration Rises in N.C.; Caswell Awaits Effects of Ruling," *Carolina Times*, January 19, 1963, 1, 5.

135. "Integration Gains in North Carolina," *Christian Science Monitor*, December 4, 1964, 3.

136. Peebles-Wilkins, "Reactions of Segments of the Black Community," 117, 119. North Carolina was barely "ahead of Alabama, Arkansas, Louisiana and South Carolina" in integrated schools. Ibid., 119.

137. "The Future of Negro Children at Stake," *Carolina Times*, June 9, 1962, 2; "Durhamites Hurt over School Board Action," *Carolina Times*, June 9, 1962, 1; "Durham Board of Education Plans Robbery of Negro School Children," *Carolina Times*, June 9, 1962, 2.

138. "School Integration Rises in N.C.," 1, 5.

139. "No Move Made to Integrate County Schools," *Carolina Times*, February 16, 1963, 2.

140. "The School Bond Issue in Saturday's Primary," *Carolina Times*, May 30, 1964, 2; "Over Million for 2 White Schools, $175,000 for 1 Negro School," *Carolina Times*, September 12, 1964, 1, 4.

141. "Integration of Schools a Two-Way Street," *Carolina Times*, September 19, 1964, 2.

142. Douglas, *Reading, Writing, and Race*, 113–14.

143. Ibid.

144. Orfield, "1964 Civil Rights Act," 89–90.

145. "Federal Supervision for Public Schools," *Carolina Times*, January 9, 1965.

146. "NCTA Protests Dismissal of Negro Teachers," *Carolina Times*, May 29, 1965, 1; "Teacher Employment in an Integrated School System," *Carolina Times*, May 29, 1965, 2.

147. "Says Teacher Problem in N.C. Worst in Nation," *Carolina Times*, August 14, 1965, 1B.

148. "Race Players Force Issue of Park Seating," *Carolina Times*, April 20, 1957, 1; "A Costly and Unnecessary Blunder," *Carolina Times*, April 27, 1957, 2.

149. Boston, "Lunch Counter Sit-In Demonstrations," 18–20, 24.

150. Douglas E. Moore to Martin Luther King Jr. (web source).

151. Tom Faison, "Theater, Library Mixed Use Sought," *Durham Morning Herald*, May 21, 1957, 1A.

152. "De-Segregation Drive Building Here," *Durham Morning Herald*, June 14, 1957, 1A.

153. Richard K. Barksdale, interview by August Meier, notes, June 5, 1958, Durham, NC, box 139, Meier Papers.

154. Davidson, *Best of Enemies*, 89.

155. Boston, "Lunch Counter Sit-In Demonstrations," 24. On Stewart, see Winford, " 'Battle for Freedom,' " 190, 199, 294.

156. Williams interview.

157. Ibid.

158. "The Lethargy of the Durham Committee on Negro Affairs," *Carolina Times*, June 15, 1957, 2; Davidson, *Best of Enemies*, 90. Moore left Durham and Asbury Methodist Church in June 1960 to serve in a mission in the Belgian Congo. "A Distinct Loss to Durham," *Carolina Times*, June 18, 1960, 2; "Rev. Moore Paid Tribute on Eve of Methodist Conference Opening," *Carolina Times*, June 18, 1960, 1, 6.

159. Austin to NC Mutual, June 17, 1964, box AC-1, Spaulding Papers.

160. Williams interview; Boston, "Lunch Counter Sit-In Demonstrations," 18–20; *State v. Clyburn*, 101 SE 2d 295—NC: Supreme Court 1958.

161. Winford, " 'Battle for Freedom,' " 295–96.

162. "Negotiations on in Tennis Case," *Carolina Times*, July 20, 1957, 1. Williams was an outstanding young tennis player. Two years earlier, he had defeated future tennis great Arthur Ashe in a tournament. Ernie Ingram, "Southeastern Tennis Tournament Closes with Local Entrants Sharing Many of the Fine Trophy Awards," *Carolina Times*, August 6, 1955, 5.

163. Winford, " 'Battle for Freedom,' " 299–304; "A New Meaning for Moderation," *Carolina Times*, July 27, 1957, 2.

Chapter Six

1. Davidson, *Best of Enemies*, 100.

2. "The A&T Students' Sitdown Strike," *Carolina Times*, February 6, 1960, 2. The first white student attended a historically black college in North Carolina in 1957, when

Rodney Jaye Miller was admitted to North Carolina A&T for summer session that year. "A&T Admits White Student for Summer," *Carolina Times*, June 15, 1957, 1.

3. Davidson, *Best of Enemies*, 99. In 1967, Callis Brown, a graduate of NCC and NCC Law School, served as director of community and intergroup relations for the National Congress of Racial Equality. "N.C. College Law Graduate Gets Important Position with CORE," *Carolina Times*, September 16, 1967, 1.

4. Sindler, "Youth and the American Negro Protest Movement," 23.

5. Davidson, *Best of Enemies*, 100.

6. Sindler, "Youth and the American Negro Protest Movement," 25.

7. "Student-Faculty Group to Talk with Council," *Carolina Times*, February 13, 1960, 1; "A&T Move Sets throughout State Chain Reaction," *Carolina Times*, February 13, 1960, 1.

8. "Yes, There Is a Better Way," *Carolina Times*, February 13, 1960, 2.

9. "Quinton Baker Interview—Notes, Interview #23," box 5, Chris D. Howard Papers, David M. Rubenstein Rare Book & Manuscript Library, Duke University, Durham, NC.

10. Barksdale, "Indigenous Civil Rights Movement," 154.

11. Claude Sitton, "Negro Sitdowns Stir Fear of Wider Unrest in South," *New York Times*, February 15, 1960, 1.

12. " 'I'm No Outside Agitator' Montgomery's Abernathy Says," *Carolina Times*, February 20, 1960, 6; Davidson, *Best of Enemies*, 104. Douglas Moore introduced Ralph Abernathy. " 'I'm No Outside Agitator,' " 6.

13. "Non-Violence Leader Speaks before 1,500," *Carolina Times*, February 20, 1960, 1.

14. "No Negotiations without Student Leaders," *Carolina Times*, February 20, 1960, 2, 6.

15. "The Power We Fight Against," *Carolina Times*, February 20, 1960, 2.

16. "An Encouraging Sign for the South," *Carolina Times*, February 27, 1960, 2; "More Student Arrests: Nine White Students Are among 21 Arrested in Winston-Salem," *Carolina Times*, February 27, 1960, 1. According to this last article, "43 students from St. Augustine's College and Shaw University were arrested" the previous week.

17. "103 at Durham School Sign AAUW Statement on Sit-Downs," *Carolina Times*, April 16, 1960, 1.

18. "The High Calling of Non-Violent Protests," *Carolina Times*, May 7, 1960, 2.

19. "Ushers Association in 36th Annual Mid-Year Session Sun., April 24," *Carolina Times*, April 23, 1960, 1. In May 1960, Austin flew to Los Angeles, California, to attend the general conference of the AME (African Methodist Episcopal) Church. "Publisher in Calif.," *Carolina Times*, May 7, 1960, 1.

20. "The Negative Vote at Wake Forest College," *Carolina Times*, April 2, 1960, 2.

21. Ibid.

22. "More Visits to White Churches Needed," *Carolina Times*, March 31, 1962, 2.

23. Rivera interview.

24. "2 Yanked from Seats in Strike at Statesville," *Carolina Times*, April 9, 1960, 1.

25. "Three Durham Counters Open Quietly," *Carolina Times*, August 6, 1960, 1.

26. Greene, *Our Separate Ways*, 81.

27. "Counters Open Now in 69 Cities," *Carolina Times*, August 13, 1960, 1, 6.

28. "Full Scale Assault on Segregated Movies May Be Forming," *Carolina Times*, January 14, 1961, 1, 2.

29. "Why the Theaters Are Being Picketed," *Carolina Times*, January 28, 1961, 2.

30. "Prepared to Stay Out, Says Student, Leaders," *Carolina Times*, January 28, 1961, 1. See also "Movie Desegregation, Equal Jobs Drive among Local NAACP Goals," *Carolina Times*, January 28, 1961, 1; "Youth NAACP Forms New Organization," *Carolina Times*, October 29, 1960, 6; "Full Scale Assault on Segregated Movies," 1, 2.

31. "Picketing Continues," *Carolina Times*, February 4, 1961, 1.

32. "A Salute to White Sit-Ins and Pickets," *Carolina Times*, February 4, 1961, 2.

33. "Support That Is More Than Lip Service," *Carolina Times*, March 18, 1961, 2.

34. "Should Be Settled without Court Action," *Carolina Times*, March 10, 1962, 2.

35. "Chapel Hill Movies Open to All; Durham Theatre Won't Negotiate," *Carolina Times*, March 17, 1962, 1, 2; "Time for the City Council to Act," *Carolina Times*, March 17, 1962, 2.

36. "Eight Students Enter Suit to Desegregate Carolina Theatre," *Carolina Times*, July 21, 1962, 1, 5.

37. Williams interview.

38. "A Bully or a Loyal American Citizen," *Carolina Times*, November 17, 1962, 2.

39. "Durham Firm Removing Jim Crow Serving Area," *Carolina Times*, March 9, 1963, 1,2.

40. "A Compromise Is Not a Victory," *Carolina Times*, March 30, 1963, 2.

41. Williams interview.

42. Bowman, "Negro Politics in Four Southern Counties," 63.

43. "Meany Attacked the Wrong Man," *Carolina Times*, October 3, 1959, 2. See also Marshall, "Unions and the Negro Community," 190.

44. "Meany Attacked the Wrong Man," 2.

45. "The AFL-CIO Attack on the NAACP," *Carolina Times*, November 24, 1962, 2.

46. "Employment Policy of Local Tobacco Workers," *Carolina Times*, June 16, 1962, 2.

47. "North Carolina's Low Wage Scale," *Carolina Times*, January 19, 1963, 2.

48. "Justifiable Causes for Striking," *Carolina Times*, July 6, 1957, 2.

49. Wilbur Hobby, "Letter to the Editor," *Carolina Times* July 20, 1957, 2.

50. "Industry, the South and Race," *Carolina Times*, December 7, 1957, 2. Walter Daye was elected president of local 208 Tobacco Workers International Union, defeating Mazyck. "Daye Wins Union Vote, Beats Mazyck," *Carolina Times*, December 21, 1957, 1.

51. "The Negro Employment Problem," *Carolina Times*, December 3, 1960, 2.

52. "The CBS 'Harvest of Shame' Television Show," *Carolina Times*, December 3, 1960, 2.

53. "The Disastrous Result of Segregated Unions," *Carolina Times*, April 29, 1961, 2.

54. "If the President Means Business," *Carolina Times*, May 6, 1961, 2.

55. "Durham Store Hires Two Clerks," *Carolina Times*, February 18, 1961, 1, 6.

56. "Boycott of Durham Stores in the Making," *Carolina Times*, March 18, 1961, 1, 2.

57. "5 Taken Off, 3 Added to Boycott," *Carolina Times*, March 25, 1961, 1. See also "Boycott Narrows to Five," *Carolina Times*, April 1, 1961, 1; "No Change in Boycott List," *Carolina Times*, April 8, 1961, 1; "Adults Join Picket Lines," *Carolina Times*, April 29, 1961, 1.

58. "Carolina Power and Light's Requests to Be Excused," *Carolina Times*, July 29, 1961, 2.

59. "Boycott of Five Stores Continues," *Carolina Times*, July 22, 1961, 1, 4.

60. "Store Officially Approved: A&P Must Prove 'Good Faith,' Boycotters Say," *Carolina Times*, October 7, 1961, 1.

61. "The Winn-Dixie Boycott Continues," *Carolina Times*, October 21, 1961, 2.

62. "Interference in Behalf of the Despised Poor," *Carolina Times*, August 5, 1961, 2.

63. "No Help for Garbage Collectors from Race Leaders," *Carolina Times*, August 19, 1961, 2. See also "Important Question in the Garbage Collectors Strike," *Carolina Times*, September 9, 1961, 2.

64. "Pickets in Durham," *Carolina Times*, August 4, 1962, 1.

65. "Four in Sit-In Sent to County Roads for 30 Days," *Carolina Times*, August 11, 1962, 1; "In Race Struggle: Durham Discovers 'New Unity': Nearly 1,500 Take Part in Bias Protest," *Carolina Times*, August 18, 1962, 1, 2.

66. "No Time for a Moratorium on Discrimination," *Carolina Times*, August 18, 1962, 2; "Another Rally Planned Sunday," *Carolina Times*, August 18, 1962, 1.

67. "The Howard Johnson Fight in Carolina," *New York Amsterdam News*, August 25, 1962, 21.

68. "No Room in Durham Cafes for Christmas Spirit Demonstrators," *Carolina Times*, December 22, 1962, 1, 2.

69. "Durham Mayor Appoints 'Good Neighbor Council,' " *Carolina Times*, April 20, 1963, 1.

70. "Needed, a 'Good Neighbor' Committee," *Carolina Times*, March 9, 1963, 2.

71. "NAACP-CORE Call Boycott in Durham," *Carolina Times*, March 2, 1963, 1, 6.

72. "Progress Noted by Leaders of Boycott against Durham Stores," *Carolina Times*, March 9, 1963, 1, 6.

73. "Support for the Student Pickets," *Carolina Times*, March 16, 1963, 2.

74. "Negro Ministers Set a Fine Example," *Carolina Times*, April 6, 1963, 2; "Ministers to Join Picket Lines: Alliance Votes to Man Lines at Sears-Roebuck on Saturday," *Carolina Times*, March 30, 1963, 1; "Six Stores on Boycott List," *Carolina Times*, April 20, 1963, 1.

75. Korstad and Leloudis, *To Right These Wrongs*, 177.

76. Ibid.

77. "New Mayor Acts Swiftly to Solve Issue," *Carolina Times*, May 25, 1963, 1.

78. "More Eating Establishments Drop Barriers," *Carolina Times*, June 22, 1963, 1.

79. "Raleigh Demonstrations Score Victory: Raleigh Firms Urge End to Segregation," *Carolina Times*, May 18, 1963, 1, 6A.

80. "Anti-Segregation Demonstrations Race through Tarheelia," *Carolina Times*, May 25, 1963, 1.

81. "Opposed to All Forms of Violence," *Carolina Times*, May 25, 1963, 2.

82. "Governor Sanford's Speech at the Boys State Meet," *Carolina Times*, June 22, 1963, 2.

83. "Governor Sanford's Meeting in Raleigh," *Carolina Times*, June 29, 1963, 2.

84. "A Gangster Sheriff in Rutherford County," *Carolina Times*, May 20, 1961, 2.

85. "Raising the Economic Level of Both Races," *Carolina Times*, December 29, 1962, 2.

86. "Williamston Citizens Girding for New C-R Demonstrations," *Carolina Times*, November 23, 1963, 1, 6; "Preaching the Gospel in Deeds," *Carolina Times*, November 23, 1963, 2. See also Carter, "Williamston Freedom Movement."

87. "Elder Won't Stop Students," *Carolina Times*, May 25, 1963, 1, 6A.

88. "A New Day for Negro Educators," *Carolina Times*, March 10, 1962, 2.

89. "Shameful Performance of Two Negro Educators," *Carolina Times*, August 10, 1963, 2.

90. Chafe, *Civilities and Civil Rights*, 132.

91. "Durham Movie Houses Approve Desegregation," *Carolina Times*, July 20, 1963, 1.

92. "Durham Theaters Open to All Patrons," *Carolina Times*, August 17, 1963, 1.

93. "City Mobilizes for 'March,'" *Carolina Times*, August 17, 1963, 1.

94. "March on D.C. Proclaimed Big Success," *Carolina Times*, August 31, 1963, 1.

95. "The March on Washington Message Was Delivered," *Carolina Times*, September 7, 1963, 2.

96. "The Mayor's Attitude Understandable to a Majority," *Carolina Times*, September 7, 1963, 2.

97. "Durham Governing Units Take Stands against Racial Bias," *Carolina Times*, October 12, 1963, 1.

98. "Harrison, Austin NAACP Council Speakers Sunday," *Carolina Times*, November 30, 1963, 3, 6.

99. "Weighed in the Balances and Found Wanting," *Carolina Times*, November 30, 1963, 2.

100. "Malcolm X Scores U.S. and Kennedy," *New York Times*, December 2, 1963, 21.

101. Roy Wilkins, "Letters to the Editor," *Carolina Times*, January 4, 1964, 2.

102. "The Fading Liberal Image of Chapel Hill," *Carolina Times*, January 11, 1964, 2. The *Times* identified the woman who urinated on the protester as a "white waitress," but at least three books report that it was Jeppie Watts, co-owner with her husband of the restaurant. The protester who endured Watts's urination was University of North Carolina student Lou Calhoun. Chansky, *Game Changers*, 62–63; Ferris, *Edible South*, 263; Pryor, *Faith, Grace and Heresy*, 366.

103. "The Efforts to Halt Street Demonstrations," *Carolina Times*, February 22, 1964, 2.

104. "A Public Official's Abuse of Public Trust," *Carolina Times*, January 18, 1964, 2; "Gov. Threatens Force against Demonstrators," *Carolina Times*, January 18, 1964, 2; Covington and Ellis, *Terry Sanford*, 341–42.

105. "Slaves Today in North Carolina," *Carolina Times*, November 5, 1955, 2. See also Burch and Joyner, *Unspeakable*, 5, 6.

106. "School Bond Elections," *Carolina Times*, April 9, 1960, 1; Hoffman, *Health Care for Some*, 64.

107. "The School Bond Elections," 1. Austin expanded his attack on segregated hospitals to Alamance County Hospital in Burlington. "The Use of Federal Funds for Segregated Hospitals," *Carolina Times*, April 16, 1960, 2.

108. Reynolds, "Professional and Hospital Discrimination"; "Nine Enter Action against Two Hospitals," *Carolina Times*, February 17, 1962, 1; "End Sought to Hospital Racial Bars," *Greensboro Daily News*, April 7, 1960; "Negro Ban to Hospital to Continue," *Greensboro Daily News*, May 5, 1960.

109. Smith, *Health Care Divided*, 89–90.

110. Ibid., 91–95. See also Reynolds, "Professional and Hospital Discrimination," 710–20.

111. "The Integration of Hospitals," *Carolina Times*, March 7, 1964, 2; "U.S. Supreme Court Outlaws Hospital Bias," *Carolina Times*, March 7, 1964, 1.

112. "When Patience Ceases to Be a Virtue," *Carolina Times*, July 7, 1962, 2.

113. "Lincoln Hospital's Plight the Result of Discrimination," *Carolina Times*, February 9, 1963, 2.

114. Mathews and Prothro, *Negroes and the New Southern Politics*, 148–50.

115. Bowman, "Negro Politics in Four Southern Counties," 169–70.

116. Mathews and Prothro, *Negroes and the New Southern Politics*, 154–55.

117. "Dismissal of Registrar in Halifax Sought," *Carolina Times*, May 5, 1956, 1.

118. Wertheimer, *Law and Society in the South*, 135–37.

119. "Registration Trouble to Court?: Complaints Mount in East as Justice Dept. Probe Is Hinted," *Carolina Times*, May 19, 1956, 1; "Finger-shaking Also 'Assault' in No. Carolina," *The Militant* (New York), January 19, 1959, 1. McLean suggested that his next step would be to "seek Federal Court action if the State Board of elections fails to correct the situation." Instances where blacks were denied voter registration included a "Northampton registrar who appeared to be intoxicated . . . turned down persons because they couldn't tell how many rooms there were in the courthouse." In other cases, blacks were forced to wait two hours and told to tell others of the long wait, were required to recite from memory sections of the Constitution, "read the entire Constitution," or were denied registration because the person was left-handed. "Registration Trouble to Court?," 1.

120. "The Right to Vote in Eastern North Carolina," *Carolina Times*, May 26, 1956, 2.

121. "Reprisals in Vote Dispute: Seaboard Nurse Loses Permit," *Carolina Times*, May 26, 1956, 1.

122. "Finger-shaking Also 'Assault,'" 1.

123. "Reprisals in Vote Dispute," 1.

124. Wertheimer, *Law and Society in the South*, 150–57; "Literacy Test Challenged," *Carolina Times*, March 2, 1957, 1; "Literacy Test Step Nearer Showdown," *Carolina Times*, July 6, 1957, 1.

125. "New Vote Denials in East N.C.: Dictation Test Said Used by Registrar," *Carolina Times*, May 14, 1960, 1.

126. "The Vice President's Forthright Stand on Civil Rights," *Carolina Times*, August 27, 1960, 2.

127. "The Most Important Issues in the Present Campaign," *Carolina Times*, October 29, 1960, 1, 6.

128. "The Negro Voter Faces a Great Decision in Tuesday Election," *Carolina Times*, November 5, 1960, 1, 2.

129. John S. Stewart and J. H. Wheeler, "Demos Point to Gains Made for Working Man," *Carolina Times*, November 5, 1960, 1; E. T. Browne and F. L. Tyson, "GOP Statement Calls for Two Party System," *Carolina Times*, November 5, 1960, 1.

130. Thorpe, *History of North Carolina Central University*, 44. Scott served as a U.S. senator from North Carolina from 1954 until his death in 1958. Pleasants, *Political Career of W. Kerr Scott*, 273, 301.

131. "Much at Stake in Saturday's Election," *Carolina Times*, June 25, 1960, 2.

132. "The Defeat of Dr. Lake for Governor," *Carolina Times*, July 2, 1960, 2.

133. Drescher, *Triumph of Good Will*, 218.

134. "Negro Voters Save Democrats: Race Provides Margin in N.C.," *Carolina Times*, November 12, 1960, 1, 6.

135. Donald C. Bacon, "Negro Vote Drive," *Wall Street Journal* November 6, 1961, 17; "What Price Party Loyalty?," *Carolina Times*, November 12, 2.

136. "Durham Strays Slightly from CONA Choice," *Carolina Times*, May 20, 1961, 1; Sindler, "Youth and the American Negro Protest Movement," 11.

137. "No Death Blow for the Committee on Negro Affairs," *Carolina Times*, May 20, 1961, 2.

138. "Time for Negroes of N.C. to Change Their Party," *Carolina Times*, March 3, 1962, 2.

139. "Strike Now for Better Employment Opportunities," *Carolina Times*, September 23, 1961, 2.

140. "A New Policy for N.C. Negro Democrats," *Carolina Times*, April 15, 1961, 2.

141. "The Seabrook and Duncan Appointment," *Carolina Times*, July 15, 1961, 2.

142. "State NAACP Head Says: 'Appointments OK, But...,'" *Carolina Times*, July 22, 1961, 1. Governor R. Gregg Cherry made the first appointment of an African American to a state commission in 1945 when he chose W. J. Kennedy of NC Mutual to serve on the Recreation Commission. Governor Kerr Scott appointed two blacks, William Rich and Harold Trigg, to state commissions in 1949. "Two Durham Men Were First Job Holders," *Carolina Times*, July 22, 1961, 1.

143. "Sanford Names Four New Negro College Trustees," *Carolina Times*, July 29, 1961, 1. In 1969, John S. Stewart became the first black chairman of the North Carolina A&T board of trustees. "John S. Stewart, First Black Man Elected Chairman of A&T Board," *Carolina Times*, November 8, 1969, 1.

144. "NCC Gets Five Negro Trustees," *Carolina Times*, August 19, 1961, 1.

145. "Another Show Window Dressing Stunt," *Carolina Times*, June 23, 1962, 2.

146. "Time for Negroes of N.C. to Change Their Party," *Carolina Times*, March 3, 1962, 2.

147. "Negro Destiny at Stake in Next Tuesday's Election," *Carolina Times*, November 3, 1962, 2.

148. "Governor Sanford at the Crossroad," *Carolina Times*, January 26, 1963, 2.

149. "Governor Sanford's 'New South' in Look Magazine," *Carolina Times*, December 5, 1964, 2.

150. "Figures Don't Lie, but Liars Figure," *Carolina Times*, August 11, 1962, 2; "N.C. Equal Jobs Claim Is Denied," *Carolina Times*, August 11, 1962, 1.

151. "County Commissioners Run-off Decision Awaited in Durham," *Carolina Times*, June 2, 1960, 1.

152. "Saturday an Important Day for Durham," *Carolina Times*, June 23, 1962, 2; "Bloc Vote Tactics Proved Fatal to Dr. Boulware," *Carolina Times*, June 30, 1962, 1.

153. "The Greatest Loss in the Run-off Primary," *Carolina Times*, June 30, 1962, 2.

154. "GOP Hopefuls Barnes, Browne Fall Short," *Carolina Times*, November 10, 1962, 1, 2; "The Trend toward a Two Party System in N.C.," *Carolina Times*, November 10, 1962, 2; "Demos in Durham Turn Back Republicans on All Levels," *Durham Morning Herald*, November 7, 1962, 1, 2.

155. *Carolina Times*, April 11, 1964, 1.

156. "Again Register and Vote," *Carolina Times*, April 18, 1964, 2.

157. *Carolina Times*, September 26, 1964, 1.

158. "More Negro Candidates Needed," *Carolina Times*, April 11, 1964, 2; Michaux interview. Michaux went to Palmer Memorial Institute in Sedalia, North Carolina, with A. D. King. When Martin Luther King Jr. visited Durham, he would stay in the Michaux home. Michaux interview.

159. "Negro Office Seekers Score Big Gains in General Election," *Carolina Times*, November 14, 1964, 1, 4.

160. "Legislator Scolds A&T Prexy for Sit-in Action," *Carolina Times*, February 23, 1963, 1; "Disgraceful Representation in the Legislature," *Carolina Times*, February 23, 1963, 2.

161. "Big Registration to Follow New Office Seekers," *Carolina Times*, April 18, 1964, 1, 4.

162. Korstad and Leloudis, *To Right These Wrongs*, 201.

163. "The Awakening in Halifax County," *Carolina Times*, April 18, 1964, 2.

164. "Negro Registration Is Pushed: Voting Power in Warren and Halifax Raised," *Carolina Times*, May 9, 1964, 1.

165. "Slow Down Methods against Registering," *Carolina Times*, May 9, 1964, 2.

166. "Mississippi Tactics Used in Warren County to Discourage Negro Registration," *Carolina Times*, May 16, 1964, 1.

167. "The Gathering Storm in Warren and Halifax Counties," *Carolina Times*, May 16, 1964, 2.

168. "News Roundup," *The Student Voice*, June 2, 1964, in Carson, *Student Voice*, 158.

169. "Ousted Enfield Teacher Is Latest 'Hood' Victim," *Carolina Times*, July 11, 1964, 1, 4; "Dismissed Negro Teacher Sues School Officials for $250,000," *Carolina Times*, July 4,

1964, 1, 4; "North Carolina Teacher Seeks $250,000 Damages in Lawsuit," *Carolina Times*, January 16, 1965, 1.

170. "Ousted Enfield Teacher Is Latest 'Hood' Victim," 1, 4. Governor Moore appointed Branch to the North Carolina Supreme Court in 1966. He was elevated to chief justice by Governor James Hunt in 1979. "Joseph Branch, Associate Justice & Chief Justice," (web source).

171. "Challenge of the Ku Klux Klan in North Carolina," *Carolina Times*, July 18, 1964, 2; "Enfield Teacher Loses C. Rights Case in United States Court," *Carolina Times*, June 12, 1965, 1; "The Case of Mrs. Willa Johnson," *Carolina Times*, June 19, 1965, 2.

172. "The Ku Klux Klan Takes Over in Enfield," *Carolina Times*, July 11, 1964, 2.

173. "The Halifax County Voters Movement," *Carolina Times*, December 12, 1964, 2; "Halifax County Board Presented 10 Requests," *Carolina Times*, December 12, 1964, 1.

174. Advertisement, *Carolina Times*, May 30, 1964, 3, 4.

175. "The Accusation of Negro 'Bloc Voting,'" *Carolina Times*, June 6, 1964, 2.

176. Fleer, *Governors Speak*, 48; Christenson, *Paradox of Tar Heel Politics*, 198.

177. "What Price Party Loyalty," *Carolina Times*, June 20, 1964, 2.

178. Advertisement, *Carolina Times*, June 27, 1964, 1.

179. "Interracial Goodwill in N.C. at Stake Saturday," *Carolina Times*, June 27, 1960, 2.

180. "Comparisons That REALLY Count!," *Carolina Times*, June 27, 1960, 5.

181. Leubke, *Tar Heel Politics 2000*, 142–43; Link, *Righteous Warrior*, 70.

182. "An Important Decision for Negro Voters," *Carolina Times*, July 4, 1964, 2.

183. "The Presidential and Gubernatorial Campaign," *Carolina Times*, July 18, 1964, 2.

184. Ibid.

185. "The Most Crucial Election in History," *Carolina Times*, October 31, 1964, 2.

186. *Carolina Times*, October 31, 1964, 3; John R. Dungee, "Letter to the Editor," *Carolina Times*, October 31, 1964, 2, 5; Claude Sitton, "Civil Rights Act: How South Responds," *New York Times*, July 12, 1964, E7.

187. "Negro Voters Save N.C. for Democrats," *Carolina Times*, November 7, 1964, 1, 4; Hansen, *1965 World Almanac*, 65–66.

188. Fleer, *Governors Speak*, 52.

189. "The Register and Vote Campaign Must Continue," *Carolina Times*, November 7, 1964, 2.

190. *Carolina Times*, November 14, 1964, 2. Editorial title was illegible in digital version.

191. "The NAACP's Ban against Mississippi Products," *Carolina Times*, January 16, 1965, 2.

192. "Lest We Forget Alabama," *Carolina Times*, March 13, 1965, 2; Garrow, *Protest at Selma*, 74–77.

193. "The Attitude of Dr. King Regarding Alabama," *Carolina Times*, April 3, 1965, 2.

194. "Economic Sanctions Extended to State of Alabama by NAACP," *Carolina Times*, April 24, 1965, 2B.

195. "Ballots and Not Bullets the Solution in Harlem," *Carolina Times*, July 25, 1964, 2.

196. "Rioting No Solution to Ills of the Negro," *Carolina Times*, August 21, 1965, 2.

197. "The Lack of Leadership," *Carolina Times*, August 28, 1965, 2; Ray Thompson, "Letter to the Editor," *Carolina Times*, August 28, 1965, 2.

198. "Monday's Meeting with Governor Moore," *Carolina Times*, September 4, 1965, 2.

199. "1200 March Protesting Death of Rev. Jas. Reeb," *Carolina Times*, March 20, 1965, 1.

200. "The President's Speech on Voting Rights," *Carolina Times*, March 20, 1965, 2.

201. Dallek, *Flawed Giant*, 218–19.

202. "Rev. Fred Shuttlesworth: C R Leader Praises FBI for Arrests in New Bern," *Carolina Times*, February 20, 1965, 1.

203. Salter, "Typical Klan Rally" (web source).

204. "Ku Klux Klan Visits and Parades in City," *Carolina Times*, May 1, 1965, 1.

205. "McKissick, Hawkins Urge U.S. Registrars for N.C.," *Carolina Times*, August 14, 1965, 1

206. "Opponents to the Right to Vote Law," *Carolina Times*, August 14, 1965, 2.

207. "Fine Exhibition of Interracial Cooperation," *Carolina Times*, June 26, 1965, 2.

208. "Governor Moore Pays His Debt," *Carolina Times*, August 21, 1965, 2.

Chapter Seven

1. "A Sordid Chapter in the History of Durham," *Carolina Times*, March 26, 1966, 2.

2. Muhammad, "Black Press."

3. Jacobs, *Race, Media, and the Crisis*, 48.

4. Muhammad, "Black Press."

5. Jacobs, *Race, Media, and the Crisis*, 6.

6. Ibid., 51.

7. David Newton, "Black Community to Honor Austin," *Durham Morning Herald*, March 17, 1970, 1B; White, "Economic and Social Development of Negroes," 202; "Thanks to Our Readers," *Carolina Times*, April 2, 1960, 1.

8. "Inspector Finds Houses of Abe Greenberg Substandard," *Carolina Times*, July 2, 1966, 1; Greene, *Our Separate Ways*, 123.

9. June Ingram to Abe Greenberg, September 18, 1965, box 371, folder 4585, North Carolina Fund Papers, Southern Historical Collection, Manuscripts Department, Wilson Library, University of North Carolina at Chapel Hill (hereafter cited as NC Fund Papers).

10. Ron Semone, "The 'Greenberg Demonstrations,'" June 21, 1966, box 371, folder 4585, NC Fund Papers.

11. "The Importance of the Primary on May 1," *Carolina Times*, May 1, 1965, 1–2.

12. "Stewart Defeats Stith in City Council Primary over Three to One," *Carolina Times*, May 8, 1965, 1; "The Wrangle over the May 1 Primary," *Carolina Times*, May 15,

1965, 2. "Stewart Re-Elected to Council Seat by 2-1 Margin," *Carolina Times*, May 22, 1965, 1.

13. "Picket Struck by Automobile at Stith Home," *Carolina Times*, June 25, 1966.

14. "Questions Raised by Picketing," *Durham Morning Herald*, June 26, 1966; Sara Lynn Wood, "Reader's Views: Appalled by Coverage," *Durham Morning Herald*, July 4, 1966; both articles in box 371, folder 4585, NC Fund Papers.

15. Inspector Finds Houses Substandard," 1; Greene, *Our Separate Ways*, 123; Ron Semone, "The 'Greenberg Demonstrations,'" June 21, 1966, box 371, folder 4585, NC Fund Papers.

16. "Better Housing for All Durham Citizens," *Carolina Times*, July 2, 1966, 2.

17. Greene, *Our Separate Ways*, 126.

18. "The Durham Housing Authority," *Carolina Times*, February 12, 1966, 2; "The Durham Housing Authority Chairman," *Carolina Times*, January 15, 1966, 2; "A Sordid Chapter in the History of Durham," *Carolina Times*, March 26, 1966, 2.

19. "The Durham Housing Authority Chairman," *Carolina Times*, January 15, 1966, 2; "Sordid Chapter in the History of Durham," 2. In October 1971, Henderson finally became chairman of the Durham Housing Authority after the reorganization of the agency. He served as chairman until 1980. "Henderson Named Commission Chairman Housing Authority," *Carolina Times*, October 9, 1971, 1; "J. J. 'Babe' Henderson," VT 4949/241, WTVD Videotape Collection, Southern Historical Collection, Manuscripts Department, Wilson Library, University of North Carolina, Chapel Hill.

20. "The Strength of the Spirit," *Carolina Times*, January 11, 1969, 2.

21. "LDF Backing Thorpe Eviction Case in D.C.," *Carolina Times*, March 25, 1967, 1A; Fuller with Page, *No Struggle, No Progress*, 67. According to Howard Fuller, the organization was called the Mothers Club.

22. Greene, *Our Separate Ways*, 113. The *Carolina Times* noted that the Supreme Court did not rule that "recipients of government benefits have a right to those benefits which are due certain procedural protection under the constitution." "Mrs. Joyce Thorpe Is Upheld U.S. Tribunal," *Carolina Times*, April 22, 1967, 1–2.

23. "What Price Token Integration?," *Carolina Times*, January 1, 1966, 2.

24. "The Plan to Abolish Lincoln Hospital," *Carolina Times*, April 9, 1966, 2; Brown, *Upbuilding Black Durham*, 155–59.

25. "Proposals for Watts and Lincoln Hospitals," *Carolina Times*, May 21, 1966, 2.

26. "A Fraud on the Community," *Carolina Times*, July 23, 1966, 2.

27. Anderson, *Durham County*, 354.

28. "About Better Hospital Facilities," *Carolina Times*, April 8, 1967, 2.

29. Anderson, *Durham County*, 354.

30. "Three Judge U.S. Court Enjoins State Officials," *Carolina Times*, April 9, 1966, 1.

31. Peebles-Wilkins, "Reactions of Segments of the Black Community," 114, 116.

32. "Enfield Teacher Is Awarded Damages in Dismissal Case," *Carolina Times*, June 11, 1966, 1; "NCTA and NEA Aid Teachers," *North Carolina Teachers Record* 38

(March 1967): 34; "Supreme Court Reinstates Ousted Teacher: Mrs. Johnson Victorious in Enfield Case," *Carolina Times*, January 14, 1967, 1; "Hampton Alumni Honors Former Enfield Teacher," *Carolina Times*, April 15, 1967, 1.

33. "Hampton Alumni Honors Former Enfield Teacher."

34. "NCTA and NEA Aid Teachers," 34.

35. "A Lesson for Eastern North Carolina," *Carolina Times*, January 14, 1967, 2. While her case made its way through the courts, Johnson worked in "the Durham office of the N.C. Fund as Technical Assistant on the community support staff." "Hampton Alumni Honors Former Enfield Teacher," 1.

36. "Palmer Charges Black Teachers Being Dismissed Enmasse under Desegregation," *Carolina Times*, June 21, 1969, 1.

37. "NCTA Secretary Scores Black Teacher in Halifax County," *Carolina Times*, June 14, 1969, 1.

38. "Protection for Black Teachers," *Carolina Times*, March 13, 1971, 2A.

39. Fairclough, *Class of Their Own*, 403.

40. "Opposition to Merrick-Moore Phase Out Voiced by Citizens," *Carolina Times*, February 15, 1969, 1.

41. "The Phase-Out Epidemic," *Carolina Times*, March 8, 1969, 2.

42. "The Nixon Administration and the Negro," *Carolina Times*, August 2, 1969, 2.

43. "The Pattern of Token Integration," *Carolina Times*, February 15, 1969, 2.

44. "New Education Chairman Faces Tough Job," *Carolina Times*, September 6, 1969, 2.

45. "Governor Moore's Budget Message," *Carolina Times*, February 18, 1967, 2.

46. "The Need of NCC Law School in N.C.," *Carolina Times*, March 11, 1967, 2A.

47. "NCC Fights Proposal to Drop Its Law School," *Chicago Defender*, December 21, 1968, 36.

48. Fuller, *No Struggle, No Progress*, 61.

49. Korstad and Leloudis, *To Right These Wrongs*, 1, 82–83, 178–79. Sanford chaired the board of the North Carolina Fund, which was incorporated by Sanford, Charlie Babcock of the Reynolds family and the Z. Smith Reynolds Foundation, John Wheeler, and C. A. (Pete) McKnight, editor of the *Charlotte Observer*. Wheeler pressed for Durham to be a center of one of the programs of the fund. Ibid., 78–85, 176. The North Carolina Fund provided $11,000 for Action for Durham Development (ADD), "a forty-seven-person ad hoc committee," created by Mayor Grabarek. Headed by white attorney Victor Bryant, who served as chair, and J. A. McLean, vice president of Central Carolina Bank and Trust Company, who "served as vice-chair," only three blacks were included in the committee, which was created to reduce poverty in Durham and focused on getting a grant from the North Carolina Fund. Ibid., 177.

50. Ibid., 178.

51. Fuller, *No Struggle, No Progress*, 63–64.

52. Howard Fuller, Book Talk at Hayti Heritage Center, Durham, North Carolina, October 12, 2014.

53. James V. Cunningham, "Resident Participation: The Struggle of the American Urbident for Freedom and Power," prepared for the Ford Foundation, August 1967, p. 163, box 74, folder 780, NC Fund Papers.

54. Bertie Howard and Steve Redbourn, "UOCI: Black Political Power in Durham," August 7, 1968, p. 235, box 369, folder 4563, ser. 4.8, NC Fund Papers; "The Case of Howard Fuller," *Carolina Times*, July 29, 1967, 2. See also "Issues to be Aired," *Durham Sun*, July 26, 1967, 1, 2.

55. Fergus, *Liberalism, Black Power*, 28–29.

56. "Class Conflict or Class Union?," *Carolina Times*, October 14, 1967, 2.

57. "The Voice of the Poor," *Carolina Times*, October 7, 1967, 2.

58. Keith Kennedy, "Durham Blacks Meet," *Duke Chronicle*, October 22, 1968, 7.

59. Belvin, "Malcolm X Liberation University," 40–41.

60. "Howard Fuller Heard by NCC Students in Address," *Carolina Times*, October 7, 1967, 1.

61. Belvin, "Malcolm X Liberation University," 41–42.

62. Wayne King, "Durham's Black Muslims," *Daily Tar Heel*, April 10, 1963, 2.

63. "The 'Black Panther' Method," *Carolina Times*, September 3, 1966, 2; "N.Y. Rally Features Guard and Negro-Unity Appeal," *Christian Science Monitor*, August 31, 1966, 11; Ogbar, *Black Power*, 80. The Black Panther Party of New York, which lasted less than one year, was not related to the Black Panther Party created by Huey Newton and Bobby Seale in Oakland, California, in October 1966. Ogbar, *Black Power*, 80, 85.

64. "Powell's Black Power Movement," *Carolina Times*, April 8, 1967, 2A.

65. "Black or White Prejudice No Different," *Carolina Times*, December 20, 1969, 2.

66. "The Black Power Movement," *Carolina Times*, July 29, 1967, 2.

67. "One of Our Blackest Hours," *Carolina Times*, August 26, 1967, 2.

68. "The Downfall of SNCC," *Washington Post*, August 17, 1967, A20; "SNCC and the Nonwhite World," *Christian Science Monitor*, August 17, 1967, 16; Carson, "Blacks and Jews," 42–46.

69. Anderson, *Durham County*, 372.

70. "The Case of Howard Fuller," *Carolina Times*, July 19, 1967, 2. See also "The Truth about Howard Fuller," *Carolina Times*, August 26, 1967, 2. It is curious that both Osha Gray Davidson and Devin Fergus claim that Austin only supported Fuller in private, not in public, when Austin wrote several editorials backing Fuller. Davidson, *Best of Enemies*, 180; Fergus, *Liberalism, Black Power*, 65. Austin praised the *Durham Morning Herald* for its August 23, 1967, article on Fuller. "The Truth about Howard Fuller," *Carolina Times*, August 26, 1967, 2.

71. "Our Stand against Violence," *Carolina Times*, April 27, 1968, 2.

72. *Carolina Times* April 30, 1966, 1; *Carolina Times*, May 7, 1966, 1.

73. "The May 28 Democratic Primary," *Carolina Times*, May 21, 1966, 2.

74. Advertisement, *Carolina Times*, May 21, 1966, 3A. M. Hugh Thompson ran for district court judge in 1966. Advertisement, *Carolina Times*, May 21, 1966, 4A.

75. "The Big Job Facing Negro Voters," *Carolina Times* June 4, 1966, 2.

76. Bertie Howard and Steve Redbourn, "UOCI: Black Political Power in Durham," August 7, 1968, 3–4, box 369, folder 4563, ser. 4.8, NC Fund Papers.

77. Stone, "Southern City," 117, 122.

78. "The Bloc Vote Question," *Carolina Times*, May 13, 1967, 2.

79. Greene, *Our Separate Ways*, 134; Stone, "Southern City," 122; Howard and Redbourn, "UOCI: Black Political Power in Durham," 4; Stone, "Southern City," 122.

80. "Another Two Years of Do Nothing," *Carolina Times*, May 20, 1967, 2.

81. "Congratulations to Durham's Voters," *Carolina Times*, May 20, 1967, 2; "Another Negro for City Council," *Carolina Times*, March 25, 1967, 2A; "The Durham City Council Election," *Carolina Times*, April 22, 1967, 2.

82. "Durham's 'On Again Off Again' Mayor," *Carolina Times*, August 5, 1967, 2.

83. *Carolina Times*, May 4, 25, June 1, October 5, 12, 19, 26, November 2.

84. "Young Dems Convene," *Duke Chronicle*, September 26, 1968, 1; Advertisement, *Duke Chronicle*, November 5, 1968, 12.

85. "3 More Negro Candidates Announce Entry in Primary," *Carolina Times*, March 25, 1968, 1; "Greensboro Attorney to Run for N.C. House of Representatives," *Carolina Times*, February 17, 1968, 1.

86. "Hawkins Candidacy for Governor," *Carolina Times*, April 20, 1968, 2.

87. "To Preserve Our Heritage," *Carolina Times*, March 16, 1968, 2.

88. Fergus, *Liberalism, Black Power*, 67–68; "J.C. 'Skeepie' Scarborough III Tops Run-off Primary June 1," *Carolina Times*, June 8, 1968, 1; "N.C. 18 District Elects Negro Judge and State Legislator; A.T. Spaulding Fred McNeill Win Offices," *Carolina Times*, November 9, 1968, 1.

89. "The Strength of the Spirit," *Carolina Times*, January 11, 1969, 2.

90. "The Approaching Mayoralty Election," *Carolina Times*, March 15, 1969, 2.

91. "The City Council Election May 17," *Carolina Times*, May 17, 1969, 2.

92. "Candidates Forum to Be Held April 30," *Carolina Times*, April 26, 1969, 1. Grabarek advertised in the *Carolina Times*, May 3, 1969, 12A.

93. "Drivers Wanted," *Duke Chronicle*, April 16, 1969, 8.

94. "Where Do We Go from Here?," *Carolina Times*, May 24, 1969, 2.

95. "The Apathy of Durham Black Leaders," *Carolina Times*, April 12, 1969, 2.

96. "Negro Winner in Race for Mayor of Chapel Hill, N.C.," *Carolina Times*, May 10, 1969, 1.

97. "Durham Sinks to Its Lowest Depths," *Carolina Times*, September 27, 1969, 2; "'Appeal' by Klansmen Disrupts City Council Session," *Carolina Times*, September 20, 1969, 1.

98. "A Coalition of Liberals, Labor and Negroes," *Carolina Times*, November 22, 1969, 2.

99. "A Candidate for Mayor," *Carolina Times*, May 15, 1971, 2A.

100. "Dr. C. E. Boulware Retains City Council Seat," *Carolina Times*, May 22, 1971, 1.

101. Eldridge, *Chronicles of a Two-Front War*, 7.

102. "The Fulbright Attack on War in Viet Nam," *Carolina Times*, February 5, 1966, 2.

103. "Tokenism and Taxation," *Carolina Times*, August 27, 1966, 2.

104. "Making Carmiachel [*sic*] a Scapegoat," *Carolina Times*, April 15, 1967, 2.

105. Shafer, "Vietnam-Era Draft," 69.

106. "The House Is Becoming Divided," *Carolina Times*, April 22, 1967, 2.

107. "The Stupidity of Modern Warfare," *Carolina Times*, September 20, 1969, 2.

108. "Time to End the Vietnam War," *Carolina Times*, December 13, 1969, 2.

109. "Little Choice between Political Parties," *Carolina Times*, April 23, 1966, 2.

110. "Representative Fountain's Opposition," *Carolina Times*, October 15, 1966, 2.

111. Fleming, *Legendary Locals*, 77.

112. "The Plight of Negro Republicans," *Carolina Times*, August 17, 1968, 2.

113. "Editorially Speaking: November 5, a Day of Destiny," *Carolina Times*, November 2, 1968, 1, 2.

114. Brundage, *Southern Past*, 236–37.

115. Gotham, *Race, Real Estate*, 82; Anderson, *Durham County*, 342; John Phelps, "All 8 Bond Proposals Approved Here," *Durham Morning Herald*, October 7, 1962, 1A, 5A; "You Have Until 6:30 P. M. . . . ." *Durham Sun*, October 6, 1962, 9; "Durham's Choice in the Bond Vote," *Durham Morning Herald*, October 6, 19620, 4A.

116. Brundage, *Southern Past*, 238–39.

117. "Urban Renewal Bond Issue Headed for Defeat," *Carolina Times*, September 15, 1962, 2.

118. "Durham's Future at Stake in Bond Election," *Carolina Times*, October 6, 1962, 2.

119. Rice, "Urban Renewal in Durham," 93.

120. Brundage, *Southern Past*, 240–50.

121. "Petitions RC of Durham to Air Problems," *Carolina Times*, April 22, 1967, 1, 2; Winford, " 'Battle for Freedom,' " 411.

122. Community Organization Not to Oppose Expressway," *Carolina Times*, April 29, 1967, 1.

123. Brundage, *Southern Past*, 255.

124. Anderson, *Durham County*, 343.

125. Davidson, *Best of Enemies*, 193–94.

126. Korstad and Leloudis, *To Right These Wrongs*, 225–26.

127. Ibid., 226.

128. Ibid.

129. "The Image of Durham's Mayor," *Carolina Times*, October 7, 1967, 2.

130. "Class Conflict or Class Union?," *Carolina Times*, October 14, 1967, 2.

131. Davidson, *Best of Enemies*, 210.

132. "The Assassination of Martin Luther King," *Carolina Times*, April 13, 1968, 2.

133. "Non-Academic Employees at Duke U.," *Carolina Times*, April 20, 1968, 2; Ludwig, "Closing in on the 'Plantation,' " 82–89.

134. Greene, *Our Separate Ways*, 166.

135. Ibid., 166–67.

136. "Durham's Present Racial Controversy," *Carolina Times*, August 24, 1968, 2.

137. "Clement III, Urges Durham Blacks Continue Boycott," *Carolina Times*, August 24, 1968, 1.

138. John B. Justice, "Fuller Calls for Boycott Support at Solidarity Mass Meeting Sun," *Carolina Times*, November 23, 1968, 1.

139. John Phelps, "Bryant Calls for Support of Black Solidarity Boycott at Meet," *Carolina Times*, January 4, 1969, 1, 5; John Phelps, "Young Leader Declares Black Community Must Stick Together," *Carolina Times*, January 11, 1969, 1.

140. "White Urges All Black People Remain Unified in Boycott Effort," *Carolina Times*, February 1, 1969, 1.

141. "Solidarity," *Duke Chronicle*, October 19, 1968, 4.

142. Keith Kennedy, "Durham Blacks Meet," *Duke Chronicle*, October 22, 1968, 7.

143. "Boycott of Durham Merchants Ends," *Durham Morning Herald*, February 17, 1969, 1.

144. Greene, *Our Separate Ways*, 183.

145. "Last Sunday a High Day in Durham," *Carolina Times*, February 22, 1969, 2; "The Black Solidarity Boycott," *Carolina Times*, November 23, 1968, 2; "Black Solidarity Boycott of Durham Merchants Is Ended: Committees to Arrange Plan for City Blacks," *Carolina Times*, February 22, 1969, 1.

146. "Temporary Cessation Boycott of Four Rocky Mt. Stores Announced," *Carolina Times*, November 23, 1968, 1.

147. "Smoke Screen," *Carolina Times*, May 24, 1969, 2; "Foundation for Community Development," *Carolina Times*, May 17, 1969, 2; Greene, *Our Separate Ways*, 134.

148. "Malcolm X Liberation University Closes Shortly after Opening," *Carolina Times* March 22, 1969, 1. Malcolm X Liberation University opened for one hour on March 17, 1969, but did not begin operations until several months later.

149. Fuller, *No Struggle, No Progress*, 104. Both locations had formerly been part of Durham Hosiery Mill No. 2. "Open Durham" (web source).

150. "Congratulations Malcolm X University," *Carolina Times*, October 25, 1969, 2.

151. "Is the Dream a Nightmare?," *Carolina Times*, November 1, 1969, 2.

152. "Classes in Session at City's First Nation Building School: Hopkins Thinks MXU Accepted by Most Blacks," *Carolina Times*, November 1, 1969, 1.

153. "Fuller Announces Opening Date for Malcolm X Univ.: School to Be Dedicated on October 27," *Carolina Times*, October 18, 1969, 1, 2.

154. Fuller, *No Struggle, No Progress*, 105.

155. "Larger Funds Predicted for NC Negro Schools," *Norfolk Journal and Guide*, June 10, 1967, A2.

156. "Carolina Times Editor-Publisher Dies," *Carolina Times*, June 19, 1971, 1, 8.

157. "Durham to Honor Veteran Editor," *Philadelphia Tribune*, March 17, 1970, 11; "Community Honors Louis E. Austin with Testimonial," *Carolina Times*, March 21, 1970, 1, 8.

158. David Newton, "Black Community to Honor Austin," *Durham Morning Herald*, March 17, 1970, 1B; "Community Honors Louis E. Austin with Testimonial," *Carolina Times*, March 21, 1970, 1, 8.

159. John Myers, "Taking a Closer Look," *Carolina Times*, June 19, 1971, 2A; Louis Ernest Austin, Death Certificate #1971001027, June 12, 1971, Durham County (NC) Register of Deeds.

160. John Myers, "Louis Austin, the Man and His Times," *Carolina Times*, June 19, 1971, 1B.

161. Davidson, *Best of Enemies*, 296.

162. "Louis E. Austin Succumbs at 73," *Durham Morning Herald*, June 14, 1971; "Carolina Times Editor-Publisher Dies," 1, 8; "Stilled Now—The Captain from the Ship of Protest and Reform," *Carolina Times*, June 19, 1971, 2A.

163. "Carolina Times Editor-Publisher Dies," 1, 8.

164. "Carolina Times Editor Dies; Last Rites Held," *Norfolk Journal and Guide*, July 3, 1971, 15.

Epilogue

1. "Our Commitment," *Carolina Times*, June 19, 1971, 1, 8.

2. Alison Blount, "*The Carolina Times*," *Duke Chronicle*, February 22, 1972, 6; "Retiring as a Teacher," *Carolina Times*, May 13, 1967, 1; Kenneth Edmonds interview, July 15, 2013; Lodius Austin and DeNina Austin interview.

3. Eric Ferreri, "She Kept Paper a Voice for the Voiceless," *Raleigh News and Observer*, May 16, 2008, 7B; Vivian Edmonds, interview by Sonia Ramsey; Kenneth Edmonds interview, May 23, 2011.

4. Valerie Whitted, "Publisher Vivian A. Edmonds Leaves Us to Carry the Torch," *Spectacular Magazine*, June 2008, 7.

5. Blount, "*Carolina Times*," 6; "Retiring as a Teacher," 1.

6. "Nixon's Economy Budget," *Carolina Times*, February 17, 1973, 2. See also "What Ever Happened to Black America?," *Carolina Times*, February 24, 1973, 2.

7. "Rights of the Poor and Black in Jeopardy," *Carolina Times*, January 5, 1974, 2.

8. "Wilmington Journal Office Building Bombed," *Carolina Times*, June 2, 1973, 1; "Wilmington Journal Bombing," *Carolina Times*, June 2, 1973, 2.

9. "*Carolina Times* Building Burns: Arson Is Charged," *Black Excellence* 3 (March–April–May 1979): 11; Godwin, *Black Wilmington*, xv; Janken, *Wilmington Ten*, 17–18, 30, 69–70.

10. Michaux, interview by Jack Bass; Kenneth Edmonds interview, July 15, 2013.

11. "County Commission Seat Is Sought by Mrs. Spaulding," *Carolina Times* February 2, 1974, 1; "Nathan Garrett to Seek Second Term as County Commissioner," *Carolina Times*, February 23, 1974, 1.

12. "Michaux, Bell, Mrs. Spaulding Successful Primary Candidates," *Carolina Times*, May 18, 1974, 1.

13. Vivian Edmonds, interview by Sonia Ramsey.

14. Kenneth Edmonds interview, July 15, 2013.

15. "Soul City: Building a Firm Foundation," *Carolina Times*, January 31, 1976, 13.

16. "Is Helms Man Enough to Apologize," *Carolina Times*, January 17, 1976, 2; Fergus, *Liberalism, Black Power*, 215–17.

17. Benjamin Chavis, "The Dialectics of Incarceration," *Carolina Times*, March 27, 1976, 1; "Is North Carolina Moving on Plot to Murder Rev. Chavis?," *Carolina Times*, March 27, 1976, 1.

18. Ray Jenkins, "Wilmington Ten: N.C. Justice on Trial," *Carolina Times*, June 12, 1976, 1; Ray Jenkins, "Wilmington Ten: N.C. Justice on Trial," *Carolina Times*, June 19, 1976, 1, 13.

19. Janken, *Wilmington Ten*, 92.

20. "*Carolina Times* Building Burns: Arson Is Charged," *Black Excellence* 3 (March–April–May 1979): 11; "*Carolina Times* Burned, N.C. Publishers Offer $1000," *Black Ink* (UNC–Chapel Hill Black Student Movement newspaper), January 29, 1979, 1; "Durham City Council Balks on Police Brutality," *Carolina Times*, November 4, 1978, 1; Pat Bryant, "U.S. Justice Dept. Probes Police Brutality," *Carolina Times*, November 25, 1978, 1, 10; "Coalition Calls for Immediate Firing of Public Safety Officer," "Duke University Police Brutality Meet Held," *Carolina Times*, December 2, 1978, 1; "Police Brutality Coalition Pickets City Hall," *Carolina Times*, December 16, 1978, 1.

21. O'Connell, "Hayti," 5.

22. "Vivian Edmonds: The Carolina Times," *Norfolk Journal and Guide* (June 2, 1982): A9.

23. "*Carolina Times* Burned," 1; Kenneth Edmonds, interview, July 15, 2013.

24. "Thank you," *Carolina Times*, February 3, 1979, 3.

25. Pat Bryant, "Police Crimes Subject of Unrest," *Carolina Times*, January 27, 1979, 1.

26. "Mass Rally Monday," *Carolina Times*, January 27, 1979, 1.

27. Whitted, "Publisher Vivian A. Edmonds," 7.

28. Stella Walker Austin, Death Certificate #1981001962, October 6, 1981, Register of Deeds, Durham, NC; "Final Rites Held for Mrs. Stella W. Austin," *Carolina Times*, October 10, 1981, 1; "Retiring as a Teacher," *Carolina Times*, May 13, 1967, 1; "Durham Society Notes," *Carolina Times*, October 30, 1954, 4; "Durham Society Notes, *Carolina Times*, January 2, 1954, 4; "Durham Socials," *Carolina Times*, June 13, 1953, 8.

29. Whitted, "Publisher Vivian A. Edmonds," 7.

30. Eric Ferreri, "She Kept Paper a Voice for the Voiceless," *Raleigh News and Observer*, May 16, 2008, 7B.

31. Whitted, "Publisher Vivian A. Edmonds," 7.

32. "Our Creed," undated, copy in the author's possession.

33. Sundquist, *King's Dream*, 5.

34. Baumgartner, Epp, and Love, "Police Searches of Black and White Motorists," (web source); Ruetschlin and Asante-Muhammad, "The Retail Race Divide," (web source); Barber, "The Retreat from Voting Rights," (web source); Aja, Bustillo, Darity, and Hamilton, "From a Tangle of Pathology to a Race-Fair America," (web source); Oppel, "Activists Wield Search Data to Challenge and Change Police Policy," (web

source); Cassandra Stubbs, "Prosecutors Still Using Race to Choose Juries," Davis Vanguard, http://www.davisvanguard.org/2016/05/60046/, accessed May 29, 2016; Engel, "Racial Discrimination Remains Plague on Criminal Justice System," (web source); Kotch and Mosteller, "Racial Discrimination and the Death Penalty," (web source).

35. Blight, *Frederick Douglass' Civil War*, 9.

Bibliography

Archival Materials

Atlanta, Georgia
    R. D. Woodruff Library, Atlanta University
        Southern Conference for Human Welfare Collection
Cambridge, Massachusetts
    Schlesinger Library, Radcliffe Institute, Harvard University
        Pauli Murray Papers
Chapel Hill, North Carolina
    Southern Historical Collection, Manuscripts Department, Wilson Library,
    University of North Carolina
        Frank Porter Graham Papers
        Guy B. Johnson Papers
        William J. Kennedy Papers
        North Carolina Commission on Interracial Cooperation Papers
        North Carolina Fund Papers
        Howard W. Odum Papers
        Thomas Pearsall Papers
        Reed Sarratt Papers
        Junius Scales Papers
        WTVD Videotape Collection
    University Archives, Wilson Library, University of North Carolina
        Gordon Gray Records
Charlotte, North Carolina
    Special Collections, J. Murrey Atkins Library, University of North Carolina
        Fred D. Alexander Papers
College Park, Maryland
    Special Collections, Hornbake Library, University of Maryland
        Tobacco Workers International Union Papers
Durham, North Carolina
    David M. Rubenstein Rare Book & Manuscript Library, Duke University
        Rencher N. Harris Papers
        Chris D. Howard Papers
        Clydie F. Scarborough Papers
        Asa and Elna Spaulding Papers
    Durham County Register of Deeds

University Archives, James E. Shepard Memorial Library, North Carolina Central
    University
    James E. Shepard Papers
Los Angeles, California
    Special Collections, Charles E. Young Research Library, University of California at
        Los Angeles
    Ralph J. Bunche Papers
Madison, Wisconsin
    Wisconsin Historical Society
        Carl and Anne Braden Papers
New York, New York
    Schomburg Center for Research in Black Culture
        August Meier Papers
Raleigh, North Carolina
    North Carolina Division of Archives and History, State Archives
        Audio-Visual Materials Collection
        Department of Public Instruction, Division of Negro Education Papers
        Governor J. Melville Broughton Papers
        Governor Luther H. Hodges Papers
        Governor W. Kerr Scott Papers
        Governor William B. Umstead Papers
Washington, D.C.
    Federal Bureau of Investigation, U.S. Department of Justice
        Louis E. Austin Files
    Library of Congress
        NAACP Legal Defense and Educational Fund Records
        NAACP Papers

Microfilm Sources

Claude A. Barnett Papers. Frederick, MD: University Publications of America,
    1984–85.
William Hastie Papers. Frederick, MD: University Publications of America, 1986.
Papers of the NAACP. Frederick, MD: University Publications of America, 1986–.

Database

Proquest History Vault: Papers of the NAACP

Oral Histories

Austin, Lodius, and DeNina Austin. Interview by Brenda Williams, January 12, 1995,
    Interview V-0003. Southern Oral History Program Collection (#4007),

Southern Historical Collection, Wilson Library, University of North Carolina at Chapel Hill.

Austin, Louis E. Interview by Anne Braden, ca. 1957, notes, box 49, folder 11, Carl and Anne Braden Papers, Wisconsin Historical Society, Madison, WI.

Edmonds, Kenneth. Interview by the author, May 23, 2011. Notes in the author's possession.

———. Interview by the author, July 15, 2013. Digital recording in the author's possession.

Edmonds, Vivian. Interview by Sonia Ramsey, May 28, 1993. Behind the Veil Collection. John Hope Franklin Research Center for African and African American History and Culture. Duke University, Durham, NC.

———. Interview by the author, August 30, 2004. Notes in the author's possession.

Hobby, Wilbur. Interview by William Finger, March 13, 1975, Interview E-0006. Southern Oral History Program Collection (#4007), Southern Historical Collection, Wilson Library, University of North Carolina at Chapel Hill.

Johnson, Guy B. Interview by Jacquelyn Hall, December 16, 1974, Interview B-0006. Southern Oral History Program Collection (#4007), Southern Historical Collection, Wilson Library, University of North Carolina at Chapel Hill.

Michaux, H. M., Jr. Interview by the author, February 9, 2015, Durham, NC. Digital recording in the author's possession.

———. Interview by Jack Bass, November 20, 1974, Interview A-0135. Southern Oral History Program Collection (#4007), Southern Historical Collection, Wilson Library, University of North Carolina at Chapel Hill.

Pearson, Conrad Odell. Interview by Walter Weare, Durham, NC, April 18, 1979, transcript, H-218. Southern Oral History Program Collection (#4007), Southern Historical Collection, Wilson Library, University of North Carolina at Chapel Hill.

Rivera, Alexander M. Interview by Kieran Taylor, November 30, 2001, Interview C-0297. Southern Oral History Program Collection (#4007), Southern Historical Collection, Wilson Library, University of North Carolina at Chapel Hill.

Spaulding, Asa T. Interview by Walter Weare, April 16, 1979, Interview C-0013-3. Southern Oral History Program Collection (#4007), Southern Historical Collection, Wilson Library, University of North Carolina at Chapel Hill.

Turner, Viola. Interview by Walter Weare, April 15, 1979, Interview C-0015. Southern Oral History Program, Southern Oral History Program Collection (#4007), Wilson Library, University of North Carolina at Chapel Hill.

Williams, Virginia. Interview by Kieran Walsh Taylor, April 6, 2002, Interview C-0300. Southern Oral History Program Collection (#4007), Southern Historical Collection, Wilson Library, University of North Carolina at Chapel Hill.

Government and School Documents

"Address by Governor Luther Hodges before Joint Session of the General Assembly of North Carolina, Meeting in Special Session." In *Journal of the House of Representatives of the General Assembly of the State of North Carolina, Extra Session 1956 and Regular Session 1957* (Raleigh: n.p., 1957), 11.

Bulletin: The National Training School, Catalogue Edition. Vol. 7, no. 3, April 1920, University Archives, James E. Shepard Memorial Library, North Carolina Central University, Durham, NC.

"Conference on Race Relations, July 10, 11, 12, 1944, North Carolina College for Negroes, Durham, North Carolina." North Carolina Room, Durham County Library, Durham, NC.

Corbitt, David Leroy, ed. *Addresses, Letters and Papers of Clyde Roark Hoey, Governor of North Carolina, 1937–1941.* Raleigh, NC: Council of State, 1944.

Department of the Interior, U.S. Board of Education. *Negro Education: A Study of the Private and Higher Schools for Colored People in the United States.* Vol. 2. Washington, D.C.: Government Printing Office, 1917.

Durham City Board of Education Minutes. Durham Schools Administrative Office, Durham, NC.

Educational Publications of the Superintendent of Public Instruction of North Carolina, Numbers 31–60, 1921–1922. Raleigh, NC: Capital Printing Company, 1921.

Jeffers v. Whitley, 309 F.2d 621, Court of Appeals, 4th Circuit 1962.

Jones, Thomas Jesse. *Negro Education: A Study of the Private and Higher Schools for Colored People in the United States.* Vol. 2. Washington, D.C.: Government Printing Office, 1917.

1900 United States Census.

1910 United States Census.

1920 United States Census.

1930 United States Census.

1940 United States Census.

1929–1939 Catalogue, 1930–1931 Announcements, The North Carolina College for Negroes, Durham, NC, 1929. University Archives, James E. Shepard Memorial Library, North Carolina Central University, Durham, NC.

North Carolina State Board of Health, Office of Vital Statistics, Certificate of Death, R. McCants Andrews, July 5, 1932. Copy in author's possession.

"Proceedings of Conference on Race Relations, North Carolina College for Negroes, Durham, NC, July 11–13, 1945." North Carolina Room, Durham County Library, Durham, NC.

Public Education in North Carolina: A Report to the Public School Commission of North Carolina. New York: General Education Board, 1921.

Standardization and Classification of Public High Schools in North Carolina, 1921–1922, Educational Publication No. 60. Raleigh, NC: State Superintendent of Public Instruction, 1921.

State v. Clyburn, 101 SE 2d 295, NC: Supreme Court 1958.
University of North Carolina Record, Catalogue Issue 1932–1933. Chapel Hill: University of North Carolina Press, 1933.

Newspapers and Periodicals

Atlanta Daily World
Baltimore Afro-American
Campus Echo (Durham)
Carolina Alumni Review (Chapel Hill)
Carolina Times
Charleston News and Courier
Chicago Defender
Christian Science Monitor
Crisis
Daily Tar Heel (Chapel Hill)
Duke Chronicle
Durham Morning Herald
Durham Sun
Ebony Magazine
Greensboro Daily News
Indianapolis Recorder
The Militant (New York)
News and Observer
New York Age
New York Amsterdam News
New York Times
Norfolk Journal and Guide
People's Rights Bulletin
Philadelphia Tribune
Pittsburgh Courier
The Progress (Enfield, NC)
The Public Appeal (Durham)
Spectacular Magazine (Durham)
Wall Street Journal
Washington Post
The Watchman and Southron (Sumter)

Published Sources, Dissertations, Theses, and Unpublished Comments

Adelson, Bruce. *Brushing Back Jim Crow: The Integration of Minor League Baseball in the American South*. Charlottesville: University Press of Virginia, 1999.
Alexander, Ann Field. *Race Man: The Rise and Fall of the "Fighting Editor" John Mitchell Jr*. Charlottesville: University of Virginia Press, 2002.

Allen, William C. *History of Halifax County*. Boston: Cornhill Company, 1918.

Anderson, Eric. *Race and Politics in North Carolina, 1872–1901: The Black Second*. Baton Rouge: Louisiana State University Press, 1980.

Anderson, Jean Bradley. *Durham County: A History of Durham County, North Carolina*. 2nd ed. Durham, NC: Duke University Press, 2011.

Aptheker, Herbert, ed. *A Documentary History of the Negro People in the United States*, Vol. 4, *From the New Deal to the End of World War II*. New York: Citadel, 1990.

Arsenault, Raymond. *Freedom Riders: 1961 and the Struggle for Racial Justice*. New York: Oxford University Press, 2011.

Baker, Scott. "Testing Equality: The National Teacher Examination and the NAACP's Legal Campaign to Equalize Teachers' Salaries in the South, 1936–1963." *History of Education Quarterly* 35 (Spring 1995): 49–64.

Barksdale, Marcellus C. "The Indigenous Civil Rights Movement and Cultural Change in North Carolina: Weldon, Chapel Hill, and Monroe: 1946–1965." PhD diss., Duke University, 1977.

Bass, Jack, and Walter De Vries. *The Transformation of Southern Politics: Social Change and Political Consequence since 1945*. New York: Basic Books, 1976.

Beezer, Bruce. "Black Teachers' Salaries and the Federal Courts before *Brown v. Board of Education*: One Beginning for Equity." *Journal of Negro Education* 55 (Spring 1986): 200–213.

Bell, Derrick. *Race, Racism and American Law*. 3rd ed. Boston: Little, Brown, 1992.

Bell, John L. *Hard Times: Beginnings of the Great Depression in North Carolina, 1929–1933*. Raleigh: North Carolina Department of Cultural Resources, 1982.

Belvin, Brent H. "Malcolm X Liberation University: An Experiment in Independent Black Education." MA thesis, North Carolina State University, 2004.

Berry, Mary Frances. "The Matt Ingram Case and the Denial of African American Sexual Freedom." *Journal of African American History* 93 (Spring 2008): 223–34.

"Black History Month." *Newsletter of the Historic Queen Street Baptist Church*. February 2010, http://qsbcva.org/news/newsletter_feb_10.pdf. Accessed June 24, 2012.

Blight, David W. *Frederick Douglass' Civil War: Keeping Faith in Jubilee*. Baton Rouge: Louisiana State University Press, 1989.

Bloom, Jack M. *Class, Race, and the Civil Rights Movement: The Changing Political Economy of Southern Racism*. Bloomington: Indiana University Press, 1987.

Boston, Jesse. "The Lunch Counter Sit-In Demonstrations in Durham, North Carolina." MA thesis, North Carolina Central University, 1975.

Bowman, Robert Lewis. "Negro Politics in Four Southern Counties." PhD diss., University of North Carolina at Chapel Hill, 1963.

Boyd, Harold Kent. "Louis Austin and the *Carolina Times*." MA thesis, North Carolina College at Durham, 1966.

Brinton, Hugh Penn. "The Negro in Durham: A Study of Adjustment to Town Life." PhD diss., University of North Carolina, 1930.

Brown, Deborah F. *Dead-End Road*. Bloomington, IN: AuthorHouse, 2004.

Brown, Leslie. *Upbuilding Black Durham: Gender, Class, and Black Community Development in the Jim Crow South*. Chapel Hill: University of North Carolina Press, 2008.

Brown-Nagin, Tomiko. *Courage to Dissent: Atlanta and the Long History of the Civil Rights Movement*. New York: Oxford University Press, 2011.

Brundage, William Fitzhugh. *The Southern Past: A Clash of Past and Memory*. Cambridge, MA: Harvard University Press, 2005.

Bunche, Ralph J. *The Political Status of the Negro in the Age of FDR*, edited by Dewey W. Grantham. Chicago: University of Chicago Press, 1973.

Burch, Susan, and Hannah Joyner. *Unspeakable: The Story of Junius Wilson*. Chapel Hill: University of North Carolina Press, 2007.

Burns, Augustus M., III. "Graduate Education for Blacks in North Carolina, 1930–1951." *Journal of Southern History* 46 (May 1980): 195–218.

———. "North Carolina and the Negro Dilemma, 1930–1950." PhD diss., University of North Carolina at Chapel Hill, 1969.

Caldwell, Arthur B., ed. *History of the American Negro, North Carolina Edition*. Vol. 4. Atlanta: A. B. Caldwell, 1921.

Cannon, Robert Joseph. "The Organization and Growth of Black Political Participation in Durham, North Carolina, 1933–1958." PhD diss., University of North Carolina at Chapel Hill, 1975.

Carmines, Edward G., and James A. Stimson. *Race and the Transformation of American Politics*. Princeton, NJ: Princeton University Press, 1989.

Carson, Clayborne. "Blacks and Jews in the Civil Rights Movement: The Case of SNCC." In *Bridges and Boundaries: African Americans and American Jews*, edited by Jack Salzman, Adina Black, and Gretchen Sullivan Sorin, 36–49. New York: George Braziller, 1992.

Carson, Clayborne, ed. *The Student Voice, 1960–1965: Periodical of the Student Nonviolent Coordinating Committee*. Westport, CT: Meckler, 1990.

Carter, David C. "The Williamston Freedom Movement: Civil Rights at the Grass Roots in Eastern North Carolina, 1957–1964." *North Carolina Historical Review* 76 (January 1999): 1–42.

Carver, Kam Owen. "The Role of the Durham Committee on the Affairs of Black People in the Pursuit of Equal Educational Opportunities, 1935–1954." MA thesis, North Carolina Central University, 1992.

Cecelski, David S. *Along Freedom Road: Hyde County, North Carolina, and the Fate of Black Schools in the South*. Chapel Hill: University of North Carolina Press, 1994.

Chafe, William H. *Civilities and Civil Rights: Greensboro, North Carolina and the Black Struggle for Freedom*. New York: Oxford University Press, 1981.

———. *The Unfinished Journey: America since World War II*. 5th ed. New York: Oxford University Press, 2003.

Cha-Jua, Sundiata Keita, and Clarence E. Lang. "The 'Long Movement' as Vampire: Temporal and Spatial Fallacies in Recent Black Freedom Studies." *Journal of African American History* 92 (Spring 2007): 265–88.

Chambers, Julius. "Impact of Supreme Court Decisions on the Desegregation of Statewide Systems of Higher Education." In *The Impact of Desegregation on Higher Education: Proceedings of the National Conference on Desegregation in Higher Education at Sheraton-Crabtree Motor Inn, Raleigh, North Carolina July 18–20, 1979,* edited by Jeff E. Smith, 183–193. Durham: North Carolina Central University, 1981.

Chansky, Art. *Game Changers: Dean Smith, Charlie Scott and the Era That Transformed a Southern College Town.* Chapel Hill: University of North Carolina Press, 2016.

Cheek, Neal. "An Historical Study of the Administrative Actions in the Racial Desegregation of the University of North Carolina at Chapel Hill, 1930–1955." PhD diss., University of North Carolina at Chapel Hill, 1973.

Christensen, Rob. *The Paradox of Tar Heel Politics: The Personalities, Elections, and Events That Shaped Modern North Carolina.* 2nd ed. Chapel Hill: University of North Carolina Press, 2008.

Claytor, Willie A. "Negro Councilmanic Office-Holders in North Carolina, 1947–1957." MA thesis, North Carolina College at Durham, 1958.

Cole, Olivia W. "Rencher Nicholas Harris: A Quarter of a Century of Negro Leadership." MA thesis, North Carolina College at Durham, 1967.

Cone, James H. *Martin & Malcolm & America: A Dream or a Nightmare.* Maryknoll, NY: Orbis Books, 1991.

Cooper, John Milton, Jr. *Pivotal Decades: The United States, 1900–1920.* New York: W. W. Norton, 1990.

Covington, Howard E., Jr. *Henry Frye: North Carolina's First African American Chief Justice.* Jefferson, NC: McFarland, 2013.

Covington, Howard E., Jr., and Marion A. Ellis. *Terry Sanford: Politics, Progress, and Outrageous Ambitions.* Durham, NC: Duke University Press, 1999.

Crow, Jeffrey J., Paul D. Escott, and Flora J. Hatley. *A History of African Americans in North Carolina.* Rev. ed. Raleigh: North Carolina Department of Cultural Resources, 2008.

Culver, John C., and John Hyde. *American Dreamer: A Life of Henry A. Wallace.* New York: W. W. Norton, 2000.

Dalfiume, Richard M. "The 'Forgotten Years' of the Negro Revolution." *Journal of American History* 55 (June 1968): 90–106.

Dallek, Robert. *Flawed Giant: Lyndon Johnson and His Times, 1961–1973.* New York: Oxford University Press, 1998.

Daniel, Pete. *Lost Revolutions: The South in the 1950s.* Chapel Hill: University of North Carolina Press for Smithsonian National Museum of American History, 2000.

Davidson, Chandler. "The Recent Evolution of Voting Rights Law Affecting Racial and Language Minorities." In *Quiet Revolution in the South: The Impact of the Voting Rights Act, 1965–1990,* edited by Chandler Davidson and Bernard Grofman, 21–37. Princeton, NJ: Princeton University Press, 1994.

Davidson, Osha Gray. *The Best of Enemies: Race and Redemption in the New South.* Chapel Hill: University of North Carolina Press, 2007.

Davis, Richard. *The Press and American Politics: The New Mediator*. New York: Longman, 1992.

Day, Richard E. "North Carolina." In *Civil Rights U.S.A.: Public Schools Southern States 1962; Staff Reports Submitted to the United States Commission on Civil Rights and Authorized for Publication*. Washington, D.C.: Government Printing Office, 1962.

Dennis, Everette E., and William L. Rivers. *Other Voices: The New Journalism in America*. San Francisco: Canfield, 1974.

Devine, Thomas W. *Henry Wallace's 1948 Presidential Campaign and the Future of Postwar Liberalism*. Chapel Hill: University of North Carolina Press, 2013.

Diaz, Sara P. "'A Racial Trust': Individualist, Eugenicist, and Capitalist Respectability in the Life of Roger Arliner Young." *Souls: A Critical Journal of Black Politics, Culture, and Society* 18 (October 2016): 235–62.

Digby-Junger, Richard. *The Journalist as Reformer: Henry Demarest Lloyd and Wealth against Commonwealth*. Westport, CT: Greenwood, 1996.

Dillard, James Hardy, Thomas Jesse Jones, Charles Templeman Loram, Jason Houldsworth Oldham, Anson Phelps Stokes, and Monroe Work. *Twenty Year Report of the Phelps-Stokes Fund, 1911–1931*. New York: Phelps-Stokes Fund, 1932.

Dittmer, John. *Local People: The Struggle for Civil Rights in Mississippi*. Urbana: University of Illinois Press, 1994.

Douglas, Davison M. *Reading, Writing, and Race: The Desegregation of the Charlotte Schools*. Chapel Hill: University of North Carolina Press, 1995.

———. "The Rhetoric of Moderation: Desegregating the South during the Decade after Brown." 1994, *Faculty Publications*, Paper 116, http://scholarship.law.wm.edu /facpubs/116. Accessed May 15, 2016.

Drescher, John. *Triumph of Good Will: How Terry Sanford Beat a Champion of Segregation and Reshaped the South*. Jackson: University Press of Mississippi, 2000.

Dries, Marion E. "Into the Lion's Den: TWIU Local 208's Fight for Seniority Rights and Civil Rights in the Liggett & Myers Tobacco Plant, Durham, North Carolina, 1937–1968." MA thesis, North Carolina State University, 1999.

Drone, Janell. "Desegregation and Effective School Leadership: Tracking Success, 1954–1980." *Journal of African American History* 90 (Autumn 2005): 410–21.

Dudziak, Mary L. *Cold War Civil Rights: Race and the Image of American Democracy*. Princeton, NJ: Princeton University Press, 2000.

Eamon, Tom. *The Making of a Southern Democracy: North Carolina Politics from Kerr Scott to Pat McCrory*. Chapel Hill: University of North Carolina Press, 2014.

Eldridge, Lawrence A. *Chronicles of a Two-Front War: Civil Rights and Vietnam in the African American Press*. Columbia: University of Missouri Press, 2011.

Ellsworth, Scott. *The Secret Game: A Wartime Story of Courage, Change, and Basketball's Lost Triumph*. New York: Little, Brown and Company, 2015.

Equal Protection of the Laws in North Carolina: Report of the North Carolina Advisory Committee to the United States Commission on Civil Rights, 1959–62. Washington, D.C.: Government Printing Office, 1962.

Fairclough, Adam. *A Class of Their Own: Black Teachers in the Segregated South.* Cambridge, MA: Harvard University Press, 2007.

Farrar, Hayward. *The Baltimore Afro-American, 1892–1950.* Westport, CT: Greenwood, 1998.

Felder, James L. *Civil Rights in South Carolina: From Peaceful Protests to Groundbreaking Rulings.* Charleston, SC: History Press, 2012.

Fergus, Devin. *Liberalism, Black Power, and the Making of American Politics, 1965–1980.* Athens: University of Georgia Press, 2009.

Ferris, Marcie Cohen. *The Edible South: The Power of Food and the Making of an American Region.* Chapel Hill: University of North Carolina Press, 2014.

Finkle, Lee. "The Conservative Aims of Militant Rhetoric: Black Protest during World War II." *Journal of American History* 60 (December 1973): 692–713.

———. *Forum for Protest: The Black Press during World War II.* Rutherford, NJ: Fairleigh Dickinson University Press, 1975.

Fleer, Jack D. *Governors Speak.* Lanham, MD: University Press of America, 2007.

Fleming, Monika S. *Legendary Locals of Edgecombe and Nash Counties.* Charleston, SC: Arcadia Publishing, 2013.

Franklin, John Hope, and Alfred A. Moss. *From Slavery to Freedom: A History of Negro Americans.* 6th ed. New York: Alfred A. Knopf, 1988.

Frederickson, Kari A. *The Dixiecrat Revolt and the End of the Solid South, 1932–1968.* Chapel Hill: University of North Carolina Press, 2001.

Freedman, Eric M. "Milestones in Habeas Corpus—Part III: *Brown v. Allen*: The Habeas Corpus Revolution That Wasn't." *Alabama Law Review* 51 (Summer 2000), http://people.hofstra.edu/eric_m_freedman/freed3.pdf. Accessed June 4, 2014.

Friedman, Andrea. "The Strange Career of Annie Lee Moss: Rethinking Race, Gender, and McCarthyism." *Journal of American History* 94 (2007): 445–68.

Fuller, Howard. Book Talk at Hayti Heritage Center, Durham, North Carolina, October 12, 2014. Notes in the author's possession.

Fuller, Howard, with Lisa Frazier Page. *No Struggle, No Progress: A Warrior's Life from Black Power to Education Reform.* Milwaukee, WI: Marquette University Press, 2014.

Galambos, Louis, and Daun Van Ee, eds. *The Papers of Dwight David Eisenhower: The Presidency. Volumes 14-17, The Middle Way.* Baltimore: Johns Hopkins University Press, 1996–2001.

Gardner, Michael R. *Harry Truman and Civil Rights: Moral Courage and Political Risks.* Carbondale: Southern Illinois University Press, 2002.

Garrow, David J. *Protest at Selma: Martin Luther King, Jr., and the Voting Rights Act of 1965.* New Haven, CT: Yale University Press, 1980.

Gavins, Raymond. *The Perils and Prospects of Southern Black Leadership: Gordon Blaine Hancock, 1884–1970.* Durham, NC: Duke University Press, 1993.

———. "Within the Shadow of Jim Crow: Black Struggles for Education and Liberation in North Carolina." In *From the Grassroots to the Supreme Court:* Brown v. Board of Education *and American Democracy,* edited by Peter F. Lau, 68–87. Durham: Duke University Press, 2004.

Gelman, Irwin F. *The President and the Apprentice: Eisenhower and Nixon, 1952–1961.* New Haven, CT: Yale University Press, 2015.

Gershenhorn, Jerry. "A Courageous Voice for Black Freedom: Louis Austin and the *Carolina Times* in Depression-Era North Carolina." *North Carolina Historical Review* 87 (January 2010): 57–92.

———. "Double V in North Carolina: The *Carolina Times* and the Struggle for Racial Equality during World War II." *Journalism History* 32 (Fall 2006): 156–67.

———. "*Hocutt v. Wilson* and Race Relations in Durham, North Carolina, during the 1930s." *North Carolina Historical Review* 78 (July 2001): 275–308.

Gilmore, Glenda Elizabeth. "Admitting Pauli Murray." *Journal of Women's History* 14 (Summer 2002): 62–67.

———. *Defying Dixie: The Radical Roots of Civil Rights, 1919–1950.* New York: W. W. Norton, 2008.

Godwin, John L. *Black Wilmington and the North Carolina Way: Portrait of a Community in the Era of Civil Rights Protest.* Lanham, MD: University Press of America, 2000.

Gotham, Kevin Fox. *Race, Real Estate, and Uneven Development: The Kansas City Experience, 1900–2010.* 2nd ed. Albany: State University of New York Press, 2014.

Greenberg, Jack. *Crusaders in the Courts: How a Dedicated Band of Lawyers Fought for the Civil Rights Revolution.* New York: Basic Books, 1994.

Greene, Christina. "'The Negro Ain't Scared No More!': Black Women's Activism in North Carolina and the Meaning of *Brown*." In *From the Grassroots to the Supreme Court: Brown v. Board of Education and American Democracy*, edited by Peter F. Lau, 245–69. Durham, NC: Duke University Press, 2004.

———. *Our Separate Ways: Women and the Black Freedom Movement in Durham, North Carolina.* Chapel Hill: University of North Carolina Press, 2005.

Greene, Robert Ewell. *A Biography: Thomas Sewell Inborden, Early Educator of Color.* Fort Washington, MD: R. E. Greene, 1996.

Griffin, Willie James. "Courier of Crisis, Messenger of Hope: Trezzvant W. Anderson and the Black Freedom Struggle for Economic Justice." PhD diss., University of North Carolina at Chapel Hill, 2016.

Haley, John H., III. "The Carolina Chameleon: Charles N. Hunter and Race Relations in North Carolina, 1865–1931." PhD diss., University of North Carolina at Chapel Hill, 1981.

Hall, Jacquelyn Dowd. "The Long Civil Rights Movement and the Political Uses of the Past." *Journal of American History* 91 (March 2005): 1233–63.

Hansen, Harry, ed. *The 1965 World Almanac and Book of Facts.* New York: New York World Telegram, 1965.

Harlan, Louis R. *Booker T. Washington: The Wizard of Tuskegee, 1901–1915.* New York: Oxford University Press, 1983.

Hine, Darlene Clark. "The NAACP and the Supreme Court: Walter F. White and the Defeat of Judge John J. Parker, 1930." *Negro History Bulletin* 40 (September–October 1977): 753–57.

Hoffman, Beatrix. *Health Care for Some: Rights and Rationing in the United States since 1930*. Chicago: University of Chicago Press, 2012.

Hogan, Lawrence D. *A Black National News Service: the Associated Negro Press and Claude Barnett, 1919–1945*. Rutherford, NJ: Fairleigh Dickinson University Press, 1984.

Inborden, Thomas S. *History of Brick School*. Typescript, 1934. Photocopy in the Author's Possession.

Irons, Janet. *Testing the New Deal: The General Textile Strike in the American South*. Urbana: University of Illinois Press, 2000.

Irons, Jenny. *Reconstituting Whiteness: The Mississippi State Sovereignty Commission*. Nashville: Vanderbilt University Press, 2010.

Isaac, Larry. "Movement of Movements: Culture Moves in the Long Civil Rights Struggle." *Social Forces* 87 (September 2008): 33–63.

Jacobs, Ronald N. *Race, Media, and the Crisis of Civil Society: From Watts to Rodney King*. New York: Cambridge University Press, 2000.

Janiewski, Dolores. "Seeking 'a New Day and a New Way': Black Women and Unions in the Southern Tobacco Industry." In *"To Toil the Livelong Day": America's Women at Work, 1780–1980*, edited by Carol Groneman and Mary Beth Norton, 161–78. Ithaca, NY: Cornell University Press, 1987.

———. *Sisterhood Denied: Race, Gender, and Class in a New South Community*. Philadelphia: Temple University Press, 1985.

Janken, Kenneth Robert. *Rayford W. Logan and the Dilemma of the African-American Intellectual*. Amherst: University of Massachusetts Press, 1993.

———. *White: The Biography of Walter White, Mr. NAACP*. New York: New Press, 2003.

———. *The Wilmington Ten: Violence, Injustice, and the Rise of Black Politics in the 1970s*. Chapel Hill: University of North Carolina Press, 2015.

Jones, Lester M. "The Editorial Policy of Negro Newspapers of 1917–18 as Compared with That of 1941–42." *Journal of Negro History* 29 (January 1944): 24–31.

Justesen, Benjamin R. *George Henry White: An Even Chance in the Race of Life*. Baton Rouge: Louisiana State University Press, 2001.

Kiser, Vernon Benjamin. "Occupational Change among Negroes in Durham." MA thesis, Duke University, 1942.

Korstad, Robert. *Civil Rights Unionism: Tobacco Workers and the Struggle for Democracy in the Mid-Twentieth-Century South*. Chapel Hill: University of North Carolina Press, 2003.

Korstad, Robert R., and James L. Leloudis. *To Right These Wrongs: The North Carolina Fund and the Battle to End Poverty and Inequality in 1960s America*. Chapel Hill: University of North Carolina Press, 2010.

Kousser, J. Morgan. *Colorblind Justice: Minority Voting Rights and the Undoing of the Second Reconstruction*. Chapel Hill: University of North Carolina Press, 1999.

———. "Progressivism-For Middle-Class Whites Only: North Carolina Education, 1880–1910." *Journal of Southern History* 46 (May 1980): 169–194.

Kruse, Kevin M., and Stephen Tuck. "Introduction." In *Fog of War: The Second World War and the Civil Rights Movement*, edited by Kevin M. Kruse and Stephen Tuck, 4–12. New York: Oxford University Press, 2012.

Kujovich, Gil. "Public Black Colleges: The Long History of Unequal Instruction." *Journal of Blacks in Higher Education* 3 (Spring 1994): 65–76.

Landers, James. "The National Observer, 1962–77: Interpretive Journalism Pioneer." *Journalism History* 31 (Spring 2005): 13–22.

Larkins, John R. *Patterns of Leadership among Negroes in North Carolina*. Raleigh, NC: Irving-Swain, 1959.

LaRossa, Ralph. *Of War and Men: World War II in the Lives of Fathers and Their Families*. Chicago: University of Chicago Press, 2011.

Lawson, Steven F. *Black Ballots: Voting Rights in the South, 1944–1969*. Lanham, MD: Lexington Books, 1976.

———. *Running for Freedom: Civil Rights and Black Politics in America since 1941*. 2nd ed. New York: McGraw-Hill, 1997.

Leach, Laurie F. *Langston Hughes: A Biography*. Westport, CT: Greenwood, 2004.

Leonard, Thomas C. *The Power of the Press: The Birth of American Political Reporting*. New York: Oxford University Press, 1986.

Leubke, Paul. *Tar Heel Politics 2000*. Chapel Hill: University of North Carolina Press, 1998.

Lewis, David Levering, ed. *W. E. B. Du Bois: A Reader*. New York: Henry Holt, 1995.

Link, William A. *Righteous Warrior: Jesse Helms and the Rise of Modern Conservatism*. New York: St. Martin's, 2008.

———. *William Friday: Power, Purpose, and American Higher Education*. Chapel Hill: University of North Carolina Press, 1995.

Ludwig, Erik. "Closing In on the 'Plantation': Coalition Building and the Role of Black Women's Grievances in Duke University's Labor Disputes, 1965–1968." *Feminist Studies* 25 (Spring 1999): 82–89.

MacDougall, Curtis D. *Gideon's Army*. New York: Marzani & Munsell, 1965.

Malone, Barry. "Divine Discontent: Nathan Carter Newbold, White Liberals, Black Education, and the Making of the Jim Crow South." PhD diss., University of South Carolina, 2013.

Maltese, John Anthony. *The Selling of Supreme Court Nominees*. Baltimore: Johns Hopkins University Press, 1995.

Marshall, Ray. "Unions and the Negro Community." *Industrial and Labor Relations Review* 17 (January 1964): 179–202.

Mathews, Donald R., and James W. Prothro. *Negroes and the New Southern Politics*. New York: Harcourt, Brace & World, 1966.

McGuire, Danielle L. *At the Dark End of the Street: Black Women, Rape, and Resistance: A New History of the Civil Rights Movement from Rosa Parks to the Rise of Black Power*. New York: Random House, 2010.

McGuire, Phillip. "Desegregation of the Armed Forces: Black Leadership, Protest and World War II." *Journal of Negro History* 68 (Spring 1983): 147–58.

McKinney, Charles W., Jr. *Greater Freedom: The Evolution of the Civil Rights Struggle in Wilson, North Carolina*. Lanham, MD: University Press of America, 2010.

———. " 'Our People Began to Press for Greater Freedom': The Black Freedom Struggle in Wilson, North Carolina, 1945–1970." PhD diss., Duke University, 2003.

Minchin, Timothy. *Hiring the Black Worker: The Racial Integration of the Southern Textile Industry, 1960–1980*. Chapel Hill: University of North Carolina Press, 1999.

Moon, Henry Lee. "The Negro Vote in the Presidential Election of 1956." *Journal of Negro Education* 26 (Summer 1957): 219–30.

Moran, "Peter William. "Border State Ebb and Flow: School Desegregation in Missouri, 1954–1999." In *With All Deliberate Speed: Implementing* Brown v. Board of Education, edited by Brian J. Dougherty and Charles C. Bolton, 175–198. Fayetteville: University of Arkansas Press, 2008.

Moreno, Paul. "Fair Employment: Law and Policy, 1933–1972." PhD diss., University of Maryland, College Park, 1994.

Morris, Aldon D. *The Origins of the Civil Rights Movement: Black Communities Organizing for Change*. New York: Free Press, 1984.

Morrison, Minion K. C., ed. *African American Political Participation: A Reference Handbook*. Santa Barbara, CA: ABC-CLIO, 2003.

Muhammad, Larry. "The Black Press: Past and Present." Neiman Foundation for Journalism at Harvard: Nieman Reports (Fall 2003), http://www.nieman.harvard.edu/reports/article/100994/The-Black-Press-Past-and-Present.aspx. Accessed February 6, 2014.

Murray, Pauli. *Song in a Weary Throat: An American Pilgrimage*. New York: Harper & Row, 1987.

———. *Pauli Murray: The Autobiography of a Black Activist, Feminist, Lawyer, Priest, and Poet*. Knoxville: University of Tennessee Press, 1987.

Murray, Pauli, ed. *States' Laws on Race and Color*. Cincinnati: Woman's Division of Christian Service Board of Missions and Church Extension, 1952.

Murray, Percy E. *History of the North Carolina Teachers Association*. Washington, D.C.: National Education Association, 1985.

Myrdal, Gunnar, with the assistance of Richard Sterner and Arnold Rose. *An American Dilemma: The Negro Problem and Modern Democracy*. Vol. 2. New York: Harper & Brothers, 1944.

Nalty, Bernard C. *Strength for the Fight: A History of Black Americans in the Military*. New York: Free Press, 1986.

"NCTA and NEA Aid Teachers." *The North Carolina Teachers Record* (March 1967): 34.

Newkirk, Pamela. *Within the Veil: Black Journalists, White Media*. New York: New York University Press, 2000.

Noble, Alice. *The School of Pharmacy of the University of North Carolina: A History*. Chapel Hill: University of North Carolina Press, 1961.

Nuruddin, Yusuf. "The Promises and Pitfalls of Reparations." In *Redress for Historical Injustices in the United States: On Reparations for Slavery, Jim Crow, and Their*

Legacies, edited by Michael T. Martin and Marilyn Yaquinto, 379–401. Durham, NC: Duke University Press, 2007.

O'Connell, Patrick. "Hayti." *Tobacco Road* 3 (October 1979): 4–6, 20.

Odum-Hinmon, Maria E. "The Cautious Crusader: How the *Atlanta Daily World* Covered the Struggle for African American Rights from 1945 to 1985." PhD diss., University of Maryland, 2005.

Ogbar, Jeffrey O. G. *Black Power: Radical Politics and African American Identity.* Baltimore: Johns Hopkins University Press, 2004.

"106 West Parrish Street," http://www.opendurham.org/buildings/106-west-parrish -street?full. Accessed June 24, 2012.

Orfield, Gary. "The 1964 Civil Rights Act and American Education." In *Legacies of the 1964 Civil Rights Act*, edited by Bernard Grofman, 89–128. Charlottesville: University of Virginia Press, 2000.

Patterson, James T. *Brown V. Board of Education: A Civil Rights Milestone and Its Troubled Legacy.* New York: Oxford University Press, 2001.

Payne, Charles M. *I've Got the Light of Freedom: The Organizing Tradition and the Mississippi Freedom Struggle.* Berkeley: University of California Press, 2007.

Peebles-Wilkins, Wilma. "Reactions of Segments of the Black Community to the North Carolina Pearsall Plan, 1954–1966." *Phylon* (2nd Quarter 1987): 112–121.

Pleasants, Julian M. *The Political Career of W. Kerr Scott, the Squire from Haw River.* Lexington: University Press of Kentucky, 2014.

Pleasants, Julian M., and Augustus M. Burns III. *Frank Porter Graham and the 1950 Senate Race in North Carolina.* Chapel Hill: University of North Carolina Press, 1990.

Prather, H. Leon, Sr. *We Have Taken a City: The Wilmington Racial Massacre and Coup of 1898.* Rutherford, NJ: Fairleigh Dickinson University Press, 1984.

Pryor, Mark. *Faith, Grace and Heresy: The Biography of Rev. Charles M. Jones.* Lincoln, NE: iUniverse, 2002.

"Queen Street Baptist Church: Our History," http://qsbcva.org/about/history.html. Accessed June 24, 2012.

Reed, Betty Jamerson. *School Segregation in Western North Carolina: A History, 1860s–1970s.* Jefferson, NC: McFarland, 2011.

Reed, Linda. *Simple Decency & Common Sense: The Southern Conference Movement, 1938–1963.* Bloomington: Indiana University Press, 1994.

Reed, Merl E. "Black Workers, Defense Industries, and Federal Agencies in Pennsylvania, 1941–1945." In *African Americans in Pennsylvania: Shifting Perspectives*, edited by Joe William Trotter Jr. and Eric Ledell Smith, 363–87. Harrisburg: Pennsylvania State University Press, 1997.

Regester, Charlene B. "From the Buzzard's Roost: Black Movie-going in Durham and Other North Carolina Cities during the Early Period of American Cinema." *Film History: An International Journal* 17 (2005): 113–24.

Reynolds, P. Preston. "Professional and Hospital Discrimination and the US Court of Appeals Fourth Circuit 1956–1967." *American Journal of Public Health* 94 (May 2004): 710–720.

Rice, David H. "Urban Renewal in Durham: A Case Study of a Referendum." MA thesis, University of North Carolina at Chapel Hill, 1966.

Rice, John D. "The Negro Tobacco Worker and His Union in Durham, North Carolina." MA thesis, University of North Carolina at Chapel Hill, 1941.

Roefs, Wim. "Leading the Civil Rights Vanguard in South Carolina: John McCray and the Lighthouse and Informer, 1939–1954." In *Time Longer than Rope: A Century of African American Activism, 1850–1950*, edited by Charles M. Payne and Adam Green, 462–491. New York: New York University Press, 2003.

Rogoff, Leonard. *Homelands: Southern Jewish Identity in Durham-Chapel Hill and North Carolina*. Tuscaloosa: University of Alabama Press, 2001.

Rosen, Hannah. *Terror in the Heart of Freedom: Citizenship, Sexual Violence, and the Meaning of Race in the Postemancipation South*. Chapel Hill: University of North Carolina Press, 2008

Rubio, Philip F. *There's Always Work at the Post Office: African American Postal Workers and the Fight for Jobs, Justice, and Equality*. Chapel Hill: University of North Carolina Press, 2010.

Scales, Junius Irving, and Richard Nickson. *Cause at Heart: A Former Communist Remembers*. Athens: University of Georgia Press, 1987.

Shadle, Douglas. "Black Catholicism and Music in Durham, North Carolina: Praxis in a New Key." MA thesis, University of North Carolina at Chapel Hill, 2006.

Shafer, D. Michael. "The Vietnam-Era Draft: Who Went, Who Didn't, and Why It Matters." In *The Legacy: The Vietnam War in the American Imagination*, edited by D. Michael Shafer, 57–79. Boston: Beacon, 1990.

Shapiro, Herbert. *White Violence and Black Response: From Reconstruction to Montgomery*. Amherst: University of Massachusetts Press, 1988.

Shenk, Gerald E. *"Work or Fight!": Race, Gender, and the Draft in World War One*. New York: Palgrave Macmillan, 2005.

Simmons, Charles A. *The African American Press: A History of News Coverage during National Crises, with Special Reference to Four Black Newspapers, 1827–1965*. Jefferson, NC: McFarland, 1998.

Sindler, Allan P. "Youth and the American Negro Protest Movement: A Local Case Study of Durham, North Carolina: A Paper Presented at the Youth in Politics Panel, Sixth World Congress, International Political Science Association," Geneva, Switzerland, September 21–25, 1964. North Carolina Room, Durham County Library, Durham, NC.

Sitkoff, Harvard. "African American Militancy in the World War II South: Another Perspective." In *Remaking Dixie: The Impact of World War II on the American South*, edited by Neil R. McMillen, 70–92. Jackson: University Press of Mississippi, 1997.

———. *A New Deal for Blacks: The Emergence of Civil Rights as a National Issue: The Depression Decade*. New York: Oxford University Press, 1978.

———. "Racial Militancy and Interracial Violence in the Second World War." *Journal of American History* 58 (December 1971): 661–81.

———. *The Struggle for Black Equality, 1954–1992*. Rev. ed. New York: Hill and Wang, 1993.

Smith, David Barton. *Health Care Divided: Race and Healing a Nation*. Ann Arbor: University of Michigan Press, 1999.

Smith, Jason Scott. *Building New Deal Liberalism: The Political Economy of Public Works, 1933–1956*. London: Cambridge University Press, 2005.

Smith, Jeff E., ed. *The Impact of Desegregation on Higher Education: Proceedings of the National Conference on Desegregation in Higher Education at Sheraton-Crabtree Motor Inn, Raleigh, North Carolina July 18–20, 1979*. Durham: North Carolina Central University, 1981.

Snider, William D. *Light on the Hill: A History of the University of North Carolina at Chapel Hill*. Chapel Hill: University of North Carolina Press, 1992.

Sosna, Morton. *In Search of the Silent South: Southern Liberals and the Race Issue*. New York: Columbia University Press, 1977.

Stillman, Richard, II. "Racial Unrest in the Military: The Challenge and the Response." *Public Administration Review* 34 (May–June, 1974): 221–29.

Stockley, Grif. *Daisy Bates: Civil Rights Crusader from Arkansas*. Jackson: University Press of Mississippi, 2005.

Stone, Ted G. "A Southern City and a County in the Years of Political Change: Durham, North Carolina, 1955–1974." MA thesis, North Carolina Central University, 1977.

Suggs, Henry Lewis. *P. B. Young, Newspaperman: Race, Politics, and Journalism in the New South, 1910–1962*. Charlottesville: University Press of Virginia, 1988.

Suggs, Henry Lewis, ed. *The Black Press in the South, 1865–1979*. Westport, CT: Greenwood, 1983.

Sullins, William S., and Paul Parsons. "Roscoe Dunjee: Crusading Editor of Oklahoma's *Black Dispatch*, 1915–1955." *Journalism Quarterly* 69 (Spring 1992): 204–13.

Sullivan, Patricia. *Days of Hope: Race and Democracy in the New Deal Era*. Chapel Hill: University of North Carolina Press, 1996.

Sundquist, Eric J. *King's Dream*. New Haven, CT: Yale University Press, 2009.

Taves, Henry V., Allison H. Black, and David R. Black. *The Historic Architecture of Halifax County, North Carolina*. Halifax, NC: Halifax County Historical Association, 2010.

Taylor, Gregory S. *The History of the North Carolina Communist Party*. Columbia: University of South Carolina Press, 2009.

Taylor, William A. *Every Citizen a Soldier: The Campaign for Universal Military Training after World War II*. College Station: Texas A&M University Press, 2014.

Thompson, John Henry Lee. "The Little Caesar of Civil Rights: Roscoe Dunjee in Oklahoma City, 1915 to 1955." PhD diss., Purdue University, 1990.

Thornton, Brian. "The Murder of Emmett Till: Myth, Memory, and National Magazine Response." *Journalism History* 36 (Summer 2010): 96–104.

Thorpe, Earl E. *A Concise History of North Carolina Central University*. Durham, NC: Harrington, 1984.

———. *The Mind of the Negro: An Intellectual History of Afro-Americans*. Westport, CT: Negro Universities Press, 1961.

Thuesen, Sarah Caroline. "Classes of Citizenship: The Culture and Politics of Black Public Education in North Carolina, 1919–1960." PhD diss., University of North Carolina at Chapel Hill, 2004.

———. *Greater than Equal: African American Struggles for Schools and Citizenship in North Carolina, 1919–1965*. Chapel Hill: University of North Carolina Press, 2013.

Tindall, George B. *The Emergence of the New South, 1913–1945*. Baton Rouge: Louisiana State University Press, 1967.

Tushnet, Mark V. *Making Civil Rights Law: Thurgood Marshall and the Supreme Court, 1936–1961*. New York: Oxford University Press, 1994

———. *The NAACP's Legal Strategy against Segregated Education, 1925–1950*. Chapel Hill: University of North Carolina Press, 2004.

Tuttle, William M., Jr. *Race Riot: Chicago in the Red Summer of 1919*. New York: Atheneum, 1980.

Tyson, Timothy B. *Radio Free Dixie: Robert F. Williams and the Roots of Black Power*. Chapel Hill: University of North Carolina Press, 1999.

———. "Wars for Democracy: African American Militancy and Interracial Violence in North Carolina during World War II." In *Democracy Betrayed: The Wilmington Race Riot of 1898 and Its Legacy*, edited by David S. Cecelski and Timothy B. Tyson, 253–76. Chapel Hill: University of North Carolina Press, 1998.

Uesugi, Sayoko. "Gender, Race, and the Cold War: Mary Price and the Progressive Party in North Carolina, 1945–1948." *North Carolina Historical Review* 77 (July 2000): 269–311.

Walker, Anders. "'Legal Means': Luther Hodges Limits *Brown* in North Carolina." In *The Ghost of Jim Crow: How Southern Moderates Used* Brown v. Board of Education *to Stall Civil Rights*, 49–84. New York: Oxford University Press, 2009.

Walker, Harry Joseph. "Changes in Race Accommodation in a Southern Community." PhD diss., University of Chicago, 1945.

Walton, Hanes, Jr. *Invisible Politics: Black Political Behavior*. Albany: State University of New York Press, 1985.

Ware, Gilbert. *William Hastie: Grace under Pressure*. New York: Oxford University Press, 1984.

Warlick, Kenneth R. "Practical Education and the Negro College in North Carolina, 1880–1930." PhD diss., University of North Carolina at Chapel Hill, 1980.

Washburn, Patrick S. *The African American Newspaper: Voices of Freedom*. Evanston, IL: Northwestern University Press, 2006.

———. "The *Pittsburgh Courier*'s Double V Campaign in 1942." *American Journalism* 3 (1986): 73–86.

———. *A Question of Sedition: The Federal Government's Investigation of the Black Press during World War II*. New York: Oxford University Press, 1986.

Weare, Walter B. *Black Business in the New South: A Social History of the North Carolina Mutual Life Insurance Company*. Durham, NC: Duke University Press, 1993.

Weaver, Bill, and Oscar C. Page. "The Black Press and the Drive for Integrated Graduate and Professional Schools." *Phylon* 43 (1st Quarter 1982): 15–28.

Wehr, Paul Ernest. "The Sit-Down Protests—A Study of a Passive Resistance Movement in North Carolina." MA thesis, University of North Carolina at Chapel Hill, 1960.

Wertheimer, John W. *Law and Society in the South: A History of North Carolina Court Cases*. Lexington: University Press of Kentucky, 2009.

White, Frank H. "The Economic and Social Development of Negroes in North Carolina since 1900." PhD diss., New York University, 1960.

Wilkinson, Edith Lewis. "Patterns of Negro Segregation in Durham, North Carolina." MA thesis, Duke University, 1950.

Williams, Margo Lee. "The History of Strieby Congregational Church and School, Union Township, Randolph County, North Carolina: Cultural Heritage Site Application." July 6, 2014, http://www.co.randolph.nc.us/hlpc/downloads/Strieby_Church_and_School_History.pdf. Accessed November 12, 2014.

Winford, Brandon. "'The Battle for Freedom Begins Every Morning': John Hervey Wheeler, Civil Rights, and New South Prosperity." PhD diss., University of North Carolina at Chapel Hill, 2014.

Wolcott, Victoria W. *Race, Riots, and Roller Coasters: The Struggle over Segregated Recreation in America*. Philadelphia: University of Pennsylvania Press, 2012.

Web Sources

Aja, Alan, Daniel Bustillo, William Darity Jr., and Darrick Hamilton. "From a Tangle of Pathology to a Race-Fair America." *Dissent Magazine*, https://www.dissentmagazine.org/article/from-a-tangle-of-pathology-to-a-race-fair-america. Accessed May 29, 2016.

Barber, William, II. "The Retreat from Voting Rights." *New York Times*, April 28, 2016. http://www.nytimes.com/2016/04/28/opinion/the-retreat-from-voting-rights.html. Accessed May 30, 2016.

Baumgartner, Frank R., Derek A. Epp, and Bayard Love. "Police Searches of Black and White Motorists." https://www.unc.edu/~fbaum/TrafficStops/DrivingWhileBlack-BaumgartnerLoveEpp-August2014.pdf. Accessed May 30, 2016.

"Biographical Note." Edward R. Dudley Papers, Amistad Research Center, Tulane University, New Orleans, Louisiana. http://www.amistadresearchcenter.org/archon/?p=accessions/accession&id=36 Accessed June 12, 2013.

"The CAROLINIAN Has Rich Traditions." http://web.co.wake.nc.us/lee/vf/caro/19901004tchr/19901004tchr.htm. Accessed November 14, 2007.

Carrie J. Austin, 1961, index, FamilySearch, https://familysearch.org/pal:/MM9.1.1/FGYZ-LX8. Accessed June 28, 2012.

Charles Arrant Death Certificate, December 6, 1922. https://familysearch.org/pal:/MM9.1.1/F3DP-MQR. Accessed June 29, 2012.

"Confidential War Department Memo, July 10, 1944." http://nuweb9.neu.edu
/civilrights/north-carolina/booker-t-spicely/. Accessed May 27, 2014.

Douglas E. Moore to Martin Luther King, Jr., October 3, 1956. "The Martin Luther
King, Jr. Papers Project." http://mlk-kpp01.stanford.edu/primarydocuments/Vol3
/3-Oct-1956_FromMoore.pdf. Accessed December 19, 2014.

Edmonds, Edwin R. Interview by William H. Chafe, ca. 1975. http://library.uncg.edu
/dp/crg/oralHistItem.aspx?i=638. Accessed May 12, 2014.

Engel, Gretchen. "Racial Discrimination Remains Plague on Criminal Justice System."
News and Observer, http://www.newsobserver.com/news/local/community
/durham-news/dn-opinion/article45478803.html. Accessed May 29, 2016.

"First Baptist Church: History." http://www.thefbch.org/history.asp. Accessed
June 24, 2012.

"Former Publisher Nanton, Dead at 81." *Carolinian* (January 29, 1991), http://web.co
.wake.nc.us/lee/vf/caro/19910129fpnd/19910129fpnd.htm. Accessed November 12,
2007.

Hill's Durham Directory, 1915–16. http://library.digitalnc.org/cdm/compoundobject
/collection/dirdurham/id/4841/rec/14. Accessed June 24, 2012.

Hill's Durham Directory, 1923. http://library.digitalnc.org/cdm/compoundobject
/collection/dirdurham/id/19657/rec/19. Accessed June 24, 2012.

Hill's Durham Directory, 1925. http://library.digitalnc.org/cdm/compoundobject
/collection/directories/id/190381/rec/6. Accessed June 24, 2012.

Hill's Durham Directory, 1926. http://library.digitalnc.org/cdm/compoundobject
/collection/dirdurham/id/11628/rec/2347. Accessed June 24, 2012.

"Jasper Brown Family Moves to Washington." ca. 1964. http://ncccha.blogspot.com
/2010/04/jasper-brown-family.html. Accessed June 19, 2013.

John Johnston Parker Papers. Finding Aid, Southern Historical Collection, University
of North Carolina. http://www.lib.unc.edu/mss/inv/p/Parker,John_Johnston.
html. Accessed June 25, 2012.

Jones, Susie. Interview by William H. Chafe, ca. 1978. http://libcdm1.uncg.edu/cdm
/singleitem/collection/CivilRights/id/743/rec/61. Accessed April 16, 2017.

Junot, Jim. " 'Huc': The Story of Henry Hucles." http://vuusports.com/news/2010/12
/14/FB_1214102819.aspx?path=football. Accessed March 27, 2016.

"Joseph Branch, Associate Justice & Chief Justice." http://www.nccourts.org/Courts
/Appellate/Supreme/Portrait/Portrait.asp?Name=Branch. Accessed May 27, 2016.

King, Martin Luther, Jr. "Remarks of Dr. Martin Luther King, Jr. for Negro Press
Week," February 10, 1958. http://www.thekingcenter.org/archive/document/mlk
-remarks-negro-press-week#. Accessed November 21, 2014.

Kotch, Seth, and Robert P. Mosteller. "Racial Discrimination and the Death Penalty:
The Racial Justice Act and the Long Struggle with Race and the Death Penalty in
North Carolina." *North Carolina Law Review,* https://www.unc.edu/~fbaum
/teaching/articles/kotch-mosteller-2010-unc-law-review.pdf. Accessed May 30, 2016.

"Lyda Moore Merrick." http://hayti.org/about-us/lyda-moore-merrick/. Accessed
March 29, 2016.

McCaffrey, Thomas O. "Memorandum for the Officer in Charge, July 11, 1944, National Archives." http://nuweb9.neu.edu/civilrights/north-carolina/booker-t-spicely/. Accessed May 27, 2014.

McKenna, Dave. "Harold Bell's Black History Month," *Washington City Paper*, February 11, 2011. http://www.washingtoncitypaper.com/articles/40387/harold-bell-black-history-mouth/. Accessed June 24, 2011.

"Memorandum for the Officer in Charge, July 11, 1944, War Department, National Archives." http://nuweb9.neu.edu/civilrights/north-carolina/booker-t-spicely/. Accessed May 27, 2014.

"Open Durham." http://www.opendurham.org/buildings/1218-fayetteville-st-fk-watkins-house. Accessed June 23, 2012.

"Open Durham." http://www.opendurham.org/buildings/durham-hosiery-mill-no-2-service-printing-company-elviras-carolina-times. Accessed October 15, 2014.

Oppel, Richard A., Jr. "Activists Wield Search Data to Challenge and Change Police Policy." *New York Times*, http://www.nytimes.com/2014/11/21/us/activists-wield-search-data-to-challenge-and-change-police-policy.html. Accessed May 29, 2016.

"Post Season Basketball Records (& special games) for the Long Island University Red Devils (through 1933–34) • Blackbirds • Busy Bees (through 1951)." http://www.luckyshow.org/basketball/Blackbirdpost.htm. Accessed March 27, 2016.

Rev. R. Spiller Death Certificate. https://familysearch.org/pal:/MM9.3.1/TH-267-12876-55110-60?cc=1609799. Accessed June 29, 2012.

"Robert McCants Andrews, Registration Card." Ancestry.com. Accessed June 6, 1917.

Ruetschlin, Catherine, and Dedrick Asante-Muhammad. "The Retail Race Divide: How the Retail Industry Is Perpetuating Racial Inequality in the 21st Century." NAACP, http://action.naacp.org/page/-/economic%20opportunity%20documents/Retail_Race_Divide_Rename.pdf. Accessed May 30, 2016.

Salter, John. "A Typical Klan Rally: Halifax County, November, 1964." http://www.hunterbear.org/a_typical_klan_rally.htm. Accessed February 20, 2015.

"Statement of Pfc. Robert C. Martin, July 8, 1944, War Department Memo, National Archives." http://nuweb9.neu.edu/civilrights/north-carolina/booker-t-spicely/. Accessed May 27, 2014.

Stubbs, Cassandra. "Prosecutors Still Using Race to Choose Juries." *Davis Vanguard*, http://www.davisvanguard.org/2016/05/60046/. Accessed May 29, 2016.

Woolley, John, and Gerhard Peters. "Election of 1956." http://www.presidency.ucsb.edu/showelection.php?year=1956. Accessed March 4, 2016.

Index

193, 206; and black nationalism, 192; and Nation of Islam, 192; and Mickey Michaux, 193; and Wensell Grabarek, 194–97, 202; and Vietnam War, 197–99; and urban renewal, 200–201; and assassination of Martin Luther King, Jr., 203; and Malcolm X Liberation University, 205–6; death of, 207. See also *Carolina Times*
Austin, Maude, 9, 15, 21, 128, 207
Austin, Stella Vivian Walker, 21, 89, 139, 207, 208, 212
Austin, Vivian. *See* Edmonds, Vivian Austin
Austin, William Louis, 9, 10, 12, 21, 221n47
Avant, Edward R., 54, 57, 104, 105
Avery, John M., 30
Axis Powers, 5, 60, 70

Babcock, Charlie, 281n49
Bacon Street Housing Project, 202
Bailey, Josiah, 55, 86, 238n247, 240n264
Baines, Bruce, 156–57
Baker, Ella, 84, 214
Baker, Quinton E., 154, 161, 165
Baltimore Afro-American, 18, 28, 83, 138, 245n99, 252n45
Bankers Fire Insurance Company, 16, 20, 46
Bankhead, Don, 123
Bank Street Baptist Church, 20
Banner Enterprise, 18
Barfield, Franklin, 114
Barksdale, Richard K., 150
Barnes, Alexander, 105, 173, 223n95
Barnett, Claude, 25, 77, 89
Barnhill, Maurice V., 38
Baseball, 121, 122, 123, 149, 242n34
Basketball, 65–66, 123
Bates, Daisy, 3
Bates, L. C., 3
Beech, Harvey, 98
Bell, William (Bill), 209–10

Bennett, Noah H., 161
Bennett College, 4, 54, 238n242
Biddle, Francis, 72
Bilbo, Theodore, 75
Biltmore Hotel, 109
Birmingham, AL, 163, 166
Bishop, P. A., 263n2
Black nationalism, 7, 192, 205
Black newspapers. *See* black press; *and names of specific newspapers*
Black Panther Party of New York, 192, 282n63
Black Panthers, 7, 282n63
Black Power, 4, 7, 183, 189, 192, 193, 206
Black press, 62, 65, 70–72, 87, 89, 127, 183–84, 197, 217–18n12, 230n130, 243n67. *See also names of specific newspapers*
Black Solidarity Committee for Community Improvement (BSC), 203–5
Bledsoe, Maxine, 143
Bloc voting, 104, 112, 177, 194
Blue v. Durham Board of Education, 91–93
Bluford, Ferdinand D., 137
Bonnie Brae Golf Course, 123
Borland, J. H., 71
Boston University, 149
Boulware, C. Elwood, 155, 173, 191, 194, 197
Boycotts, 26, 54–55, 124–25, 158, 160, 162–63, 176, 179, 203–4
Brame, Charlotte, 143
Branch, Joseph, 176, 278n170
Breece, A. B., 234n183
Brewer, James, 191
Brick, Joseph Keasby, 13
Brick, Julia Brewster, 13
Brooklyn College, 66
Brooklyn Dodgers, 122–23
Brotherhood of Sleeping Car Porters, 68
Broughton, J. Melville, 64, 65, 73–74, 97, 112
Brown, Callis, 153, 271n3

Mangum, T. V., 102

March on Washington for Jobs and
  Freedom, 164, 214

March on Washington Movement, 6, 61,
  68–69, 86, 119, 214, 248n183

Marsh, William, Jr., 144, 150, 151, 152

Marshall, Thurgood, 34, 82–83, 144

Martin, Davis B. (Dan), 52, 106, 214,
  256n121

Mass incarceration, 214

Mays, Benjamin, 75

McBean, Adelene, 65

McCann, John, 212

McCarthy, Joseph, 129

McCord, Jim, 95

McCoy, Cecil, 1, 34–38, 98, 214,
  228n104

McCray, John, 2–3

McDonald, Ralph W., 236n208

McDougald, Richard L., 21, 41, 43, 51, 82

McDougald Terrace, 186

McGee, Willie, 260n210

McKaine, Osceola, 3

McKinney, T. E., 25

McKissick, Floyd, 98, 143, 151, 154, 160,
  181, 210, 214

McKissick, Joycelyn, 4, 143, 161

McKissick v. Carmichael, 98

McKnight, C. A. (Pete), 281n49

McLean, Charles A., 169, 275n119

McLean, J. A., 281n49

McLendon, John, 65–66

McMullan, Harry, 94, 96–97

McNeil, Dave, 19

McNeil, James, 57–58, 239n263

Meany, George, 158–59

Mechanics and Farmers Bank, 4, 16, 17,
  20, 21, 24, 41, 51, 151

Medicaid, 209

Meier, August, 150

Merrick, Edward, 36, 230n141

Merrick, John, 16, 20, 74

Merrick, Lyda Moore, 43, 230n141

Merrick-Moore County School, 188

Michaux, Henry McKinley, Jr. (Mickey),
  174, 191, 193, 195, 202, 209, 277n158

Michaux, Henry McKinley, Sr., 16, 174,
  221n51

Militant, The, 170

Miller, Rodney Jaye, 270–71n2

Mills, Joseph N., 19, 39

Mississippi, 2, 75, 130, 132, 138, 141, 148,
  159, 166, 170, 175–76, 179

Mississippi State Sovereignty Commission, 2

Monroe, NC, 76, 130–31

Montgomery Bus Boycott, 2, 5, 149, 167

Moore, Aaron M., 15, 16, 225n40, 230n141,
  234–35n187

Moore, Dan K., 176–82, 189, 195,
  278n170

Moore, Douglas, 4, 149–51, 270n158,
  271n12

Moore, E. J., 187

Moore, Harry T., 119

Morehouse College, 75

Morgan v. Virginia, 102

Morrison Training School for Negroes, 130

Morrow, Anna, 64

Morrow, E. Frederic, 76

Moses Cone Memorial Hospital,
  167–68

Moss, Annie Lee, 129

Mount Vernon Baptist Church, 19, 84,
  204

Movie theaters, 125, 235n192, 257n138; and
  boycotts, 4, 54–55, 124, 213, 263n268;
  and desegregation, 5, 7, 26, 150, 156–57,
  162–64, 167

Muhammad, Larry, 183

Murdock, W. H., 57

Murphy, Carl, 138

Murray, Pauli, 41–43, 65, 89, 98, 126, 214

Murrow, Edward R., 159

Mutual Savings and Loan Association, 16

Myers, John, 207